QUEBEC WOMEN

CLIO – THE MUSE OF HISTORY

The Clio Collective comprises four historians who have tried to write history in a different way. Micheline Dumont has taught women's history at the University of Sherbrooke since 1970. Michèle Jean is a specialist in adult education and is presently an assistant deputy minister in Quebec's Ministère de la Main-d'oeuvre et de la Sécurité du revenu. Marie Lavigne is the director of the Regional Offices, Quebec Ministry of Cultural Affairs. Jennifer Stoddart was at the time of writing the research director for the Canadian Advisory Council on the Status of Women. She is currently the director of investigation for the Quebec Human Rights Commission.

QUEBEC WOMEN

A History

by
The Clio Collective

Micheline Dumont
Michèle Jean
Marie Lavigne
Jennifer Stoddart

translated by
Roger Gannon and Rosalind Gill

The
Women's
Press

CANADIAN CATALOGUING IN PUBLICATION DATA

Quebec women

Translation of: L'Histoire des femmes au Québec
depuis quatre siècles
Bibliography: p.
Includes index.

ISBN 0-88961-101-7

1. Women – Quebec (Province) – History.
I. Dumont-Johnson, Micheline, 1935-   .

HQ1459.Q8H5813 1987   305.4'09714   C87-094139-9

Originally published in French as *L'Histoire
des femmes au Québec depuis quatre siècles*
by Les Quinze, Editeur (Division of Sogides Ltd.)

Cover illustration by Suzanne Duranceau
This book was produced by
the collective effort of
The Women's Press

Printed and bound in Canada

Published by *The Women's Press*
229 College Street No. 204
Toronto, Ontario   M5T 1R4

The Women's Press gratefully acknowledges
financial support from The Canada Council
and the Ontario Arts Council.

CONTENTS

Preface 11

PART I: BEGINNINGS 1617-1701 13

CHAPTER ONE
THE HEROIC PERIOD 17
First Came the Men *17* Indian Women in the Seventeenth Century *19*
Living in a Cabin *20* The Proximity of the Indian Tribes *23*
Madeleine de Verchères *26* Leaving France *28*

CHAPTER TWO
UNSUNG HEROINES 31
Founding Women *31* Taking the Veil *37* Girls for Marriage *40*
Women from the Lesser Nobility and from the Bourgeousie *16*
A Society Begins to Emerge *48*

PART II: STABILITY 1701-1832 53

CHAPTER THREE
FAMILY LIFE 59
Little Girls *59* Serving Others *63* Courtship and Marriage *64*
Maternity *77* Sickness and Death *82*

CHAPTER FOUR
WOMEN UNDER THE ANCIEN REGIME 85
Never-Ending Work *85* Beliefs of all Kinds *93*
Unmarried Women: Religious Lay *94*
Living on the Fringe of Society *97* Democratic Rights *103*
A Traditional Society in the Process of Change *107*

PART III: UPHEAVALS 1832-1900 111

CHAPTER FIVE
THE GREAT COMMOTION 117
When a Man's World Begins to Fall Apart *117*
The Defeat of the Traditional Rights of Women *122* On the Move *127*

CHAPTER SIX
GETTING MARRIED 131
Finding a Husband *131* Getting Married and Having Children *134*
Having Fewer Children *136* Bringing up Children Alone *140*
Sending Daughters to School *142* Becoming a Housewife *145*
New Work Instruments *149* Sewing at Home *151*

CHAPTER SEVEN
WORKING UNDER ANOTHER ROOF 155
Servants *155* Factory Workers *160*
Pioneers or Schoolmistresses *164* Prostitutes *169*
Women and Work *170* Brides of Christ *173* Speaking Out *176*
A Tiny Little Place for Women *180*

PART IV: CONTRADICTIONS 1900-1940 183

CHAPTER EIGHT
MODERN WOMEN 189
Emulating Mommy and Grandma *189*
Large Families: A Disappearing Species *192*
1914-1918: World War One and the Growth of New Attitudes *195*
Pulling Through in Bad Times *196*
When Science Gets Involved: Health and Charity *197*

CHAPTER NINE
PULLING THROUGH 205
The Perfect Homemaker *205*
Earning a Living: Serving Capital and Patriarchy *208*
Factories *210* Domestic Service *213* In the Shops and Offices *216*
A Job to Make Ends Meet *217*
In the Service of God: Religious Celibacy *218*
Female and Male Professions *220*
Present but Absent in Writing and in the Arts *224*
Women Unionists and Strikers *226*

CHAPTER TEN
WOMEN WORKERS: INVISIBLE, OR ALMOST 233
Spreading the Rural Idea *233*
Domestic Chores: "Dear God, Send Me to Heaven
With a Broom in My Hand" *234* Women Colonists *235*
Stopping the Exodus from the Land *236*
More Than Housewives: Women as Participants *237*

CHAPTER ELEVEN
GETTING AN EDUCATION AND ORGANIZING 241
Access to Education: The Long Haul *241* Continuing Education *248*
The Women's Movement: Social Feminism and Christian Feminism *249*
Getting the Law Changed *252*
A First Commission of Enquiry into the Status of Women *255*
Women's Solidarity *261* Suffragettes and the Struggle for Equality *262*
Almost Equal but Still on the Sidelines *265*

PART V: THE IMPASSE 1940-1969 271

CHAPTER TWELVE
YOUR COUNTRY NEEDS YOU: FROM BOMBS TO BABIES 277
The War, A Decisive Experience *277* War: Men's Business *278*
Military Service *279* Each Woman Worker Counts *281*
Women Hostages in a Political Guerrilla War *283* Family Allowances *284*
The "Fermières" Dispute *287* Wartime Restraint *289*
Women's Organizations in Time of War *291*
Returning to the Home *293* Working Women Protest *294*
The Education of Women: Dishpans or Diplomas *297*

CHAPTER THIRTEEN
CONTEMPORARY WOMEN 301
The Feminine Mystique *301* Family Planning *304*
The Schools Open Up *307* Marriage or Work *309*
Committed Women *313* The Fabricated Women *318* And Politics *321*

CHAPTER FOURTEEN
QUIET FEMINISM 325
Women's Abilities to Go Unrecognized *325*
From Nursery School to University *327* The Pink-Collar Workers *331*
The Rebirth of Organized Feminism *336* The Birth Commission *341*
Orchestra Wives Go on Strike *347*

PART VI: THE EXPLOSION 1969-1979 351

CHAPTER FIFTEEN
THE TURBULENT YEARS: FEMINISM IGNITES 355
Debunking the Feminine Mystique *355*
The New Feminism: An International Movement *357*
Feminism Gains Footing in Quebec *359*
Feminism Becomes a Social Institution *363*
The New Feminism Takes Root *366*   What Do Feminists Do? *368*
"I am not a feminist, but ..." *375*

Epilogue 377

Glossary 379

List of Acronyms 379

Index 381

TABLES

TABLE 1
The "King's Daughters"
42

TABLE 2
Names Given to the First Girls Born in Canada
46

TABLE 3
Number of Children in Nurseries Run by
the Grey Nuns in Montreal
142

TABLE 4
Variation in Weekly Wages in Certain Trades in
Montreal, Summer, 1881
162

TABLE 5
Diplomas Granted by Teachers' Training Colleges
165

TABLE 6
Budget for a Man, Woman and Three Children, 1926
207

TABLE 7
Percentage Distribution of Female Work Force
by Main Occupational Group
Montreal, 1911-1941
209

TABLE 8
Differences in Wages by Sex and Age
Montreal, 1930-1931
209

TABLE 9
Legal Status of Married Women as Defined in
the Quebec Civil Code, 1866-1915
254

TABLE 10

Increase in the Labour Force in Quebec, 1941-1971

311

TABLE 11

Nurses in Quebec, 1941-1971

312

TABLE 12

Novels Published in Women's Magazines

319

TABLE 13

Women in a Male Domaine: Number of Candidates in
Provincial and Federal Elections
Since 1945 (Quebec only)

222

TABLE 14

Changes Brought About by Bill 16

323

TABLE 15

Subjects Chosen by Female Cégep Students

329

TABLE 16

Percentage Distribution of Women Teaching in the School System,
by Level, 1977-1978

330

TABLE 17

Female Occupations

332

TABLE 18

Inequality in Male and Female Wage

332

PREFACE

Seven-year-old Anne was sitting in the corner of the kitchen, tracing her family tree. She named people as if reciting a nursery rhyme. "My mother's name is Juliette, Juliette's mother was called Rebecca, Rebecca's mother was Maria, Maria's mother was Emilie ..." but she could not remember any further.

"Mommy, who was Emilie's mother?"

"Mommy, what did Emilie's mother do?"

Like thousands of children, Anne liked to journey back in time. In history classes, nobody could tell her what Emilie, her great-great-grandmother, had done. They would tell her only about the great men who had changed the course of history. Had she been bold enough to ask about the women who had played a role in this history, they would have proudly read through the short list of famous women, from Marguerite Bourgeoys to Thérèse Casgrain. Had she dared ask if Emilie, her ancestor, was part of history, they probably would have answered: "Why should Emilie be mentioned in history? Did she do anything special?" For historians, Emilie had no historical importance: she had simply lived her life and was therefore non-significant.

What brought us to write this synthesis of the history of the women who have lived in Quebec during the past four centuries was our refusal to accept that the hundreds of thousands of Emilies were non-significant. We were not prepared to see women dispossessed of our own history. None of us was willing to let the history of men and a few illustrious women be passed off as the collective history of a whole population. Women had also made history. We had to find them, to find out where and why they were overshadowed. We had to put the facts in their true perspective.

We were not the first to attempt to make women part of history. During the past twenty years or so, work in social, urban and rural history and research on the history of workers and women has multiplied. We decided it was time to gather the scattered information accessible only to experienced researchers in books, theses and learned journals. In spite of recent efforts by historians to compile a history of these anonymous people, there are still large gaps in our collective memory, especially regarding women. Indeed, the historical role of Native women and women immigrants has hardly been researched. The limited attention they receive in this book reflects the scant material available on the subject, not the place they hold in our history.

A similar problem exists for the thousands of peasant women, mothers and women workers who did nothing "special," unlike the heroines, founders of religious communities and feminists. They left no written material, or if they did, only traces of it have been found. Therefore, we are often forced to reconstruct their lives by looking at changes in the organization of domestic work or changes in the role and size of families.

Reconstructing four centuries of history is somewhat like making a quilt: the pattern that emerges depends on the material you have and the way you decide to assemble the pieces. We decided to stitch the quilt of this history outside the framework of strictly male spheres of activity – the fur trade, war, ministerial responsibility, construction of the railways – usually dealt with in history books. This history takes an entirely different approach. What was the significance of changes in ways of being born, growing up, giving birth and working? These questions became the focus of our attention, not changes in governments. We were also looking for significant events that involved all women, and not only those who were first to penetrate male bastions. That is why, in many cases, we chose to base our history on experiences common to all women.

We will discuss subjugation and liberation, equality (or, rather, inequality) and differences; restrictions and accomplishments. In attempting to reconstruct the collective past of women, we asked the same question again and again: Why was it like that?

Although the rhythm of woman's life seems not always to have beat in time with the periods described in history books, women were affected by or participated in the events of "general" history. For this reason, we begin each section of the book with a resumé of important historical events as a backdrop to the history of the women of that era. We have limited the footnotes at the end of each chapter to quotations from historical figures, primarily women. At the end of each section is a list of works of the historians whose material we have drawn on in writing this book.

Now that we have completed this project, which took thirty-six months (four times nine months, but that is pure coincidence), we would like to thank all those who helped us write our book. Space permits us to mention only those who played an essential role: Joanne Daigle did a great deal of research in the archives in an attempt to throw light in some very dark corners. Louise Dechêne, Alison Prentice, Paul-André Linteau and Agnès Bastin made many valuable comments. Solange Lettre, Nicole Brossard, Monique Roy and Suzanne Cloutier transmitted their enthusiasm and encouragement. Pauline Léveillée, Sarah Porter, Pauline Vaillancourt, Jacqueline Perrault and Louise Rousseau typed the numerous drafts of the manuscript. Our children and our partners did without us for so many Saturdays and Sundays that we gave up counting. To all, our sincerest thanks.

Micheline Dumont   *Marie Lavigne*
Michèle Jean   *Jennifer Stoddart*

I
BEGINNINGS
1617-1701

THE SIXTEENTH CENTURY was the century of the great explorations that revealed to Europe the then unknown territories of America, Africa and Asia. Two vast colonial empires arose: those of Portugal and Spain. France was also attracted by these territories and sent explorers across the seas. The voyages of Jacques Cartier, between 1534 and 1541, were part of the French initiatives in North America. Yet, it was not until the seventeenth century, that the new colonial empires of France and England competed for dominance in North America.

We owe the existence of New France to geographer-colonizer Samuel de Champlain and to King Henry IV of France. In 1608, more than sixty years after Jacques Cartier's first discoveries, Quebec was established by Champlain. The colony was able to survive only because New France had considerable reserves of a single precious commodity: furs. Moreover, the colony was cut off from the great maritime sea lanes for six months of the year because its link to the sea, the St. Lawrence River, was frozen. Thus, New France was perceived to offer little scope for development, despite the vastness of explored territory that stretched from the mouth of the Mississippi to Hudson Bay.

Several themes characterized the history of seventeenth-century New France. First and foremost, the activities of the fur merchants clashed with the efforts of those attempting to set up a permanent colony. Their efforts were also hindered by the ongoing opposition of the Iroquois, who, throughout the seventeenth century, waged a successful war of attrition against the Hurons, allies of the French.

We can also observe between 1635 and 1665 the direct involvement of religious societies in the process of colonization. This period is traditionally referred to as *l'épopée mystique* (the mystical period), a remarkable title, given

15

the pervasive lack of interest in the colony on the part of French authorities of the day.

However, in 1663, Louis XIV began to provide his colony with centralized institutions. For about a dozen years – while Jean Talon was Intendant – notable progress in immigration, exploration and economic development took place: the seigneurial system, which controlled immigration and land distribution and which had been introduced in 1628, expanded rapidly.

Even this improved level of progress, however, compared poorly with the progress made by the English colonies on the shores of the Atlantic, whose population increased twenty-five times more rapidly than the population of New France. The proximity of the colonies led swiftly to a struggle between England and France for possession and control of the territories in the interior; and an English alliance with the Iroquois only served to increase the conflicts.

A combination of factors in the seventeenth-century gave rise to a New France that was unique. It was a time of beginnings, of inventive energy. Women and men could attempt to leave misery behind, to fulfil their religious aspirations or to make their fortunes. Into a new land without frontiers came women of all social classes to take up the challenge.

CHAPTER ONE

THE HEROIC PERIOD

FIRST CAME THE MEN

FOR MORE THAN A QUARTER of a century, there was no place in New France for European women. Quebec was a summer trading post, for sailors, merchants, *engagés* (indentured labourers), soldiers, interpreters and Indians. In this resolutely male environment, Champlain considered French women as just so many superfluous mouths to feed.

Moreover, the first settlement was very near the encampments of Indian groups that had been living on American soil for thousands of years. How the first contacts between whites and Indian women came about is unknown. The first documents either did not speak of this taboo subject; contained voyageurs' exaggerated boasts of their sexual prowess; or were written by missionaries scandalized by the conduct of the French. It seems that from the very beginnings of the colony, men took advantage of what they perceived to be the sexual freedom of the Montagnais and Algonquin women. This, as well as the specialized and seasonal nature of the Quebec fur trading post, postponed the need for French women.

In 1617, the family of Marie Rollet and Louis Hébert arrived in New France. Until 1634, the official beginning of settlement, they were almost the only family to live permanently in Quebec and to own a house. The family was both typical and exceptional. As was common practice at the beginning of the seventeenth century, Marie Rollet closely participated in the work of her apothecary husband. Apothecaries were the medical specialists in this isolated post; yet the Hébert family could not save their daughter Anne, who died giving birth to her first child. Although this was the unfortunate fate of many women during this period, the Héberts' second daughter, Guillemette,

---

THE DOWRY

"The dowry is an asset that a woman brings to her marriage," according to the Robert dictionary. This is only a partial definition, for the dowry is also proof that the relationship between the sexes has an economic basis. A dowry can take the form of goods or money, but doesn't always have the same function. In primitive societies, the dowry is paid to the wife's father by the husband as compensation for the loss of an economic asset. Among the upper classes, the dowry is paid to the husband by the father, to compensate for taking over an economic burden. In some circumstances, the dowry may be paid by a third party. This would be the case in New France for the *filles du roy* (King's Daughters). Today, however, the most common form of dowry is the woman's trousseau.

---

the wife of Guillaume Couillard, bore ten children, also common during the *Ancien Régime.**

What was exceptional, however, about this family was that the eldest daughters of Guillemette married when they were eleven and twelve years of age. Demographic studies show that early marriages for both women and men were more frequent at the lower end of the social scale. But in certain social classes marriage was postponed for economic and family planning considerations. In New France, during the first two generations, the scarcity of women frequently led to the marriage of preadolescent girls.

The Hébert-Couillard family was exceptional in being highly extended: it took in Indians, the Montagnais girls, Charity and Hope, who had been adopted by Champlain. It also took in a Black boy from Madagascar, who had arrived in Quebec on a ship belonging to the Kirkes, adventurers who attempted to control the French colony from 1629 to 1632. The boy was New France's first slave, but seems to have been considered a servant – slavery was not permitted until the beginning of the eighteenth century. Among its many other domestic servants the Hébert-Couillard family counted a number of Indians. The Jesuits found this household somewhat turbulent and highly independent; yet, they happily attended a banquet at Marie Rollet's house, in honour of the first baptism of an Indian – at which fifty-six wild geese, thirty ducks, twenty teal and other game were consumed.

But what is one single family in such a vast colonial venture?

---

* *Ancien Régime* is a phrase that refers to the system of government in France before the revolution of 1789.

INDIAN WOMEN IN
THE SEVENTEENTH CENTURY

Two types of Indian peoples lived near the settlements of the first French colonists: hunter-gatherers and horticultural peoples. The hunter-gatherers were most often nomadic and part of the great Algonquin language family. (The principal sub-groupings were the Abenakis, the Ottawa, the Algonquins, the Micmacs, the Montagnais, the Nascapis and the Cree.) They inhabited what is now the province of Quebec, as well as the forests bordering the Atlantic. The horticultural peoples, who led a semi-sedentary life, had more permanent settlements. They grew corn, pumpkins, tobacco, beans and sunflowers. These peoples belonged to the Huron-Iroquois language family; they inhabited the St. Lawrence River valley during the sixteenth century and the Great Lakes region thereafter.

The position of the women of these peoples was unlike anything the Europeans had encountered. Iroquois women, in particular, seemed to dominate their social units. The Jesuit Lafiteau would say of them, a century after the arrival of the white man: "Nothing, however, is more real than the superiority of these women. It is they who truly constitute the nation; and it is through them that the nobility of the race, the family and the tribe are perpetuated. They are the ones who hold the real power. The land, the fields, the harvests, everything belongs to them.... The children are their property and the order of succession is passed down through their blood."[1] The society was matrilineal – descent was handed down from mother to daughter – and also matrilocal – the husband left his household and came to live with his wife's family. The men, hunters and warriors, were away for long periods; it was the women who grew the crops and thereby assumed the greater responsibility for feeding the family and the survival of the group.

Women also held the real political power. The matrons, senior women of the matrilineal lines, elected and deposed the Council of Elders, which regulated the tribe. Hereditary admission to this council was transmitted through women. Some anthropologists hold that women also had the right of veto in matters of war and peace.

It is more difficult to give a general description of the Algonquin-speaking peoples, as the groups vary greatly. However, recent research indicates that among hunting and gathering peoples there was little formalized political and social structure; early anthropological works assumed the superiority of men. In a society of hunters, men played the most important economic role. In fact, the opposite is true; later research shows that gathering was more important for survival than was hunting.[2]

The sexual customs of the Indians were very different from those of seventeenth-century Europeans: Native women, in particular, were very free before marriage; divorce was by mutual consent; and, among hunting-gathering peoples, polygamy was common. Such sexual and marital mores scandalized the European, Catholic missionaries, for whom conversion included the imposition of European-style submission to civil authority. The missionaries, therefore, attempted to impose on the Native peoples European family structures, which were built on the concept of male authority, female fidelity and the sanctity of marriage. Yet, the ethical and social order of these societies was based on personal freedom, a concept the missionaries did not understand. In fact, they totally failed to comprehend the nature of Indian society.

The role of women in Native societies is also evident in the Indians' choice of trade goods: saucepans and metal utensils, blankets and, of course, firearms – mostly products related to the craft making and daily work of women.

Yet in the clash of cultures that followed the arrival of the Europeans in North America, Indian women were the most directly affected; for their craft was threatened by ready-made products. Their position in the family and as individuals was thereby undermined and their political power challenged.

LIVING IN A CABIN

In 1634, French colonists began to arrive. Most of them were men but there were some families and the occasional young woman who arrived on her own and immediately found a husband. It was almost impossible for well-to-do families to keep young women as servants and even if work contracts were signed, the women quit to get married. The first civil suits were in fact actions against women servants who had broken their contract in order to marry. On average, there were three or four marriages per year, and in the same period approximately ten children were born. Occasionally, families followed the Hébert-Couillard example, taking on Indian servants – most often Algonquins – an old woman who looked after the children or an adolescent who helped with the hunt. Other families adopted Indian children, although they did not treat them exactly like their own children. The closeness of Native camps and the continuous Iroquois threat created bonds of mutual need between the French and Native communities.

The Indians shared with the colonists their practical knowledge of clothing, use of medicines and food, and modes of winter transport, protection from the swarms of mosquitoes in the spring and adaptation to life in the forest. Unfortunately, little specific information on this temporary cohabitation has survived, although it appears to have existed only at the very beginning, when the French population was smaller than the Indian population camped nearby.

French women had to learn how to fire a musket and do heavy work. When a family moved into its house, traditionally male chores were done by both sexes: burning and clearing land, using a pick, building, harvesting, skinning animals and insulating houses. New colonial buildings were primitive: only the second or third generations would have the luxury of improving their living conditions. These hard, early times are exemplified in the list of effects left by Marie Poulliot and Anthoine Mondin after thirteen years of working their land on the Ile d'Orléans. The only utensils in the simple cabin were "one pot without a cover or spoon, one copper boiler, one frying pan, one grill pan, two old blankets." No change of clothes, not one piece of furniture: the bed and table were fixed crudely to the wall. In a shed, "two *minots* of peas, twenty *minots* of wheat, one *minot* of barley. [A *minot* is eight gallons.] In another shed, two young steers, one cow eight years old, half a barrel of lard, and one hundred and a half (sic) eels, six or seven pounds of butter, four pounds of fat and sixty bales of hay. The only equipment was a pair of straps, a gun, two axes, one hoe, one sickle and an old pair of snowshoes."[3] In thirteen years, the couple had cleared nineteen acres of workable land and cut down six acres of wood. We can barely imagine such a Spartan life, without crockery, without furniture, without even a storage chest. Yet most women who came to New France in the first years led a life of such privation. The children slept on the floor, on straw mattresses or beds of bullrushes, wrapped in blankets of dog hair, bear skins, moose skins or ox hides.

Only a privileged few possessed a change of clothes. An inventory drawn up after a woman's death reports, "There is nothing left to count as far as the clothes of the deceased are concerned, the better part of which remain at the Hôtel-Dieu de Québec. What remained was used to make clothes for small children."[4] Clothes brought from France had to serve for many years and the women sewed only dresses and undershirts. During the first decades, all other clothing was imported from France, ready-made, and the clothes of the dead were sold for a small fortune. Spinning wheels and weaving had yet to appear in New France; and some administrators, observing that the women were idle during much of the winter, accused them of being lazy.

We have already seen that a frugal diet was the norm: peas, bread made from wheat or barley, fat, eels. However, hunting was a source of additional protein and, as a result, the population enjoyed better health than their contemporaries in France. Women, in particular, were more robust, died less often in childbirth and, if they survived their first pregnancies, lived remarkably long lives.

As there was no furniture to polish, crockery to wash, windows to clean, meat to salt or curtains to sew, domestic chores were minimal. True, sewing and cooking fell to the females, but women's sphere of activities coincided largely with that of the men, in the fields and in the bush. (Of course, this sharing of chores was one sided: women could do any chore, but men did not touch anything in the house, although they had managed well enough, before women arrived.) The wives of the colonists, less occupied in the house than were women in Europe, did heavy work. When the men left, the women could hold the fort at home. That, according to Marie de l'Incarnation, is why men hoped to marry "village girls as good for work as any man." In the nineteenth and even in the twentieth century, those responsible for colonization would continue to see women in this same light.

Twentieth-century women often interpret the performance of male work by women in the seventeenth century as an example of growth and liberation; but for some of these women, life must have seemed abnormal. To take on "male" tasks as well as "female" tasks seemed to them a heavy burden. The occasional accounts left by women bring out their anxiety in the face of the unfamiliar. Every woman secretly longed for the life she had left behind in France.

Moreover, the colony was very dependent on France. "Without commerce the country is worthless. It can do without France for its food, but it is entirely dependent on it for its clothes, its tools, its wine, its brandy and for an infinity of little comforts," wrote Marie de l'Incarnation.

It was women, for the most part, who ran the small businesses that sold the imported material, clothes, furs, brandy and utensils. From a famous lawsuit in the Trois Rivières region in 1666 over the sale of brandy, we learn that women were running the most important trading post in the area, and that they were skilled in circumventing administrative constraints to guarantee the prosperity of their business. It was common practice in the seventeenth century for "the wives of merchants to learn to keep the books, to run the business in the absence of their husband," and these absences were frequent. In *Ancien Régime* society, especially in the working class, women took part in family decisions and accompanied their husbands to the lawyers for matters such as assigning property, signing a lease or arranging for the apprenticeship of one of their children, according to historian Louise Dechêne.

Widows and artisans' wives made ends meet by keeping inns or taverns. This appealed to many because of the easy profits to be made from cheating Indians, getting soldiers and servants drunk and serving wine at Sunday mass. Some even secretly turned taverns into gambling dens or places of debauchery. Several tavern owners turned to prostitution, taking with them their daughters or female servants. In New France, as everywhere else, the two

---

JEANNE ENARD, THE WIDOW CREVIER

Jeanne Enard, wife of Christophe Crevier, arrived in Trois Rivières in 1639. She was recognized, very early on, as a good businesswoman and her house became the centre of a flourishing traffic in brandy with the Indians. In time, she established a veritable network, her servants and farmers serving as intermediaries. She organized several trading expeditions. Her victims were Indians who had been assembled at Cap-de-la-Madeleine by the Jesuits to remove them from the bad influence of the French. In 1666, the Jesuit Gabriel Druillette demanded an enquiry into her business activities. During these proceedings, Indians presented moving testimony on the atrocities they had committed after having drunk "fire-water." Cynical and overbearing, Jeanne Crevier denied any responsibility for these excesses. Her connections would guarantee her immunity from prosecution.

---

occupations were often connected; however, very few madams got into trouble with the law.

Studies of civil actions bear witness to the participation of women in almost all social occupations. In addition, a study of criminal proceedings provides us with a gallery of determined, outspoken women – skilled at inventing insults, ready to defend themselves and to wield a poker in disputes, and given to stealing and to causing bodily harm if need be. This atmosphere of violence was characteristic of early North American settlements – New France was no exception – and women were in the centre of the picture. Life was crude, bitter, almost wild, but the hope of bettering oneself made it all bearable.

THE PROXIMITY OF THE INDIAN TRIBES

To complete this picture of daily life, we must turn to the Iroquois resistance, which profoundly affected the everyday life of colonists in the seventeenth century. This permanent threat sometimes forced colonists to spend weeks on end inside the forts, especially in Trois Rivières and Montreal, and to abandon clearing the land and farming. Even everyday domestic chores were left undone; everybody – French and Native – in the fort lived off supplies sent from France or whatever could be prepared communally in the fort. Such occurrences were common between 1642 and 1666, when two hundred and ninety people – more than 10 percent of the population – were killed or captured by the Iroquois. After a lull of approximately twenty years, war broke out again and every settlement felt threatened. News of attacks sustained the tense atmosphere.

From 1634 to the end of the seventeenth century, such circumstances made women's lives in New France rather different from those of their contemporaries in France. This difference was not the result of a particular ideology but was created by the painful necessity to which the whole population had been reduced. The proximity and example of the Indians also probably influenced the colonists; for, however miserable they were, they saw an even more deprived population living nearby. Their self-image was thus transformed. The women, in particular, considered their fate to be more enviable than that of the "savages." The onerous work done by Indian women more than outweighed their influence in the councils and family clans; following Christian moral principles, the colonial women judged the "savages" harshly. Even the Indian woman's great sexual freedom before marriage was not perceived to be an advantage, for the French women were no more able than the missionaries to see Indian women with the eyes of today's anthropologists!

There were few real marriages between whites and Indians, although there were, of course, "marriages" in the treaty territories. The Hurons, in particular, wanted to cement their political connections with the French through family ties. Thus, each Frenchman – including missionaries, who were considerably embarrassed – was adopted by a family and presented with a "wife." Missionaries tried to "marry" Frenchmen to Huron women, especially their own servants, to avoid scandal; but this policy had very little success.

Indian women who did submit to these unions lost out on all counts. Only adolescents were in demand – the men disdained those who were older than twenty – and such women were easily abandoned. In the end, they were also rejected by members of their own tribe. Some turned to prostitution, a social phenomenon unknown to American Indian tribes before the arrival of the whites. In some cases missionaries ordered prostitutes' heads shaved as punishment.

Native women were more difficult to convert than Native men for several reasons: their closer ties to the religious rites of their tribes, their reluctance to adopt Catholic morality, and the loss of status they would incur when they conducted their lives according to the dictates of the missionaries. From this perspective, the cult devoted to Kateri Tekakwitha the "Lily of the Mohawk," who died in saintly circumstances in 1680, takes on new meaning. The life of this Iroquois virgin was to compensate for the so-called licentious behaviour of Indian women so harshly condemned by the missionaries. It was no accident that the religious and political authorities promoted her cult: Kateri Tekakwitha was proof that missionary endeavours had succeeded. Kateri Tekakwitha was the exaltation of a mythic virginity designed to weaken the resistance of Indians to Christian morality, one more document to add to the file of the "Noble Savage."

There were only six recorded interracial marriages in the colony in the seventeenth century. All were between Frenchmen and Indian women. It is possible that there were more but that such unions were kept secret. How do we explain this small number of marriages between whites and Indians? To be sure, Frenchmen enjoyed the sexual freedom given young Indian women and the help that they gave them in their daily lives; but Indian women found it difficult to accept the constraints of a Christian marriage and a European life-style. And there were so few Frenchwomen in the colony that there were never any available to marry an Indian.

Life in the bush appealed to many French colonists; however, only the men were allowed to live Indian style. The women, it appeared, did not – or could not – even consider the idea. It is significant that the first women to live in the bush were Métis women; of these, Isabelle Montour was the most famous. However, documents are silent on whether Frenchwomen were forbidden or chose not to live Indian style.

During the years of war with the Iroquois, considerable zeal was put into buying back young French girls captured by the Iroquois, who unhesitatingly exchanged them for valiant Onondagua warriors. Such was the fate of Elizabeth Moyen, who was captured in 1665 at the age of sixteen and who had to marry her rescuer, Lambert Closse. If, by chance, the Iroquois brought captured women back to camp, they tortured them as if they were soldiers: this is what happened to Catherine Mercier in 1651. Perhaps this was because many women colonists participated in the defence of the settlements, whereas Indian women did not take part in combat, confining themselves to torturing prisoners. Children taken prisoner were adopted by the tribes and there are numerous reports of children raised in the bush who found it impossible to readapt to a European way of life once found by their families.

History has not recorded the names of all the women who helped fight the Iroquois. However, contemporaries were particularly struck by the exploit of Martine Messier who, in 1652, succeeded in warding off the attacks of an Iroquois by violently grabbing his testicles. Nevertheless, it was the singularity of the exploit that made her famous, not the fact that she had defended herself.

From 1634 to 1666, the Iroquois war darkened the lives of those few women who came to settle in New France. After the temporary peace between the Indian tribes in 1666, however, daily life would be delivered from what Pierre Boucher considered the greatest drawback of the country. "A woman," he

---

ISABELLE MONTOUR

Elizabeth Couc was born at Cap-de-la-Madeleine in August, 1667. Her father, Pierre Couc, had once been a coureur des bois known as "Fleur-de-Cognac" and eventually settled down on a parcel of land; her mother, Marie Métiouamègougoue, was an Algonquin. In 1673, when there were four daughters and two sons in the family, they went to live on the other side of the St. Lawrence, on the banks of the St-François river. In 1679, Elizabeth witnessed the rape and murder of her eldest sister, Jeanne. Elizabeth's mother reminded her that, in the memory of women, in Indian society, rape was unheard of before the arrival of the whites. In 1684, Elizabeth Couc married Joachim Germano, a coureur des bois. For eleven years she led a life of loneliness and domestic chores typical of the wife of a voyageur. She had only one child. Her husband, her brother and her brothers-in-law were all engaged in the fur trade around the Great Lakes. The whole clan, including the women and children, ended up at Michilimakinac in 1693. The Couc sisters, now bearing the name Montour, were the first "white women" to settle in the Great Lakes region. A widow at twenty-eight, Elizabeth Couc (Montour) became famous for her exploits and her talents as an interpreter. Finally, she married an Iroquois chief and put her life in the hands of her new family. Madame Montour died in 1749 in Pennsylvania.[5]

---

wrote in 1663, "is always worried that her husband, who has set out in the morning to work, will be killed or taken prisoner and that she will never see him again."[6] With the resumption of the Iroquois war at the end of the century, a new generation of Canadians built themselves a reputation as heroes.

MADELEINE DE VERCHERES

The concept of heroism has been developed essentially from male experience. It is also a concept used by historians when they make judgements about certain events of the past. Evidently, most people who came to New France did not consider themselves to be heroes or heroines. Some, taking advantage of this image in order to obtain a pension, exaggerated the courage they had displayed in service of their king.

In fact, there were many heroines; but only one woman in the seventeenth century who claimed that status for herself: Madeleine de Verchères. Her case is worthy of study, since it tells us about women's collective self-image.

Let us briefly recall the facts: on 22 October, 1692, Madeleine de Verchères was present at the capture by Iroquois of about twenty settlers working in the fields. Pursued by an Iroquois, she escaped his grasp by untying her neckerchief and shutting herself inside the fort. She organized its defence, alerted the neighbouring forts by firing off a cannon and succeeded in holding the Iroquois at bay until reinforcements arrived.

There is nothing surprising about this story so far, since attacks had been frequent between 1686 and 1701 and the "heroine's" mother had herself put up a similar fight two years previously. However, the episode became interesting when Madeleine de Verchères decided to seek a pension as a reward for her heroic exploit. She thought of doing so first seven years after the event, in 1699, and revived her claim sometime between 1722 and 1730, when she was at least forty years of age. The second time she presented a much more dramatic version of her exploit, which by general consent lacks credibility. But the credibility of her story is not the real issue here.

The two versions written by Madeleine de Verchères were very revealing. "Although my sex does not permit me to have attributes other than those required of me," she wrote, "however, permit me to say that I have feelings which lead me to glory, just like many men."[7] Or again: "French Canadian women would not be less passionate in displaying their zeal to glorify the King, if they had occasion to do so." And recounting her exploit, she stated: "At that fatal moment, I maintained the little confidence of which a girl is capable and with which she can be armed." She distinguished herself from the woman who was "extremely afraid, as is natural with all Parisian women;" and she refused to "stop for the groans of several women overcome with grief at the sight of their husbands being carried off."

Finally, we should note the heroine's endorsement of values based on a male, military and elitist concept of courage; she tacitly accepts the general inferiority of women and their confinement to "naturally" female roles; she justifies her heroism above all by the fact that she escaped the confines placed on women. However, the mere fact that she was able to write the account and make her claim indicated that she was a member of a social class with access to royal pensions.

In the final analysis, the story of Madeleine de Verchères tells us that there were women of character in seventeenth-century New France; above all, however, it shows us that women's collective self-image was hardly different from that of traditional societies. Then why did some women come to Canada knowing of the Iroquois attacks? Why did they become heroines despite themselves?

LEAVING FRANCE

Historical studies are gradually revealing how difficult the daily life of the lower classes in sixteenth-century and seventeenth-century France was. In his authoritative *La France moderne,* Robert Mandrou has attempted an outline of historical psychology. The picture he paints is full of greys and blacks. Diet is characterized by chronic undernourishment, punctuated by occasional surpluses and long periods of privation, if not actual famine. Numerous seventeenth-century accounts describe pitiful scenes in which families were reduced to eating grass or earth. Epidemics were frequent and caused severe reductions in the population. And fear seems to have been characteristic of the period: fear of shortages, famines and epidemics was increased by the fear of war, which filled the roads with thousands of soldiers and outlaws.

We shall not attempt a detailed analysis of the economic situation in France during this period; we will, however, detail factors that affected the daily lives of the general population: a considerable rise in the cost of living, a spectacular leap in the price of bread in times of crisis, the difficulty young men had in apprenticing for a trade, girls' problems finding a husband, and an increased number of poor people and abandoned babies. Moreover, seventeenth-century society was characterized by great chasms between the social classes that, in certain regions, provoked popular rebellions and acts of sedition.

As few systemic solutions were offered, people began to look for their own ways out. One, favoured especially by men, was the nomadic life – a flight toward greener pastures, leaving behind wife and children. This was the attraction of the sea, of adventure, of pilgrimage, of war, of exile. Seaports were inundated with people on the move, ready to do anything to improve their lot. In Honfleur, Cherbourg, Saint Nazaire, La Rochelle and Saint Mâlo, shipowners easily found volunteers for a voyage to New France or an expedition to the Caribbean. The ships that arrived each summer in Quebec were filled with men, but carried few women.

The nomadic life was not the only means of escape. Drunkenness (distilled spirits had just been discovered); the theatre (l'Illustre Théâtre, Molière's theatre company for example); and feast days provided the poor with respite from the anxiety of daily living. The more educated had access to the exotic accounts of geographers and missionaries that inspired voyages of imagination.

For the upper classes, mystical experiences were an acceptable means of expression and escape. Within the Catholic Church, numerous mystical movements grew up. Large numbers of religious orders, lay movements, convents and secret societies were founded. "This exaltation of the mystical affected more women than men.... Battered unceasingly by long years of war, they turned towards prayer and love of God as their refuge," Robert Mandrou tells us. "Lord, I am prepared to do anything to follow you," wrote a Port-Royal nun, "I am even prepared to go to Canada."

The combination of nomadism and mysticism would lead to an exceptionally high level of female immigration to New France. Yet in seventeenth-century France, there was no room for religious dissent. Protestants and other heretics were hunted down and exiled or compelled to convert. As Cardinal Richelieu had forbidden heretics to settle in New France, one does not find there any of the religious sects that sought refuge on British American soil. The fact that England permitted Puritan, Quaker and Catholic settlements in its colonies explains the incredible difference in immigration patterns of New England and New France. British immigration was more dense, occurred more rapidly and, above all, included more families; those who settled on the shores of the Atlantic came from established communities. On the banks of the St. Lawrence immigration was a fragmented affair.

Unfortunately, we don't know what prompted women and girls to emigrate. Whether they followed husbands, whether they went in search of husbands or whether they went to establish a convent or a hospital, theirs were acts of independence that neither custom nor established practices in the seventeenth century permitted. Many of these women seem to have displayed exceptional determination and independence. We should not, therefore, be surprised that the first women who settled in New France were somewhat out of the ordinary. Their desire to escape from poverty or to improve themselves led them to choose an unorthodox solution that would affect their whole lives. There is, then, good reason for dwelling on the type of women who came here. For the choice they made transformed most of them into heroines, to be sure, albeit anonymous heroines.

NOTES

1 Joseph F. Lafiteau, *Moeurs des Sauvages américains, comparés aux moeurs des premiers temps,* 2 volumes (Paris: 1724). This quotation is taken from volume 2, chapter 2. The value of Lafiteau's ethnological observations is fully recognized today.

2 Several studies even credit women with contributing from 60 to 80 percent of the labour necessary for survival. Eleanor Leacock, who studied the Montagnais and the Nascapis and who based her work principally on the writings of Jesuit missionaries, found excellent arguments to support the principle of matrilocal residence.

3 According to a post-mortem inventory drawn up by notary Paul Vachon on 23 January, 1681, quoted by Sylvio Dumas in *Les Filles du Roi en Novelle-France,* Société historique de Québec, 1972, pp. 115-116.

4 Ibid.

5 Simone Vincens, *Madame Montour et son temps* (Quebec/Amérique, 1979).

6 Pierre Boucher, *Histoire véritable et naturelle des moeurs et productions du pays de la Nouvelle-France, vulgairement dite le Canada* (Paris: 1664), p. 151. (A new edition was published in 1964 by the Société historique de Boucherville.)

7 Madeleine de Verchères, writing to the Comtesse de Maurepas, on 15 October 1699 (sic), in the *Supplément au Rapport des archives canadiennes,* 1899, pp. 6-7.

CHAPTER TWO

UNSUNG HEROINES

FOUNDING WOMEN

IN SEVENTEENTH-CENTURY FRANCE, the Church assumed most social responsibilities. Traditional historians have awarded a prominent place to the women who played a role in the Church of New France. Indeed, their glorification of patriotism and the past has inspired any number of edifying stories about the piety of French-Canadian heroines. Marie de l'Incarnation, Jeanne Mance, Marguerite Bourgeoys and Marguerite d'Youville, to mention only the most famous, are major figures in all the histories of New France, right alongside the Champlains, the Maisonneuves, the Frontenacs and the Montcalms. But it is time to look for the real women behind these heroines.

First of all, let us place this wave of religious zeal in its historical context. There is no denying that the history of New France was both religious and fervent, at least for the first few generations. However, such a movement was not unique to New France; it could be found behind almost every seventeenth-century attempt at colonization. The Mayflower Pilgrims, who landed in America in 1620, were part of this religious colonization, as were William Penn's Quaker colonists, who settled in Pennsylvania in 1682. European nonconformists, weary of the wars of religion, saw seventeenth-century America as ideal terrain for the perfection of Christianity rather than as a land of religious liberty. In fact, tolerance was not a concept with which seventeenth-century colonists were familiar. Rather, a large number of them wanted to lead a pure and perfect life in the virginal surroundings of the New World. This religious zeal was prevalent throughout the entire seventeeth century.

A twentieth-century reader may find it difficult to understand the all-pervasive nature of religion and the universal influence it had over women, men and children in the early days of the colonies. There were as many different religious sects then as there are today, but whatever their beliefs, people were more devout than their descendants. This is not to say that our ancestors were more virtuous than we are, but that they feared God more. Communities of religious women in New France were part of this vast religious movement; to understand them, we must see them in this Christian context.

What was unique, however, about New France was the remarkable number of women who played a vital role in the colony's spiritual and material beginnings. One would search in vain for similar deeds in the annals of British American history. "The ecclesiastical structure of the Puritans, at any rate, allowed for no female participation, in contrast to the Catholic Church where ... as members of monastic orders dedicated to education and to care of the sick, women could exercise some of the most noble prerogatives of their sex," wrote one Anglo-Saxon historian. But the proliferation of female communities in New France also has an historical explanation.

New France was fortunate to have an effective propaganda machine: the *Relations des Jésuites* (published in English as *Jesuit Relations and Allied Documents*). Each year, the Jesuits published letters from their missionaries, who were scattered across the continents of the world. These texts aroused great interest; they were read in the refectories of convents and monasteries and discussed in religious brotherhoods. Through *The Jesuit Relations,* a number of women, both aristocratic and bourgeois, heard about Canada; nuns heard the call to evangelize the "savages"; and women were invited to join religious communities in America. The mystical atmosphere of the period proved very helpful to such institutions.

The influence of the *The Jesuit Relations* provides us with a most illuminating explanation for all the visions, occurrences of divine inspiration, miraculous events and premonitions revealed in dreams that abound in early accounts of the communities. If divine intervention did play a role in these undertakings, it did so within a social climate that fostered the most spiritual forms of escapism and gave rise to many charitable deeds.

The women who responded to the call were not dreamers, for their mystical inspiration was accompanied by a strong sense of reality. This is seen in the way women who read *The Jesuit Relations* initiated their projects, and obtained their necessities: authorization to locate within the town of Quebec, seigneurial titles, a fief on the outskirts of the town, and funds for the transportation of nuns, their servants and a great deal of furniture, dishes, fabrics and various utensils. Four distinct institutions were established within thirty years: the convent of the Ursulines de Québec, founded by Marie Guyart (Marie de l'Incarnation) in 1639; the Hôtel-Dieu de Québec, founded in 1639 and operated by the Hospitalières de Dieppe, under the supervision of Marie Guenet and Marie Forestier; the Hôtel-Dieu de Montréal, begun in 1643, the work of Jeanne Mance, who made use of the services of the Hospitalières de la Flèche; and the Congrégation des Filles séculières de Ville-Marie, founded in 1669, the great achievement of Marguerite Bourgeoys, who arrived in Montreal in 1653.

The history of these institutions demonstrates the diverse talents of these determined and highly resourceful women. Marie Guyart had had ten years' experience as the manager of a transport company on the docks of the Loire River. Her talents as a businesswoman proved indispensable in the successful foundation of the Ursuline convent. She sorted out the rather vague financial agreements made by her sponsor, Madame de La Peltrie, and oversaw the construction of the first convent, "... which was built entirely from stone and measured 92 feet in length and 28 feet in width. The manner in which it was built made it the most beautiful and the grandest house of its period." She was responsible for the cutting of the 175 cords of wood that the building's four chimneys consumed every year. After the building was destroyed by fire in 1650, she raised the necessary funds to reconstruct it. A good part of the thirteen thousand letters she wrote constitute a veritable colonial history, assessing and describing with great insight the fledgling French-Canadian society.

THE EDUCATION OF INDIAN WOMEN

It is ... very difficult if not impossible to francisize or civilize them. We have more experience with them than anybody else and yet, of the hundreds who have passed through our hands, we have scarcely civilized one. They are docile and thoughtful, but when they are farthest from our minds, they climb the fence and take off into the bush with their relatives, finding more pleasure there than in all the attractions of our French homes. The Savage temperament is such that they cannot be restrained; if they do submit, they become melancholy and fall a prey to sickness. Moreover, the Savages love their children deeply, and when they know that they are sad, they will do anything to get them back, and they must be returned. We have come to know the Huron, Algonquin and Iroquois women. The Iroquois women are the prettiest and the most docile of all. I do not know if it will be easier to civilize them than the others, nor if they will retain the French civility in which they are being raised, for they are Savages and, as such, we cannot expect too much of them.

Marie de l'Incarnation to her son,
1 September, 1668.[1]

She disagreed with Monseigneur de Laval over the regulations of her order, opposed her bishop vigorously and openly deplored the authority he exercised over the religious communities. In fact, it was not until after the death of Marie de l'Incarnation that the bishop of Quebec was able to impose his rule on the Ursulines of the town.

Finally, Marie de l'Incarnation was distinguished by her exceptional intellectual and spiritual vigour. She left eight books of religious writings, which specialists study with interest even today.

Nor did Jeanne Mance escape the mysticism that drew women to service in New France. "When she decided to come to America, she was a woman of 34, matured by war and all its misery," historian Micheline D'Allaire tells us. She first made sure that her decision had been a solid and realistic one; then she put her social position and her talents as a fund-raiser to good use, obtaining donations from rich women anxious to do good deeds. Only then did she join the company of founders of Ville-Marie, where she became bursar, nurse and supervisor of provisions.

Her hard work led to an increase in membership in the Société Notre-Dame-de-Montréal from eight to thirty-seven; eight of the members were women. Within this society Jeanne Mance played an important diplomatic role.

She arrived in Quebec in 1641 and prepared for her new responsibilities by studying how the Hôtel-Dieu de Québec was managed and by becoming familiar with the Huron language. The next year she began to organize the first temporary dispensary at Ville-Marie inside the fort and then built a hospital (measuring sixty feet by twenty-four feet), a barn and a stable. She brought in furniture, clothing, utensils, medicines and domestic animals.

The Hôtel-Dieu was able to continue its work with the successful foundation of Ville-Marie. Jeanne Mance made three voyages to France, in 1649, 1658 and 1662, on behalf of these two enterprises. On each of these voyages she conducted delicate negotiations concerning new funds, the upkeep and eventual dissolution of the Société Notre-Dame-de-Montréal and the arrival of the Hospitalières de la Flèche in New France. This led to a lengthy disagreement with the archbishop of Quebec, who did not want two distinct congregations of hospitalers in the colony. But Jeanne Mance chose her allies well. With the Sulpiciens' consent, she obtained autonomous status for her hospital and for the community she had brought from France. For the fort of Ville-Marie had been a private venture for twenty years. Its development had been thwarted by Iroquois attacks, which had killed 51 percent of the population, and by the lack of practicality of its first leaders. Historians agree that, in fact, until Ville-Marie became an integral part of New France, Jeanne Mance played

THE FOUNDING WOMEN DISPUTE
THE AUTHORITY OF THE BISHOP

If it is to be done, it should be done with the consent of, and through all the bishops in whose dioceses there are Convents; for we are under their authority. And what is annoying is that in their freedom to make Constitutions and Customaries they have acted in such a way that there are several Customs in one Congregation. In addition, each Congregation has its first and fundamental Constitutions; the whole situation has, however, been altered and thrown into confusion by all the changes the Bishops are making. Today, things have disintegrated to such a point that it would take this union of Bishops, the agreement of the Holy See and a Constitution approved by His Holiness to restore unity.

Marie de l'Incarnation to her son,
3 October, 1645.

He has given us eight months or a year to think about it. But, my dear Mother, the matter has already been thoroughly considered and a definite decision taken: we will not accept [his decision] unless our refusal is seen as an act of total defiance. Nevertheless, we are not saying anything that might sour relations, for we have to deal with a Prelate who is extremely pious and who, if he is convinced that the glory of God is at stake, won't change his mind and we will have to go in that direction which will seriously affect our observance of our vows.

Marie de l'Incarnation to Mother Saint-Ursule,
13 September, 1661.[2]

As to the commitments that Monseigneur wants us to make, all that we can promise his Eminence on this point, after having consulted those who know our community extremely well, is that while we remain in the Congregation we will continue to make our vows; and because of our position, we do not believe that we can bind ourselves otherwise.... We do not seek other bonds than those of pure love. As for the promise to obey him, that Monseigneur wants all sisters to make on the day they take their vows, everybody knows well enough that until now he has been absolute master in our community.... Therefore, we do not feel obliged to demonstrate further our dependence on him, except by stating that we are under his authority.[3]

a more decisive role than Maisonneuve in its development. In 1663, Ville-Marie became Montreal.

Marguerite Bourgeoys played an equally important role in the early years of New France. This young Frenchwoman heard of Canada from Maisonneuve's sister, Mother Louise de Chomedey-de-Sainte-Marie. The founder of Ville-Marie refused to bring a religious community to Montreal, but agreed to bring Marguerite Bourgeoys in 1653 if she would devote herself to educating children. However, Maisonneuve's mission was primarily to recruit colonists. The first woman writer in New France, Soeur Morin, described Marguerite Bourgeoys's role in the following manner:

> There [in Nantes] she went to Monsieur le Coq's, where she purchased most of the goods and provisions that she needed to equip the 100 men for whom she was responsible. My sister Bourgeoys can do anything; she is equally successful in temporal and spiritual matters, because her love of God guides her actions and gives her wisdom. She has all the character of the proverbial wise woman and it would be very difficult to find another like her.[4]

When she arrived in New France, Marguerite Bourgeoys could not devote herself to teaching. "Life is so precarious in Ville-Marie and infant mortality is so high that it was almost 8 years before we managed to raise any children at all," she wrote. Nevertheless, in April 1658, Bourgeoys welcomed her first pupils in a building near the hospital. Subsequently, she would go to France in search of co-workers and, in 1671, she would obtain letters patent for the Congrégation Notre-Dame, the first congegation of non-cloistered nuns to be founded in the seventeenth century. Today, it is difficult to appreciate the

---

MARIE MORIN

Marie Morin was born in the town of Quebec in 1649. When she was thirteen, she joined the Hospitalières de Montréal, holding a number of positions (including bursar and superior) until her death in 1730. In 1697, she decided to write the history of her community: *Histoire simple et véritable de l'établissement des religieuses hospitalières de Saint Joseph en l'isle de Montréal diste à présant Ville Marie, en Canada, de l'année 1659* ... Her mother, Hélène Desportes, was the first child to be born in the town of Quebec. Marie Morin was the first nun who was born in Canada; she was also the first writer born in New France.

THE SECULAR AND THE CLOISTERED

Since 1556, canon law had required that a nun take solemn vows and lead a cloistered life. After 1563, women teachers and hospitalers had to conform to Church laws, formulated at the Council of Trent, if they wished to be accepted by Church authorities.

New religious orders in the seventeenth century opposed these laws, which they saw as obstacles to their apostolic mission. These women described themselves as "secular." Marguerite Bourgeoys was the first in Canada and one of the first in the Church to obtain permission to create a secular community, one that did not require the sisters to be cloistered.

---

significance of the audacious innovations introduced by this "secular" community, which had to work to support itself, wore a lay uniform and advocated avant-garde educational principles. Marguerite Bourgeoys advocated training for teachers, free instruction, education for girls and "... prudent and moderate use of corporal punishment, remembering that one is in the presence of God." She also recommended that children learn to read in French and not in Latin – a daring innovation for the time. Sisters travelled on foot, by canoe and on horseback; and they founded a number of convents, usually under extremely difficult conditions.

The most original aspect of Marguerite Bourgeoys' work lay in her creation of a community that did not have to be cloistered. Twice, she had to resist, albeit respectfully, her bishop's wish to amalgamate the congregation with the Ursulines de Québec. All the women who founded institutions in the seventeenth century opposed the bishop. This was a sign of real independence, and their example would be followed in the eighteenth century by Marguerite d'Youville, founder of the Soeurs Grises de Montréal (Grey Nuns of Montreal).

TAKING THE VEIL

The women who founded the orders form quite an impressive group. Can the same be said for the young French-Canadian women who chose to enter the convent after 1646? In the early days of the colony, the scarcity of women made for very few entrants; but after 1680, there was a steady stream of postulants, which increased in proportion to the population until 1722, when the King tried to raise the dowry price for taking the veil. Why did these young

---

IN OPPOSITION TO THE CLOISTERING OF NUNS

We are asked why we do not take solemn vows. We reply that the Blessed Virgin, our dear Teacher, gave herself to God of her own accord; her vow of chastity was known only to the angel and her other vows only became known when she put them into practice – and from this she never strayed throughout her life, in the same way as we take our vows of our own accord, but it is good that people see our vows being put into practice.

We are asked why we prefer to be vagabonds rather than cloistered nuns, since the cloisters offer protection to persons of our sex. We reply that the Blessed Virgin was never cloistered but [sic] she never refused a voyage which allowed her to carry out some good or charitable deed. Because we see her as our teacher, we are not cloistered, although we live in a Community. In this way, we can go everywhere we are sent to educate girls.[5]

Marguerite Bourgeoys

---

women enter the convent? The proportion of novices was greatest in the upper classes. Piety was most conspicuous among the elite, and young women of this class often had to wait a long time before they could find a suitable husband.

Rich girls entered as choir nuns, with a dowry from their families or from a priest. Poor girls entered as lay sisters and, in lieu of a dowry, paid for their upkeep in kind (firewood, wheat or straw mattresses). A few Indian women were admitted into the communities, but they frequently died within months of taking the veil, because they were unable to tolerate life in the cloister.

It is extremely difficult to know the real reasons girls took the veil, and much research is still to be done. Besides the undeniably religious motives, there were sometimes more prosaic reasons: a desire for material security, a comfortable life and social recognition; and family pressures (from aunts and elder sisters). Although in seventeenth-century Quebec, not as many girls became nuns as did after 1850, nevertheless, there was a steady flow into the convent during the *Ancien Régime*. We can, however, get a better understanding of this aspect of seventeenth-century women's history if we examine the various roles a nun's religious vocation opened to her.

The Ursulines educated the daughters of good families. The Filles de la Congrégation did something new and, for the period, exceptional: they intro-

CHOIR NUNS AND LAY NUNS

There were two social classes of nuns in the convents. The cloistered nuns (*moniales*) took solemn vows and enjoyed special prerogatives in the workings of the community. They led the services. These were the choir nuns.

To look after them, there were domestic sisters, so-called lay sisters. The lay sisters also took solemn vows and lived the cloistered life; but their vocation was the hard work: gardening, cooking, washing and housework. Lay sisters had to be strong and docile.

These distinctions did not apply to the Filles de la Congrégation, who were secular.

duced boarding schools into the parishes. A dozen convents were founded in this way in the seventeenth century and most would continue to function throughout the eighteenth century.

The participation of women in education was not unique to New France; however, education in New France was uniquely structured. Instruction for girls was quite limited. It was primarily religious, but also involved learning to read, to write, "jeter" (to count with tokens) and to do all sorts of things appropriate to their sex – everything a girl should know. There were four levels of education, which corresponded to the social status of the pupils. At the top of the hierarchy were the boarding-school pupils of the Ursulines; then came the day pupils; lower down the scale were the boarders from the schools of Marguerite Bourgeoys and at the bottom of the ladder were the

ON THE EDUCATION OF GIRLS

Experience demonstrates that all these girls are slow and so we will not take them until they are 12. In this way, they will be in a better position to benefit from their classes ... and to pay for their keep ... as for writing, this is not necessary for poor girls; it would be a waste of time, which could be better spent on other things. If some were found that we thought capable of becoming nuns, they could be sent to school to learn how to write....[6]

pupils of La Providence, a sort of domestic-science school founded by Marguerite Bourgeoys. At this school, nuns took lower-class girls and taught them how to perform household chores.

The nuns played an extremely active role in community social work. Their duties seem to have been carried out according to *Ancien Régime* traditions but, once again, the subject has not been systematically studied. It is worth noting, however, that New France subscribed to traditional Catholic views of charity, in this respect at least profiting from structures and models nonexistent in Protestant countries. Moreover, charitable foundations in New France were unique and, compared to what was happening in British North America, played an important social role. Although they had much larger populations, it was a long time before a similar movement grew up in the British American colonies. At the end of the seventeenth century, communities of women in New France assumed responsibility for everything relating to public charity: helping the poor, the old, the invalid, the sick, the mad, women prisoners, prostitutes and orphans.

From research on the Hôtel-Dieu de Québec, we know that the hospital, on average, housed about forty people, and more when there was an epidemic. Care was free and, it appears, very good. (According to the registers of the hospital, 92 percent of men and 90 percent of women who were admitted were cured.) In Montreal, Judith Moreau de Bresoles, the hospitaler brought over by Jeanne Mance, had such a good reputation as a nurse that patients naïvely believed it would be impossible for them to die if she looked after them.

Thus, New France was, for certain seventeenth-century French women, a privileged place where they could express their independence and initiative. Whether aristocrats or bourgeoises, nuns or lay women, these women found in America a new milieu, free from the constraints of tradition; and they found a life that demanded every ounce of energy they possessed. As long as the colony remained underdeveloped, the women enjoyed relative independence. For example, both Jeanne Mance and Marguerite Bourgeoys crossed the Atlantic seven times, a feat that few male administrators, lay or clerical, could claim and one that few women in the eighteenth century would repeat.

But was such the case for all the women who came here?

GIRLS FOR MARRIAGE

At this point we might take a closer look at the fate of one group of immigrant women to New France – the single women who came here for the express purpose of getting married. Historians have long argued about the morality of these women, both prior to and after their arrival in Quebec, and presented contradictory evidence. (We might point out that they devote much more energy to examining the virtue of women than of men. Nevertheless, the question remains: Were they "girls of average virtue" (Baron de la Hontan), "very-well educated women" (*Journal des Jésuites*), "women of easy virtue" (Boucault), "girls who were very vulgar and very difficult to control" (Marie de l'Incarnation), or "very fine girls, taken from honorable homes" (*Jesuit Relations*)?[7] In reality, the issue has been approached from the wrong direction, with the result that people have spent time examining value judgements and opinions. We shall approach the question from another perspective.

Why were they induced to come? It would appear that there was a desire to encourage the indentured labourers and the soldiers – men who otherwise would return to France or go off into the bush – to remain in the colony. Women were a stabilizing element in a social unit made up primarily of bachelors. Where there were women, there would eventually be houses and children – in other words, a future; a reason for building towns and schools and for writing laws; a motivation for clearing land, for growing crops and for establishing farms. Demographers Charbonneau and Landry estimate that of the men who came, 56 percent stayed on. However, of the women who came to get married, the figure is above 90 percent. Is there an explanation for this discrepancy?

Of course there is. It lies in the types of contract offered to male and female immigrants. A man arrived in New France and signed an *engagé* contract, which bound him to his employer for three years. Thus, such men were nicknamed "Trente-six Mois" (Thirty-six Months). At the end of this period the man was free. But a woman signed a marriage contract that bound her for life to her husband. Therefore, few women returned to France. The King's Daughters were sent specifically for the purpose of procreation. Thus, we hear Colbert informing Talon of the despatch of "400 good men, 50 girls, 12 mares and two stallions," and Talon rejoicing "that the women of New France have a child every year." These fine administrators contrived regulations to force bachelors to take a wife within fifteen days of the arrival of the boats, failing which their licence to trade would be revoked. Demographers have shown, however, that the policies of the administrators (bonuses for large families, presents for couples who married young) had no effect on the behaviour of the population.

Did the King's Daughters know what was in store for them? We must believe that they did. Most got married in the weeks or even the days following their arrival in the colony. Between 1634 and 1662, 230 were recruited by religious communities and by the agents of the *Cent Associés* (the One Hundred Associates), a group involved in commercial activities in New France. The course of events is easy to follow: young women would be recruited for

TABLE 1
The *King's Daughters*

Where did they come from?

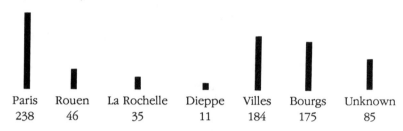

Paris	Rouen	La Rochelle	Dieppe	Villes	Bourgs	Unknown
238	46	35	11	184	175	85

How old were they?

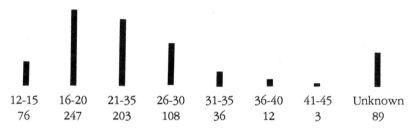

12-15	16-20	21-35	26-30	31-35	36-40	41-45	Unknown
76	247	203	108	36	12	3	89

When did they arrive?

Emigration of the 'King's Daughters'

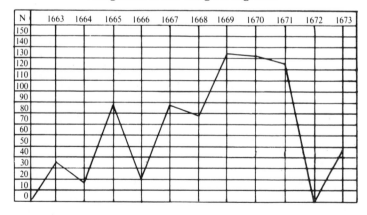

Source: Sylvio Dumas, *Les Filles du Roi en Nouvelle-France* Cahiers d'historie. no 24, La société historique de Québec, 1972.

unmarried colonists, who had come four or five years earlier to make the colony habitable for families. However, this mode of colonization produced a severe imbalance in the population. By 1663, there were six bachelors for every girl who had reached puberty.

Between 1663 and 1673, the State took control of immigration and recruited, amongst others, nearly eight hundred girls for marriage; these were named the *filles du roy*, (King's Daughters) because their transport and their keep were paid for by the King. Most often, their dowry was paid in clothing and supplies suitable for their household. Some privileged girls received a cow, utensils and seeds. Sylvio Dumas estimates that one-third of the King's Daughters received goods to the value of two or three hundred *livres,* and that only 247 received a gift of fifty *livres* from the King. Recruiters had to make sure that the young women were not already married, and received a fee for every girl they persuaded to venture overseas. "Whether they were sent by parents who wanted to get rid of them or by the directors of the Hôpital-Général, who took in orphaned or poor girls, they undoubtedly escaped a miserable fate," states Louise Dechêne. It is possible that girls imprisoned for prostitution managed to melt into the crowd in various contingents, particularly those from La Pitié or La Salpêtrière.

Even allowing that marriage was not endowed with the psychological and emotional refinements it has today, the marriages of these young immigrant

---

SALPETRIERE AND LA PITIE

In seventeenth-century France, the Hôpital-Général was an institution that looked after the disadvantaged: poor people, abandoned children, the sick, orphans of both sexes, tramps, pregnant women and single mothers, insane people and prostitutes. In 1656, an edict established the Hôpital-Général de Paris, which consisted of several buildings. La Salpêtrière and La Pitié were part of this institution. La Salpêtrière took in mostly abandoned children, orphaned girls and pregnant women. The bourgeoisie in Paris easily obtained servants from La Salpêtrière. La Pitié consisted of two buildings for the "incarceration of debauched girls," a house of protection rather than correction. La Salpêtrière sometimes housed more than eight thousand people of all ages and social conditions. More than 50 percent of the King's Daughters came from La Salpêtrière.

women seem to have occurred rather hastily. The girls were considered lucky, because it was difficult for a girl to marry in France at that time; but we must remember that along with their good fortune came very difficult living conditions.

It would appear that, as soon as they were signed up, the King's Daughters were most likely sent off on foot toward a seaport, either Dieppe or La Rochelle, where they embarked for Canada. A woman was placed in charge of them for their two-month crossing. The boats were not very comfortable and the girls travelled in contact with the other passengers: sailors, *engagés* and soldiers. On the rare occasion they were pregnant when they arrived, they were returned to France.

Usually, most were provided with a husband within days of their arrival. We may assume that the girls did the choosing, and as there were fewer of them, they could choose as they wished. In this situation, men who had somewhere to live had the edge. "This was the first thing the girls made enquiries about and they acted wisely, because those men who were not established suffered a great deal before they could lead a comfortable life," wrote Marie de l'Incarnation. Moreover, documents record that nearly 13 percent of the King's Daughters signed more than one marriage contract before committing themselves to a religious ceremony, which bound them for the rest of their days. Yet there were only four requests for a separation out of the large number of hastily contracted marriages. As a rule the King's Daughters clearly took charge of their own lives, enabling them to meet the challenges of the harsh life that awaited them in a cabin in Canada. They were equal to the demands made on them and, in fact, eight years after the arrival of the last convoy, only forty-three had died. (Demographic studies, however, demonstrate that the King's Daughters became infertile sooner than women born in Canada.)

The life awaiting these girls was exceptionally harsh, but met the most basic needs. This was an improvement over France, where not even these needs were met. It seems also that the scattered population in New France considerably reduced the effect of epidemics, which were so frequent in seventeenth-century Europe.

The exceptional circumstances of colonization gave rise to distinctive social behaviour that lasted for nearly two generations. We have already mentioned the most striking example of such distinctive behaviour under the *Ancien Régime*: the marriage of just-adolescent or even prepubescent girls. However, by the end of the seventeenth century, the age for marriage would rise and would soon follow the custom in France. The position of widows, too, was interesting: there is every reason to believe that they were much sought after and that they used the advantage of their assets (a house, tools, land already half cleared) to marry a man who was still young and had no children. In France, widows were usually doomed to poverty; in Quebec, as colonization progressed, it would not be as easy for widows to remarry.

Another distinctive social feature was the small number of babies born out of wedlock. Demographers put the figure at 4.5 percent of all births – half the rate during the following century and low even for the seventeenth century. This phenomenon was due, it appears, to the young age at which the girls married: among widows, the percentage of babies born out of wedlock reached 20 percent. In New France, it was circumstance rather than sentiment that dictated when marriages took place. In France, one got married in October (before Advent) or in winter (before Lent); in New France one got married when the boats arrived, between August and October. After 1680, however, the marriage calendar would become more like that of France, which followed the rhythm of agricultural work.

Current research has not provided precise figures on infant mortality rates or mortality rates amongst women in childbirth. Demographer Hubert Charbonneau is of the opinion that infant mortality increased as the seventeenth century progressed. He estimates that fewer babies died in Quebec than in France and hypothesizes that those women who survived the rough crossing were strong and thereby contributed to the hardiness of the population in the new land. Yet his research also shows an above-average death rate amongst women between the ages of thirty and forty-five, perhaps because women who died during childbirth tended to be most vulnerable at the beginning and at the end of their fertile period. It also seems certain that families were large, with six or seven children on average, and that in most cases a woman had a child every two years. When they reached forty, women ceased to have children. Menopause seems to have come earlier and puberty later in the seventeenth century than today. Also, as was generally the case in pre-industrial society, couples tended not to use contraception.

Seventeenth-century French-Canadian society had another distinctive characteristic: the large proportion of sexual offences that were brought before the courts. It was two times as high as during the following century. André Morel states: "It is certain, moreover, that real crime in this area, far from decreasing, must have in fact increased." It appears that in the seventeenth century, breaches of the sexual code were a source of indignation and scandal, which explains why so many charges were brought before the courts. Social control in this area would have been much greater during the seventeenth century than during the following century.

For all that, anecdotes concerning the "debauchery in New France" tell us more about sexual customs than they do about the morality of the population. The language of those involved seems to be remarkably frank and crude, especially among peasants. Yet there was a double standard in all classes of society; fidelity was essentially a woman's duty.

These social characteristics were prominent amongst the working classes, but it seems the situation was only slightly different amongst the more well-to-do.

WOMEN FROM THE LESSER NOBILITY AND FROM THE BOURGEOISIE

Marguerite Legardeur de Repentigny, the wife of Jacques LeNeuf de la Poterie, disembarked at Quebec on 11 June 1636; she was part of a family of about fifteen who came to New France with the declared aim of making a fortune, as the avenues to power and riches in France were too crowded. Because she was only a wife, she has not attracted the interest of historians. However, like other women in her social group, she played a not-insignificant role in the management and success of the financial and property ambitions of her family. Examples of such female participation are to be found among ambitious people from all walks of life who were seduced by the American adventure.

We know very little about these women. To find out about them, we must take a fresh look at historical documents and at studies dealing with their husbands, their fathers and their sons. It is clear this relatively affluent immigrant group was not large in number, but they played a considerable role between 1634 and 1663, when colonization was principally in the hands of private companies. In 1682, after Talon's intendancy, during which France provisionally took over development and settlement of New France, the merchants resumed even tighter control, with the self-serving complicity of the authorities. On the one hand, the role of these people in the economic development of the colony was decisive. On the other hand, this group is overrepresented in the archives and studies of past eras have largely ignored "ordinary people." What is interesting about this social group is not its numbers but the female archetype that emerges from it.

The primary role of women in the families of the lesser nobility or of the bourgeoisie, often ennobled by the King, was to bear children. Families with eight, ten or twelve children were not uncommon. Children were a useful means of increasing the number of land concessions made to parents: in 1663, there were eight cases of concessions granted to *seigneurs* younger than six years of age and six cases that involved adolescent *seigneurs*. These concessions, it should be noted, never went to females. It was only a death in the family – usually that of their husbands – that would bring them seigneurial property.

Since the French-Canadian nobility had hardly any interest in the improvement and exploitation of their land, children became a pretext for claiming pensions. Their sons dressed in Indian style, played highwayman, went off into the fur trade and sought positions in the army, while daughters were used to strengthen family fortunes through arranged marriages. After two generations, the great families formed a closely knit society, in which daughters' dowries forged strong links that would be increasingly difficult to break.

In this small society, girls had character and "they were more knowledgeable, for the most part, in dangerous subjects than those in France," wrote Marie de l'Incarnation. "Thirty girls gave us more work in the boarding school

TABLE 2

Names Given to the First Girls Born in Canada
(*Canadiennes* Receiving Baptism)

First Names	Total	Percentage
Marie	808	9.6
Marie-Madeleine	683	8.1
Marie-Anne	586	7.0
Marguerite	617	7.3
Jeanne	397	4.7
Catherine	385	4.6
Anne	371	4.4
Geneviève	327	3.9
Françoise	295	3.5
Louise	255	3.0
Elisabeth	234	2.8
Marie-Françoise	209	2.5
Marie-Catherine	193	2.3
Marie-Jeanne	161	1.9
Angélique	139	1.7
Other given names	2746	32.7
Total	8406	100.0

Source: R. Roy, Y. Landry, H. Charbonneau,
"Quelques comportements des Canadiens au XVIIe
siècle d'après les régistres paroissiaux" in *Revue
d'Histoire d'Amérique française,* vol. 31, no 1 (juin
1977), p. 71.

than 60 in France." Brought up in freedom, these "little savage girls" were sent to the Ursulines to learn a few social graces. Most often they received bursaries, since their families could not pay the whole cost of their board. The girls left the convent to get married soon after they had completed their studies, which were largely concerned with preparing them to be wives and mothers. If they did not find suitable spouses, they entered the convent.

Many women were forced to nurse their babies themselves, at least in the seventeenth century, since there were not enough women to act as wet-nurses. Once freed from having and nursing babies, they took part in managing business affairs and actively sought to give their children a good start in life through suitable marriages and positions in the army or in public administration. Widows were still considered eligible marriage partners; consequently, they increased their efforts to remarry in order to guarantee that their children had a guardian. Consider the case, for example, of Eléonore de Grandmaison, who had four husbands, one after the other, and displayed undeniable talents as a businesswoman. Although, by 1663, 54.5 percent of the *seigneuries* belonged to widows, it does not necessarily follow that the women had control of the management of the property. They owned the *seigneuries,* but in the full knowledge that they would hand over the property to their sons. Furthermore, women were never found on councils or in key positions in the colony.

The houses of such people appeared to be crowded with furniture. Each ship that arrived in Quebec brought to these privileged but indebted families cushions, tables, candlesticks, armchairs, mirrors, linen and silver platters, which trumpeted their social status. Women reigned supreme in these households, pale imitations of homes in France. Yet, if they survived their husbands, women often found themselves close to poverty once their children had been well provided for. In this era, no son would interrupt his career to come to the assistance of his mother; no daughter would take her mother into her family. The State and the Church looked after them, either by granting them pensions or by housing them in convents.

A SOCIETY BEGINS TO EMERGE

New France provided an opportunity for women and men to escape: by crossing the Atlantic, they ended a life of poverty and wandering on French soil. Moreover, in the seventeenth century, mystics found in New France a land in which they could give vent to their aspirations and adventurers a new place to try their luck. The beginnings of the colonial period were an exceptional period, demanding the energy of everyone involved. It was to be expected that women would go beyond their culturally determined limits.

Because there was a need, women founded religious institutions, became merchants, soldiers, administrators and missionaries. Because there was a land to be opened up, hundreds of women "as capable of work as any man" cleared land and helped to populate the colony.

What characterized this century was not so much the heroism or the unfamiliar or nontraditional activities of women, but the many independent and individual deeds they accomplished. In 1698, there were only 15,355 people living in New France. Nevertheless, in such a small society, and in only three-quarters of a century, a large number of women played a role worthy of recording in official histories.

The beginning of the eighteenth century would be another turning point in Quebec history. The Iroquois wars ended in 1701, putting an end to decades of fear in the community and freeing women from carrying muskets. There was less and less contact with the Indians. The tribes had been decimated by war and disease and had either been driven into the interior or had been literally shut up in villages, where the missionaries kept them semidependent and tried to impose a European moral code on the women. Marriageable girls were no longer in short supply, and slowly the population became more balanced. The *seigneuries* began to fill up as the colonists cleared the land and pushed back the forest. There were, however, still families in New France who lived in poverty and isolation as there are in Quebec in the twentieth century. But from the beginning of the eighteenth century, the number of households that achieved a certain level of prosperity increased and a stable parish life slowly came into existence. Institutions and social classes became more secure; however, at the same time, dreams of colonial fortunes were beginning to fade. Even the fur trade was entering a period of crisis.

But the new circumstances would create for women a normalized society, closer to that of the *Ancien Régime,* in which women were restricted to family life. The most obvious sign of these changes in society seems to have been the appearance of a new social group, the destitute. After 1676, they crowded into Quebec and means had to be found to assist them. By 1685, they had reached Montreal.

Bureaux des pauvres (shelters for the poor), administered by the laity, were opened in Quebec and Montreal. But the religious authorities managed to change them into general hospitals, run by nuns or monks, as in France.* Two-thirds of the poor who went to the Montreal shelter were women. In the stable society that was emerging, women figured prominently among its rejects. The heroic period was well and truly at an end.

---

* The Hôpital Général opened its doors in 1701. It was run by the Hospitalières de Saint Augustin, who had left the Hôtel-Dieu.

NOTES

1 Marie de l'Incarnation, Ursuline (1599-1672), *Correspondance,* new edition by Dom Guy Oury, Abbaye Saint-Pierre, Solesmes, 1971, p. 809.

2 Ibid.

3 Marguerite Bourgeoys to Monsieur Tronson, in Faillon, *Vie de la Soeur Bourgeoys,* vol. 2, pp. 31-32.

4 Marie Morin, *Histoire simple et véritable, les annales de L'Hôtel Dieu de Montréal,* 1659-1725, critical edition by Ghislaine Legendre (Montreal: Presses de l'Université de Montréal, 1979), p. 64.

5 *Marguerite Bourgeoys* texts selected and annotated by H. Bernier in the series Classiques canadiens, no. 3 (Montreal, Fides, 1958), p. 66.

6 Contract for the donation of 13, 300 *livres* by Jeanne Leber to the Congrégation Notre-Dame, 9 September, 1714, ibid., Le Pailleur. Quoted in Louise Dechêne, *Habitants et Marchands de Montréal au XVIIe siècle,* in the series "Civilisations et Mentalités," (Paris: Plon, 1974).

7 For views on the *filles du roy* see the following:
——— *Jesuit Relations and Allied Documents.* (ed. Thwaites), volume XXI, pp. 107-109; volume XLI, pp. 185-187.

——— Pierre Boucher, op. cit., pp. 155-156.

——— De Baugy. *Journal d'une Expédition contre les Iroquois en 1687,* (Paris, 1883) (letter of 23rd November, 1683).

——— Marie de l'Incarnation. *Correspondance,* new edition by Dom Oury, 1971: letter of October 1668, p. 832; letter of October 1669, p. 862.

——— Lahontan. *Nouveaux voyages de Mr le Baron de la Honton dans l' Amérique septentrionale* (La Haye, 1703), vol. I, pp. 10-12.

——— *Le Journal des Jésuites,* (Quebec, 1871), p. 335.

FURTHER READING

Charbonneau, Hubert. *Vie et mort de nos ancêtres.* Demographic Study, in the series *Démographie canadienne,* no. 3. Montreal: PUM, 1975.

D'Allaire, Micheline, "Jeanne Mance à Montréal en 1642" in *Forces,* 1973, pp. 38-46.

Daveluy, Marie-Claire. *Jeanne Mance* Montréal: Fides, 1962.

Dechêne, Louise. *Habitants et marchands de Montréal au XVIIe siècle.* Plon, 1974.

Desrosiers, Léo Paul. *Les Opiniâtres*. Montreal: Fides, 1980.

Dickinson, John A. "La guerre iroquoise et la mortalité en Nouvelle-France, 1608-1666" in *Revue d'histoire d'amérique française,* vol. 36 no. 1, June 1982, pp. 31-54.

Dictionnaire biographique du Canada, vol. 1.

Douglas, James. "The Status of Women in New-England and New France" in *Queen's Quarterly,* 1912, pp. 359-374.

Dumas, Sylvio. *Les Filles du Roi en Nouvelle-France.* Cahiers d'histoire, no. 24. La Société historique de Québec, 1972.

Jamieson, Kathleen. *Indian Women and The Law in Canada: Citizens Minus.* Ottawa: Advisory Council on The Status of Women, 1978.

Jean, Marguerite. *Evolution des communautés religieuses de femmes au Canada de 1639 à nos jours.* Montreal: Fides, 1977.

Lachance, André. "Le Bureau des pauvres de Montréal." in *Histoire sociale,* no. 4, November 1969, pp. 97-110.

Leacock, Eleanor. "Montagnais Marriage and The Jesuits in the Seventeenth Century; Incidents from The Relations of Paul Le Jeune" in *The Western Canadian Journal of Anthropology,* vol. VI, no. 3, 1976.

Leacock, Eleanor. "The Montagnais-Nascapi Band" in Cox, Bruce ed., *Cultural Ecology.* Toronto: McClelland and Stewart, 1973.

Mandrou, Robert. *Introduction à la France Moderne.* An Essay in Historical Psychology, 1500-1640, in the series L'Evolution de l'Humanité. Albin Michel, 1961.

Morel, André. "Réflexions sur la justice criminelle canadienne au XVIIIe siècle" in *Revue d'Histoire d'Amérique française,* vol. 29, no. 2, pp. 241-253.

Oury, Dom Guy. Marie de l'Incarnation (1599-1672), Quebec: P.U.L., 1973, 2 volumes.

Rousseau, Francois. "Hôpital et société en Nouvelle-France: l'Hôtel Dieu de Québec à la fin du XVIIe siècle" in *Revue d'Histoire d'Amérique française,* vol. 31, no. 1, pp. 29-47.

Seguin, R. L. *La vie libertine en Nouvelle-France au XVIIe siècle.* Montreal: Leméac, 1972.

II
STABILITY
1701-1832

AFTER ITS INITIAL DIFFICULTIES, New France entered a period of prosperity and relative stability. However, conditions at the beginning of the eighteenth century did not augur well for the colony. The war with the English colonies did not end until 1713. The fur trade, the economic base of the colony, collapsed and had to undergo a radical transformation. Attempts were made to diversify the economy, but a period of inflation, caused by a crisis in the colony's finances, devastated the lives of the poor. Finally, however, in the 1720s an era of greater prosperity began.

France was interested in its colony in Canada for economic and military reasons. The fur trade, a vast enterprise based mainly in Quebec and Montreal, allowed French investors to make generous profits. New France was a vital military base for furthering the ambitions of Louis XIV and Louis XV in America.

The rivalry between the English and French explains the numerous wars that occurred. North America, like Europe, India and the high seas, was another battlefield for the colonial powers. France maintained a vast military machine in Canada, which was reinforced in times of military need. The war economy was one of the driving forces behind the development of the St. Lawrence Valley. It has been estimated that close to a quarter of the total population of New France worked for the military complex.

After the defeat of the French on the Plains of Abraham in 1759, Canada was unconditionally handed over to Britain in 1763 under the terms of the Treaty of Paris. The British continued to fortify the colony and French troops were replaced by British troops – who were often, in fact, Scots or Germans.

In the eighteenth century, war was one of the scourges, along with epidemics, floods and famine, which afflicted a population. The actual battles scarcely affected the people, but their standard of living and family unity were particularly disrupted, and, of course, a siege that cut citizens off from their sources of supply was always catastrophic. Moreover, armies indulged in destructive acts that were harmful to the civilian population; but even if the citizens supported one side or the other, in the long term, their traditional way of life was little modified by events over which, in any case, they had no control. Popular history has, nevertheless, kept alive the memory of the darkest years: 1759, when Quebec was bombarded and besieged, and when hundreds of farms were burned and destroyed; and the winter of 1775-76, when the Americans tried to take Quebec and Montreal.

In spite of these wars, Canada experienced a period of general stability and prosperity, as evidenced by an extraordinary population increase. Demographer Jacques Henripin has estimated that the Francophone population alone increased twenty-fold between 1700 and 1830.

From the beginning of British rule, English and Scots – merchants, craftsmen, adventurers and farmers – sought their fortune in Canada. Other ethnic groups also began to arrive. After the American Revolution, the Loyalists came to seek political asylum in Canada; and other Americans came looking for cheap land. A number of British soldiers stayed in Canada and married local women. After the Napoleonic wars, waves of Protestant and Catholic Irish immigrants arrived.

In spite of these events, there was little change in the lives of most inhabitants of the St. Lawrence Valley, who lived in *seigneuries* and farmed their land. The social organization was basically feudal, although the obligations of the French-Canadian peasant were not as onerous as those of his French cousin. Some historians think the seigneurial system was a brake on the development of agriculture and an obstacle to the growth of a modern, nineteenth-century outlook. Other historians believe that the seigneurial system provided institutional protection for the Francophone community faced with the arrival of other ethnic groups.

In the eighteenth century, most of the population lived in a rural setting. Many families were unable to produce a surplus to exchange for imported goods; they made most of the articles they needed. But, generally speaking, the period before 1815 was a prosperous one: there was plenty of arable land and harvests were good. The picture became darker when war took away a part of the work force needed for agricultural work or when there were poor harvests. A bad year often meant sudden increases in the death rate: an underfed population was more vulnerable to mortal illnesses.

The end of the War of 1812-14 marked an end of the farmer's prosperity. The price of wheat exports to supply the vast British army in Europe fell suddenly. Disease ruined much of the crops. The population had grown so large that there was no longer enough land in the old *seigneuries,* and people were forced to settle farther and farther from the river. Farmers sub-divided their farms among their children: in 1831 on the Ile d'Orléans, 40 percent of the heads of family were not landowners.

For the few townspeople of Quebec, Trois Rivières and Montreal, the eighteenth century brought abrupt changes. They made their living from trade and from the military establishment: they were administrators, merchants, minor civil servants, officers, soldiers and craftsmen; religious orders ran hospitals, schools and hospices for the local population. The change of political régime in New France in 1760 directly affected all these people. Those who held high positions in the administration or in the army saw their careers in the French bureaucracy compromised and many lost no time in returning to the motherland with their families. Merchants dependent on the French government – selling furs or supplying food to the army – saw their businesses collapse. Of the three male religious organizations, only the Sulpiciens would survive. The Jesuit and Récollet communities were no longer authorized to recruit new members and were doomed to extinction, for too many Catholic priests were a threat to the new Protestant authorities. (The female religious communities, on the other hand, were hardly affected by the change of régime and immediately gained the sympathy of the British rulers.) The secular clergy, greatly reduced in number, looked after the Catholic population in the parishes.

The eighteenth century was the age of the aristocratic ethic. The colony was governed by the personal representative of the King who often served both as military commander and administrator. Prestigious positions in the government were filled by friends of the monarchy or, under English rule, of the party in power in England. This hierarchy, based on social rank acquired through birth or wealth, would be perpetuated throughout the century.

The first half of the eighteenth century was not an easy time for the Catholic Church. The King of France was jealous of his power and kept a close eye on the bishops; the court at Versailles discouraged the foundation of new religious communities in the belief that the colony already had too many. The British takeover of the colony left the Church in a very delicate position. A recent attempt to place a Catholic king on the British throne had been thwarted, and the Catholic Church was seen as a subversive force. As a result, it took the Bishop of Quebec several years to convince the British authorities of his loyalty and to be recognized by them. Moreover, during the eighteenth century, a wave of anticlericalism was being spread by philosophers amongst educated people. In such a social climate, a priest would often have difficulty controlling the irreligious behaviour of his flock.

The arrival of vast numbers of Protestants during the nineteenth century would bring about the creation of Protestant institutions, which still exist in Quebec. They demanded not only separate churches for each sect, but also schools, hospitals, hospices and even charitable associations run by Protestants.

From 1701 to 1832, the life of most women in the St. Lawrence Valley changed very little. Whether she was a farmer or a merchant, a woman led her life entirely within the family context. Marriage and family life provided security; the only other secure life was that of a nun.

To understand what life was like during the *Ancien Régime,* one must appreciate the great importance of the family. All activities – domestic, economic and social – centred on the family: thus, women held an important place in society. There was inequality between the sexes, but this was not called into question, for the survival and well-being of the family unit depended on both men and women fulfilling their complementary roles.

A woman's life, from birth through childhood, courtship and old age was totally consumed by the needs of the family. For both men and women, success in the social, economic, political and cultural spheres was defined not in terms of individual advancement, but by the success of the family group.

CHAPTER THREE

FAMILY LIFE

LITTLE GIRLS

PARENTS HAVE NOT ALWAYS greeted the birth of girls and boys with equal joy. In traditional societies, where frequent births threatened the family's standard of living, more girls than boys were victims of infanticide. A boy would carry the family name and could more easily provide material security for his parents in their old age. A girl, when very young, would have to begin to acquire a dowry or at least a trousseau and would inevitably go to live with her future husband's family. Yet there is no evidence that parents of that period were happier when they had a boy than a girl. In any case, until the middle of the eighteenth century, most immigrants were men; therefore, parents did not have to fear that they would be left with unmarried daughters on their hands.

Some parents have left evidence of their affection for their daughters. At the end of the seventeenth century, Pierre Boucher spoke in his will of his youngest daughter, Geneviève, with great tenderness. Elizabeth Bégon, an *épistolière* (a prolific letter writer) and a member of upper-class Montreal society at the end of the French régime, took great interest in the progress of her granddaughter, Marie-Catherine de Villebois de la Rouvillière, who lived with her after the death of the child's mother. The little girl seemed to be the centre of attention for the adults around her. Her grandmother wrote: "We pass the time with less boredom than we would if she weren't with us." Marie-Catherine was a particularly pampered daughter, as she was the only child in a wealthy family.

Parents had little reason to worry about having too many children. The abundance of arable land and of game and fish almost always provided sufficient food for the family in New France – frequently not the case in Europe. In certain quarters in Europe and America during the eighteenth century, people began to inquire more openly about methods of birth control, but there is no evidence that French Canadians practised birth control with any success. Some contraceptive methods were known at the time – for example, self-restraint and coitus interruptus; but demographic statistics seem to show that such methods were not used in Canada, at least not by the married Francophone population. In the eighteenth and nineteenth centuries in Europe, infanticide was employed to limit the number of children in a family. The child was either killed (smothered "by accident" while sleeping in his parents' bed), or abandoned in a public place. Abandoning the child seemed to be most common among unwed mothers, while married mothers seemed more likely to smother unwanted babies. It is not known whether this form of infanticide was practised in Canada; but one might well ask if it was because of this danger or for moral reasons, that the Church hierarchy preferred that children not sleep with their mothers.

THE MIRACLE OF THE NEWBORN CHILD

1. There were three reapers in the field; (repeat)
   Where three young girls were making hay.
   • Refrain: I am young; I hear the woods resound
   I am young and pretty.

2. Three young girls went making hay (repeat)
   And one gave birth to a child that day.
3. She wrapped it in a big white cloth;
4. And threw it in the river.
5. The child began to talk to her.
6. – My good mother, you are sinning.
7. – But, my child, who told you so?
8. – Three angels in heaven told me so.
9. One was all white and the other grey;
10. The other looked like Jesus Christ.
11. – Oh, do come back, my dear child.
12. – My dear mother, it is too late.
13. My little body is sinking fast;
14. My little heart is dying;
15. My little soul is in heaven.

• Refrain after each stanza.[1]

A CIRCULAR TO PRIESTS IN ACADIA

7. I am also told that mothers take their children to bed with them on the pretext that nothing has ever happened to them and that the risk of a child dying of cold is a greater worry. I am asking every missionary to give his opinion on this matter in particular so that we may consequently come to a decision. We are fully aware that in several dioceses in France this is not condoned. This practice could be followed, at least during the summer, until our decision is made in the winter.[2]

In the preindustrial era, a high birth rate was balanced by an equally high death rate; and a large percentage of those who died were children. In the colony, only three of four children in a family could hope to reach adulthood. A large family provided labour for the farm or family business and gave parents hope that a few children would survive and help them in their old age.

According to the traditional division of chores within the family, a little girl had to help her mother and learn to do "women's work." Girls could do light chores, such as picking berries or tending sheep, with the little boys; but chores in the house or chicken coop were allotted specifically to girls at a very early age. To relieve her mother, the eldest girl often looked after the younger children. The training young girls received was limited to practical knowledge, which they could make use of throughout their lives.

As a woman spent her life within the family, a formal education hardly seemed necessary for a young girl. However, boys were no more educated: reading and writing were considered essential only for the wealthier classes. Like many upper-class children, Marie-Catherine de Villebois de la Rouvillière received her first lessons at home. But her grandmother, who was an educated *épistolière,* displayed an attitude rare for her time: she informed Marie-Catherine's father that she was allowing the child to study before learning traditional women's work, sewing and housekeeping.

> She helps me pass the time.... I explain to her everything she wants to learn: the history of France, Rome, geography, basic reading in French and Latin, writing, verses, history, anything she wants to know in these areas if it will encourage her to write and to learn. But she does not like housework at all: I leave her alone, preferring her to learn her lessons, rather than to do household work – she will learn that when I decide.[3]

Elizabeth Bégon was born in Montreal. A knowledgeable woman, she is evidence that at least a few girls from wealthier families had access to a broad education most other women could not provide for their daughters. At most, they were able to send them to a convent, where the girls received several years of primary schooling from the nuns.

It was thanks to these religious teaching communities that education for girls had been provided uninterrupted since the very first days of the colony – even after the English invasion. Of the seven communities of women in New France, three – the Ursulines at Quebec and Trois-Rivières and the Soeurs de la Congrégation in Montreal – devoted themselves almost entirely to educating girls. At the end of the French régime, there were even boarding schools in the countryside. Access to education for girls seems to have been widespread: even today it is asserted that, in the old days, women were better educated than their husbands.

There is no proof that this was true. Research has shown that, in the eighteenth century, approximately the same number of women as men could sign their names in their parish register or on notarized documents. However, those who could sign represented only a small portion of the population, perhaps 10 percent.

Yet several European travellers remarked that women were better educated than men. There are two possible explanations for this. On the one hand, at that time in certain regions of France, England and New England, illiteracy was two to three times higher amongst women than amongst men. Visitors to Canada must have been impressed by the very small difference between male and female literacy levels. On the other hand, it seems that more women than men were able only to read, while more men than women could read and write.

Education was more widespread and more accessible to ordinary girls than to boys because of the number of convents and the importance within the Church of the tradition of teaching girls. Nevertheless, in the eighteenth and at the beginning of the nineteenth century, a convent education hardly went beyond learning to read and write and being taught the "feminine" subjects considered essential to a girl's upbringing.

One such subject was religious education, which was especially important for women, whose behaviour, according to the morality of the times, had to be more disciplined than men's. Girls also had to learn the basic skills of good housekeeping, particulary sewing, which was a necessity, a pastime and an expression of feminine creativity. The best seamstresses were most often nuns, who embroidered vestments for the clergy or decorated items to be sold. If a woman could sew, her family was guaranteed to be clothed. In the towns, a woman could make a little money by sewing and mending. Also, upper-class women devoted some of their spare time to embroidery.

Social status dictated which female educational institution a girl would attend. The Ursuline convent at Quebec accepted only girls from the upper classes, daughters of aristocrats or rich merchants, who were taught music, art, singing and a foreign language, all necessary to the education of a girl who was to marry a rich man. There was great respect for women musicians, even though women were not allowed to become professionals. Society women sang or played an instrument at family gatherings or at small social receptions.

Those who did not possess sufficient social standing to be taught by the Ursulines might go to small, country schools. During the nineteenth century, there were also lay teachers in the towns. Some were governesses; some went daily to their pupils' homes; and others ran little schools in their own homes. In 1825, one third of the lay teachers working in Montreal were women.

It would appear, then, that formal education for women was never very highly developed. In the convent, a woman was trained to become a nun or a mother and wife. There was no training for trades or professions that would allow women to make a living outside the domestic setting. By the eighteenth century, access to nearly all jobs and professions had been closed to women for a long time. The exceptions – the jobs of seamstress and midwife – were related to women's work in the family. By contrast, a few boys were able to learn a trade at a school founded at Saint-Joachim by Monseigneur de Laval; or, if they intended to become priests, they could attend what would later be called the first university in America, the Séminaire de Québec. Also, before 1760, the Collège des Jésuites de Québec accepted a small number of boys for "classical studies."

SERVING OTHERS

In preindustrial times, few women spent their days alone at home. Most families organized the sharing of household chores. At a time when almost no girls went to school, mothers were helped by their eldest daughters; and all the children had to contribute to the well-being of the family. Less-well-off families apprenticed their children at nine or ten years of age. Although this enabled boys to train as blacksmiths, carpenters or coopers, one of the few apprenticeships open to girls was housekeeping.

In a study of female domestics in the town of Quebec around the middle of the eighteenth century, historian Francine Barry states that these young servants were often the youngest or eldest daughters of a large family, who were sent out to work by their parents. *Habitant* families who lived near the town most often sent their daughters out as servants. Growth in big families occurred in a cyclical way: after the birth of six or seven children, it became imperative to send the eldest away to make ends meet. Furthermore, when parents grew old or fell ill, the fact that the youngest worked outside the family meant fewer mouths to feed. Also, parents hoped that sending their daughters away might increase their chances of making a good marriage.

A girl was hired when very young, before puberty, and often had to work "until she was married or otherwise provided for." If such a provision was not made, the contract was to be terminated when the girl reached eighteen, twenty or twenty-five. The young servant girl was not paid in cash and simply agreed to serve her masters; the exact nature of her duties was not specified. In return, the masters promised to treat her as one of their own children, to raise her in the Catholic faith, to provide her with board and lodging and to clothe her adequately. Often, contracts stipulated that at the end of her service, the masters should provide her with new clothing and, in some cases, give her a small trousseau.

Unlike servant girls, apprentice seamstresses in the eighteenth century were generally not hired until they were nineteen. Their apprenticeship was very short, lasting just over a year. It was very expensive, costing the apprentice up to one or two hundred *livres*.

The job of domestic seems to have assumed a very different status at the beginning of the nineteenth century. From historian Claudette Lacelle's description of the life of a maidservant in the town of Quebec around 1820, it seems that domestics were becoming more like paid workers and less like apprentices.

At that time, the growth of urban centres meant that women could work as servants during the day and return home in the evening. In fact, by then, most servants came from the towns. But the wealthier the household, the more servants were required to live in. Francophone girls went to work in Francophone houses; Anglophones hired Anglophones. Few families could afford more than one servant. Most had a sixteen- or seventeen-year-old all-purpose maid who lived in a tiny room in the basement or attic or in the kitchen. Her wages were half those of a male servant. The workday started at dawn and finished only when all the family had gone to bed. Under such conditions, it is not at all surprising that many servants changed jobs frequently, moving from house to house in search of a better position.

COURTSHIP AND MARRIAGE

In eighteenth-century New France, people did not rush into marriage as they had in the early days of the colony. By the beginning of the century there was an equal proportion of men and women, and girls put off marriage until they were adults. Demographer Hubert Charbonneau has estimated that between 1700 and 1729, half the brides were older than twenty-two; the corresponding age for grooms was nearly twenty-six. People in Canada could afford to marry earlier than those in France, where the scarcity of land and periods of severe shortage forced them to put off marriage until they felt they could provide some material security. The higher standard of living in America allowed for earlier marriages, in that it permitted couples to take on the extra burden of the children who were inevitably born during the first or second year of marriage.

Depending on the level of society they came from, some people found it advantageous to postpone marriage. This delay would give women time to prepare a trousseau and men time to ensure financial security; it also enabled couples to limit the number of children. Indeed, around 1750, Montreal merchants were taking such an approach. Historian José Igartua has estimated that, on the average, merchants were over thirty when they married and that their wives were twenty-five. Both husbands and wives in this group married later than the population as a whole.

The number of marriages remained relatively high throughout the eighteenth century. Periodic drops in the annual rate often reflected bad times, when war or disease killed off potential spouses or made courtship difficult. According to demographers Jacques Henripin and Yves Peron, during the period 1711 to 1835, the marriage rate was lowest between 1776 and 1785. The American invasion, the threat of war with the Thirteen Colonies, several years of bad harvests and falling agricultural prices were reasons for not marrying or for postponing marriage.

Most French-Canadian women chose their husband from a relatively small circle of acquaintances. They married someone from their own social class and parish or from a neighbouring parish. In the early eighteenth century, French Canadians usually married other French Canadians; immigrants, for the most part, married immigrants. Soldiers were billeted in private homes in the winter, and as a result French-Canadian women had a chance to meet young Frenchmen. There were periods when French authorities encouraged soldiers to get married and settle in Canada; at least 15 percent of the soldiers from the La Sarre and Royal Roussillon regiments who came to fight with Montcalm were married in Canada. These European husbands were, on the average, over twenty-eight, according to demographer Yves Landry, though their wives married at the same age as other French-Canadian girls – between twenty-one and twenty-two. From the very beginning of British occupation, French-Canadian women from all social classes married soldiers in the British army: A British officer or merchant was considered a good catch. For example, Marie-Catherine Fleury-Deschambault, the widow of the Baron de

Longueuil, married William Grant in 1770, and her two sisters took John Frazer and William Dunbar as husbands.

As marriage was terminated only by the death of one of the spouses, it was important to choose carefully. Material considerations took precedence over all others. For merchant, seigneurial and administrative families what counted, above all, were family origins, the bride's dowry and the wealth of the husband-to-be. In *Ancien Régime* society, where social status depended on birth, it was important not to marry beneath one's station. The great families of New France married amongst themselves, thus keeping a firm grip on the privileges of their rank. Sometimes there was an alliance of wealth and social status – a rich merchant would marry a girl less well-off but from a distinguished family. In this way, the first families of New France were successfully revitalized in the seventeenth and eighteenth centuries.

Among the ruling classes, the social position of women was important. A wife's social contacts, family wealth and dowry were assets that could prove crucial to the career of her husband or her sons. In letters to her son-in-law in 1749, Elizabeth Bégon tells of the various marriage plans amongst the upper classes of New France; she does not hesitate to repeat the widespread opinion of one marriage: "They say that it is a fairly bad match as far as money is concerned."

The higher the marriage stakes, the more closely parents needed to supervise their children's choice of fiancé. The *Coutume de Paris* (the Custom of Paris, the law governing New France during the *Ancien Régime*) set the age of majority at twenty-five, and younger couples wishing to marry had to obtain parental consent. In practice, few young people attempted to marry without family approval because the sanctions could be severe. For example, at the beginning of the eighteenth century, when a young member of the family of Governor Vaudreuil dared marry without permission, the governor banished him and his wife to Cape Breton Island.

Because of the strictures of the Coutume de Paris, clandestine marriages were quite rare. Marriages *à la gaumine,* in which a man and a woman married before witnesses in a mass during the elevation of the Host, did not please religious and civil authorities one bit. In 1718, Monseigneur de Saint-Vallier issued a *mandement* (pastoral letter) threatening to excommunicate men and women who resorted to this marriage practice. In the same year, in defiance of the threat, Elizabeth Rocbert de la Morandière, aged twenty-two, eldest daughter of the King's quartermaster in Montreal, married chevalier Claude Michel Bégon, twenty-nine, career soldier and youngest brother of Intendant Bégon. As there were no barracks in Montreal at that time, Claude Michel lived with Elizabeth's family. A large number of these marriages *à la gaumine* seem to have involved officers of the French army, who were forbidden to enter into marriages that would limit their availability for service. The Bégon family disapproved of their son's marriage because they felt that Elizabeth's social rank was not high enough for their ambitions. For this reason, some of them nicknamed Elizabeth the "Iroquoise" and the family put pressure on the civil and military authorities under whose jurisdiction the couple came. The marriage lasted for thirty years, but it is not known if it was always a happy one. Of Elizabeth Bégon's three or four children only a son who left for France when very young survived his parents. And, of course, there was the granddaughter, Marie-Catherine.

Hardly anybody seemed to marry for love in those days. Parents whose children married for love – and did so without their knowledge – begged the authorities to annul these marriages. When the two daughters of *seigneur* François Picoté de Belestre, Marie-Anne and Mariette, married captains in the English army a few years after the English invasion, their parents tried to have both marriages annulled. In her husband's absence, Marie-Anne's stepmother, second wife of the *seigneur,* sued her step-daughter and the latter's husband, John Warton. She refused to recognize the marriage because it lacked a marriage contract, a proper Catholic ceremony and the father's consent. The affair ended up in a military court, where Governor Gage dismissed the charges on the grounds that annulment of the marriage would damage the reputation of the Warton couple and of any future children. It would appear that the two sisters had simply been married by the chaplain of their husbands' regiment.

The *habitants* did not have the same exaggerated concern for social rank and connections. But a girl with a fine trousseau had a clear advantage over other girls. In 1797, in Chambly, Pierre Thomas Perot The Younger refused to marry the mother of his child. According to a witness under oath:

> ... Pierre Thomas Perot The Younger had been seeing the said Marie Anne Collet behind her Father's and Mother's back and he had said to him and to others, If the child's nose had not been so big, he would have kept him, and if the said Marie Anne Collet were richer he would marry her....[4]

All evidence seems to suggest that dowries were rare amongst the lower classes. A girl hoped that she could accumulate enough linen to make a trousseau. In the marriage contract, parents would often promise an advance on the girl's inheritance, to be paid if the funds became available. Even in wealthy families, dowry promises were often not met because of lack of funds. On the 21 December 1748, the Baron de Longueuil confessed to Elizabeth Bégon that he was worried about his son's relationship with young

Mademoiselle de Muy because, given the state of his son's finances, he feared that her family was encouraging the couple to marry too early.

> I fear that he is being pressured into marriage; Madame de Muy is a very strong woman, who wants me to consent to this; but I will not allow my son to marry early, I have my daughter's future to consider.[5]

French-Canadian peasants must have been much like French peasants – they were looking for strong, healthy, hard-working, untiring spouses rather than languid beauties. Pehr Kalm, a Swedish traveller in Canada in 1749, remarked that courtship of young girls was strictly supervised. A man could court a girl only if he intended to marry her. This concern for the honour and reputation of young women explains, in part, the low rate of illegitimate births and prenuptial conception. According to demographer Hubert Charbonneau, only 8 percent of children in a group surveyed at the beginning of the eighteenth century were conceived before marriage. But it is also possible that contraceptive methods were used within extramarital relationships. (In theory, these methods were not to be used within marriage, as the Church disapproved of couples who indulged in sterile carnal pleasures.) In any case, in small communities, everyone knew when a couple was courting and the probable father of a child was public knowledge. Social disapproval and the shame that was attached to a bastard child encouraged women to have sexual relations only with their husbands (or at least only with their fiancés). There is no doubt that pregnancy was the cause of more than one hasty marriage. For example, in a group of 141 soldiers who were married in the Quebec area between 1748 and 1756, it seems that fifteen had had sexual relations, because their children were born shortly after marriage. In two or three of these cases, the children had already been born and were legitimized by the marriage.

Nearly all couples went to the notary's to sign a marriage contract, even those who possessed almost no worldly goods. Until 1866, the *Coutume de Paris* regulated the civil rights of the individual in New France and Lower Canada, and established the legal primacy of the husband as head of the family over the wife and children. The rights of individuals, especially women, were restricted in the name of the family.

THE CHURCH AND ILLEGITIMATE CHILDREN

When the Couple have had children before their Marriage, whom they wish to legitimize, they will be put in a particular place under the veil with the Bride and Groom and the Priest will say....[6]

Unless there was a special clause in the marriage contract, the couple was married under a system of community of property. After marriage, all chattels or moveable goods and real estate purchased or obtained by the spouses became their joint property, but were administered by the husband alone. He could sell, give away or pledge these possessions, as long as it was for the common good of the community formed by husband and wife. The only assets that remained legally the wife's were properties received as an inheritance or gift from her parents. Even then, the husband had access to profits made on these assets and could, for example, collect rent or sell a harvest without his wife's consent. However, he could not sell the inherited property.

If one of the spouses died, the survivor received half the estate and the other half was divided in equal parts amongst the children. The widow could claim customary dower rights, a sort of pension designed to protect her from poverty. It consisted of the *usufruct* or enjoyment and use of certain immoveable properties belonging to the husband, which remained outside of the community.

Couples could make changes to this standard arrangement in the marriage contract. Most couples had no property to serve as a basis for dower rights when they got married. Instead, they substituted an agreed-upon sum of money, which was drawn from the husband's entire estate and paid to the wife after his death. A couple could also agree that the survivor would receive a *préciput* – certain chattels or a fixed portion of the estate – before it was divided up or, if there were no children, they could agree that the surviving spouse would keep everything. When spouses were expecting inheritances, these were mentioned in the contract and it was decided whether they would be included in the community property. In any case, the widow could refuse her share of the estate when it was in a deficit, a privilege designed to compensate for poor administration on the part of her husband.

The clauses of the marriage contract were important because, given the high death rate, there were many widows and orphans in New France. Freedom to write a will was introduced by the English. Until then, a marriage contract had been the only way to control one's property after death. The *Coutume de Paris* forbade a married couple to give each other any gifts except food or small items; it was thought that gift-giving would diminish the estate left to the heirs of each spouse. For the same reason, other legal strictures placed limits on what an individual could give to anyone except family members. After 1801, women and men were free to make wills in which they could dispose of their assets, even share their part of the community property. However, in the early nineteenth century, very few women made wills.

Marriage laws in the eighteenth and nineteenth centuries denied wives a number of individual rights. Without her husband's authorization, a married

BENEDICTION OF THE NUPTIAL BED

The blessing of a bed can be performed at any time. But if the newly married couple asks to have their bed blessed, We decree that in that case the Benediction be performed after the Celebration of Marriage before the feast; to ensure that modesty is protected in such a way, that nothing destroys the Sanctity of this Ceremony.

The Priest will speak in a solemn and chaste manner to the Couple as follows:

We must not fail to tell you along with Saint Paul that Marriage must be treated by everybody with respect and the Nuptial Bed be pure and without stain; remember that you are the children of the Saints and God himself: That your flesh through the union of the Word of God with mankind, has become the body of Jesus Christ. Remember too that your bodies are the Temple of the Holy Spirit, that you must only touch them as you would the Sacred Vessels; that is to say with modesty and restraint. Remember that your Nuptial Bed will one day be your death bed, from which your souls will be taken on high before the Judgement Seat of God, to receive the terrible punishment of the Seven Husbands of Sara, if you become slaves to your body, your passions and your lust.

Join in Prayer with us, and ask God to guide you away from such a terrible fate, and to keep the spirit of impurity away from your bed and your hearts, and to cause chastity to reign in your bed.

Then the Priest will instruct the Couple and everyone to kneel....[7]

woman could not take any legal action or start a business. The husband had absolute control over family assets. However, when the *Coutume de Paris* is compared to Common Law, which governed immigrants in Upper Canada after 1791, the situation in Quebec appears to have been very favourable for women. The *Coutume de Paris* gave priority to claims made by the wife and children over those made by creditors, and gave them the right to buy back certain assets that had been sold outside the family. But after 1760, Anglophone men in New France, true to the spirit of capitalism, would complain that these laws made it difficult for them to accumulate money.

A few weeks before their wedding, a couple would go to the notary's. The marriage date was chosen according to Catholic and rural traditions. It was difficult to be wed during Lent or Advent, when the Church discouraged cele-

CAPITALISM CLASHES WITH WOMEN'S RIGHTS

Anglophone immigrants did not accept the principle that assets should be shared by husband and wife. They were used to English Common Law, which gave few rights to wives and allowed assets to be controlled by the husband, who could thus amass capital more quickly. A certain Mr. Grey, who travelled in Lower Canada at the beginning of the nineteenth century, remarked that civil law, which provided for joint ownership, ran counter to capitalist development. But he noted that many spouses had already found a way around the laws by signing a contract of separation of property.

> When one of the parents dies, an inventory is made of the property, and each child can immediately insist on the share of the property the law allows. The French law supposes that matrimony is a co-partnership; and that, consequently, on the death of the wife, the children have a right to demand from their father the half of his property, as heirs to their mother. If the wife's relations are not on good terms with the father, a thing that sometimes happens, they find it no difficult matter to induce the children to demand *a partage*, or division, which often occasions the total ruin of the father, because he loses credit, equal, at least, to his loss of property, and often to a greater extent. His powers are diminished, and his children still have a claim on him for support....
>
> The law, making marriage a *co-partnership*, and creating a *communité de bien*, is sanctioned by the *code of French law* called *Coutume de Paris*, which indeed is the *text book* of the Canadian lawyer; the wife being by marriage invested with a right to half the husband's property; and, being rendered independent of him, is perhaps the remote cause that the fair sex have such influence in France; and in Canada, it is well known, that a great deal of consequence, and even an air of superiority to the husband, is assumed by them. In general (if you will excuse a vulgar metaphor), *the grey mare is the better horse*.
>
> British subjects coming to this country are liable to the operation of all these Canadian or French laws, in the same manner that the Canadians themselves are. They are not always aware of this circumstance; and it has created much disturbance in families. A man who has made a fortune here (a thing by the bye which does not very often happen), conceives that he ought, as in England, to have

the disposal of it as he thinks proper. No, says the Canadian law, you have a right to *one half* only; and if your wife dies, her children, or, in case you have no children, *her nearest relations*, may oblige you to make a *partage,* and give them half your property, were it a hundred thousand guineas, and they the most worthless wretches in existence. Nothing can prevent this but an antinuptial contract of marriage, barring the *communité de bien*.[8]

bration. There were also few weddings during planting and harvest times; most weddings occurred in January, February and November. A few took place in April, after Easter, or in September and October, when work on the land was completed for the year.

A marriage was both a solemn religious occasion and an opportunity for festivity. The mass and the benediction of the nuptial bed – the symbol of fertility in the marriage – were followed by the wedding celebration which, in wealthy families, might last for several days.

Weddings allowed a family to display its prosperity and social rank, a very great concern to the ruling classes, whose weddings were society events. The bride wore her finest, which, in the style of the time, would be brightly

AN ORDONANCE ON
THE CELEBRATION OF MARRIAGE

So that Priests can more effectively deal with scandalous acts of disrespect and profanation that occur very frequently during the celebration of Marriage, We have deemed it appropriate to order them to inform all those wishing to marry that they have received an order from Us not to admit into Nuptial Benediction any ladies who are immodestly dressed, whose head is not covered, whose breasts are exposed or only covered with transparent material. We order them also to ensure as much as possible, that there is no impiety, jesting or insolence in the Church, either during arrival or departure on the day that the Sacrament is performed or on the day after the Wedding. And to ensure that this behaviour does not occur, We allow them to address themselves to The Secular Arm if necessary.[10]

coloured. On the day she was married, in about 1749, Mademoiselle de la Ronde was spirited enough to prompt the following remarks:

> Before administering the sacrament, the priest must know if the couple has received any instruction. The curé de Québec who is a young man newly arrived from France this year and a scrupulous man, questioned Monsieur de Bonaventure who answered every question very politely. After that, he asked him to bring in Mademoiselle de la Ronde, as he had done in the sacristy, and he asked her if she knew what the sacrament of marriage was. She answered that she didn't know anything about it, but that if he was curious she could tell him about it in four days time. The poor priest bowed his head and did not question her any further.[9]

Neighbours would draw attention to second marriages between people from different social backgrounds or age groups with a *charivari*. The neighbours would assemble beneath the window of the newly-weds' house and sing and dance until the husband came out or threw a small sum of money. This custom, which began as a way of showing the community's disapproval of such a marriage, persisted until the twentieth century, but in a somewhat less rowdy form.

Romantic love as it is known today appears to have been largely absent from relationships between men and women, or at least between husbands and wives. But in some marriages there was a certain affection, a kind of love, which can be detected in correspondence between husbands and wives at the end of the eighteenth century. Only the writings of the upper classes have survived; and these do not indicate what was happening in other classes of society.

In the eighteenth century, the dependence of both sexes on the division of daily labour must have taught them to appreciate each other. It was difficult to conceive of life without one's partner. Most women without a husband were destined to live on the periphery of society and in financial insecurity. A single man found it hard to do his work and keep house. The complementarity of roles and the near impossibility of ending a marriage must have persuaded many women to put up with imperfect marriages.

It was particularly useful for voyageurs and merchants who lived on the fur trade to have a woman by their side. Indian women, who served as interpreters and guides, made snowshoes and dressed the furs, proved to be essential to the survival of whites in the North-West. Anglophones and Francophones scandalized the missionaries by choosing Indian women as their common-law spouses. These marriages *à la façon du pays* (according to the custom of the country) lasted as long as the husband stayed in the west. When the husband left, the Indian woman and her Métis children went back to her tribe.

However, Indian society began to disintegrate through contact with white civilization, and soon métis children could not be assimilated. At the beginning of the nineteenth century, women and children abandoned at trading posts were the responsibility of the fur companies who ran the posts. The

---

A "MANDEMENT" CONCERNING CHARIVARIS

François, by the grace of God and of the Holy See, first Bishop of Quebec.

Having been informed that as a consequence of a marriage celebrated in Quebec, for the last six days a great number of people of both sexes have been assembling every night under the pretext of holding a charivari and have in their disorder and scandalous liberties, as normally happens, committed very impious acts, which make a total mockery of the mysteries and of the truths of the Christian religion and of the most holy ceremonies of the Church, which has forced us to seek help from the secular arm to put a stop to these types of gathering, which secular arm has used its authority to repress them, notwithstanding which we have learned that not only do these gatherings continue but also that they are getting bigger day by day and they are getting more impious, which forces us in the exercise of our duty to join the authority of the Church with that of the secular arm, and to oppose with all our power, these sorts of impiety and such assemblies which are expressly forbidden to all the faithful of either sex and even by civil ordonance, as they are most prejudicial to religion, good morals, and the public good and to the peace of all families. For these reasons, and to arrive at an appropriate solution to such a great evil that could only lead to very tragic consequences, We expressly forbid and inhibit all parishioners of both sexes in our diocese, to be found in the future at any of these so-called charivaris: We also forbid fathers and mothers to send or allow their children to attend them, masters and mistresses to send their servants or to allow their servants to go there of their own full will, on pain of excommunication. And so that no one may plead ignorance, it is Our wish that this ordonance be read publicly during the sermon in the parish church of Quebec and other places in our diocese and affixed to church doors.

Issued in Quebec on the 3rd of July sixteen hundred and eighty-three.

François, Bishop of Quebec.[11]

half-Indian, half-white girls from these unions cohabited with employees of the North-West or Hudson's Bay companies, and became increasingly unwilling to accept the almost inevitable desertion of their children by the father. A number of whites showed real affection for their Indian or métis spouses, and tried to provide for the education of their children. But many rejected their mate as soon as they made their fortune and could afford to become engaged to a white woman.

Historian Sylvia Van Kirk cites a number of examples of the casual manner with which men treated women. J.G. McTavish, one of the chief administrators of the Hudson's Bay Company, abandoned his Métis spouse; as a result, she killed her child. Then, around 1813, McTavish entered into a *mariage à la façon du pays* with Nancy McKenzie, the natural daughter of Roderick McKenzie of the North-West Company. The union lasted for seventeen years and produced at least seven children. Then, in 1830, McTavish went to Scotland, where he married a young lady. On his way home with his new wife, he stopped in Montreal, where his thirteen-year-old daughter, Mary, was at school. Mary was publicly introduced to the new Mrs. McTavish, who became upset and left the room in tears, humiliated by this brutal reminder of her husband's former liaisons. Mr. McTavish's former spouse, Nancy, very depressed by the turn of events, continued to exert pressure on him. McTavish tried to quiet her by finding her a new husband. In 1831, he gave a week's holiday to one of his employees in Rivière Rouge, Pierre Leblanc, and promised him two hundred pounds sterling if he would marry Nancy McKenzie. Leblanc accepted the offer and married her in the Saint Boniface church.

The husband was the head of the family and his wife was supposed to obey him, but it seems that many women often defied their husbands. For example, at the end of the French régime, a well-known public figure in Montreal disapproved of his wife's behaviour, but did not seem able to make her change. On 14 February 1749, Elizabeth Bégon recounts:

> De Muy was telling me after dinner that he no longer wanted his wife and daughter to attend and that it was not at all appropriate to spend the nights dancing and the days sleeping while the holy sacrament is exposed. I do not know if it will be easy for him to keep to this.[12]

Several days later, she learned that a charming young widow had refused the hand of a member of the La Vérendrye family

> ... who thought he only had to ask for her hand to be successful. But he was wrong: all she wants is someone to amuse her and keep her company and not a master.[13]

Many husbands were unfaithful, and some women did not always live up to the ideal of the chaste and obedient wife. Witness the following extract from Madame Bégon's journal:

> Madame Vassan, whose husband left her at her father's house when he went to Fort Frontenac, found she did not have enough freedom there. She has taken rooms at Martel's where she has found her match in her own lady servant, who is just as wild as she is; she is out night and day.[14]

Historian Jean-Pierre Wallot describes life at the beginning of the nineteenth century, when upright citizens were scandalized by cases of bigamy and cuckolded husbands found solace in seducing chambermaids. As far as we know, upper-class French Canadians did not resort to duels to defend male honour in such cases, as was the custom in Europe. Is this a sign of a certain permissiveness as far as women's behaviour was concerned?

Records indicate that, between 1700 and 1760, only one woman was convicted of adultery. In 1733, Geneviève Millet, wife of Pierre Roy, was sentenced to make amends for the scandal she had caused. She was whipped in the public square and at crossroads in the town of Quebec and was then locked up with prostitutes in the Hôpital-Général. Such charges were rare, so perhaps there was a certain tolerance of these so-called conjugal offences. However, it should be noted that women never seemed to take their husbands to court for adultery. Furthermore, an adulteress could be deprived of her dower rights but an unfaithful husband did not place his inheritance in jeopardy. This double standard, which forced women to be chaste and only suggested that men be so, formed part of the laws and religious practices of all European societies at the time.

Male brutality toward women seemed both to be accepted and inevitable. Women rarely lodged complaints against their husbands for assault; however, many women were beaten. Charlotte Martin-Ondoyer was walking in the market square in Montreal one day in 1734 under the influence of alcohol, as she admitted. She took a wallet from the pocket of Demoiselle Godefroy de Linctôt. When her husband, drum-major Antoine Laurent, was told of her crime, he beat her. In 1744, another husband found it necessary to discipline his wife when she lost her temper and gave her brother a black eye. The brother was an accountant with the religious community of the Charron Brothers'. Marie-Madeleine César, known as "Lévard," was beaten by her husband, who wanted to show her that he was "opposed to all violence."

We know of these incidents because they happened under exceptional circumstances: when there was a judicial enquiry into a wife's behaviour, it was very much in the husband's interest to show that she had been sufficiently disciplined for her evil ways. In separation trials, which were rare, women complained of their husbands' brutality. There was a great deal of physical violence at the time but, except in unusual situations, no one thought of drawing attention to male violence in the family.

Women preferred to keep their husbands by their sides. In 1749, the military authorities of the colony were harassed by women who wanted their husbands to be exempt from military service. Were there reasons of sentiment for this, in addition to material concerns? It is hard to say. In 1780, Marguerite Bender was upset that her new husband had been attached to a mobile regiment and complained to her cousin, the widow Baby. The next year, she was still complaining that she missed her husband.

History is also silent on the question of sexual relations between men and women. The myth of female frigidity was only invented quite recently and *Ancien Régime* society recognized women's sexuality, and their need to express themselves sexually, as long as they did so within marriage.

The Church, in the eighteenth century, did not seem to make any distinction between the sexual needs of the husband and the wife – paradoxical in a religion that otherwise subordinated the wife to the husband. Each spouse was mutually expected to perform the duties of marriage. But it was recognized that:

> there are ... reasons that may legitimately excuse one of the two parties from performing their marriage duty; such as adultery by one of the parties, serious illness, pregnancy, when there is a danger of harming the child, and the risk of contracting a contagious disease.[15]

The "danger of harming a child" probably refers to the fact that a new pregnancy would cause the mother's milk to dry up. This could endanger the life of a child who was still nursing. However, the modesty that characterized eighteenth-century society hid the intimate behaviour of people from public view, just as the thick curtains around the parents' bed concealed its occupants. Moreover, a *mandement* from the bishops at the end of the seventeenth century ordered parents to ensure that boys and girls slept in different beds.

Some rare accounts lead us to believe that sexual relations, especially when forbidden, took place as much during the day as at night, in out-of-the-way places: behind the maple-sugar shack, in the woods or in a ditch. Some heads of households, such as Pierre Gardeur de Repentigny, quite shamelessly took advantage of their wives' absence to rape the servant girls.

MATERNITY

Between marriage and menopause, women in the eighteenth century and at the beginning of the nineteenth century could expect to give birth at regular intervals and sometimes every twelve months. During their fertile years, women were so occupied with maternity that we may well ask how they accomplished their other chores. There was a high death rate among young mothers, perhaps because of successive births and ensuing complications.

During the eighteenth and nineteenth centuries, the French-Canadian population grew steadily. Fluctuations in the birth rate between 1711 and 1835 show how the economic and political situation affected the number of births. For example, the highest birthrates from 1736 to 1835 were between 1761 and 1770, when war was no longer taking *habitants* away from their land. Periods when the birthrate was at its lowest were characterized by economic crises, which postponed marriages and increased the death rate. Marriage and death had a direct effect on the number of births: chronic malnutrition made women less fertile and increased the number of miscarriages. Miscarriages during the first months of pregnancy are not included in historical statistics; it is probable, therefore, that there were more pregnancies than have been recorded. Demographers calculate that eighteenth-century women had an average of eight children (if the marriage was not prematurely cut short by death), but it is possible that they had even more. Children were usually conceived at specific times of the year and according to the dictates of the Church calendar. The Church refused to celebrate marriages on days of penitence and encouraged couples to abstain from sex during these periods. Nevertheless, if one of the partners demanded his or her spousal rights, the other was obliged to comply. Most children were conceived between May and September and in January and February, a fact that contradicts the belief that husbands left every spring for the fur trade.

Even though repeated childbirths were an inevitable part of a wife's life, women had good reason to be afraid of childbirth. In the seventeenth century, the only century for which we have exact figures, the death rate for thirty- to forty-year-old women was extremely high. In fact, there was a greater risk of death for women of this age group than for men: surely complications caused by multiple childbirths can be the only explanation.

Childbirth was painful, difficult and often fatal. It was a time for women to help and comfort one another. The correspondence of the widow Marie-Thérèse Baby gives us some sense of the shadow cast by childbirth over a woman's life. In 1762, Marie-Thérèse's sister died in childbirth, leaving eight children. In 1765, Marie-Thérèse relates how she went to Chambly to help a friend who had been "dangerously ill" after giving birth. In a letter dated 1771, she says that Madame Longueuil gave birth to a boy and that "she paid dearly for the satisfaction of a second marriage." In the same year, she reports that a friend "had given birth to a boy" and that "she was in grave danger." Two years later, she confided:

Madame Ryves has been very ill as a result of giving birth, the details of this birth (and what happened afterward) have made us cry a lot.[16]

Women giving birth were attended by the parish midwife. Under the French régime, the midwife was often elected by the assembly of the women of the parish. For example, in February 1712, the women of Boucherville elected Catherine Guertin, who was approximately forty-six years old. She had to take an oath before the priest, as decreed by the Bishop of Quebec. In the newly settled regions, where a family could be very isolated, the husband sometimes assisted his wife in childbirth. In the towns, at the end of the eighteenth century, there were obstetric surgeons who specialized in delivering babies and who offered their services to women who could afford them. The doctors had instruments such as forceps to facilitate difficult births. Knowledge of gynaecology and obstetrics was very rudimentary; witness the initiative taken by the curé Boissoneau from the Ile d'Orléans. In 1813, the curé was worried by the high death rate in his parish and purchased

a treatise on women's illnesses by François Mauriceau, second edition, published by the author in MDCLXXV [1675], to help instruct women who are to give birth in the parish of St-Pierre and which must be passed from hand to hand without any women claiming it as their property.[17]

It is difficult to know how parents felt about their newborn children. Antoine Foucher, who was married in 1743, took care to register the births and deaths of all his children in a notebook with the title "Age of the children that the Lord has seen fit to send us since our marriage." Between 1744 and 1767, he made fifteen entries, two of which recorded miscarriages: "My wife gave birth in her third month of pregnancy, as a result of an accident." In 1792, only four of Foucher's children were still living. In 1804, the widow Faribeault of Saint-Henry de Mascouche wrote to her daughter, who was pregnant for the fifth time:

Every time you make me a grandmother I feel I have grown younger, what upsets me however is that it makes you grow older, all things considered I hope that you will take things easily, or at least that you will rest for the next 20 years or so, which will allow you to start again with greater vigour when your spirit is renewed.[18]

There is little information about the practice of breast-feeding in the eighteenth century. Wealthier citizens could place their child in the care of a wet nurse, as was the custom in France. Montreal merchant Pierre Guy noted scrupulously the births and deaths of all his children and the sum paid to the midwife and wet nurse for each. Guy's children were put out to nurse, on the day they were born or the next day, with families in parishes as far away as Saint-Léonard, Saint-Michel and Sault-aux-Récollets. Madame Guy gave birth to seven daughters and seven sons, but few of them lived very long. Those who survived stayed with a nurse until they were two.

> Marie-Louise, my third daughter, was born on the 31st of March 1776 and she was put out to nurse on the first of April with Sénée at la Chine for 12″ a month and she stayed until the 29th of August which makes 5 months and one day for which I paid him.... On 30 August 1766, I left Marie-Louise at the home of Joseph La Chapelle of St. Léonard she died the same day she arrived at the said Chapelle home Paid the midwife 48.″ [19]

At the end of the eighteenth century, motherhood assumed a more important status in France, and mothers were encouraged to look after their babies themselves. Farming out a child to a wet nurse was increasingly condemned as a murderous practice. Mothers were expected to breast-feed their newborn children and to watch over the cradle day and night. It would no longer be acceptable for a mother to leave a young child. Doctors, demographers and male politicians hoped that such care would increase the number of citizens who could serve the nation. Perhaps because of this new attitude toward maternity, Julie Bruneau breast-fed her children in the 1820s.

> I see no reason to wean my little girl she is still too young and moreover does not have any teeth yet which is usually the main reason for not weaning children unless there are other reasons, and I don't have any I am well and breast-feeding does not tire me.[20]

In the eighteenth century, the rate of illegitimate births remained relatively low. Illegitimate children were severely sanctioned by the Church and the *Coutume de Paris*; a man was strongly encouraged to marry the woman who was pregnant by him. Under the *Coutume de Paris,* an illegitimate child was an outcast and could inherit from his parents only under very restricted circumstances. Furthermore, the law prevented a man from providing his concubine, as the law termed a mistress or common-law spouse, with more than a living allowance during his lifetime. Considerable shame was attached to illegitimacy, but this was not the worst of it: mother and her baby had to face the problems of material existence. Keeping one's virginity until marriage was as practical as it was virtuous.

The right to make a will, introduced under the English régime, would allow the harsh illegitimacy laws of the *Coutume de Paris* to be relaxed. A study of wills drawn up in Montreal at the end of the eighteenth century shows that some men left legacies to their illegitimate children as well as to the mothers

---

*LA GUIRLANDE OU LE RECUEIL
DE CHANSONS CANADIENNES*

(Published in 1853 in Trois-Rivières by George Stobbs)

82

THE POOR GIRL

To The Tune of "Autrefois J'aimais une belle"

(Once I Loved a Beauty)

Nothing on this earth belongs to me
I didn't even have a crib;
I was found on a rock
In front of the village church.
Pushed away from my mother's breast,
I have cried for 14 springs;

Refrain
Come back, mother, I await you
On the rock where you left me

---

of the children. As long as communities stayed small, it was difficult to hide the fact that two people were courting, and even more difficult to conceal pregnancy. When women were away from the surveillance of their family and neighbours, they were more likely to become involved in illicit sexual relations. A number of women, no doubt seduced by the promise of marriage, discovered too late that their lovers wanted nothing to do with them or their children. Women immigrants crossing the Atlantic from France were particularly vulnerable to such seduction. When troops were billeted near towns, children abandoned by prostitutes or girls who had been seduced filled the hospices, as did the children of servant girls who were victims of sexual harassment – a phenomenon that seems to be a constant in history.

During the French régime, the government placed illegitimate children in the care of nurses and illegitimate girls became servants as soon as they were old enough. Later, the British authorities gave money to the Grey Nuns to pay for the care of abandoned children. But at the beginning of the nineteenth century, trade with England and immigration caused a rapid expansion of the towns, in which there was a large population of unsettled, unmarried males: immigrants, soldiers, sailors, *engagés* and day labourers. There was a remarkable increase in illegitimate births. In 1801, the Legislative Assembly of Lower Canada modified the laws concerning concubines and illegitimate children. Previously, only two solutions were open to a woman for whom the birth of an illegitimate child was an insurmountable social and material burden: she could kill the child and run the risk of being accused of infanticide; or she could leave the child at the gates of a church or a religious community, in the hope that it would be picked up before it died.

SICKNESS AND DEATH

Women, in particular, were sensitive to the high incidence of sickness and early death. They often came close to death while giving birth and the children they brought into the world frequently died before their mothers. Because of the high death rate amongst adults, there were many widowers and widows. In a letter to a woman in France, Marguerite d'Youville announced the death of Madame Mackay, the recipient's daughter:

> Madame, I would like to be able to tell you something pleasant but, on the contrary, I have the most upsetting news caused by the death of Madame Macailye [Mackay], your dear daughter, which occurred on the 13th of this month at noon. Our consolation is that she suffered with heroic patience, that she received all the sacraments and that she herself asked for the last rites, after which she still wanted to make a general confession. Her husband and her brother made sure that she had everything she needed, both spiritual and temporal. Their distress is indescribable ... the two children are in the care of their uncle, do not worry about them. They are very dear children. As for the dear departed, she gave birth in the month of February, I believe, to a boy who died two months later. She was ill from then on and completely incapacitated after mid-April. Her husband took her out in the carriage for some air a few times. Madame de Bayouville did not leave her side during all that time and from May until August when she was in Laprairie where she died. She constantly needed the nurses here to care for her, I sent the old Champigny woman who lives here to care for her at Laprairie. She has not come back yet. Monsieur Mackay made me promise that I would leave her there for a few more days, which I did willingly. He gave her beautiful dress to the church at Laprairie.[21]

There were many second and even third marriages. These were often necessary for women whose husbands had left them no means of supporting their family – a widow with small children could hardly farm her land alone. Women with an inheritance remarried quickly: as landowners, they were attractive partners to bachelors. Notarial records are full of references to the friction these marriages caused among the children.

But not all widows remarried. Usually, being a widow meant being poor, and a man was reluctant to marry a poor widow who had no inheritance, especially if he would have to feed her children. Older women often did not find a husband. They kept body and soul together by sewing or taking in boarders. In 1744, 5 percent of the servants in the town of Quebec were widows, with an average age of forty-eight. It would appear that their only place to live was in their master's house.

The few widows who could afford to do so went to live with the nuns, where they rented rooms and lived out their lives in prayer and devotion.

A few widows were young and wealthy enough to do what they wanted. (It was no coincidence that Madame de la Peltrie, Marie de l'Incarnation and Marguerite d'Youville were all widows.) Freed from the fetters of marriage, widows could become active outside the home. They enjoyed full rights according to the *Coutume de Paris* and were no longer under marital or paternal legal authority.

As parents grew older, they made plans for their children's futures; these plans included preparations for the parents' old age. The *Coutume de Paris* provided for equal division of estates, but this provision could be circumvented by gifts and, later, through wills. Usually, sons were favoured: they received land, farming equipment or buildings. Daughters often received their part of the inheritance in the form of personal possessions, which were given to them when they married.

Eighteenth-century notarial deeds demonstrate that family members often distrusted one another, since they stipulated that, in return for the gift given a child, the child was to look after the parents until their deaths. The deeds carefully detailed what had to be supplied: a furnished room, winter and summer clothing, tobacco and favourite foods. Some parents kept several animals and a wagon or carriage for transportation. Under these arrangements, many women spent their last years in their children's homes.

All things considered, even though a woman was busy with numerous pregnancies, her life consisted of much more than childrearing. During the *Ancien Régime,* women filled a role which was considerable by today's standards.

NOTES

1 M. Barbeau, *Vieilles Chansons du Vieux Québec,* Musées nationaux du Canada, Bulletin no. 75, 1962, pp. 46-47.

2 *Mandements des Evêques du diocèse de Québec,* Vol. I (Quebec, 1887, 20 April 1742).

3 Elizabeth Bégon, *Lettres au cher fils,* Nicole Deschamps ed. (Montreal: Hurtubise, HMH, 1972), 9 January 1749, p. 64.

4 Testimony of Nicolas Demers, 10 June 1797, *Collection Baby,* Archives de l'Université de Montréal, series A2, box 4.

5 Elizabeth Bégon, op. cit., 21 December 1748, p. 54.

6 Monseigneur de Saint-Vallier, *Rituel du Diocèse de Québec, 1703.*

7 Ibid.

8 H. Gray, *Letters from Canada Written During a Residence there in the years 1806, 1807 and 1808* (London, 1809).

9 Elizabeth Bégon, op. cit., 6 February 1749, p. 79.

10 Monseigneur de Saint-Vallier, op. cit.

11 *Mandements des Evêques du diocèse de Québec,* vol. I (Quebec, 1887).

12 Elizabeth Bégon, op. cit., 14 February 1749, p. 83.

13 Ibid., 25 February 1749, p. 89.

14 Ibid. 20 February 1749, p. 87.

15 Monseigneur de Saint-Vallier, op. cit., p. 331.

16 "Marie-Thérèse Baby à François Baby," 17 October 1765, *Collection Baby,* Archives de l'Université de Montréal, box 115.

17 *Livre des comptes de l'église et fabrique de la paroisse Saint-Pierre en l'Isle d'Orléans commencé l'année 1789.,* Cad-Fabrique, Canada 3, 40-1, Archives Nationales du Québec.

18 Jean-Pierre Wallot, *Un Québec qui bougeait* (Montreal: Boréal Express, 1973), p. 222.

19 Cahiers des comptes divers de Pierre Guy, 1785-1810, *Collection Baby,* Archives de l' Université de Montréal, series G2 192.

20 "Julie Bruneau à Louis-Joseph Papineau," 24 January 1829, *Rapport de l'archiviste de la province de Québec,* 1957-58, p. 69.

21 "Marguerite d'Youville à Madame de Liguery," 23 September 1770, quoted in A. Ferland-Angers, *Mère d'Youville, Première Fondatrice Canadienne* (Montreal: Beauchemin, 1945), p. 256.

CHAPTER FOUR

WOMEN UNDER
THE ANCIEN REGIME

NEVER-ENDING WORK

THE *HABITANTS* CONTINUED to clear the land and began to settle farther from the river. As they ran out of arable land inside the old *seigneuries,* each generation relived the colonizing experience. Moving to new land meant cutting ties of affection and mutual help with relatives; women as well as men found themselves alone, particularly where work was concerned. The daily effort to recreate a normal life proved difficult and exhausting.

In preindustrial society, most people spent their time struggling to obtain the bare necessities of life. Having enough to eat, providing adequate shelter, dressing warmly enough for the winter and protecting the family against numerous diseases were daily preoccupations. Only a tiny minority – those who lived in the towns or in the seigneurial manors – could enjoy a life of material security and leisure.

The work done by each woman and man was a crucial contribution to the well-being of the family. A woman's work was indispensable: she was responsible for the stable and the henhouse, for the vegetable garden, for preparing food, for making clothes and tending to the sick. Without a woman in the home, a family would have trouble surviving.

Towards 1750, hearths and fireplaces were replaced by cast-iron stoves, which were easier to use and which revolutionized housework. The stoves were made at the St. Maurice Forge or at the Batiscan Smelter. Women had to learn how to cook all over again because the new stoves required a different technique from hearth cooking. Marcel Moussette, an expert on domestic heating, suggests that it was because of this technological change that the recipes of the French régime have not become part of our own tradition.

MEALS AND HOUSEWORK

The never-ending preparation of food was a woman's most important chore. Unlike in Europe, relatively few people in New France died of hunger. However, poor harvests caused periodic food shortages. For example, 1769, 1789, 1833 and 1834 were bad years: the scarcity of wheat and other grains severely disrupted eating habits and resulted in a high death rate. However, there were few real famines, mainly because game and fish were readily available until the nineteenth century.

The preparation of food was a long and fastidious chore, but meals were simple and varied little, except for celebrations or in rich people's houses. The main foods were bread, pork, vegetables and fish, and game and fruits when in season.

Cooking was time-consuming, not because meals were elaborate but because it took a long time to prepare food for cooking. To turn a newly-killed pig into stewing meat, ham or sausages for the winter took several days.

Bread formed the basis of all meals in New France. In the eighteenth century, the *habitants* ate two or three pounds of bread a day; even during food shortages, as happened in 1820, they ate at least one pound. It took a whole day to make bread; women had to knead the bread, maintain the right temperature for it to rise, put it in the oven – outside the house – and keep an eye on it while it baked. And women made bread at least once every week.

Household utensils were rudimentary. It was impossible to prepare a number of dishes for each meal because most women had only one or two pots and a few spoons, forks, knives, plates and bowls.

HISTORY OF EMILIE MONTAGUE

When her husband, John Brooke, was sent to the town of Quebec in 1763, Frances Moore Brooke accompanied him. During her stay, she wrote *The History of Emilie Montague,* the first Canadian novel. Brooke describes the relationship that develops between a young English girl and a British army officer in the town of Quebec; the young couple insist on marrying for love rather than for money. The book provides an amusing and insightful portrait of the life and preoccupations of the well-to-do inhabitants of the town of Quebec. Its success led to the printing of a French edition in Paris in 1770.

Affluent women had more culinary equipment and could put some variety into their meals. Some *habitants* used roasting pans, funnels and cheese vats, which suggests that they were cooking relatively elaborate meals.

Women were responsible for the quality of food they put on the family table. In times of war or economic disruption, they complained in their letters that supplies were expensive. In the towns, where women were particularly dependent on merchants, a shortage of supplies might provoke street riots. In November 1757, during the English invasion, meat was scarce, and the government distributed horsemeat. French Canadians did not like the idea of eating horsemeat: to show their discontent, the women of Montreal went to Governor Vaudreuil and threw the meat at his feet:

> ... they were repelled by the idea of eating a horse, a friend to man; their religion forbade them to eat horsemeat and they would rather die than eat it.[1]

They were shown that the meat was of good quality, but they refused it, saying that "they would not eat any and neither would anybody else, not even the troops." In 1758, women demonstrated in the town of Quebec when the daily bread ration was cut to two ounces. The Marquis de Montcalm noted:

> Uprising of Montreal women starving to death, protesting that flour is sold for 20 *sols* a pound ... the Marquis de Vaudreuil promises to increase by 30 pounds the 75 that he distributes to poor families.[2]

People took pride in serving good meals, especially when there was a distinguished guest at the table. Traveler Pehr Kalm noted that women preferred to remain standing near their guests so they could better attend to their needs and to make sure that the food was served properly.

A long agricultural crisis preceded the Rebellion of 1837, and forced the peasants to change their eating habits: housewives did not have enough wheat to prepare their recipes. Pea soup and buckwheat pancakes probably date from this period; tea and molasses, which were imported in British ships, were introduced into the French-Canadian diet. A sizeable part of the family budget was spent on food, especially in the towns, where women had to choose among very expensive products.

Eighteenth-century housewives do not appear to have been obsessed with cleanliness, which would not assume much importance until the nineteenth century, when the connection between germs and disease would be discovered. Floors were washed rarely; it was considered sufficient to sprinkle them with water to keep the dust down. Keeping the house, clothes and children clean certainly did not consume a large part of a woman's time. There was very little furniture in houses – poor families owned only a few chairs, a table, a trunk, a large bed, a few straw mattresses and, perhaps, a cupboard. Lower-class houses were small and people lived mostly in one big room, which served as both kitchen and bedroom. The more affluent – prosperous merchants, for example – owned much more furniture, sometimes imported, as well as silverware and carpets. People were also unconcerned about the cleanliness of beds; many people possessed only one or two sets of sheets. Madame Bégon says that, in 1749, her neighbour wanted the *intendant* to sleep in bedclothes "covered with all kinds of stains." Bégon hastened to offer him "a cleaner bed."[3] There were no bathrooms. Only the rich owned latrines; most people used chamber pots or buckets, which were sometimes emptied out the windows.

CLOTHING

Women did not often wash their clothing: shifts and petticoats were washed only when the owner possessed a change of clothes to wear while their garments dried. Although people had few clothes, dress was enormously important in traditional Francophone society. The dress of the nobility, in particular, had to reflect their social rank, and men as well as women invested considerable sums in their wardrobes. In the eighteenth century, clothes were a reflection of a person's sex and social class. It was not until the nineteenth century that capitalist ideology would transform women into symbols of their husbands' success. Nineteenth-century husbands dressed soberly in black, but their wives would subject their bodies to the torture of corsets, crinolines and bustles. In the eighteenth century, fancy dress was not as restrictive physically. Eighteenth-century men and women, particularly the wealthy, wore lace, jewelry, embroidery and trinkets.

Most women wore outer clothes made from local materials, which they spun, wove, dyed and cut themselves. Undergarments (shifts and petticoats) were made of linen that women spun from flax. Before the middle of the nineteenth century, neither sex wore underpants. A woman wore an undershirt, a camisole and several petticoats, which she could take off and wash in turn. During menstruation, women used rags, which they washed carefully from month to month. According to historian Robert-Lionel Séguin, some women probably made their own tampons, using a method described in pharmaceutical books of the time. Women in New France wore skirts much shorter than in Europe. This was a great source of amusement to visitors from Europe, who found that, despite efforts to keep up with European fashion, women in Quebec were far behind contemporary style. Women who lived in the countryside wore cowhide shoes, which were often home-made; women in the towns wore more dainty, high-heeled shoes. At home, a woman wore a big smock; when going out, she put on a long hooded cloak. Women who could afford some luxury bought imported material, especially material from India, which was very colourful and had imaginative designs. Women in mourning wore black. Dresses were often the only wealth a woman possessed and some women took care to bequeath them to relatives and friends.

In the eighteenth century, upper-class women and men wore wigs. Even ordinary people never went without hats; peasant women wore bonnets or straw hats winter and summer. They also wore silver crosses around the neck.

Some observers were struck by the charm and beauty of the women in Quebec. Others remarked that peasant women seemed to age prematurely; their skin became brown and wrinkled from working in the fields and bending over hot fires. Pretty or not, they aimed to please; on holidays, they dressed in their finery. This interest in fashion aroused the wrath of the clergy and the more puritanical elements of society. The priests urged women to wear more modest clothes and to pay less attention to the way they dressed; but, judging by the regular occurrence of these warnings throughout the eighteenth century and well into the 1820s, they had little success.

OUTSIDE WORK

Women's work extended beyond the house. Women and children looked after the barn, the barnyard and the vegetable garden. Daily work in the barn was one of the most arduous of women's tasks. There was not much livestock, but the work was hard because their tools were primitive. Every autumn, they preserved vegetables in ice pits or root cellars; some women had cold attics to preserve game or fowl. If a woman lived near the market, she could dispose of surplus vegetables or eggs. Even in the towns, every house had a little garden, as the first maps of Montreal indicate.

When extra help was needed, French-Canadian women worked with their husbands in the fields, especially during haymaking, which required days of intensive work. Traveler Pehr Kalm observed that an almost equal number of women and men worked in the fields. Furthermore, it would appear that many women worked in the fields as much as men did. Service in the French militia and, in the nineteenth century, logging took sons and husbands away from home. During their absences, women did the agricultural work. Some men went into the fur trade, particularly young bachelors, whose sisters replaced them in the fields.

In the towns, women often worked with their husbands in the family business. Wives of innkeepers and tavern owners worked alongside their husbands; wives of craftsmen supervised young apprentices. Wives of day labourers and women whose husbands did not make enough money to support the family could take in boarders, sew or wash clothes to make ends meet. Between 1700 and 1760, half the shoemakers in the town of Quebec received extra income from wives who worked as maids, laundry women or nurses.

In 1825, Jacques Viger conducted a census of the town of Montreal. According to his figures, one Montreal woman in five had employment outside the home; almost 27 percent of the active work force in the town was female. Of the women who had a job, more than half were domestic servants and more than a quarter were day workers. Forty percent of teachers were women. Women also worked as governesses, washerwomen, midwives, seamstresses and milliners. Viger cited other occupations in his census – family businesses in which a few women worked as blacksmiths, coachbuilders, gardeners, innkeepers, corsetmakers, weavers, merchants, landlords, haberdashers, farmers and nurses.

Papers left by merchants and administrators show that upper-class women were involved in their husbands' businesses. Even though a superficial reading of the *Coutume de Paris* would lead one to believe that wives were not part of the business world, in reality women worked everywhere. Women were legally authorized by their husbands to participate in business negotiations and to represent them in legal disputes when the husbands were away.

Marie-Anne Barbel is a good example of an eighteenth-century businesswoman. In 1723, at the age of twenty, she married Jean-Louis Fornel, a bourgeois merchant. Between 1724 and 1741, she bore fourteen children; of these, only three would survive her. While her husband was alive, she acted as his authorized representative. After his death in 1745, instead of dividing and liquidating the joint assets, Marie-Anne decided to keep the medium-sized business intact. She obtained a permit to trade in furs; she invested in real estate; she filed suit against a number of businesses; and she bought a pottery factory. She did not consent to the final settlement of the joint estate between herself and her children until thirty-six years after her husband's death. In the meantime, she used the capital to make investments and continued to support several of her adult children.

The wives of civil servants cultivated the social contacts necessary to further their husbands' careers. In a society in which upward mobility often depended on friendships rather than performance, personal connections among members of the aristocracy and the bourgeoisie were carefully nurtured, and it was the woman's duty to maintain these connections. Women did not exercise any real political power, but they enjoyed considerable influence.

Madame Bégon's journal shows us how social and political life were intertwined. She tells the story of Elizabeth Joybert de Soulanges, who was born in Canada. When she was seventeen, she married the Marquis de Vaudreuil. After bearing eleven children, she decided, in 1709, that she could advance the family fortune by representing the family directly at the Court of Versailles. She successfully thwarted a plot against Vaudreuil, and she had herself appointed governess to the King's children.

Madame Bégon also describes Angélique Renaud d'Avène des Méloizes, another Canadian-born woman. She was educated by the Ursulines in Quebec, and, in 1746, married the Chevalier de Livaudière, Monsieur Péan, right-hand man of Intendant Bigot in the last days of the French régime. Madame Péan became the most popular hostess in upper-class French society. Rumours spread about the friendship between the Péans and the Bigots, a friendship reinforced by Madame Péan being Bigot's mistress. When they returned from France, Péan and Bigot were imprisoned while an enquiry was conducted into the corruption of the Bigot régime. Madame Péan used her influence to obtain permission to visit her husband frequently and to keep his reputation and fortune intact in spite of his misdeeds. (She had no scruples, as was evidenced by the letter Marguerite d'Youville wrote her after she left Canada, in which d'Youville tried – unsuccessfully – to get Péan to pay back the money she owed the Grey Nuns.)

During the English régime, Lady Dorchester, wife of the governor of the province of Quebec at the end of the eighteenth century, carefully cultivated contacts between the governor and the established Francophone families. She spoke French, paid regular visits to religious institutions and sent her children to be educated by the Ursulines in the town of Quebec.

Julie Bruneau, daughter of a member of the Legislative Assembly, married a politician, Louis-Joseph Papineau. Correspondence between the two reveals that Julie Bruneau followed politics very closely and totally supported her husband's activities. In 1835, she wrote to him:

> The only thing that amuses me and interests me is politics when I can get some news about it but there is scarcely any. The newspapers only give us a few debates and those are not very accurate.[4]

She expressed great admiration for him as a political leader but, in their private life, she was not always the compliant wife.

> I fully agree with you that there are few totally disinterested men who sacrifice, in every situation, their own interest for the sake of public good as is the duty of all men who hold public office ... that is what I admire about you and what surprises me because I don't know any others like you except your father and Monseigneur Viger.[5]

As Papineau's wife, Julie Bruneau was a public figure in the small world of Lower Canada. Her slightest gesture could have political repercussions and she was obliged to take this into account.

It was normal practice for women to accompany armies, although history ignores their presence. In the eighteenth century and at the beginning of the nineteenth, women followed the armies from France and England. A small minority of soldiers were allowed to get married during their military service and to bring their wives to the camp or barracks. Under the English régime, women were given half of a man's ration and children an eighth. Women worked at tailoring, looked after sick soldiers and cooked for the troops. Soldiers who married without permission were severely punished, so the few women present, married or unmarried, were often a source of contention.

Whether noble or peasant, a woman worked within the context of family activities defined by her husband. Family finances determined whether she participated in her husband's activities or did extra work, such as sewing or cleaning, to make ends meet. As well, the number of mouths to feed in relation to the number of children old enough to work would influence the wife's activities. A family of small children required a lot of care. Later, these children could contribute to the family income: an older daughter could look after the younger children and the wife could help her husband. Adolescents could replace their mothers in the fields.

A RECEPTION AT THE PAPINEAU RESIDENCE

... at half past Eight we arrived there and found the Grounds and Portico of the house very prettily illuminated with coloured Lamps, the Band of the 15th in attendance, and a large party of Canadian Ladies and Gentlemen assembling, so that a brilliant fête and *soirée dansante* awaited us. This surprise was particularly gratifying as coming from Monsr Papineau, and his Wife, who does not enter into society at Montreal (where people indulge too much in divided societies), received her company nevertheless with much Ease and did the honours (I thought) remarkably well. It certainly is quite in the character of a French Woman, whatever be her birth or Rank in life, to possess tact in society, and to bear herself as if it was quite natural to her to live in Evidence and they have self possession, and are generally speaking graceful, so that *les Nuances* of Manner between the Various ranks of life are more gradual and not so decided as with us. A French Woman who is unaffected and inclined to please, will contrive to be pleasing.[6]

BELIEFS OF ALL KINDS

Religious sentiment amongst women in preindustrial society was profound. But it is difficult to say whether the priests had as much influence on women as they would have by the end of the nineteenth century. In Quebec, as in France, whatever anticlericalism there was seemed to manifest itself amongst men. As they knew very little about the philosophy of the Enlightenment and were excluded from political power, women were less motivated to question the control exercised by the Church. Many women belonged to lay orders, such as the Confrérie de la Sainte-Famille, a religious society that encouraged its members to respect the good works and teachings of the Church. Elisabeth Bégon and Marguerite d'Youville occupied important positions in this society in Montreal.

But until the 1830s, priests continued to criticize women's behaviour, which leads us to believe that their influence was not always very strong. What were the criticisms leveled against women? They dressed in immodest fashion and spent their time at balls and social events of dubious morality. For if women worked hard, they also knew how to enjoy themselves. In all social classes, dancing was very popular. Women of all ages, married or single, drank, ate and danced until the wee hours of the morning at country weddings and society parties. This exuberance, which was noticed by travelers, contrasted with women's repressed behaviour during the Victorian era, when ladies of good breeding were expected to refuse alcohol and restrain themselves in public.

In the middle of the eighteenth century, people began to hold evening gatherings in their homes. This allowed women to continue sewing or spinning while singing and exchanging news.

In the eighteenth century, peasants still believed in witchcraft. Although curbed by the Church, this belief found expression in tales and legends. There were no longer witch hunts in France when New France was being settled. (The famous witch hunt in Salem, Massachusetts, at the end of the seventeenth century is attributable to local conditions, particularly the control of the Puritan clergy.) In Canada, no women were executed for witchcraft. But medieval demonology was still familiar to women – consider the hallucinations of Mother Catherine de Saint-Augustin, a nun in the town of Quebec, who during the 1660s, believed she was tormented by devils.

Women were not persecuted as witches, but the image of the evil witch remained one of the strongest stereotypes applied to women who did not conform. In 1671, Françoise Duberger, widow of a man named Galbrun, was condemned to death by the Sovereign Council for killing her first husband. There was also an investigation "of a child smothered by la Galbrun, and other evil practices." She was:

found guilty of a crime in fact and law for having concealed her pregnancy, for having been treated on two or three different occasions and for having taken medicine to lose the fruit of her womb and finally for having given birth, killed her child and buried the latter immediately.[7]

Marie-Josephe Corriveau, according to her own testimony, refused to tolerate further beatings from her husband. In 1763, she was condemned to death for the murder of her husband, and was hanged. At the beginning of the nineteenth century, novelist Phillipe Aubert de Gaspé portrayed "La Corriveau" as a horrible ghost who haunted nighttime travelers. Folklorists and historians in the nineteenth and twentieth centuries would exaggerate the legend of La Corriveau, and each new version would be more horrifying than the last.

Women who killed their husbands or the children of unwanted pregnancies were questioning male authority. Men could produce few explanations to account for this defiance: such women were witches, evil persons and knew the secrets of the devil and the supernatural. Thus, female rebellion was denied or sublimated so that men no longer felt threatened.

UNMARRIED WOMEN: RELIGIOUS AND LAY

The necessity of sharing work encouraged young girls to look for husbands. Without a husband, a woman had scarcely a chance of attaining a satisfactory standard of living and could not have her own household. Women who did not marry had no choice but to live with other families as domestics. Daughters of wealthy families or women who had an inheritance were exceptions: they had an income, and did not need to marry. One such woman was "la vieille fille de Lanaudière," described by Philippe Aubert de Gaspé. At the beginning of the nineteenth century, de Lanaudière ran her *seigneurie* alone. At the end of the French régime, Louise de Ramezay, a daughter of the governor of Montreal, also remained unmarried. She ran the family sawmill, started a new sawmill with another woman and administered vast estates.

The other alternative for those who did not marry was a life of religious celibacy. The religious life offered material and psychological security, as well as the opportunity to do jobs not normally undertaken by women and to escape immediate male authority. But it is likely that most women who entered the religious life were motivated by a desire to serve God.

Three new communities of women were founded in the eighteenth century. In addition to the Hôpital-Général de Québec, which was officially founded in 1701, the Ursulines de Trois-Rivières were founded in 1702. This new autonomous community would teach young girls and look after the sick.

Marguerite Dufrost de Lajemmerais, widow d'Youville, had for a long time been aware of the need to feed the poor and abandoned people of Montreal. In 1737, she joined with three friends, rented a house and began to take in the poor. Marguerite d'Youville did not want to found a religious order: she and her friends were not interested in monastic life, with its cloisters and solemn vows, although they did want to lead a pious existence. When the Charron brothers went bankrupt, Madame d'Youville and her associates took over their hospital and ran it for the benefit of the people of Montreal. Because they were running a hospital, the women were forced to form a secular association conforming to the laws of the Church. They were called "desmoiselles de la Charité chargées par Sa Majesté de la direction de l'Hôpital-Général de Montréal," and were known generally as the Grey Nuns. The community devoted itself exclusively to providing "social services." They looked after the poor, the old and the sick of both sexes. But their most important work was looking after and educating abandoned children, whose numbers increased sharply between 1750 and 1770, due to the presence of first the French and then the English armies.

In the eighteenth century, religious communities grew very slowly. French authorities limited their growth because they considered religious communities unproductive in a colonial setting. Nuns had no political power because most religious communities did not allow their members to leave the cloister. Unlike male communities, such as the Jesuits, women's communities did not get involved in political intrigue and contented themselves with providing services to the surrounding community. They posed no threat to the new English authorities. In 1760, they looked after soldiers from both armies – the Ursulines even knitted winter stockings for the bare legs of Scottish soldiers. They were also quick to elect a woman of American origin as mother superior, hoping to consolidate relations with British authorities. Later, the Ursulines would accept young Anglophones into their convents. In 1764, there were no more than 190 nuns in Quebec; in 1800, there were 304. In 1825, according to Jacques Viger, there were only 93 nuns in the city of Montreal.

Life in the convent was serene but austere. The hierarchy in the convent community more or less reproduced the class structure of society at large. Choir sisters devoted themselves to community work: teaching, hospital care and embroidering of vestments for the clergy. Women of more humble origin were servants: they did the housework in the convent and looked after the other sisters. Every religious community was associated with a distinct social group. In the first half of the eighteenth century, the Hôpital-Général de Québec attracted daughters of the minor nobility, while the postulants in the Ursuline convent or at the Hôtel-Dieu came from more modest backgrounds, although they had larger dowries, which often took the form of land or goods. Lady Simcoe, the wife of the Governor-General of Upper Canada, visited the Ursulines and described her experience:

> I had an order from the Catholic Bishop for admittance to the Convent des Ursulines, where I went today with Madame Baby. The Superieure is a very pleasing conversible woman of good address. Her face & manner reminded me of Mrs. Gwillim. The nuns appeared cheerful, pleased to see Visitors & disposed to converse & ask questions. Their dress is black with a white hood & some of them looked very pretty in it. They carry cleanliness & neatness to the greatest pitch of perfection in every part of the Convent, & are industrious in managing a large garden.
>
> They educate Children at this Convent, taking both pensionnaires & day boarders. They make many decorations for their altars & Church, & gild Picture frames. They shewed a fine piece of Embroidery worked by an English nun, since dead. Some of them make boxes & pin cushions of birch bark worked with dyed hair of the *Orignal*. It is so short that it must be put through the Needle for every stitch which makes it tedious. All sorts of Cakes & Sweetmeats are made here & all the Deserts in Quebec are furnished by the Nuns. They dry apples in a very peculiar manner, they are like Dried apricots. All these things are of use to maintain them, their finances being very moderate.
>
> Another Convent is called the Hôtel Dieu for the reception of the Sick, whether French or English. It is attended by the Medical Men on the Staff, who speak highly of the attention payed by the Nuns to the Sick people. The General Hospital is a Convent a mile out of Town, where Sick and Insane people are received.[8]

The correspondence of Soeur Thérèse de Jésus at the end of the eighteenth century suggests that the daily preoccupations of nuns were scarcely different from those of lay women. The greatest worry for all women was their health. Almost a hundred letters written by this Ursuline from Trois-Rivières to her brother François Baby have been preserved, and in almost all of them she complains of her health and gives a detailed description of her vomiting, headaches, chest pains, intestinal problems, colds and so on. In this respect, her letters are hardly different from those of her contemporaries. Soeur Thérèse seems to be in constant communication with her family and often asks for news of each member. Unlike married women, who worried more about the health of a mother who was giving birth, she was more interested in the newborn child. In May 1787, she was less concerned about her sister-in-law's condition than she was about the baby's; she hoped that she "would soon have the satisfaction of hearing that she has given me a little nun." Soeur Thérèse held a series of responsible positions in the convent. When she was put in charge of provisions, she worried about bad harvests and used her brother to intervene so that she might obtain the lowest prices. Sometimes she asked her family for money, something that few nuns could do: "yes I am the only nun who benefits so much from her own family."[9]

LIVING ON THE FRINGE OF SOCIETY

Slavery was authorized in Canada in 1709 and not abolished until 1833. During both the French and English régimes, slave women worked as domestic servants. In 1744, in the town of Quebec, 5 percent of the female servants were Black slaves and 10 percent were Indians. The death rate amongst these slaves was high and adapting to white society was difficult; consequently, they did not always make ideal servants, even if they did not have to be paid for their work. Their status in families varied from that of an adopted child to that of a harshly exploited beast of burden. Marie-Joseph, a Black slave, was probably exploited: outraged by the treatment she received, she set fire to her mistress's house in Montreal in April 1734. The fire spread and forty-six houses burned down. Marie-Joseph was hanged in the market square; then her body was burned at the stake and her ashes thrown to the wind, the ultimate degradation for criminals, who, under the *Ancien Régime,* were denied a religious service.

Although there were some marriages between whites and Indians and also between Indians and Blacks, more than half of the children of slaves were born outside marriage and were, in the words of the parish register, of 'unknown fathers'. These children were born into servitude and belonged to their mother's owner. Marguerite d'Youville owned a slave; so did a merchant named Pierre Guy. The husband of Madeleine de Verchères, Governor Vaudreuil, and the Bishop of Saint-Vallier were also slave owners.

According to historian André Lachance, during the first half of the eighteenth century, only 20 percent of those accused of criminal offences were women, even though women constituted almost half the French-Canadian population. The rate of female criminality seems low, and it would decrease. (Since the mid-nineteenth century, the rate has not been higher than 15 percent. In 1967, it was only 11.5 percent in Quebec.) What were women charged with? From 1712 to 1759, almost half the charges involved crimes of "violence against the person," a category that included murder (especially infanticide), insults, slander and defiance of the law. The relative ease with which French-Canadian women appeared to resort to violence would lead one to believe that the ideal of the submissive, fragile female had very little hold on women of the time.

Between 1712 and 1748, four women, two of them servants, were sentenced to be hanged for infanticide, a crime of which only women could be found guilty. One was saved from the gallows when the father of her child, who had refused to marry her, changed his mind. Another, who managed to escape, was hanged in effigy. A third, the mother of a family whose absent husband was not the father of the smothered child, had her sentence commuted to a whipping and perpetual exile.

More than 14 percent of all charges against women were for insult, defamation of character, slander and libel. Although they were excluded from power, in a society where honour and reputation meant everything, women's tongues were their most effective weapons.

Almost a third of all charges involved theft. Robberies were carried out in broad daylight, most often without break and entry. In the towns, servants had easy access to their masters' possessions. They usually stole small objects: smocks, ribbons or cutlery. Theft in the home was punished severely because the servant who had been taken into the family had dared to violate the family's trust.

The low crime rate can be explained by the restrictions of the domestic setting. Most crimes were committed outside the home, and, therefore, most involved men. Men were the heads of families and could make whatever rules they wanted in their own households; they did not need to resort to the judicial system. Women were restricted to the home and therefore had less opportunity to commit crimes.

Generally speaking, women received more severe sentences than men: more corporal punishment (excluding the gallows) and more degrading punishment (branding and public reprimand and atonement) as if those few women who challenged masculine authority were punished as examples to other women.

Marie-Josephe Corriveau, a battered wife, paid with her life for her transgression of the male order. She admitted her guilt at her trial in April 1783.

> Marie-Josephe Corriveau, the widow Dodier, declares that she killed her husband Louis Hélène Dodier during the night while he was sleeping in his bed; that she did it with a small axe that she was neither aided nor abetted by anyone to do it; that no one knew about it. She realizes that she deserves to die. She only asks the Court to give her a little time to make her confession and to make her peace with heaven. She adds that it is really due in great part to the way her husband treated her if she is guilty of this crime.[10]

The British authorities, who wanted to intimidate a recently conquered populace, sent La Corriveau to the gallows. As was the custom in the eighteenth century, her body was put on public display: she hung for more than a month in an iron cage above the crossroads at Lauzon, near Quebec. Many men killed their wives, but none gained the reputation of La Corriveau, who is still a legend two hundred years after her death.

Rape also seems to have been passed over in silence. The only rapes brought to the attention of the authorities during the French régime were those of very young girls. French soldiers were punished for a variety of crimes, but almost never accused of rape. However, historian William Eccles recounts that in 1760, while Commander Murray was trying to subjugate the countryside between Quebec and Montreal, his soldiers slipped his control and raped several French-Canadian women.

THE CONCEALMENT OF
PREGNANCY AND INFANTICIDE

In sixteenth-century France, the royal authority, alarmed by the number of infanticides, probably of illegitimate children, had an ordonance published that charged all girls and women to declare their pregnancies. This made it difficult for mothers to abort a fetus secretly, or clandestinely kill a newborn child. Since a respectable woman had no reason to "harbour" or hide her pregnancy, this ordonance was aimed at those who, finding themselves pregnant outside of wedlock, tried to hide their mistake by killing the child. The ordonance, issued by Henri II in 1556, stated:

> That every Woman who finds herself guilty of crime in fact and law for having harboured and hidden her pregnancy as well as the birth of her child without declaring one or the other, and without seeking witness to one or the other, the life or death of her Child, when it came out of her belly, and having deprived the child of the Holy Sacrament and Baptism as much as public burial, which is customary, may this Woman be held and accused of murdering her Child and as atonement sentenced to death and executed....[11]

In New France, some *intendants* had the ordonance read out every three months in the churches. This made it difficult for a woman on trial for concealing pregnancy or infanticide to plead ignorance of the law. Under the English régime, a woman who concealed the birth of her child or who tried to dispose secretly of the body of her stillborn child could be sentenced to at least two years' imprisonment.

There is no reason to believe that women were not the victims of sexual aggression; but in a society in which honour was everything and female chastity an essential virtue, a woman who complained that she had been raped would only raise questions about her own behaviour. The shame a rape victim felt made her keep quiet about the circumstances surrounding the brutal attack. When a woman brought charges against her attacker, it was she who was put on trial.

Susannah Davis, a seventeen-year-old servant who worked in nine houses in three years, recalled how she was raped on the evening of Mardi-Gras in 1813, when she was living in the house of a man called Roussel:

> I did not know him before, he is a married man, the wife of the P— had left ... at two in the afternoon leaving in the house of the P— myself and two little children, the eldest of whom was five – at eleven o'clock I went to bed I put out the Candles – and two hours later the P— came to the Bedroom where I was with a candle in his hand which he put on the table where he began to eat. He asked me to eat also but I did not want to. He came close to my bed and told me he wanted to sleep with me – I told him no – And then I got up ... he put out the candle took me in his arms and threw me on his bed – I resisted I started to shout he grabbed me by the throat to stop me from crying out he also stopped me from getting up, the children were crying out he told them to be quiet and to stay in their beds – and he said to me get up if you can – I continued shouting and he asked me if I wanted the neighbours to hear me ... the first time he only wet me on my buttocks with his private parts – the second time he hurt me with his organ in my body, in my private parts – ... all that was done against my wishes – ... I never consented – it was done with violence and by force –.[12]

But the testimony of Susannah Davis was confused, and her hope for financial compensation was naive. Her behaviour had been overly familiar in the past, and people did not believe in her virtue. Only the woman next door, who had given her shelter the day after the rape, testified in her favour. The accused was a solid citizen, father and eminently respectable man, as eleven members of the community testified; six of those who appeared in court as witnesses on his behalf were men. In short, Susannah Davis's word had little credibility. The accused was found not guilty.

Between 1712 and 1748, "moral" crimes committed by women – adultery, debauchery, cohabitation, prostitution, and so on – comprised only a small part of officially recognized female crimes. There was much greater tolerance of such behaviour than there had been in the seventeenth century. According to historian André Lachance, no legal action was taken against prostitutes during the last decade of the French régime. When prostitution became flagrant, the authorities in Quebec would lock up a number of women in the Hôpital-Général. In Montreal, the same procedure was followed, but without much success, according to Elizabeth Bégon, who noted in 1749:

> Today my dear son, we saw Madame Bouat, who as I informed you has been at the Frères Charon since the *Saint-Martin* with madame d'Youville. It is very amusing to see her: she does nothing but preach and talk about the pleasures of life away from society. She assured us of the conversion of four women who were put into the Jéricho; she visits them from time to time. I think I told you their names: Madame Guiniolète and her daughter, Madame Sans-Poil and one from Quebec whose name I do not know. The only thing that Madame Bouat fears is that the soldiers might want to remove these women from captivity, but I do not think they want to do anything inappropriate.[13]

At the end of the nineteenth century, prostitution was still beyond the control of the authorities. Historian Wallot quotes estimates from 1810: four to six hundred prostitutes for the town of Quebec, which had a population of thirteen to fourteen thousand. Even though the Legislative Assembly voted annual sums of money for the rehabilitation of prostitutes, no institution was capable of dealing adequately with the problem. In 1825, in Montreal, 6 percent of all women who declared a profession said they were prostitutes. Perhaps for many women, prostitution was the best if not the only way of earning a living.

Poverty condemned many women to a marginal existence. Lucrative jobs were beyond the reach of most women: they lacked specialized training, and many were responsible for small children. Moreover, the average salary for a woman was approximately half that earned by a man – a constant throughout the history of Quebec. A woman with no inheritance could hardly support herself. A woman whose husband died, was sick, or abandoned her became solely responsible for her family; she would rapidly slip into poverty. In the eighteenth century, a woman would turn to religious communities for help. Sometimes the government would give a meagre pension to widows of war veterans or loyalists.

At the beginning of the nineteenth century, female poverty increased in the towns. Part of the population consisted of unmarried women, orphans, unemployed women and those suffering from chronic diseases. As well, there were immigrant women, who became more numerous after 1850. A number of these were wives of former British army officers or of colonial administrators. For the most part, women who immigrated with their families were poor. In the early 1830s, Irish immigration increased and brought poor people to

SUSANNA MOODIE ARRIVES IN MONTREAL IN 1832

I was not a little amused at the extravagant expectations entertained by some of our steerage passengers. The sight of the Canadian shores had changed them into persons of great consequence. The poorest and the worst-dressed, the least-deserving and the most repulsive in mind and morals exhibited most disgusting traits of self-importance. Vanity and presumption seemed to possess them altogether. They talked loudly of the rank and wealth of their connexions at home, and lamented the great sacrifices they had made in order to join brothers and cousins who had foolishly settled in this beggarly wooden country.

Girls, who were scarcely able to wash a floor decently, talked of service with contempt, unless tempted to change their resolution by the offer of twelve dollars a month. To endeavour to undeceive them was a useless and ungracious task. After having tried it with several without success, I left it to time and bitter experience to restore them to their senses. In spite of the remonstrances of the captain and the dread of the cholera, they all rushed on shore to inspect the land of Goshen, and to endeavour to realize their absurd anticipations.[14]

Lower Canada; sometimes these immigrants brought cholera or other contagious diseases to the colony.

Women already established in Lower Canada did what they could to relieve the distress of the thousands of immigrant women who arrived without money or friends. The government largely left the work of relieving poverty to private initiatives, but the problem soon became far too big for the nuns to handle. Individual charity, which had been practised for a long time, was not sufficient, especially in the congested urban environment. In 1817, bourgeois women in Montreal organized the Female Benevolent Society, a charitable lay organization; in 1821, the society established the Montreal General Hospital. In 1822, upper-class ladies in Quebec organized one of the first charitable lay societies, the Female Compassionate Society, to assist Catholic and Protestant married women in childbirth. In the same year, Protestant ladies were administering the Montreal Protestant Orphan Asylum, a counterpart of orphanages run by nuns. In 1824, the Montreal Ladies' Benevolent Society started to aid destitute women and children.

Women were vulnerable to poverty and easily excluded from society for committing moral offences. They often found themselves with no family to

---

REGULATIONS OF THE FEMALE
COMPASSIONATE SOCIETY

Regulations of the Female Compassionate Society, established for the relief of poor married women in their confinement:

III. The Articles of clothing and nourishment shall be issued by the Storekeeper, on a Ticket from the Acting Directress, and the clothing shall be returned to them within thirty days. On the Storekeeper's Certificate of their being complete and properly washed, a gratuity of half a dollar, or a suit of baby linen shall be given to the poor woman, at the discretion of the Acting Directress. If not returned within the time or not in proper order, the gratuity shall be forfeited, and the woman excluded from future relief. The allowance shall consist of
Half a pound of tea,
Two pounds of Oatmeal,
Two pounds of Rice or Barley,
Two pounds of Sugar,
Six pounds of Beef,
Two loaves of Bread,
Two pounds of Soap,
Three suits of Baby Linen,
Two changes of Linen for the woman.
Medicine, Wine, Nutmegs, Wood and Bedding to be added at the discretion of the Acting Directresses.

Quebec City, Lower Canada, 1822[15]

---

turn to: without a father, husband or brother, a woman could barely survive. A relatively young woman could get by on her own, but as soon as she fell ill, grew old or found herself alone with children, her existence became precarious. The most she could hope for was assistance from other women. Providing food and clothes, comforting and caring for others were the women's tasks and it was often other women who needed this attention the most.

DEMOCRATIC RIGHTS

Women did not participate in the political life of the colony except when their own family or community interests were directly affected. Although they could not hold positions in the government, it appears that many women followed politics closely. From their letters, we learn that women kept abreast of current events, often because their men were in the army or the government or, under the British régime, were members of the opposition. In the eighteenth century, working-class women sometimes took to the streets to protest unpopular measures. In 1795, the government levied extra taxes on the *habitants* for the upkeep of roads in Quebec. The *habitants* resisted but, in spite of threats made by five hundred women, their leader was arrested.

The exclusion of women from political life had no legal basis, although it was an established custom. For example, the Constitution of 1791 fixed the franchise for property owners at quite a low level and made no distinction according to sex. As a result, certain female property owners obtained – and exercised – the right to vote. But the nineteenth century, which would enshrine the woman as queen of the household and guardian angel of family values, would not easily accept women's direct participation in the political process. Anglophone women and women close to power were over-represented amongst women voters; this partially explains why the Parti canadien, led by Louis-Joseph Papineau, wanted to take away women's right to vote. The Parti canadien feared that if women voted, the party would lose seats to the opposition.

Women do not seem to have expressed themselves on the question of their political rights. Mary Wollstonecraft's *A Vindication of the Rights of Women,* published in 1792, was read by a few individuals, but its contents remained unknown to the vast majority of women in Lower Canada. Few Francophone

---

PETITION IN 1828 ON THE VOTE FOR WOMEN

That the Petitioners, therefore, deem this refusal to take a vote offered in terms of the law, a most dangerous precedent, contrary to law, and tending to subvert their rights and constitutional privileges. That the Petitioners represent on the second head, that, as the votes of the Widows were not taken, the return of Mr. Stuart is void, inasmuch as the free choice of all the electors was not made known. That the Petitioners may presume to trouble the House with the reasons that they deem conclusive as to the right of Widows to vote; neither in men nor women can the right to vote be a natural right; it is given by enactment. The only questions are, whether women could exercise that right well and advantageously for the State, and whether they are entitled to it. That the Petitioners have not learned that there exist any imperfections in the minds of women that place them lower than men in intellectual power, or that would make it more dangerous to entrust them with the exercise of the elective franchise than with the exercise of numerous other rights that the law has already given them. That in point of fact, women duly qualified have hitherto been allowed to exercise the right in question. That the Petitioners conceive that women are fairly entitled to the right, if they can exercise it well. That property and not persons is the basis of representation in the English Government. That the qualifications required by the Election Laws sufficiently shew this. That the same principle is carried into our own constitution. That the paying of certain taxes to the State is also a basis of representation; for it is a principal contended for by the best Statesmen of England, that there can be "no taxation without representation." That the duties to be performed to the State may also give a right to representation. That in respect of property, taxation and duties to the State, the Widow, duly qualified by our Election Laws, is in every essential respect similarly situated with the man: her property is taxed alike with that of the man: she certainly is not liable to Militia duties, nor is the man above forty-five: she is not called to serve on a jury, nor is a physician: she cannot be elected to the Assembly, nor can a Judge or Minister of the Gospel. It may be alleged that nature has only fitted her for domestic life, yet the English Constitution allows a woman to sit on the Throne, and one of its brightest ornaments has been a woman. That it would be impolitic and tyrannical to circumscribe her efforts in society – to say that she shall not have the strongest interest in the fate of her country, and the security of her common rights: It is she who breathes into man with eloquent tenderness his earliest lessons of religion and of morals; and shall it be said that his country shall be forgotten, or that she shall mould his feelings while smarting under hateful laws. That the Petitioners allege that Widows exercise, generally, all the rights of men, are liable to most of the same duties towards the State, and can execute them as well. And they pray from the premises: 1. That the House declare Mr. Scott, the Returning Officer, guilty of malversation in office, and take measures to enforce the law in such case provided. 2. That the proceedings of the late Election for the Upper Town of Quebec, concluded on the fifteenth August One thousand eight hundred and twenty-seven, by the Return of Mr. Stuart, be declared void.[16]

women had the intellectual training or the time to become involved in politics. Lady Simcoe, an Anglophone, gained a reputation as a bluestocking while in Montreal because of her intellectual curiosity, which was considered too pronounced. Other Anglophones with obvious literary talent, such as Jane Ellice, wife of Lord Durham's secretary, the seigneur de Beauharnois, were perhaps too close to power to question the political process.

The rights accorded women in Lower Canada under the *Coutume de Paris* may partially explain why women did not complain. In contrast to British Common Law, which was practised in the Maritimes and in Upper Canada,

---

THE UNFORTUNATE JANETTE BILODEAU-PARENT

Janette Bilodeau-Parent was, at the turn of the nineteenth century, the mistress of Judge de Bonne. When he discarded her and married to further his career, she retaliated in the press. She published the following letter in the paper, *Le Canadien*, in which she urged voters to be wary of her former lover. In spite of her warning, Judge de Bonne, an opponent of the Parti canadien, was reelected in May 1808.

To the voters of the county of Quebec

Although it is not the custom for women to address you during the elections, I hope that you will see fit to pardon an unfortunate woman for taking this liberty, because she has no other way of obtaining justice but by addressing you. What else could I do, for the scoundrel I complain about is the Judge himself.

You know, Sirs, the trouble I went through for him in the Charlesbourg election ... I was interested in him out of pity, as a number of you were, and I did all I could to get him elected and see that he triumphed. You, Sirs, have seen this triumph which he boasted about so much. But this scoundrel had hardly triumphed, before he forgot what I had done for him, he cowardly abandoned me. He had the treachery to tell me that I was bringing him down in your esteem, and he shamelessly betrayed me so that you would see him in a good light.

The scoundrel has got married and has suddenly become religious; this is to obtain your votes. This is not a true conversion, I assure you; I know him, he will do anything to get what he wants.

The Unfortunate Janette Bilodeau-Parent[17]

---

the *Coutume de Paris* did not eradicate a woman's legal existence the moment she got married. A husband's control over his wife's assets had established limits: dower rights and a married woman's statutory lien on her husband's property were designed to protect her against fluctuations in her husband's finances or poor administration of the joint estate by the husband.

A TRADITIONAL SOCIETY IN
THE PROCESS OF CHANGE

For more than a hundred years, the colony on the banks of the St. Lawrence revolved around agricultural and family life. Families grew in size and children were set up on new lands extending to the perimeters of the *seigneuries*. Life was disrupted by the English invasion and the War of 1812, but eventually went back to normal without fundamental changes.

Women, men and children lived within their families and worked for the family. Matrimonial, professional, legal, financial, and even political choices were made according to family dictates. This social structure negated the individuality of women and men. In such a context, there was no abstract definition of a woman's role: women simply carried out the demands made on them by their families. As there was no strict distinction between private and public spheres, there was often a tendency for family, political and economic affairs to be intermixed. Women and men alike participated.

Nevertheless, society did not believe that the family estate could be jointly managed. Every family had a head who held the authority – the male, the husband, the father, whose position allowed him to pass off his personal interests as family interests. As head of the family, a man had greater control than did a woman over the family assets; he was also accorded more sexual freedom. Because he was head of the family and registered as owner of the family assets, he was given political rights when the parliamentary system was introduced.

For the women of Lower Canada, this long period ended in a climate of crisis. The economic and political troubles of the colony paved the way for a new economic system. On the one hand, the bases of the traditional economy were disintegrating; the good land was all occupied and falling agricultural productivity lowered the standard of living of the *habitants*. On the other hand, the industrial revolution had reached North American soil. Traditional society would have to change. Women were entering a century of upheaval.

NOTES

1 "Journal des Campagnes du Chevalier de Lévis, 1756-60," quoted in R.-L. Séguin, *La Civilization traditionelle de l'habitant au 17e et au 18e siècles* (Montreal: Fides, 1967), p. 75.

2 "Journal du marquis de Montcalm," quoted in R.-L. Séguin, *La Civilization traditionelle de l'habitant au 17e et au 18e siècles* (Montreal: Fides, 1967), p. 109.

3 Elizabeth Bégon, *Lettres au cher fils,* Nicole Deschamps ed. (Montreal: Hurtubise, HNH, 1972), 31 January 1749, p. 74.

4 "Julie Bruneau à Louis-Joseph Papineau," 2 November 1835. *Rapport de l'archiviste de la province du Québec,* 1957-1958, p. 66.

5 Ibid., 15 December 1831, p. 65.

6 *Lady Aylmer's Journal,* published in Rapport de l'archiviste de la province de Québec, 1934-35 (1935).

7 "Jugements et délibérations du Conseil souverain de la Nouvelle-France 1660," quoted in R.-L. Séguin, *La sorcellerie en Nouvelle-France* (Montreal: Leméac, 1971), p. 160.

8 *Mrs. Simcoe's Diary* (Toronto: Macmillan, 1965), p. 43.

9 "Soeur Thérèse de Jésus à François Baby," 2 August 1786 and 8 May 1787. *Collection Baby,* Archives de l'Université de Montréal, box 115.

10 Quoted in Lacoursière, L. "Le triple destin de Marie-Josephe Corriveau, 1733-1763," *Cahiers des Dix,* vol. 33, pp. 230-231.

11 J.-L. Flandrin, *Le Sexe et L'Occident* (Paris: Seuil, 1981), p. 168.

12 Extracts from "Sur Indictment for a Rape on Susannah-Eliza Davis, 23 February 1814," 7 May 1814, Quebec, Oyer & Terminer & General Gaol Delivery, *Sewell Papers,* Public Archives of Canada, Series 17 G 23, G II, 10, vol. 13, folio 6117 to 6128.

13 Elizabeth Bégon, op. cit., 9 January 1749, p. 64.

14 S. Moodie, *Roughing It In The Bush, or Forest Life in Canada* (Toronto: McClelland and Stewart, New Canadian Library, no.31, 1970).

15 Female Compassionate Society of Quebec (Quebec, 1822), 14-5. Bibliothèque de la ville de Montréal, Salle Gagnon.

16 "Petitions to House of Assembly, Lower Canada, 4 December 1828," in

Documents Relating to the Constitutional History of Canada 1819-1828, edited by Arthur G. Doughty and Norah Story (Ottawa, 1935), pp. 520-521.

17 *Le Canadien*, 21 May 1808.

FURTHER READING

Allard, M., ed. *L'Hôtel-Dieu de Montréal 1642-1973*. Montreal: Hurtubise HMH, 1973.

Barry, F. "Familles et domesticité féminine au milieu du 18e siècle" in *Maîtresses d'école, Maîtresses de maison*, selected articles, with an introduction by Micheline Dumont and Nadia Eid. Montreal: Boréal Express, 1983.

Bégon, E. *Lettres au cher fils*. N. Dechamps, ed. Montreal: Hurtubise HMH, 1972.

Brooke, F. *The History of Emilie Montague*. New edition by McClelland and Stewart, Toronto, 1961.

Charbonneau, H. *Vie et Mort de nos ancêtres*. Montreal: P.U.M., 1975.

Charbonneau, H., ed. *La population de Québec: Montréal*. Montreal: Boréal Express, in the series Etudes d'histoire du Québec, no. 4, 1973.

D'Allaire, M. *L'Hôpital-Général de Québec, 1692-1764*. Montreal: Fides.

Dictionary of Canadian Biography, Volume II. Toronto: University of Toronto Press, 1969.

Dufebvre, B. *Cinq femmes et Nous*. Quebec: Bélisle, 1950.

Igartua, J. "Le comportement démographique des marchands de Montréal vers 1760" in *Revue d'histoire de l'Amérique française*, vol. 33, no. 3 (December 1979), pp. 427-446.

Jean, M. *Evolution des communautés religieuses de femmes au Canada de 1639 à nos jours*. Montreal: Fides, 1977.

Lacelle, C. "Les domestiques dans les villes canadiennes au XIXe siècle; effectifs et conditions de vie" in *Histoire sociale*, vol. XV, no. 29 (May 1982), pp. 181-208.

Lachance, A. "Women and Crime in Canada in the Early Eighteenth Century, 1712-1759" in L.A. Knafla, *Crime and Criminal Justice in Europe and Canada*. The Calgary Institute for the Humanities, Wilfrid Laurier Press, 1981, pp. 157-178.

Landry, Y. "Mortalité, nuptialité et canadisation des troupes françaises de la guerre de Sept Ans" in *Histoire sociale*, vol. XII, nos. 23-24, 1979, pp. 298-315.

Light, B. and A. Prentice, eds. *Pioneer and Gentlewomen of English North America 1713-1867*. Toronto: New Hogtown Press.

Ouellet, F. *Histoire économique et sociale du Québec, 1760-1850*. 2 volumes. Montreal: Fides, 1971.

———. *Le Bas Canada, 1791-1840 Changements structuraux et crise*. Ottawa: University of Ottawa Press, 1976.

Plamondon, L. "Une femme d'affaires en Nouvelle France: Marie-Anne Barbel, veuve Fournel" in *Revue d'histoire de l'Amérique française*, vol. 31, no. 2 (September 1977), pp. 165-186.

Séguin, R.-L. *La civilisation traditionelle de l'habitant au 17e et 18e siècles*. Montreal: Fides, 1967.

———. *La sorcellerie du Québec du XVIIe au XIXe siècle*. Montreal: Leméac, 1971.

Van Kirk, S. "The Impact of White Women on Fur Trade Society" in Trofimenkoff, S.M. and A. Prentice. *The Neglected Majority*. Toronto: McClelland and Stewart, 1977.

Wallot, J.-P. *Un Québec qui bougeait*. Montreal: Boréal Express, 1973.

III
UPHEAVALS
1832-1900

FOR QUEBEC, THE NINETEENTH CENTURY was one of change, upheaval and radical transformation. Politically, the Constitutional Act gave way to the Union Bill, which was then replaced by the Act of Confederation. Industrialization gave rise to a restructuring of the Quebec economy; the period was characterized by frequent economic crises, by unemployment, and by waves of emigration to the United States and influxes of immigrants. Quebec became an urban society: customs and living conditions changed, despite resistance from an omnipresent clergy. At the beginning of the century, politics in Lower Canada was marked by parliamentary confrontation, and the agricultural economy was in an unprecedented crisis. By the 1830s, the economic situation had become alarming: in 1832, wheat production in Lower Canada collapsed totally; farmers could not pay their agricultural workers or set up their sons in farming. The countryside became overpopulated, and there was a shortage of land; merchants could no longer find customers for their imports or for the products made by artisans in Montreal and Quebec. People began to feel the effects of the economic crisis in their daily lives. Parliamentary agitation increased and, in 1837 and 1838, uprisings broke out.

Historians are divided as to the causes of the insurrections: some think they resulted from political conflict; others believe that they derived from an economic crisis, class struggle or abrupt change in modes of production. However, one thing is certain: the uprisings in Lower and Upper Canada were harshly put down by the British, who imposed a political solution on the conflict – the political union of Upper and Lower Canada. Between 1840 and 1867, the representatives of the people of Quebec and Ontario would sit side by side in the same assembly.

During the same period, England modified its economic policies and transformed the administration of its colonies. For a time, England intervened in the political problems of Lower Canada; however, the colony's economic problems were not addressed. Canadian products on the imperial market had benefited from preferential tariffs. When those tariffs were abolished, the Canadian economy had to be restructured. The Union government undertook a major reform: modernization of its transport system. In an economy based primarily on the export of wheat and wood, transport was of vital importance. The St. Lawrence canal was finished in 1848 and work was begun on extending and improving the road system; finally, railways were constructed. Agriculture, the mainstay of the Quebec economy, changed profoundly and emerged from the crisis of 1870-1880 specializing in milk production. Commercial farming also developed, and subsistence farming continued to be important.

The uprisings of 1837 and 1838 marked a social turning point: legal, social, educational and religious institutions were reformed. New municipal and educational structures were set up between the government and the people: in 1840, a government order established twenty-two municipal districts in Canada East (Quebec); subsequently, the government passed laws that would regulate the educational system in Quebec for more than a century. In addition, land-registry offices were created and, in 1866, a new Civil Code was introduced to supersede the confusing mixture of French and English law and to solve the problems posed by a legal system designed during the *Ancien Régime*.

There was also a change in the men who controlled Quebec society. The failure of the rebellion considerably weakened the liberal petite bourgeoisie and enabled the clergy to entrench its position, with great consequence to education. Monseigneur Bourget, Bishop of Montreal, gave new life to the Church in Quebec when he succeeded in ridding it of the restrictions imposed on it since the English invasion: he brought back the Jesuits, encouraged French religious communities to establish themselves in Quebec and backed the creation of new Canadian communities for women. The Church produced competent, talented individuals who worked their way into public life: education, health, social assistance, culture and information services attracted many women and men from the Church. Monseigneur Bourget was an Ultramontane and promoted a nonegalitarian, rigidly hierarchical society in which the state would submit to the Church and the Pope. The bishop missed few opportunities to give advice to politicians. Power in Quebec finally passed into the hands of the conservatives; liberalism suffered a serious blow.

The changes introduced immediately after the rebellion did not solve Quebec's social problems or mark the end of conflict and change. During the nineteenth century, the basis of the economic system changed. By the end of the century, Quebec had been transformed from a preindustrial and agricultural economy to an industrialized society. This restructuring was not entirely smooth and the crises that hit the economies of the western world in the second half of the nineteenth century had repercussions on the emerging industries of Quebec.

Quebec industrialized rapidly. Historians Hamelin and Roby have calculated that between 1851 and 1896, the value of production in secondary industry rose from $2 million to more than $153 million – more than 7000 percent. The chief industries were food, clothing, iron and steel. Thousands of women, men and children went to work in the factories, which produced thousands of different products.

Markets and an abundant work force were needed to develop the fledgling industries, and the political structure of the Union Bill became obsolete. This same structure was being attacked for ethno-political reasons in Upper Canada where the English-speaking majority preferred to have a separate state. In 1867, under the British North America Act, a group of former English colonies became separate provinces of one country, and Canada became a confederation. There were no longer barriers between the provinces; workers, goods and capital could circulate freely from one province to another.

During the nineteenth century, the colonial way of life was abandoned, democratic practices were introduced in education and municipal and provincial politics; the legal system was changed; the Church took over important sectors of community life, and a national market was created; last but not least, was the rise of the bourgeoisie and the working class.

These changes came about slowly. Before the new factories were ready to absorb the rural unemployed, thousands of women and men of Quebec found themselves without work and had to seek a living elsewhere. During this period also, thousands of British immigrants arrived at the port of Quebec; some had enough money to buy property in the Eastern Townships, but most made their way to other provinces or the United States. In 1901, scarcely 5.5 percent of the Quebec population had been born abroad. Not only was there little immigration to Quebec, but people tended to leave.

Thousands of Québécois boarded trains for the United States and settled in the industrial towns of New England. Nearly a hundred thousand emigrated to other Canadian provinces, especially Ontario. Between 1850 and 1901, more than half a million French Canadians had emigrated, an exodus so great that, by the turn of the century, there were as many Québécois outside Quebec as there were inside. Other Québécois imitated their colonial ancestors and went to work in the regions the big forestry companies were opening up. Areas north of Montreal, in the Ottawa Valley, St. Maurice and Saguenay-Lac-

Saint-Jean regions were settled. New stretches of land were cleared and wood was cut for the big companies.

Despite the exodus, towns and villages of Quebec continued to grow. During the first quarter of the nineteenth century merchants, artisans and professionals went to live in villages. In 1851, Montreal and Quebec were still the only towns of any importance, with populations of 57,715 and 42,052 respectively. The province was still rural: 85 percent of its citizens lived in municipalities with fewer than a thousand inhabitants. As industries grew up in the towns, the demographics changed rapidly. By 1901, Montreal had a population of 268,000; only 64 percent of the population of Quebec was rural.

Massive migration to the towns made existing urban structures inadequate: there was a shortage of housing and concentrations of people around factories; sanitary conditions were poor; public transport was inadequate and the risk of fires was high. In Montreal, where working-class families constituted two-thirds of the population, daily survival was closely linked to industrial production. Numerous economic crises and seasonal layoffs plunged thousands of families into destitution.

People became cogs in the new economic system. Industrialization demanded of women considerable adaptation. The traditional solidarity of the rural community was shaken to its very foundations. To survive, women had to create new forms of mutual aid and support; they were forced to modify their behaviour, to abandon the rhythm of work in a preindustrial society, to conform to the discipline of the new factories, to live in cramped, overcrowded dwellings, to buy what they once had made and to do different work. They had to relearn how to be women in a world in which they were marginal yet indispensable.

CHAPTER FIVE

THE GREAT COMMOTION

WHEN A MAN'S WORLD
BEGINS TO FALL APART

SOME WOMEN FOUND IT impossible to stay out of the political crises in Montreal. In 1832, during a by-election in the west of Montreal, British troops were called in and left a number of dead and wounded in their wake. In 1833, women with a keen interest in politics founded the Club des femmes patriotes and held regular meetings on Bonsecours Street.

While bourgeois women were forming literary or political societies and developing strategies that laid the foundation for late-nineteenth-century feminism, most women in Lower Canada were struggling with more down-to-earth problems. In 1832, the year of the decisive drop in wheat production, the economic crisis was at its worst. Fluctuations in the price of wheat particularly affected the population, for wheat was still the most widely consumed foodstuff. In 1833, only one-third of the inhabitants in the parishes of the district of Quebec had sufficient food reserves to survive until the next harvest.

The year 1832 was also the year cholera, which had been ravaging Europe, reached Quebec and Montreal. In Quebec, 3,292 people died and the town of Montreal lost a tenth of its population. There was a second cholera epidemic in 1834, which spread to the towns. According to the newspaper *Le Canadien*, the Saint-Roch district of Quebec

> ... has 95 to 110 widows who are paid by the day, and of whom a large number frequently have problems finding work at this time of year. There are also about 200 orphans. Age, sickness, and various infirmities render a large number of these poor women incapable of working for part of the winter.... In St-Roch there are still 100 to 110 poor families. [A]

certain number, it is true, have been reduced to destitution by alcohol, the use of which is so common and so disastrous amongst the working classes.... Aside from these families, whose terrible poverty is the fault of the Head of the household, there are a great many others whose poverty is brought about by contagious diseases which seem to prey relentlessly on our poor....[1]

Ni bled ni épouseurs (neither food nor husband), goes the old saying. Poverty in the towns and countryside caused many young women to postpone marriage. Between 1836 and 1840, the lowest number of marriages since 1711 was recorded, and the birthrate reached its lowest level.

The great majority of women lived in abject poverty throughout the period. In their misery, they heard of the rebellion that was brewing in the political world of men. Amongst the ruling classes in Lower Canada, were those few women fortunate enough to know how to write and with sufficient leisure to record accounts of their lives. Although excluded from political life, they took a lively interest in contemporary issues. It was impossible to remain uninterested in events, explained Cordélia Lovell to her sister-in-law, for everybody was caught up with politics, and politics was the subject of every conversation.

Julie Bruneau, a keen observer of the political scene, wrote to her husband Louis-Joseph Papineau, leader of the Parti patriote: "if conditions in Montreal don't change ... if nothing gets done force will inevitably have to be used...."[2] Rebellion appeared imminent. However, Julie Bruneau was somewhat anxious about her compatriots: she was disturbed by their weakness and their lack of political will. Upper Canada would succeed, she believed, in obtaining the desired reforms, but England would continue to oppress Lower Canada: "we help them to forge our own chains."

The political patriarchy excluded women from the militia and from direct involvement in political action: women were certainly active, but on the fringes. The permanent central committee of the Parti patriote gave Madame Girouard permission to found the Association des dames patriotes du comté des Deux-Montagnes. The women met to "work toward, as much as the weakness of their sex would allow, ensuring victory for the patriotic cause."

Before armed revolt broke out, the population of Lower Canada was called upon to boycott English goods, especially fabrics and fine imported materials. People wore coarse cloth and grey homespun woven by French-Canadian women; eminent citizens stopped wearing their elegant clothes. In Montreal, Mesdames Lafontaine and Peltier wore locally-made materials in public.

No one expected to see women directly involved in the conflict and Hortense Globensky, from the county of Deux-Montagnes, emerges as the exception. She helped her brother in his campaign for election to the legislature; she belonged to the *bureaucrate* party, was a supporter of the status quo and opposed the Patriotes. One day during the upheavals, she spoke in public, exhorting her fellow parishioners, as they were leaving Mass, to remain faithful to the government. When Patriotes attempted to silence her, she threatened them with a pistol. The Patriotes had her arrested for possession of an illegal weapon, and she was taken to prison in Montreal. On another occasion, she singlehandedly defended her house against attack. Her bravery on this occasion was recognized by some of her contemporaries, who presented her with a tea urn inscribed with the following epigraph: "in recognition of the heroism displayed above and beyond the call of her sex, on the evening of the 6th of July 1837."

Amongst the Patriotes, too, were women who went "above and beyond the call of their sex." A number carried arms, among them Emilie Boileau-Kimber of Chambly, who held Patriote meetings in her house. Another woman set fire to her own house to show the English that she was not afraid of them, and to prevent them from taking her property.

Such active involvement was the exception; most women confined themselves to a supporting role. Some made bullets and cartridges; some designed and wove tricolour flags for the Patriotes; others looked after or hid Patriotes and their family members in their homes, often at the risk of seeing their own homes burned to the ground.

The great majority of women did not participate actively or collaborate in the rebellion. They were left alone, unarmed, with the children and the elderly to confront the British troops who pillaged and set fire to the houses of the Patriotes and to whole villages, such as Saint-Denis, Saint-Benoît and Saint-Eustache.

A number of British women and children were taken prisoner by the Patriotes; sixty-two people were imprisoned in the presbytery of Beauharnois for a week; they were freed when British troops arrived. Jane Ellice, *seigneuresse* of Beauharnois, describes the liberation in her diary:

> We thought the rebels were coming to murder us & locked in Tina's arms I was trying to compose my mind when Mr Parker pushed thro' the crowd & told us that we were safe ... they did not expect to find us alive. Till 4 o'clock we stood watching the village in flames; an awful sight but very beautiful.[3]

Women did not have to endure the suffering of the front, or direct military involvement with the enemy. However, the subsequent military repression profoundly affected their lives. Only twelve Patriotes were executed, but hundreds of homes were torched: hundreds of mothers and children lost homes and possessions and had no food. The British authorities responded to the armed uprising by punishing the civilian population. Even Jane Ellice, who was rescued by the British, dwelt upon the severity of the repression: "the village was still burning; women and children flying in all directions. Such are the melancholy consequences of civil war."[4]

In documents pertaining to the troubles of 1837 and 1838, we find women left destitute by the death or imprisonment of their husbands appealing to Sir John Colborne. Sophie Mailloux reveals that she and "her family find themselves reduced (sic) to the most appalling misery through lack of food, and cannot even get the wood needed for heating." Josette Leboeuf wrote that as soon as her husband had been made prisoner, her house and all that it contained were burned; she then "found herself wandering homeless on the highway with her children and two young orphans that they were rearing, with no clothes on their backs and nothing to eat." Mary Gillecey, recently widowed, asked for her husband's hotel-keeper's licence to be transferred to her name: "the only means your Petitioner has of maintaining her Children is by Continuing to keep a Hotel."

Rosalie Dessaulles, the *seigneuresse* of Saint-Hyacinthe, described the conditions in the countryside immediately after the troubles.

> We are beginning to feel keenly the damage caused by the pillaging. The market is not getting enough meat to satisfy the needs of half the village and the little that does come is very expensive and of the worst quality. Moreover, unlike previous years, we don't have the advantage of being able to find at the farm what we cannot get at the market. They have killed, carried off, and destroyed bulls, cows, pigs, sheep and poultry of all kinds and there are others worse off than me. How many who are responsible for a family or who are old or infirm have received the same treatment and have been deprived of the means to obtain the bare necessities of life ...[5]

The period of rebellion was one of anguish and family breakdown. Many men died in battle; hundreds were taken prisoner; ninety-eight were condemned to death; fifty-eight were deported to Australia (of these, forty-four had children), and twelve were executed. Eugénie Saint-Germain, the wife of J.-N. Cardinal, member of the Legislative Assembly for Laprairie, pleaded with Lady Colborne when Cardinal was condemned to death: "You are a woman and a mother! A woman ... is on her knees before you, with a broken heart and trembling with fear. She asks you to spare the life of her beloved husband and the father of her five children! The death warrant is already signed!!" The next day, pregnant with her fifth child, Saint-Germain became a widow.

Henriette Cadieux, wife of the notary Chevalier de Lorimier, had three sons, the eldest of whom was only four. She also approached Lady Colborne, reminding her, amongst other things, that to live and support her three children she had only "what their father's work and profession had produced." Her husband was executed.

Women were not expected to take part in military action, but they were called upon to attend court to give evidence. Some testified in an attempt to exonerate a prisoner. The most frequently employed tactic was to state that the prisoner had been forced to follow the rebels and had taken part in the rebellion against his will. Others provided the prisoner with an alibi, claiming that he could not have taken part in the troubles because he had been with or had been seen by the witness. In an attempt to exonerate Josepht Roy, Josephte Merleau and Catherine Roy stated that the Patriote tricolour flag found at the prisoner's house had been made by them. It was pure coincidence that they had woven a green, red and white flag "since they made three-coloured flags ... during periods of political calm, and therefore with no thought of revolution nor with any hint of it, but simply as an expression of good taste."

A certain number of women who were politically naïve and unsympathetic to the nationalist cause testified against rebel prisoners. One woman told the court that a prisoner had stolen some pipes from her son's hardware store, and that another had uttered seditious statements. A second woman complained of having been forced to cook for the rebels; a third claimed that she had to make cartridges. One woman expressed no desire to intercede on behalf of her prisoner husband. She stated that he held secret meetings in their house and that she was testifying against him because he beat her and had punched and kicked her, and because he had "threatened to do away with her and this without any provocation on the part of the said witness who states that she is afraid that Jean-Baptiste may make an attempt on her life."

Not all women lacked patriotic feeling. Euphrosine Lamontagne-Perrault lost two sons – one killed and the other in exile. Nonetheless, she said, "If it had to be done all over again and if my children wished to act as they had done, I would not try to dissuade them because in no way did they act out of ambition; they were motivated by patriotism and by hatred of the injustices that they were suffering." Though it was men who were discontented and who took up arms, the repression was universal; the private and domestic lives of women were not spared.

When women participated in political struggles, they employed different means than men. Their participation has not been recorded in our history, which restricts itself to the deeds and actions of the few men in power. That women acted according to their interests and their personal and family priorities was only to be expected. Moreover, the Patriotes should have been grateful for any sympathy from women, since the party had tried to revoke women's right to vote in 1834.

THE DEFEAT OF THE TRADITIONAL RIGHTS OF WOMEN

It is always a source of amazement to anyone interested in women's history that, beginning in 1791, there were women who went to the polls. Were the political élites who allowed women to vote therefore less chauvinistic than other politicians? Were our politicians more egalitarian than others in Europe and America?

The logic of political liberalism demanded that all citizens, female and male, have the right to vote. But women everywhere waited long and lobbied hard before they were granted this right.

Nineteenth-century logic required that women be excluded from politics. When the parliamentarians of Lower Canada revealed their desire to exclude women from the voters' list in 1834, they were attempting to correct a historical anomaly and acting in character for their time. The attitude of the leader of the Parti patriote, Louis-Joseph Papineau, is revealed in a letter he wrote to his wife in 1830:

> I received your fine and charming letter this morning. Although it exudes a little too much independence in the face of the legitimate and absolute authority of your husband, I am not so much surprised as hurt. I see that this harmful philosophy is infecting everybody and that Rousseau's *contrat social* makes you forget St. Paul's Gospel. "Wives, be subject to your husbands."[6]

In 1849, the right to vote was taken away from women in Quebec. At a meeting of American feminists held at Seneca Falls, New York, in 1848, the participants passed an official resolution demanding the right to vote. Historian Catherine L. Cleverdon hypothesizes that this demand may have prompted the removal of the franchise in Quebec. Feminist agitation in North America was beginning to grow, and parliamentarians may have feared that Quebec women would increasingly exercise their right to vote. (Many women had not voted since 1834.) The parliamentarians decided that the electoral law should be amended to strip women of their political rights.

The legal position of women also changed. The law in Quebec was still French law; it was known as the *Coutume de Paris* and governed relations between individuals at the time Quebec became a British colony. This unfamiliar legal system was not without its problems for the new leaders; more-

---

BECAUSE OF THESE LAWS,
THEY ASSUMED AN AIR OF SUPERIORITY....

Hugh Gray was an Englishman who spent some time in Canada at the beginning of the century. In a letter written from Quebec in 1807, he commented on community of property, which he found harmful to the interests of landowners, merchants, shop owners and artisans. He also believed the system had harmful effects upon the behaviour of women:

> The law making marriage a partnership in common, and creating a *communauté de biens* is sanctioned by the code of French Law called "Coutume de Paris" which is indeed the text book of the Canadian lawyer; the wife being invested with a right to half the husband's property; and being rendered independent of him, is perhaps the remote cause that the fair sex have such influence in France; and in Canada, it is well known, that a great deal of consequence and even an air of superiority to the husband is assumed by them. In general (if you will excuse a vulgar metaphor) the grey mare is the better horse....

It was therefore because of these laws that French-Canadian women acquired the reputation of wearing the pants in the family....[7]

---

over, certain provisions were not favourable to real estate speculation. As capitalism (spearheaded by British interests) expanded in Quebec, the government came under pressure to make changes in the law relevant to women's rights.

One change led to the abolition of rules concerning dower rights, which had entitled a woman and her children, after the death of a husband, to the use of some of his property, even if the property had been sold or mortgaged. At the beginning of the nineteenth century, an owner in Lower Canada might discover that the building he had acquired several years previously was subject to dower rights after the death of the seller. British businessmen protested vigorously against dower rights, which, they said, put a brake on property speculation.

As soon as the new Union government was formed, the law was modified. Women could henceforth renounce the traditional protection offered them and their children under dower rights and thereby free up the titles of their husbands' property. Neither women nor children were indemnified or compensated for giving up their dower rights. Even if women were not forced to renounce their rights, in practice they had no choice – what informed buyer would be interested in owning a property he was not allowed to enjoy?

The introduction of land-registry offices in 1841 reinforced the pressure on women to renounce their dower rights. The system of registry offices, which had not existed under the *Coutume de Paris,* enabled a prospective buyer to consult the registry to discover who was the true owner of the property he wanted to buy, and with what liens or dower rights it was encumbered. The conflict between dower rights and the principle of land registration ended in defeat for the traditional rights of women, ironically, when a woman, Queen Victoria, was sitting on the British throne.

In 1866, the new Civil Code was made even more specific: no dower right was valid unless it had been registered. However, many women did not know they were required to go through the registration procedure. By the beginning of the twentieth century, feminists declared that, for most women, dower rights were a fiction.

The family also saw its rights eroded by the new, more individualistic conception of property. For example, the right of certain members of the family to buy back certain properties sold to non-family members was abolished in 1855.

In Lower Canada, the change from a rural society to an industrial one called for a coherent and uniform legal system, and it was decided to bring order to the patchwork of French civil law, Common Law and statutory law that governed the province during the first half of the nineteenth century. Laws in force at the time were systematized and organized into a code, which came to replace the *Coutume de Paris.*

The Civil Code of 1866 ensured historical continuity in women's legal rights. Most of the clauses of the *Coutume de Paris* relating to the status of women were reproduced in their entirety. Although the compilers of the Civil Code took the Napoleonic Code of 1804 as their model, they sometimes found it difficult to adapt the French code to the customs of Lower Canada and preferred to keep to local practices. For example, the Civil Code of Lower Canada permitted a natural child to launch a paternity suit against the alleged father. The Napoleonic Code rejected the principle that men should be responsible for their illegitimate offspring – in its desire to protect the legitimate family, the Napoleonic Code had forbidden such lawsuits. In France, a child could be legitimized when its parents recognized the child as theirs. In Quebec, a child remained a bastard until its parents legitimized it by getting married. The new code would push more than one couple into marriage, and into rejecting common-law arrangements.

Despite the severity of the new code, Lower Canada was less prudish than

France. The Civil Code allowed marriages to be annulled in cases of impotence, grounds rejected by the Napoleonic Code because proof was "difficult and scandalous." The legal age at which a Quebec woman could be married was twelve; in France the age was fifteen. The Civil Code in Lower Canada did not include the article of the Napoleonic Code that forbade a widow from remarrying within ten months of her husband's death; it was believed that public opinion was sufficient control over the behaviour of widows.

All in all, the civil rights of women were not changed very much by the Civil Code of 1866. Wives remained subject to the principle of legal incapacity during their marriage. However, certain provisions made the daily lives of women less difficult. For example, a woman who was separate as to property no longer required the formal and express permission of her husband to sell, mortgage or buy real estate. A general consent, in whatever form, was valid and no authorization was necessary for such simple administrative tasks as collecting rent or paying taxes. A wife needed her husband's consent to conduct affairs, but once this consent was given, she was free to run her business affairs as she saw fit. Finally, a housewife needed no specific legal authority to shop and make small purchases for the home. However, even though the 1866 Code contained certain concessions, the courts preferred to maintain the principle of male primacy in marriage, and obliged women to seek permission from their husbands before disposing of their own assets.

The principle of legal incapacity posed problems for women involved in charitable associations: their husbands were constantly being called upon to sign for them. The absurdity of such a situation is only too apparent. To remedy this, associations included a clause in their laws of incorporation to allow married women who sat on boards to act in their own capacity, with no need for their husbands' authorization. This was done in 1841 at the Montreal Orphan Asylum and the Asile de Montréal for old and infirm women. The Civil Code of 1866 did not modify the situation: even as late as 1908, the founder of the Saint-Justine hospital, Justine Lacoste-Beaubien, was forced to ask the Quebec legislature to exempt her from the ruled legal incapacity so she might attend to hospital business.

In the nineteenth century, the principal change in the legal status of women was the "modernization" of clauses relating to the transfer of property. Traditional dower rights were a barrier to the free circulation of capital, and women were gradually deprived of the protection accorded them under the *Coutume de Paris*. In spite of a number of changes, the Civil Code of 1866 merely perpetuated the principle of the legal incapacity of the married woman.

There is no evidence that people were critical of the clauses that reaffirmed the subordinate status of women. One explanation for the silence may be that, until the end of the nineteenth century, women in Quebec enjoyed more rights than their counterparts in Canada's other provinces, which were governed by Common Law. Under Common Law, a wife had no legal existence separate from her husband; at the time of marriage, the man obtained absolute control of the woman's person and assets.

In the middle of the nineteenth century, women subject to Common Law exerted pressure to change the law. Toward the end of the century, the law was amended several times with the passage of the Married Women's Property Acts. At the beginning of the twentieth century, the only marriage régime in most of the Canadian provinces was that of separation of property, under which, a married woman disposed of her assets as she saw fit. The situation had reversed itself: it was the women of Quebec who had the least enviable legal status. Anglophone women were particularily conscious of this inferior legal position, as other Anglophone women now enjoyed more liberal conditions. At the end of the nineteenth century, some women in Quebec – particularly women who owned property, bourgeois women, intellectuals and professionals – began to question their political and legal status.

Quebec women of European origin lost their dower rights to the "rationality" of the new economic system, which was put into place in the nineteenth century. But the greatest losers, as far as legal rights were concerned, were Native women. There were not many in Quebec (they made up only about .05 percent of the population during the last decades of the century), but they were scattered over a considerable area of the province.

Furs were no longer central to the Canadian economy, and much of the land where fur-bearing animals had their habitat was also suitable for agriculture or forestry. After the 1850s, several laws were passed with the aim of restricting Indian territory; it was hoped that the Indians would settle in one place. By introducing increasingly restrictive definitions of "Indian" status, the government reduced the number of people with the right to live on reserves and to benefit from allowances granted under certain treaties. In 1851, it was decided that Indian status descended through the paternal line. The federal law of 1869 confirmed this, and stated that any Indian woman who married a non-Indian lost her status, as did her descendants. (Such laws ran contrary to many Indian traditions. For example, the Iroquois lived in a society in which descent was traced through the woman.)

In addition, if a woman married an Indian from another band or from another tribe, she immediately became a member of her husband's tribe and had to leave her parents' house and her place of origin. If the superintendent of the reserve decided to expel a man, his wife suffered the same fate. The law also stated that a woman could not inherit upon the death of her husband: only her children could inherit from their father, and it was up to the children to support the mother. (However, this last clause was modified in 1874: one-third of the husband's assets went to the mother and two-thirds to the children.) Finally, the law stated that band councils would be elected only by adult males; women would no longer have an official voice.

Indian women found themselves with fewer rights than Indian men had under the law. The Grand Council of Indian bands in Quebec and Ontario opposed this downgrading of the status of women; in 1872, it petitioned the Prime Minister of Canada to amend the law so that Indian women could marry whomever they wanted, without being liable to expulsion from their community of origin and without losing their rights. The request fell on deaf ears.

Western "civilization" had deprived Indian women of their traditional rights and had placed them, like other women in the country, under the power and control of men.

ON THE MOVE

Living space was at a premium; all the fertile land had been taken. Thousands of Quebeckers left their native soil and went in search of a living. They had three options: they could clear new land in the hinterland; they could immigrate to the towns; or they could leave Quebec.

The Quebec authorities tried to persuade its citizens, who were especially attracted to the United States, to stay in Quebec. The provincial government encouraged a new wave of frontier settlement to the north of Montreal. St. Maurice the Saguenay and Lake Saint John areas were settled. The new settlements, which were far from commercial centres and usually on poor land, were more closely tied to the developing forestry industry than to agriculture. The colonists would work as land-clearers, farmers and lumberjacks in the camps of the big lumber companies.

Becoming a settler meant beginning again in a hostile land. A woman had to create a new mutual support network, as she was far from her women friends and her parents. She had to live in a makeshift dwelling with only the bare necessities until the new farm was ready. When the men went to cut wood, the women were left alone to look after the household and the farm. Life in a new settlement also meant having lots of children, as it was in the family's best interests to have an abundant supply of family labour.

Gérard Bouchard's analysis of the village of Laterrière, ten miles from Chicoutimi, reveals the population's tendency to reproduce a demographic behaviour that was already disappearing in other parts of Quebec. From the middle of the nineteenth century until the stock-market crash of 1929, the birthrate in this area (Latevière) was much the same as under the *Ancien*

Régime: women were having children every two years. The State introduced a number of policies to encourage large families. For example, in 1890, parents with at least twelve living children were offered one hundred acres of land or fifty dollars in cash. By the time the offer lapsed in 1906, more than five thousand families had claimed their bonus from the provincial government.

According to historian Normand Séguin, the agricultural-forestry economy of these new settlements reinforced the basic features of rural society, and accentuated certain of them. Such was the case with the birthrate. While thousands of Quebeckers were having fewer children, in the newly settled areas the birthrate reached unprecedented levels. Certain people saw the high birthrate as an indication of the power of the Catholic clergy to impose their views on family size. However, historian Chad Gaffield, who has studied the colonization of the Ottawa valley, states that there was little difference in the birthrate amongst the farming population, whether they were Anglophone or Francophone. For these families, who were involved in both agriculture and industry, a large family was a guarantee of prosperity. This suggests that women settlers had so many children not so much from fear of the clergy as from a need to adapt to the economic realities, which made it advantageous to have a large family.

The literature on colonization, and the "edifying" novels of writers such as Antoine Gérin-Lajoie, paint a bucolic image of life in the *terres neuves* (new lands). Louise Routhier is depicted by Antoine Gérin-Lajoie as the happy wife of Jean Rivard; she is the perfect mother, courageous and hard working. Normand Séguin's study of the village of Hébertville paints a different picture, in which the settlers were not always happy. Séguin reports that, in this one village, four men seriously mistreated their wives. The priest made examples of these men by denouncing them from the pulpit. In 1885, the priest condemned drunkenness in a church bulletin: "Drunkenness makes a woman throw her child into the street and attempt to do the same with another ... I am determined that temperance shall reign here."

The legal dependence of married women presented serious problems. A husband might sell everything or lose everything to his creditors, and his wife and children would be left "destitute in the bush." The Homestead Act of 1882 was passed to prevent such situations. It stated that family assets could not be seized to pay off debts incurred before the family moved to a settlement; and the assets could no longer be surrendered free of charge or for valuable consideration without the consent of the spouse.

The attractions of the settlements were few. Nearer to hand were the industrial towns of the American northwest, which were recruiting labour. Ten times as many Québécois responded to the call of the American industrial towns than to the exhortations of the colonizers. The exodus to the United

States began around 1830; by 1860, entire families were crossing the border. During the nineteenth century, half a million women and men from Quebec moved to the United States, to work primarily in textile and shoe factories.

At the turn of the century, Amoskeag Corporation in Manchester, New Hampshire, was the biggest textile factory in the world. Before World War One, fourteen thousand workers were employed there; Québécois constituted 40 percent of the work force. Historian Tamara K. Hareven explains that, during the 1870s, Amoskeag discovered that workers from Quebec were hardier and more docile than other workers. The company recruited systematically in Quebec, and paid for the transportation and accommodation of the families of those it had hired for its mills.

Women, men and children worked together in the factories and reproduced in the work setting the family patterns of their farms in Quebec. Although they had big families and the clergy disapproved of women going out to work, two-thirds of the married women of the towns worked in the factory. Little girls learned weaving and industrial spinning from their mothers, who had been taught weaving and craft spinning by their mothers.

In the industrial towns, large families were an economic asset: as soon as children reached eleven or twelve, they went to work in the factory with their parents to increase the family's income. In some towns – for example, in Lowell, Massachussetts – mothers worked at home and contributed to the family's income by taking in lodgers.

In time, however, women had fewer children. At the beginning of the twentieth century, compulsory education and child-labour laws, which regulated the employment of children, made it less practical to have a lot of children.

Another Quebec outside of Quebec grew up in New England. The clergy

---

MARIA CHAPDELAINE'S MOTHER TALKS ABOUT THE 1880s

When I was a girl, said Mother Chapdelaine, pretty nearly everyone went off to the States. Farming did not pay as well as it does now, prices were low; we were always hearing of the big wages earned down there in the factories, and every year one family after another sold out for next to nothing and left Canada. Some made a lot of money, no doubt of that, especially those families with plenty of daughters; but now it is different, and they are not going as once they did.[8]

were at first hostile to emigration, but finally they had no choice; they followed their flocks and transplanted their social institutions: parishes were created, and schools and convents founded in the United States.

Professionals, lawyers, doctors and businessmen saw in these "little Canadas" a market to be exploited. The Franco-American communities had their own institutions, schools and French-language newspapers; during the nineteenth century, it was possible to live and die in one of these communities without ever having to speak English.

Finally, a number of people left the farms where they were born for the towns of Quebec, which were absorbing part of the surplus rural population and could offer employment in manufacturing. Young people from the countryside who could not find work as lumberjacks or as agricultural labourers sought work in the towns. By the end of the century, the urban population was twice as large as it had been in the 1850s. However, girls often found themselves alone in the towns: between 1844 and 1901, there were more women than men in Montreal and Quebec City.

NOTES

1 *Le Canadien*, 23 January 1837, quoted in Fernand Ouellet *Histoire économique et sociale du Québec 1760-1850* (Montreal: Fides, 1966).

2 Letter from Julie Bruneau to L.-J. Papineau, 17 February 1836, in *Rapport de l'Archiviste de la Province de Québec*, nos. 38-39.

3 Patricia Godsell, ed., *The Diary of Jane Ellice* (Ottawa: Oberon Press, 1975), 10 November 1838.

4 Ibid., 11 November 1838.

5 Rosalie Dessaules, 13 April 1839, quoted in F. Ouellet, op.cit.

6 Letter from L.-J. Papineau to Julie Bruneau, 15 February 1830, in *Rapport de l'Archiviste de la Province de Québec*, nos. 34-35.

7 Beth Light and Alison Prentice, eds., *Pioneer and Gentlewomen of the British North America 1713-1867* (Toronto: New Hogtown Press, 1980), p. 103.

8 Louis Hémon, *Maria Chapdelaine*. Translated by W. H. Blake (Toronto: Macmillan), p. 48.

CHAPTER SIX

GETTING MARRIED

FINDING A HUSBAND

MOST WOMEN EVENTUALLY left their parent's home and gave up their jobs to assume the role of wife and mother. But did they have any choice? Could a woman live without a man and survive in the nineteenth century?

Most women had few or no personal assets, although there were, of course, exceptions amongst the bourgeoisie. A farmer's daughter received only a symbolic dowry – among the farming community it was felt that the new husband should provide the capital. Women who worked as teachers, artisans, factory workers, seamstresses and servants, earned extremely low wages and therefore could not survive independently. Thus, most women looked for men who owned land or who had an income much larger than their own.

But not all those who wanted to get married were successful. In Montreal, there were more women than men; consequently, not all women could find husbands and competition was keen. In rural Quebec in 1851, there were almost as many agricultural labourers (63,365) as farmers (78,437), and a woman was considered lucky if she married someone who would inherit land. The woman who found a rich and prosperous farmer from a good family to marry was the exception, since three-quarters of farmers owned less than a hundred acres. Nevertheless, women were willing to marry, and hoped to find the best possible partner. In the countryside, courting amongst the young took place during traditional "bees," such as berry picking, sugaring off, corn husking or the crushing of flax. In the towns, work mates got together after work. Parish life (vespers, Sunday mass, choir practice or charity bazaars) also provided occasions for young people to meet.

A BED AND BEDDING, A CUPBOARD, TWO SHEEP, A COW. THAT IS ALL ...

The father and mother in a joint will sworn before a lawyer have made Charles their second son their sole heir.... As for the other children, in addition to their clothing and body linen, they will receive the following: the boys on reaching twenty-one, a horse, a harness and a wagon; the girls on their wedding day, a cupboard, two sheep, a cow. That is all.... Even in well-off farming families, the daughters receive only a quite modest dowry to take with them. In effect, it is not thought that they will have to found a new family community, but that they will simply have to attach themselves to some community already in existence or one that is being formed.[1]

Social gatherings provided opportunities for young people to meet. Whether dancing or sitting in rocking chairs, courting couples always tried to get as close to each other as possible. When a young girl's suitor was visiting her, she would offer him a rocking chair and the suitor would rock himself closer and closer. Although priests issued numerous edicts against dancing, dances were frequent. Léon Gérin noted that even as far back as 1886, the most popular dance steps in the country were introduced by young people returning from the United States. Under the American influence traditional songs were being abandoned and people were humming the "modern and cosmopolitan love songs" of the United States.

In the 1830s, courtship had its sentimental and romantic side, but it was also approached with caution. In Madame Gosselin's literary revue, the *Museum of Montreal*, there were as many moral tales as there were beautiful romantic poems. Women were warned of the dangers of passionate love. A story entitled *Folly of Marrying* told the tale of the elegant suitor who became a brandy tippler after his marriage. "No, No!" wrote the female author, "no more marrying for love in the family. While it may be important to love, it is even more important to make a good marriage."

In general, little is known about parents' attitudes to courtship. Did they influence their children's choices? Did they object to certain suitors? Henriette Dessaulles, a young girl from the bourgeoisie, born at Saint-Hyacinthe in 1860, kept a diary from age fourteen until her marriage at twenty-one. At fourteen, she fell in love with a childhood friend, whom she would eventually marry, and was kept under constant surveillance by her mother. She was not

---

WHAT THEY THINK OF IT ALL ...

Montreal, 8 January 1890

My dear Arthur,

Our companion from the North has been here and had words with me....

His sister, a girl of thirty-three, wants to marry and she hopes that she will have more luck here. He told me, as he will tell you – quite bluntly.

The poor girl seems incapable of understanding the beauty of voluntary celibacy in this world. She seems to be unaware that many young girls have not married, out of a sense of dedication and by choice, in order to fulfil their dreams of doing charitable work, developing their intelligence, pursuing higher education and performing their filial duty, or else they have not married to avoid being united with just anybody, it being easy for even the most wretched of women to find a husband like that.

Will you allow me – you who know my horror of matrimonial agencies – to recommend her to you. She is slipping into maturity, as you see; she is sweet and at ease in society. I do not know if she is ugly: that is none of my business and that will depend on your love; she is nice and would be even more so if she walked rather than galloped – with a slight gallop which in no way suggests she is out of breath. Merely looking at her makes one breathless. One always gets the impression that she is running after someone. Given her age, she must have missed quite a number at this speed. And what makes her so deserving is that she has hunted so many hares – with such gusto – and always drawn a blank.

To think that she has run so much and has only ever shown her weariness and resignation in affectionate sighs!

On Monday evening, at the Victoria skating rink, she began her search once more. She has hunted for fifteen years in shoes or slippers and now she wants to continue the hunt on skates. Perhaps she will find someone, but ... she is on a slippery slope.[2]

---

allowed to *tutoyer* the young man (use the intimate "tu" form for "you") nor was she allowed to write to him.

It was noticed that I was using "tu" when addressing Maurice, that we were both doing so and I was told that this kind of speech was unacceptable, too intimate etc.

... To my great amazement, Maman spoke to me about my friendship for Maurice and told me that I would perhaps be tempted to receive letters from him and to respond to them and that this would be quite improper.... She insisted I promise not to write to him during his three years at university. I had to promise or otherwise I was admitting I intended to write to him.... Tomorrow is Saint-Maurice's day and I will go to mass for him ... I am waiting for them to tell me that I must not pray for him![3]

Henriette's meddling mother seemed to have preferred another suitor for her daughter and the young man was often invited to the Dessaulles home. Madame Dessaulles even left them alone in the living room, much to Henriette's great annoyance.

Her confessor also kept an eye on her; Henriette was told at confession that she must not try to meet her lover alone; she had to appear to be cold to him, and even to avoid looking at him.

The Dessaulles, who were once *seigneurs* in Saint-Hyacinthe, were wealthy; and Henriette's woes reflected the typical bourgeois attitude towards the marriage of their children.

But things seem to have been different among farmers and agricultural workers. A number of observers report that young farm workers had less respect for their father's authority than had men in the cities. Père Bourassa wrote in 1851 that, after living in the lumber camps, young men "... saw the paternal yoke as harsh and intolerable.[4] Sociologist Léon Gérin observes that the opportunity to earn a living in American factories, combined with the scarcity of land, made the young more independent of their parents. How could parents impose their choice of partner on their children? Only children who were to inherit their father's land had any motivation to bow to their parents' wishes; children who did not stand to inherit were relatively free to court whomever they wished.

GETTING MARRIED
AND HAVING CHILDREN

When she was twenty-one, Henriette Dessaulles was married in white, the latest fashion, to Maurice Saint-Jacques. She would have five children. In this respect, she was typical of Quebec women: in 1851 they had an average of seven children each, but by the end of the century the average was five.

Births were not always a happy event:

Madame Blanchard gave birth last night after 3 long painful days. The child died at birth it was a little girl; they are very sad the mother is so-so and giving some cause for anxiety.[5]

Being born and giving birth presented the same risks as in earlier centuries. However, in the nineteenth century, control of the "malady" was gradually taken over by doctors. Although there were still many midwives, obstetricians – who were going to the United States for training – were becoming increasingly important. In 1845, a government order forbade anyone who was not a qualified doctor, or who was not officially authorized by the government, to practise obstetrics in the towns of Quebec and Montreal. By 1847, responsibility for the training of midwives was handed over to the College of Physicians and Surgeons.

In the 1871 census, only about forty women claimed to be midwives; after 1891, "midwife" did not appear in the census. Midwifery itself had not disappeared: throughout the twentieth century, midwives would help thousands of rural women to give birth. However, the introduction by the College of Physicians of very difficult examinations prevented women from trying to make a career as midwives. Nevertheless, some women still acted as midwives and assisted the doctors or, on occasion, replaced them.

This invasion by men of an area hitherto the province of women was achieved in the name of science through government orders concerning the practice of obstetrics; it was reenforced by the virtual exclusion of women from medical science. A few women in Quebec were admitted to the Faculty of Medicine at Bishop's University; but by 1900, women were not permitted to

---

BEING BORN IN QUEBEC BEFORE 1850

When the time comes to *acheter** all the children are sent to a woman neighbour; they are told that "the Savages" or "the crow" are going to pay a visit and that when they return, they will have "a little brother or a little sister." The mother of the pregnant woman or an old aunt helps the *pelle-à-feu*** or the doctor.... Women have been in charge of this event for a long time; in fact, it has often been only women who have participated. After the baby is delivered, each participant receives a small glass of wine to celebrate the birth.

* "To buy," a popular expression for giving birth.
** "The coal shovel," a popular name for a midwife.[6]

---

take courses in medicine in Quebec. Women were excluded from the process of professionalization that medicine was undergoing. Childbirth became a male and "scientific" sphere of activity. In 1900, the editors of *Women of Canada* stated that, although it was still possible to obtain training as a midwife and a licence to practise, midwifery seemed to be a thing of the past. Hereafter, tending to women in childbirth in urban communities would be the job of doctors, who would be assisted by nurses. In the countryside, however, large numbers of "nonaccredited" midwives continued to practise.

In general, women gave birth at home, and childbirth was very much a part of family life for most people. Only "fallen" women, unmarried mothers or women living in dire poverty had their children in maternity hospitals which first appeared during the nineteenth century. In 1840, Mademoiselle Métivier opened the Maison Notre-Dame-de-la-Merci in Quebec. In Montreal, Anglophones founded the Montreal Lying-in Hospital. These maternity hospitals were at first charitable institutions where medical students could apprentice. Women admitted into certain maternity hospitals with university affiliation served as guinea pigs for courses in obstetrics. By the end of the century women close to medical circles were applauding the merits of having one's baby under scientific conditions in a hospital. To gain credibility for their beliefs, they had their own children in hospitals.

HAVING FEWER CHILDREN

I think, dearest Uncle, you cannot REALLY wish me to be the "Mamma d'une famille nombreuse," for I think you will see as I do the greatest inconvenience a LARGE family would be to us all, and particularly to the country, independant [sic] of the hardship and inconvenience to myself. Men never, at least seldom think what a hard task it is for us women, to go through this very often.

Queen Victoria
5 January 1841

In the eighteenth century, French-Canadian women had, on average, just over eight children. The women born around 1825 were the last generation of women to have so many children. Their daughters, born around 1845, would have only six children and their daughters, born around 1867, would have only five children. Demographer Jacques Henripin estimates that there was a 41 percent decrease in fertility amongst Quebec women between 1831 and 1891. The birthrate declined less rapidly in Quebec than in Ontario, but it was nonetheless empirically observable among certain social groups. Francophone women from the bourgeoisie had fewer children than their mothers

---

I SUPPOSE THAT SHE IS NO BETTER INFORMED THAN I ...

Some time before her marriage, Henriette Dessaulles discussed with her girlfriend Jos how many children she would have. She believed strongly that limiting the size of one's family made good sense but she does not seem to have received any information on the subject before her marriage. She wrote in her diary:

> Jos said to me "I hope, my dears that you will enjoy your happiness for two or three years before having a child?" ... I suppose that Jos is no better informed than I, but I hope that she was implying that one should have children only if one wants them; this would make good sense, but what happens in poor families makes me suspect that this is not what happens. Last week, father and mother X were discouraged by the birth of a sixth child, for their five other children were suffering from hunger.[7]

---

had. (Marie Gérin-Lajoie was just such a case: she was born in 1867 into a family of thirteen children, but she had only four.) In the towns, the bourgeoisie kept the birthrate down. Léon Gérin notes that, in villages along the St. Lawrence, certain families were limiting the number of their children.

Limiting births implies the use of contraception. To space births, couples could practise restraint or coitus interruptus. Women could reduce their chances of getting pregnant by breast-feeding for long periods, by employing artificial means or by having or inducing an abortion. Until quite recently, women could limit the number of their children only by relying on their own information networks and by acting against the teachings of the Church or in defiance of Canadian law. The Church was extremely vigilant in preventing the circulation of information on sexuality: Monseigneur Bourget would have a French publication on sexuality placed on the Index.

The State, which had been relatively discreet on the question of birth control, now decided that what had been a private concern of women was indeed a public matter. For example, in 1869, abortions were harshly dealt with: the abortionist or the pregnant woman could receive life imprisonment, and a woman who self-aborted risked seven years in jail.

In 1892, the distribution of information and material relating to contraception or abortion became illegal. If a woman wanted fewer children, she had to rely on her husband (restraint or coitus interruptus) or she had to break the law.

Between 1869 and 1916, English-language publications recommended abstinence during menstruation. Until 1920, there was no real understanding of how the menstrual cycle worked. Indeed, the proponents of birth-control theories identified the time when a woman normally ovulates as an infertile period, and thus advised couples to have sexual relations when the probability of conception was greatest.

Artificial birth-control devices certainly lowered the chances of conception, but they were specifically forbidden by law. Historian McLaren observes, however, that pharmacies in the large towns sold condoms, advertising them under the prudish designation "rubber products." French-Canadian women must also have used the diaphragm and vaginal spray; personal papers of women of the time have contained instructions for making diaphragms. In its 1901 catalogue, Eaton's announced the "Every Woman Marvel Whirling Spray," a vaginal spray. But how many Quebec women knew enough English to read this advertisement, and of these who did how many understood that this "vaginal hygiene" product could be used as a contraceptive?

THE CRIMINAL CODE OF CANADA
AND WOMEN'S BODIES

Every one is guilty of an indictable offence and liable to imprisonment for life who, with intent to procure the miscarriage of any woman, whether she is or is not with child or causes to be taken by her any drug ... uses any drug....

(55-56 V. c29 art 272)

Every one is guilty of an indictable offence and liable to two years' imprisonment who ... offers to sell, advertises, publishes an advertisement of, or has for sale or disposal, any medicine, drug or article intended or represented as a means of preventing conception or causing of abortion or miscarriage.

(63-64 V. c46 art.3)

THE CHURCH AND SEXUALITY

In the nineteenth century, the Church ensured that all information on sexuality and contraception was kept well away from parishioners. When a handbook on sexuality and reproduction for couples was distributed in Montreal in 1871, Monseigneur Bourget condemned it as dangerous and despicable, "harmful to the sacredness of virginity and celibacy." (*Mandements, lettres pastorales et circulaires au clergé, vol. vi, pp. 213-4.*)

The book, called *Hygiène et physiologie du mariage, histoire naturelle et médicale de l'homme et de la femme mariés dans ses plus curieux détails* (Hygiene and Physiology of Marriage, a Natural and Medical History of Married Men and Women in Most Curious Detail), was written by a French doctor, Auguste de Bey, probably around 1850. It appears to have been very popular: in 1876 it was already in its ninetieth edition. It was published again in 1891.

The book teaches that women and men are equal, that the pleasures of marriage are necessary and that the clitoris is a woman's centre of pleasure. The author does not approve of excision, except for those who masturbate, as masturbation is a cause of sterility. While the husband is advised not to be brutal and to learn how to awake the desires of his wife, the wife is nevertheless counselled to give in to her husband and to feign pleasure if necessary. The book also says that if intercourse lasts long enough, the woman may also achieve orgasm.

Traditional contraceptive methods had only limited success; artificial contraceptives were sold under the counter and it was difficult to obtain information because their distribution was illegal. Declines in the birthrate in Quebec and Ontario would suggest that women were ignoring the law and distributing the information.

Unwanted pregnancies were probably frequent. A woman who wanted an abortion would probably try to bring on her period by taking infusions or abortificants produced at home or commercially. These products were made from substances traditionally known for their abortive properties; McLaren mentions sabine as being especially popular and says that penny royal, quinine, cotton root, tansy (mugwort), the Christmas rose and ergot were used. (Ergot was used by midwives to relieve the contractions of women in labour.)

A glance through English-Canadian newspapers of the 1890s reveals that eleven potions and abortion pills were being advertised as products for female irregularity. One of these, the "Ladies Safe Remedies: Apoline" was manufactured in Montreal by Lyman and Sons. We do not know if the products were effective, but they were popular and must have sometimes produced the desired results.

Women could also resort to the quack abortionist, who advertised discreetly in the newspapers, or to doctors who advertised themselves as specialists in "sexual problems."

BRINGING UP THE CHILDREN ALONE

In the nineteenth century, in spite of the decline in the birthrate, married women still had large families. A sizable part of a woman's life was spent in one pregnancy after another and being kept busy by a swarm of children, all very young and very dependent. Help from relatives or support from the community was essential for any woman with a large family.

Often, large families would share accommodation with grandparents, maiden aunts and uncles, and the mother could count on some help. However, most families in rural or urban areas were "nuclear" families – wife and husband and their children – who relied on outside help. Prosperous farmers or well-to-do families took on one or two servants, who helped the mother look after the children and do the housework. However, it was hardly likely that a woman who married a labourer would have such help.

The early days of industrialization were difficult for working-class families. The average worker could not support his family on his wages, and the arrival of one child after another prevented the mother from working for wages. The working-class family had the greatest number of mouths to feed, yet the minimum number of breadwinners.

Historian Bettina Bradbury states that, to make ends meet, a quarter of the working-class families in the Saint-Jacques district of Montreal shared accommodation with other families or took in lodgers. The family's stability was still tenuous: a lay-off of the father, an accident at work, the illness of the mother, the arrival of a new child or the death of one parent destroyed the family unit. The children would be placed with relatives or put in an orphanage.

Bradbury has established that, at the orphanage of Saint-Alexis de Montréal, most of the girl "orphans" had living parents, and they returned home after an average stay of less than two years in the orphanage. (Only 1 percent of the girl orphans had no parents.) In 1863, Montreal had a dozen similar institutions housing 750 children, about 3 percent of all children in the city.

ABANDONED CHILDREN

A number of women did not raise their own children: they placed the children in charitable institutions in the hope that someone would look after them. In 1875, an average of two children a day were placed in the care of the Grey Nuns. Of the 719 children they took in only 88 survived.

> Seven hundred and nineteen children were taken in by the Révérendes Soeurs Grises last year: 81 of these children came from Quebec and Rimouski, 34 from Saint-Hyacinthe, 96 from Upper Canada – of these 44 were from Ottawa, 47 from the United States, 11 from France, 2 from Ireland, 37 from the parishes around Montreal and 421 from Montreal. Six hundred and thirty one of these died during 1875. The high death rate amongst abandoned children resulted from the bad treatment and the terrible conditions that they had endured before their arrival in this charitable institution.

In 1880, the Grey Nuns were still taking in children:

> We estimate that five to six hundred children are abandoned in this way [left at the Convent gate] every year. Terrible to say, these poor, numb creatures are half frozen when they are taken in and almost all of them die. The children who survive are put out to nurse and when they are weaned, the sisters take them into the house and later place them as apprentices with the bourgeoisie in town.[8]

Charitable institutions also looked after children by the day. In 1858, the Grey Nuns founded a number of *salles d'asile* (shelters), which provided care for preschool children. They were set up in the working-class districts of Montreal and in the towns of Longueuil, Saint-Jean, Quebec, Saint-Jérôme and Saint-Hyacinthe; they took in thousands of children before the turn of the century. The shelters allowed mothers to take on paid work, and helped families to overcome difficult periods in their lives.

The existence of orphanages and shelters suggests that new strategies were devised by families to survive difficult times. In these institutions, women who were nuns supported women who were mothers: without them, Quebec women, like other Canadian women, would perhaps have had to produce fewer children.

TABLE 3
Number of Children in Nurseries Run by
the Grey Nuns in Montreal

Name of Nursery	Period	Number of Children	Daily Average
Saint-Joseph	1858-1899	9793	242
Nazareth	1861-1914	14925	?
Bethléem	1868-1903	12853	350
Saint-Henri	1885-1920	16700	450
Sainte-Cunégonde	1889-1922	6000	?

Source: ASGM, Fonds particulier à chaque salle d'asile, in Micheline Dumont Johnson, "Des garderies au XIXe siécle," R.H.A.F., vol. 34, no 1, p. 40.

SENDING DAUGHTERS TO SCHOOL

By the time orphanges were organized, society had already begun to integrate children into an educational system. Since the early days of the colony, a certain number of schools and convents had been educating girls and boys, but education remained mainly a family matter. Parents imparted to their children the knowledge they needed to get by in life. Illiteracy was widespread, as neither the artisan nor the farmer needed to know how to read and write.

In the middle of the nineteenth century, the illiteracy rate in Quebec was the same as that of Italy, Spain or the Balkan states. However, the situation changed rapidly. Statistics compiled by historian Allan Greer demonstrate the improvement among Quebec Francophones: in 1838 and 1839, 13 percent of women could read and write; 42 percent were semiliterate. (They could read but could not write.) By 1891, 87 percent of girls ten to nineteen years of age knew at least how to read. This spectacular rise in literacy may have been a result of the laws of 1845, which reorganized the school system according to parish; increasing expansion of religious teaching communities; and new economic structures, in which children worked less. Popular tradition has always maintained that women in Quebec were better educated than men; in 1838 and 1839, almost as many French women (13 percent) as men (15 percent) could read and write; more women (42 percent) than men (29 percent) were semi-literate. This was unusual: in Europe, there were two to three times as many literate men as literate women.

After 1845, mothers sent their daughters and sons to other adults to be educated. Although school attendance was not compulsory in Quebec until 1943, official records estimate that 85 percent of boys and 90 percent of girls of school age were officially enrolled in school during the last decade of the nineteenth century. Numerous documents show, however, that attendance was irregular, both in the towns and in the countryside.

Children went to public or to private schools. Public schools, which were not free, mostly provided a primary-level education, but in some places it was possible to receive two years of secondary instruction. (These two years were referred to as the "academic" program.) Secondary education was not what it is today; the modern concept of secondary education did not appear in the public-school system until the twentieth century. The complete program in the public system lasted approximately nine years, but very few girls and boys were still at school when they were fourteen. The extent of education and regularity of attendance took second place to the economic needs of the family, and school attendance figures were regularly inflated by authorities making sure children were at school the day the inspector arrived. In the countryside, children were often kept at home to work on the farm. The working mother took her daughters out of school as soon as they were old enough to look after the younger ones at home or earn money as a servant or factory apprentice.

During the nineteenth century, various social groups denounced child labour in Quebec. Children constituted 8 percent of the industrial work force of Quebec in 1891; many more children worked at home as seamstresses without being classified as workers. Official school-attendance figures notwithstanding, illiteracy amongst the children of the working class was alarming. Following requests from workers' associations, night schools were opened in 1889. The schools offered workers a basic elementary education, and free courses were provided by the government. However, women who tried to enroll were told that they were ineligible.

The Quebec public-school system had little to offer a Francophone girl who wanted to pursue her studies beyond the elementary level. Her only option was to enter a private convent, where she would receive the equivalent of eleven years of schooling, the most education a girl could receive. There was no possibility of attending a classical college, an industrial college or a university; these were open only to boys. Only Anglophone women could pursue their studies in public high schools or schools run by religious communities and then go on to university: In 1888, McGill University granted bachelor degrees to women for the first time.

Nevertheless, remarkable progress was made during the century. Through the efforts of religious communities, education became available to girls in most urban centres and neighbouring regions. Schools and boarding schools run by nuns sprang up everywhere: by the end of the century, they numbered more than two hundred, compared to fourteen in 1830. Boarding schools accepted day students – most girls lived with their families. Historian Marta Danylewycz has calculated that, during the last three decades of the nineteenth century, between 7 and 11 percent of girls were boarders, a percentage higher than that in Anglophone provinces. Although private, these boarding schools were not necessarily restricted to the children of well-to-do families. Nor did they have the pretention or reputation of a Villa-Maria or a Mont-Sainte Marie, which prepared girls from the bourgeoisie to "sparkle in the best salons and perhaps in the most refined circles of Europe." Most schools had students who paid their school fees in agricultural produce or firewood. This was particularly true in rural Quebec, where most boarders came from the large families of farmers or artisans.

Marie-Paule Malouin's thesis on the Académie Marie-Rose examined the curricula of the academy between 1857 and 1894. A pupil who completed the whole program would have a secondary-level general knowledge; her knowledge of philosophy would be of a college standard. Malouin observes that there was a progressive adaptation of the curricula to the needs of women and the work place: bookkeeping, shorthand, typing and telegraphy were incorporated into the curriculum in 1894. The convent was not a teachers' training college, but it prepared those wanting to teach for the teachers' certificate examination.

WHAT DID CONVENT GIRLS LEARN AT SCHOOL?

The constitutions of the soeurs des Saints-Noms-de-Jésus-et-de-Marie were quite clear on the subject:

> The nuns of Saints Noms de Jésus will open schools wherever they have established themselves. They will teach reading, writing, grammar, geography, history, arithmetic, etc.... They must also teach their pupils to look after a house and to use their hands in such activities as knitting, sewing, embroidery and the like. They will teach singing, music, drawing, and other subjects and social graces that round out a solid and most careful education in boarding schools where such activities are thought to be useful and necessary; but these subjects, of which so much is made in this world, will be viewed by the Sisters simply as an agreeable way of exposing their pupils to the knowledge of salvation.[9]

The Académie Marie-Rose, in spite of its preoccupation with training in the humanities and professional skills, gave courses in domestic science and sought to develop manual skills essential to the housewife. The nuns were not the only ones who wanted to turn out good housekeepers. Public-school curricula provided boys with courses in civics, the political and administrative structure of Canada, and an introduction to the Canadian economy, its agricultural and industrial production and its business. Girls in public schools were given courses in "domestic science," knitting, sewing and embroidery.

In its 1873 report, the Department of Public Instruction indicated that even the convents placed too much emphasis on "pleasurable" subjects at the expense of truly practical subjects, such as domestic science, sewing and bookkeeping. According to the report, bookkeeping was important because the future wife had to be able to keep household accounts and to introduce organization and thrift into the running of the household. Moreover, some convent girls would have to supervise servants; others would be obliged to keep accounts and take care of the correspondence for their husband's grocery store, business or office. A good housewife, then, doubled as her husband's business partner.

The same report stressed the importance of sewing and, in addition the need to know how to cut out clothes: the girls would have to do things in life other than preside over a salon: "The cost of essentials has become so high that a wife will in future have to rely on herself for making a mass of things that previously she had other people do for her." (These observations suggest that a convent education was now within the reach of girls of modest backgrounds.)

As more and more mothers allowed their daughters to attend school, some of the responsibility for teaching domestic skills passed to the schools. Mothers who invested in their daughters' education thought that an educated daughter, although poor, had a better chance of marrying well. If the daughter did not marry or enter a convent, she would at least have received some education, which would allow her to earn a better living than that of a factory hand or servant.

BECOMING A HOUSEWIFE

Before 1850, most people were engaged in subsistence farming. A woman's work was determined by the seasons, pregnancy and the number of mouths she had to feed. By the end of the century, this way of life still existed in only a few regions of Quebec. The lives of thousands of women in the countryside and the towns were slowly changing and they were being transformed into housewives.

In mid-century, rural life in Quebec had been organized on traditional lines: women, men, children and the elderly produced in and around the house what was necessary for the survival of the family. Job specialization, based on age and sex, did exist; but women took part in production as much as men did.

Each person worked to produce essentials for the survival of the group. Relations between parents and children and between women and men primarily reflected the interdependence of various producers. Pure self-sufficiency was rarely found: since the beginnings of the colony, Quebec farmers had periodically taken part in the fur trade, sold wheat or cut wood. The men in the family had seen a market value for their own production, but products made by women were consumed mostly by the family. Only occasionally would women sell their products on the open market.

AT SAINT-JUSTIN, THE WOMEN OF THE CASAUBON FAMILY TOOK PART IN A WIDE VARIETY OF PRODUCTIVE ACTIVITIES

Most important were spinning and weaving. In 1886, eighteen or twenty bundles of flax were subjected to the preliminary processes of heating, crushing, stripping, combing, spinning and bleaching. Forty-five pounds of wool, dried at the house and then carried to Karl's factory on the Maskinongé River to be carded, were also spun during the winter by the mother, two aunts, the daughter-in-law and the eldest of the daughters using treadle spinning wheels. Eighteen of the forty-five pounds of wool were dyed – also at the house.

A small quantity of the woolen or flaxen thread obtained in this way was left in this state; a small amount was knitted, but most of it was put on the warping frame then on the loom and made by the mother, her two daughters and her daughter-in-law into cloth, flannel, material and sheets. Only pressing and fulling of material was done outside the home. Sewing and knitting completed the above list of jobs and allowed the family to provide its own household linen, cloth or flannel, bed sheets, tablecloths and hand towels, of which there were dozens and dozens piled up in the cupboards. The family also made most of its own workclothes. The women did not weave and sew to meet only the needs of the family. They produced custom-made clothes from homespun cloth. The mother sold half wool, half cotton quilts decorated with fringes. Philomène produced large woolen shawls and large footwarmers made of cotton or printed calico as well as rag rugs, which were used either as carpets for the floor or as bedspreads.

At harvest time, old aunt Marguerite, assisted by Julie and Philomène, gathered the best stalks of wheat straw and made long plaits out of them, which she then passed through the rollers of a small press. Two hundred lengths of approximately five feet were made in this way each year. From them Julie made hats for the whole family.

The remains of slaughtered animals provided the family with tallow candles and soap. Hides from cows, calves and sheep were taken to the tanner. The leather was used to repair harnesses or to do minor shoe repairs. Sheepskins were used to make workgloves and kneepads. The family went to the village cobbler only for shoes. Finally, from the hair of slaughtered pigs, mother Casaubon made curry combs, stove brushes, clothes brushes and brushes for whitewashing.

In July, they brought the hay in; in August and September, they were involved in the harvest and the threshing. In these last three operations, the women – the mother, daughter-in-law, Philomène, Eulalie and even aunt Julie – carried forks and rakes and helped the men.

The women milked the cows and were responsible for the dairy. On occasion, they even helped look after the livestock. The women were solely responsible for the vegetable garden, which required the use of a spade or fork. Mother Casaubon's special role was taking care of the tobacco crop. In the spring, she put the seedlings in boxes; later she transplanted, weeded, watered and pruned them. The women were also almost entirely responsible for growing flax; the men helped only with the harvesting and threshing of the crop. In addition, the women sheared the sheep, while the men held them still.[10]

In preindustrial society before mid-century, work was an integral part of family life. The family lived and worked in the same place and the two activities were interwoven. This close connection was evident amongst farmers who owned their farms but it also existed amongst the families of female and male artisans: seamstresses, shoe repairers, blacksmiths and bakers worked in their homes. When the first factories were built, piecework continued to be done at home and the productive character of the family unit was maintained. However, with the arrival of large factories, machines altered many of the artisans' tasks, and both women and men left their homes to work in the factories. Increasingly part of the family's productive labour had to be performed outside of the home if the family was to be fed, housed and clothed. For some family members, the home became the place where they did not work. Gradually, it would become the work place only for mothers.

Industrialization also changed the structure of rural life. Factory products were sold even in the most remote corners of Quebec. After 1880, it was possible to shop by catalogue anywhere in the province and goods were delivered by mail or rail. Thus, the rural family lost a little of its self-sufficiency and became a consumer of products of the new industries. The traditional work of women changed. Almost everywhere, as Gérin observed, "The homespun cloth is being increasingly replaced by cotton fabrics, printed calico, tweeds and commercial fabrics."

Families abandoned certain modes of production and became consumers, but the transformation affected the lives of women and men differently. Quebec farmers who supplied dairy products for the urban market received cash for their output, which enabled them to buy manufactured goods. The work of rural women, however, was still essentially centred on self-sufficiency and producing children for the continued survival of the family group; and it was unpaid work. As agriculture became commercialized, rural women no longer had the same economic function as men. Henceforth, all family members would serve different economic purposes. Interdependence gave way to dependence: those who were not paid relied on those who were paid. The

---

A "CREATURE" WHO DID NOT CONSIDER HERSELF INFERIOR TO HER HUSBAND ...

In 1886, Léon Gérin observed the Casaubon family at Saint-Justin.

Madame Casaubon is an energetic and competent woman. She appears to occupy in the family a position very nearly equal to that of the father.... Many times she may not eat with the men; but this is because there is work to be done, rather than because the table is too small and there are not enough utensils. She does not consider herself inferior to her husband.... A significant fact – her husband rarely fails to consult her before undertaking the smallest transaction.

And Léon Gérin noted that here as in the Vendée, it was customary to refer to the women as "creatures" but, he added, "this term does not have a derogatory connotation...."[11]

rural woman was slowly transformed from a producer to a housewife, although in some regions, women resisted these changes and continued well into the twentieth century to produce the necessities of life for their families.

In industrial towns, change was more rapid. The development of towns was accompanied by land speculation, and all urban space was used. Row houses of more than one storey were constructed; workers' accommodation was built in whatever space remained between houses. The process was most rapid in Montreal, because most people who lived there were tenants. As vacant land disappeared, housewives abandoned their gardens and small-scale agricultural production; during the decades of industrialization, work done by women in the home gradually became invisible.

NEW WORK INSTRUMENTS

The work previously done by artisans was now performed in factories on new machines. The new technology expanded into all sectors of production, including housework. Inventors patented many household appliances, all of which were supposed to reduce housework. American historian S. M. Strasser notes the considerable lapse between the time a household appliance was invented and the time it was distributed. Although many appliances were invented before 1900, only a few fortunate women felt the "beneficial effects" of the technology. In the United States, technological innovation spread slowly, and had little impact on domestic life before 1920. Women in cities were the first to be affected; women in small towns would have to wait until after 1930. Some inventions such as electricity and gas, had no effect on women's lives. The Compagnie du gaz de Montréal (Montreal Gas Company), established in 1847, concentrated at first on street lighting, as did the electric companies established in Montreal after 1878. Private electrical and gas companies, primarily served industrial concerns, municipalities and a few fortunate citizens.

The 1901 Eaton's catalogue tells us what was available to prospective customers. Eaton's offered only a few electrically powered products such as fans, bells and lamps, and there were as many oil and gas lamps as there were electric lamps. (Electricity was not yet the primary source of lighting in Canadian homes.)

Technological innovations were slow to appear in the kitchen. In Montreal, Meilleur & Co produced a coal-fired stove in 1864. The new stove was much more efficient than the traditional wood stove, but the housewife's work was hardly less onerous. Lighting the fire, for example, was a time-consuming and dirty chore. Strasser mentions an experiment conducted at the Boston School of Domestic Science in 1899: bringing in the coal, lighting the fire, and cleaning and maintaining the stove took five hours and twenty-six minutes of each of the six days of the experiment. By contrast, a gas stove needed one hour and forty minutes' attention, most of it spent on cleaning. This was every housewife's dream! Unfortunately, the gas stove was beyond the means of most households.

A large part of a housewife's time was spent in the preparation of meals. In countryside and town alike, there were preliminaries to the actual making of the meal. If food had been salted to preserve it, it had to be desalted before it could be eaten. There was poultry in the market, but the housewife had to pluck and eviscerate it. Various cuts of meat ready for cooking were available, but they were expensive. Most of the time, only marinated, salted or smoked meat was available: fresh meat would not become regularly available until refrigerators became widespread.

Diet in Quebec changed considerably during the nineteenth century. A series of crises in wheat production prompted people to grow potatoes and oats. The Casaubon family, whose lives were examined by Léon Gérin in 1886, ate mostly bread, which they baked once a week, pea soup, bacon and potatoes. They also ate rice soup, cabbage soup and buckwheat cakes, and many of the farm animals and fowl ended up on the family table. Pastries and berry jams were kept for Sundays, holidays or celebrations. The family drank mainly tea and milk. The Casaubons were still a self-sufficient farming unit which resisted the pressure of the consumer market.

A number of farms had abandoned small-yield mixed crops in favour of specialization; they, like many people in towns and villages, had to buy their provisions from a local store. The development of a railway network brought variety into the diet. Fruits and vegetables could be transported in refrigerated cars, which appeared in the United States in 1865, after the Civil War. The canning industry also experienced some growth during the last decades of the century. Canneries started up in Quebec after 1870, and their products entered the market. They were, however, expensive: in 1901 a can of corned beef or peaches cost fifteen cents approximately an hour's wages. The working-class housewife could not afford to give her children ready-to-serve food.

Many household chores required water. Montreal modernized its aqueduct system in the 1850s, creating a water-distribution system. But there was no running water as we know it today. Instead, water was available near the house, and the housewife carried buckets of water to the house. Houses in Montreal acquired running water by the turn of the century, but even then more than five thousand dwellings had outside toilets. During certain seasons and during the night, people used chamber pots.

The introduction of running water into every house changed domestic life. Swiss historian Geneviève Heller notes that doing the washing, which hitherto had been a social activity, became a private, individual activity; thus one of the communal bases of housework was destroyed. (Research has not yet revealed whether domestic work in Quebec had a similar communal basis.)

Running water definitely changed people's notion of cleanliness. Clothes and other items were washed more often and bodily cleanliness became a favourite theme of hygienists. However, although washing was the most tedious of household chores, it was affected very little by technological innovation. Two thousand patents for washing machines were registered in the United States around 1869, but most were made for the commercial market. Strasser emphasizes that the few machines designed for domestic use saved only a little time and labour, as many women had their washing done outside the home.

Dressmaking technology did however change the lives of most women. Fifteen years after the invention of the sewing machine in 1846 the Quebec ready-to-wear industry came into existence. By 1871 the value of goods produced was nearly six million dollars, and it tripled during the next thirty years. More and more ready-made clothes appeared on the market, although, until the end of the century, they were mainly men's clothes. Most mothers continued to make clothes for themselves and their children; but the sewing machine enabled women to make clothes more rapidly and to stay at home and to do work sent out to them by industry.

SEWING AT HOME

In many families, the husband's wages were insufficient and men were often out of work. Women from working-class families took on paid employment. During the first years of industrialization, many women and mothers worked in factories. Still more did paid work at home to support the family while continuing to do the domestic work that was essential for the survival of the family.

The garment industry depended mainly on work done in the home. The industry was the fourth largest in Quebec in terms of production. It had a unique structure: there were few large garment factories, but those that did exist concentrated on cutting the clothes. The pieces were then sent out for sewing. Historian Suzanne Cross states that, in 1892, the J. W. Mackedie company employed nine hundred women in the home; the H. Shorey company, which employed only one hundred thirty women in its workshops, employed fourteen hundred women at home. "All our work was done by families, mother and daughters working together and we paid them so much per piece," explained an entrepreneur before the Royal Commission on the Relations of Labour and Capital in Canada in 1886. The phenomenon was widespread: W. L. Mackenzie King's inquiry in 1898 discovered that three-quarters of the clothes made in Montreal were produced in hundreds of small workshops and in thousands of homes by Jewish and French-Canadian women.

The railroad enabled garment factories to employ a rural labour force. Pieces to be sewn were sent by train, as far as thirty miles from Montreal. A number of women owned their own machines, but many others worked on machines rented from or provided by the manufacturer.

Such work is frequently referred to as "the sweating system." The term also describes other practices. For example, clothing companies employed subcontractors who recruited women, handed out work, supervised it and then paid the women, keeping a sizeable commission for themselves. In other companies, women workers were assembled in makeshift premises to meet special orders: working conditions in the small, improvised workshops were unhealthy, and workers were so exploited that the shops were referred to as sweatshops.

The sweating system was a glaring form of economic exploitation. In the enquiry report, Mackenzie King revealed that "a woman slaving away for 60 hours a week, earns two to three dollars per week, while a carpenter earns three dollars per day." It would have been impossible, King said, for women to survive on their wages alone.

The Quebec Factories Act of 1885, which marked the first intervention of the provincial government in labour relations, applied only to businesses that employed more than twenty people. Milliners and seamstresses, who worked mostly at home or in small workshops, were not protected by the law and could be forced to work longer than the ten hours a day set by the act.

The Quebec Industrial Establishments' Act, which was passed in 1894, applied to all businesses. While certain sweatshops were regulated by the act, work done in the home was exempted. Factory inspector Louisa King, who owed her position to pressure from feminists, stated in 1898:

> Concerning the "sweating system" I may say, in my district, I have been unable to discover where it is carried on.
>
> I have asked again and again the manufacturers to give me the addresses of those who work for them and who employ others. They have almost invariably answered that their work was done in family shops, over which the inspector had no control. I would recommend that the family shops be brought under the law and that every manufacturer be compelled to furnish the inspector with the names and addresses of all who work for him. Such a procedure would enable the inspector to reach many places where the public safety is endangered and where people work under unfavourable conditions.[12]

Rural and urban women continued to work under these terrible conditions for a long time – it was one of the few ways they could reconcile housework, child care and earning a wage. Taking in boarders had enabled thousands of women to balance their budgets, but not all women could have boarders when the children were young; the family needed all the space in its cramped urban house. Taking in washing was difficult to integrate into the schedule of domestic chores, and it took up considerable space when the weather made it impossible to dry clothes outside.

Women were probably aware that working at home was badly paid and exploitative, as they were quite well informed about industrial wages. However, in preindustrial societies, women were not expected to live on their wages alone, as the survival of family members was the result of the combined efforts of the family as a group. These traditional views remained when women began doing industrial work at home and became aware of the great advantage of being able to reconcile housework and a paying job. Moreover, apart from times of economic hardship, when women had to support the whole family on their wages alone and had to work very long hours, women working at home could generally organize their time as they saw fit, since they were paid by the piece and not by the hour.

What today appears to be exploitation of women in their homes can be viewed as a strategy that enabled women in an industrializing society to delay the time when they would be transformed into housewives, economically dependent on their husband-providers.

NOTES

1 *Léon Gérin et l'Habitant de Saint-Justin* (Montréal: Presses de l'Université de Montréal, 1968), pp. 72 and 89.

2 *Entre Amis,* letters from Pére Louis Lalande s.j. to his friend Arthur Prevost, 1881-1900 (Montreal, Imprimerie du Sacré-Coeur, 1907).

3 Extracts from the diary, 7 April and 21 September 1875, Fadette, *Journal d'Henriette Dessaulles 1874-1880* (Montreal: Hurtubise HMH, 1971).

4 *Le Journal de Québec,* 20 May 1847, quoted in F. Ouellet, *Histoire écomomique et sociale du Québec 1760-1850* (Montreal: Fides, 1966).

5 Letter from Julie Bruneau to L.-J. Papineau, 23 February 1836, in *Rapport de l'Archiviste de la Province de Québec,* nos. 38-39.

6 J. Provencher and J. Blanchet, *C'était le printemps* (Montreal: Boréal Express, 1980), p. 102.

7 Fadette, *Journal d'Henriette Dessaulles 1874-1880* (Montreal: HMH, 1971).

8 Extracts from Jacques Bernier, *La Condition ouvrière à Montréal à la fin du XIXe siècle, 1874-1896* (Master's Thesis, Université Laval, 1971), pp. 75-76.

9 Marie-Paule Malouin, *L'Académie Marie-Rose (1876-1911)* (Master's Thesis, Université de Montréal, 1980), p. 141.

10 *Léon Gérin et l'habitant de Saint-Justin,* op. cit., pp. 59-62.

11 Ibid., pp. 86-87.

12 Quoted in J. De Bonville, *Jean-Baptiste Gagnepetit, Les Travailleurs montréalais à la fin du XIXe siècle* (Montreal: Editions de l'Aurore, 1975).

CHAPTER SEVEN

WORKING UNDER
ANOTHER ROOF

IN THE NINETEENTH CENTURY, most women who wanted to earn a living had to leave home, and find employment as servants, factory workers or teachers. In 1891, 13.4 percent of the work force in Quebec was made up of women. Ten years later, the proportion had risen to 15.1 percent. In the female population as a whole, one Quebec female in ten, ten years of age and older, was doing paid work in 1891. The figure would be 12.8 percent in 1901.

Jobs for women were limited. In 1891, 45 percent of female workers were in "domestic and personal service" and the vast majority of these were servants. A large number of women – 33.6 percent of all women workers – worked in factories. One job predominated: more than half the factory workers were seamstresses. The so-called "professional sector" comprised 10.3 percent of the female work force, and nine-tenths of these "professionals" were teachers. The remaining 10 percent of women workers worked in agriculture and fisheries (5.4 percent) or in commerce and transport (5.6 percent), as farmers, clerks or saleswomen.

SERVANTS

Domestic service was the major source of employment for women. There were the farm servants, general-purpose servants who worked for town families, cooks in large bourgeois homes or hospitals, and housekeepers in the homes of parish priests or convents. But their living conditions and daily work differed radically from one place to another. Some worked full-time; others did an occasional day's work for families that could not afford full-time servants.

We know little about these female workers. Their work, like a mother's work, was unseen outside the family. We do know, however, that domestic service decreased as the century progressed; in Canada in 1891, domestic servants represented only 41 percent of the female labour force. In a study of urban domestic service, historian Claudette Lacelle found that, in Quebec City at the beginning of the century, one household in five employed a servant. In 1871, the proportion had fallen to one household in ten. Employers were shopkeepers, professionals, civil servants or people of independent means. However, they were usually not rich enough to keep several servants, and two-thirds of women servants worked alone with their mistress as all-purpose help.

At the beginning of the century, servants' contracts were very general. The servant undertook to obey her master "and to do anything legal and honest that he asked of her." In the second half of the century, however, duties were carried out according to increasingly precise rules. Attempts were being made to rationalize domestic work. Numerous treatises on domestic economy and manuals for servants, published in Europe after the 1840s, were used by those who employed servants in Quebec.

Servants were usually responsible for food supplies, the kitchen, keeping the house clean, tending the vegetable garden (which some masters kept even in town) and sometimes looking after the children. The washing was often done by a woman hired especially for the job, but servants also had to do washing on occasion. Especially heavy or tedious chores, such as lighting the fire in the early morning and cleaning the stove, were left to the servant.

A servant's day was long: sixteen to eighteen hours a day, six days a week, under the same roof as her employer. Nighttime did not necessarily bring relief from further work: comforting young children who woke in the night or looking after the sick were sometimes part of her work. Her free time was restricted to Sunday afternoons.

For some servants, doing the shopping provided a rare period of freedom and relaxation. There was more to the market than goods for sale. Sometimes there were attractions – entertainers and tightrope walkers. One might meet acquaintances, a lover, women friends and other servants. One could chat, exchange news, perhaps find a husband.

The layout of nineteenth century towns allowed for considerable social contact. Toward the end of the century, however, wealthy families moved out to the suburbs, taking their servants with them. Far from the town centres and from the market, a servant would increasingly experience the isolation of the modern housewife.

Domestic service provided a job and a roof over one's head. In 1871, according to Lacelle, 70 percent of urban female servants lived in their masters' houses; thus, when they were dismissed, they lost their lodgings as well as their livelihood. Generally, they lived in an attic or near the kitchen in a small, sparsely furnished room. When a house had several servants, the women's rooms were smaller than those of the men; the men also sometimes had an entrance hall leading to their rooms.

We have little information about relations between masters and servants. In the Papineau family correspondence, there are, however, occasional references to domestic staff. Certain servants, like Marguerite, who raised almost all the Bruneau-Papineau children, were treated as members of the family. Indeed, Marguerite was so much part of the family that she followed the Bruneau-Papineaus into exile in Paris. Occasionally, she is mentioned in Julie Bruneau's letters to her children, who remained behind in America.

Although many servants were probably treated as part of the family, the practice was not universal. In houses where the mistress was demanding, personnel turnover was high. Louis-Joseph Papineau scolded his daughter Azélie because "she cannot keep her servants.... She will always fail to do so," he said, "because she doesn't know how to give orders tactfully!" If even Louis-Joseph Papineau got involved in the domestic problems of his daughter, it was because when Azélie lost her servants, the family had to bail her out. Papineau's remarks reveal the problems caused by servants who quit their jobs, and indicate that servant girls did not hesitate to leave mistresses who were overbearing.

Servants working in the household lived amongst people of a different class, but did not live like them. For it was the work done by servants that allowed their masters to live a life different from their own. Furthermore, servant girls often came from a rural background. Domestic service was the most common way of bringing girls into the towns.

The distance between servants and masters probably increased as more foreigners became domestics. At the beginning of the nineteenth century, servants were usually of the same nationality as their masters. In 1871, servants from Ireland and Scotland constituted nearly 70 percent of the live-in servant population in the well-to-do sections of Montreal; in Quebec City, 59 percent were French-Canadian women and 33 percent were Irish. Immigrant women were looked down on. In 1903, *Le Journal de Françoise* criticized the negative reactions to the arrival of a "cargo" of female immigrants "picked up off the streets of the cities of Britain."

In the nineteenth century, there were often service stairs between the kitchen and the maid's bedroom – a clear indication of the barriers, physical and human, between families and their servants. (Generally, servants ate in the kitchen, apart from the family.) Families no longer seemed to think that they had social responsibilities towards their servants. In Montreal, a number of servants were let go when the bourgeoisie left the city to spend the summer months in the fashionable resorts of Charlevoix or Cacouna, or in times of economic recession. Women servants had to move out when they were given notice; they had to find lodgings and, if possible, a new job. This was a far cry from the family that used to welcome a young country girl into its home and protected her from the corruption and dangers of the town.

The precarious and vulnerable position of servants who had been laid off or dismissed illustrates that, though domestic service offered a roof over one's head, it did not necessarily offer security, warmth and the protection of family life, as was claimed by those who recruited servants. At this time, Canadian society was attempting to solve what was called the "domestic crisis" or the "crisis in domestic service." Although 41 percent of the female labour force in Canada in 1891 were servants, servants had become hard to find. Domestic service was no longer the only option for working women: the factory offered much better wages and working hours and young women were entering factories in large numbers.

The domestic crisis was also a result of increased employee mobility. Leaving or changing one's job was often the only means of protesting bad working conditions and improving one's situation. There was also a crisis because "good" servants were rare, and there were increasing complaints from mistresses about the lack of training for servants.

A number of attempts were made to resolve the crisis; these ranged from rural recruitment to immigration and from professional training to a domestic-service labour pool. Recruiting Portuguese women had been common practice since the beginning of the eighteenth century. During the nineteenth century, recruitment concentrated on the British Isles. Emigration societies were formed in Great Britain and associations for welcoming and placing immigrants sprang up in the colonies. Between 1880 and 1920, the British Women's Emigration Association was the principal agency for recruiting domestic-service personnel from the British Isles. The women who selected emigrants applied certain criteria. Like Canadian bourgeois women, English bourgeois women were experiencing a domestic crisis. The servants they sent to the colonies were not experienced; they were untrained, unemployed or rural women, victims of the land shortage, who had flocked to the towns.

Female immigrants were welcomed in Canada and even encouraged by the State, which gave financial support to groups such as the Women's National Immigration Society. The State even promoted immigration: agents sang the praises of Canadian society, which, they claimed, was more democratic than that of the Old Country: in Canada, servants were treated as one of the family. Agents also attracted recruits by promising them wages twice what they would actually receive.

The immigrants were welcome only if they became servants. To make sure

AND ARE YOU HAPPY IN YOUR SITUATION?

Henriette Dessaulles, a fifteen-year-old girl from a bourgeois family, describes in her diary for 23 October 1875 a conversation with the seamstress who worked for her family six days a week, twelve hours a day:

I have discovered a beautiful soul. Rosalie, our seamstress (she is very old, 30 at least ...), is always alone in her sewing room and yesterday I was passing by quite casually when she said: "You are very pale, mamzelle Henriette, are you tired?" "I am fed up, Rosalie." "What with?" "Oh, myself, I suppose!" "But you are very happy, mamzelle." "Me, happy?" "But of course, you have good parents, everything you could wish for, you are rich, you live in a beautiful house, you are waited on as if you were helpless, you are being given a good education. There aren't many as happy as you!" I didn't reply immediately. What could I say to her? "And you, Rosalie," I asked her, "are you not happy?" "If I may say so, mamzelle, I am very content with my lot." "Do you live with your family?" "No, they are all dead. I rent a little room where I live all alone, but not for long periods," she added with her lovely smile, "since I work here, every day from seven to seven. When I do leave here in the evening I go to church to say my prayers and then when I get home I go to bed so I can get up at five o'clock the next day." "And Sunday?" "I spend a lot of time at church and I write to my nephew who's a curate in the United States." "And are you happy like this?" "Yes. I do my job as well as I can and I know that the Good Lord will do what he can for me." I left, deep in thought....[1]

that the women arrived safe and sound and that they were not diverted toward other types of employment or toward prostitution, emigration societies sent a chaperone to accompany them. When they arrived in Canada, they were looked after by associations, who provided temporary board and lodging until they could be placed with a family.

Recruiting abroad did not solve the domestic crisis. Immigrant women turned out to be as "unstable" as native-born servants. Bourgeois women wanted fewer but more efficient servant women who had received formal training. They also hoped that professional education for servants would relieve them of the need to train their own and would make the job more attractive to young women. The movement to upgrade the status of the domestic servant gave rise to various experiments. For example, early in 1860, young women were sent to the Home and School of Industry to be trained in domestic work. Orphanages run by religious communities also provided such training. In 1895, the Young Women's Christian Association founded a sewing and cooking school. Feminist associations recommended the inclusion of a domestic-science program in the schools, and the first domestic-science schools opened in Quebec.

The domestic crisis continued and worsened during the first decades of the twentieth century. Attempts to steer female workers toward domestic service had limited success, as new career opportunities were opening for women.

FACTORY WORKERS

There were a few industries before 1850, but industrialization did not really gain momentum until the second half of the nineteenth century. A limited number of industries, in Montreal and elsewhere in Quebec, hired women: garment industries; textile factories (cotton, wool, and silk); and shoe, tobacco, and leather manufacturers. Outside of Montreal, women worked in match factories, fish-canning plants, and fruit- and vegetable-canning plants.

In 1891 one Quebec factory worker in five was a woman. A large number of the industries employing women were in the towns where nearly one worker in three was a woman.

Historian D. S. Cross notes that, between 1871 and 1891, the proportion of women in the industrial work force declined from 33 to 28 percent. New jobs, she explains, were offered less often to women than to men.

There were few trades open to women – then as now, the few exceptions often camouflaged the range of job opportunities for women. In 1900, the feminist editors of *Women of Canada* noted:

> Women are finding employment in many types of work that were considered until now to be the exclusive preserve of men.... Among these jobs are house decoration (painting the interior), fresco painting, market gardening.... Some women are operating horse stables, others are selling ice.

The few women in these nontraditional jobs were held up by the magazine's editors as proof of what a woman could achieve. Although the editors noted that women earned less than men, this did not mean that women's work was less valuable, merely that they were given different jobs to do. Thus, wage discrimination remained hidden behind an accepted sexual division of labour.

The life of a woman factory worker was a hard one. Six days out of seven she was at the factory by 6:30 AM. If she was late, her wages were cut. In the cotton mills, a woman usually looked after four looms. Her work did not require great strength, but it did demand sustained attention and unfailing concentration. The woman had to notice defects in fabrics and had to work quickly. Carelessness, mistakes and clumsiness were punished by fines, deducted from her wages. The most severe fines were levied in shoe factories: the worker, who received a cent for each sole, was docked four cents for each imperfect sole. It was hot in the mills; machines were noisy and the air dusty. Workers had a break at midday after which work continued until 6:30 or 7:00 PM. In 1885, work for women was limited to ten hours a day, sixty hours a week; but the law was rarely observed: twelve- or thirteen-hour days were common until the end of the century.

Regulations and punishments in factories were decidedly paternalistic. If a factory worker used a piece of toilet paper to curl her hair, she was fined twenty-five cents. Georgina Loiselle, an eighteen-year-old apprentice in a cigar factory, was beaten by her employer because she refused to make an extra one hundred cigars. In the same factory, apprentices found guilty of stealing cigars or of absenteeism were sent to the Black Hole, a sort of dungeon in the factory basement. The owner, who appeared before the Royal Commission on the Relations of Labour and Capital, said that he punished apprentices at the request of their parents. The severity displayed by employers toward children must have been considered an extension of family discipline, which was still characterized by parental authoritarianism.

Most women were paid by the piece, not by the hour. Some companies paid women according to output while paying men by the week. A woman doing piecework had to increase her speed if she wanted to increase her wages or to benefit from bonuses. Pieceworkers also were at the mercy of the machine: they lost wages when it broke down, and faced idle machines when the factory had a surplus. Average wages for women were very low, less than those of men, as the table below indicates. (It is impossible to work out a yearly average on the basis of these weekly wages, however, as periods of unemployment were frequent, particularly in winter, when firings were common.)

A woman's wages varied considerably depending on her age and her job. Historian Trofimenkoff, who has analyzed the evidence of women who appeared before the Royal Commission on the Relations of Labour and Capital, reports that a fourteen-year-old girl earned two dollars a week in a printing shop; a twenty-year-old woman working in a cotton mill earned four dollars; an experienced seamstress seven dollars; and a woman supervisor in a tannery ten dollars a week. Historian Harvey estimates that a family needed nine dollars a week to survive. Given such wage rates, it is easy to imagine the poverty of widows or of women who were the only breadwinners in the family.

The wages of female apprentices or young, inexperienced female factory workers were even lower. As boarding houses and institutions charged boarders two dollars a week, it is probable that many female factory workers were forced to live with their families. Moreover, their meagre wages were probably essential to the survival of their parents, brothers and sisters. Certainly, working outside the home did not bring independence and freedom. Unable to live alone on her wages, a woman often had only one means of escape from home and misery – marriage to a man who earned twice the amount she did. One woman supervisor claimed "the young seamstresses in her workshop are more interested in getting married than in getting a permanent job." Some historians think that women's attachment to marriage and to the family is at the root of their lack of interest in their work and in union struggles. No research has yet been done on women and unionization in the early days of industrialization, but the little information we have indicates they were not completely indifferent to their working conditions.

For example, in 1880, the first important strike in the textile industry took place at the Hudon mills at Hochelaga, just outside Montreal. It was led by five hundred women workers who wanted increased wages and reduced working hours. In 1900, at the Montreal Cotton factory in Valleyfield, where the majority of workers were women, there were seven strikes, several of which turned violent. There were also several small, spontaneous conflicts: Harvey

TABLE 4

Variation in Weekly Wages in Certain Trades
in Montreal, Summer, 1881*

Trade	Minimum	Approximate Average Wage	Maximum
Shoemaker(m)	$5.50	$8.00	$15.50
Shoemaker(f)	$1.00	$4.00	$7.00
Cotton Worker(m)	$3.50	$5.00	$6.00
Cotton Worker(f)	$2.00	$4.50	$5.00
Tailor(m)	$4.50	$8.00	$10.50
Tailor(f)	$2.00	$3.00	$5.00

Source: Fernand Harvey, *Révolution industrielle et travailleurs,* Montréal, Boréal Express, 1978, p. 150.

* Wage averages based on evidence given to the Royal Commission on the Relations of Labour and Capital.

reports, for example, that, at Saint-Hyacinthe, fifteen women working in the Granite wool factory walked out because the foreman insisted that they do a job that halved their income per piece. Such spontaneous strikes were frequent during the nineteenth century; protests by women often took place independently and without union organization.

The union known as the The Knights of Labour, which organized workers according to job and by industry, was sensitive to the problems of the female work force. Some of its members were housewives or unemployed women. Its manifesto, published in 1887, demanded "implementation of the principle of equal wages for equal work for both sexes." The Parti socialiste ouvrier adopted a similar resolution in its 1894 manifesto, and demanded "universal and equal suffrage for all, regardless of colour, creed or sex."

These expressions of militant support coincided with a growing distrust and hostility toward working women. The lower wages of women exerted a downward pressure on men's wages, since the women were in direct competition with the men for jobs in several sectors of industry. One group within the workers' movement wanted to do away with competition by claiming equal wages for women; another group inclined toward denouncing working women and advocating their return to the home.

The Royal Commission on the Relations of Labour and Capital, whose mandate was to study working conditions, for the most part ignored the problems of working women. Women made up only one tenth of the witnesses who appeared before the commission in Quebec, although they constituted one fifth of the work force. This numerical underrepresentation was compounded by a bias in the questions asked of women. Trofimenkoff reports that the commissioners looked for the scandalous or immoral aspects of factory work: Were there separate toilets? Did girls get pregnant? they asked. There was little evidence to confirm any immorality in factory life. The commission asked questions about the morals of female factory workers, and yet overlooked their living and working conditions. Moreover, by treating the conditions of working women as a moral issue, the commission avoided the fundamental question: were women workers exploited? But the commission's portrayal of women factory workers as indifferent or docile was perhaps not unjustified. Women working for Stormont Cotton Mills in Cornwall who protested their working conditions were told that they could be easily replaced. One woman factory worker who testified against her employer in court lost her job. Activists were quickly dealt with. Forty-two percent of the women from across Canada who testified before the commission did so anonymously, while only 2 percent of the men withheld their names.

The women were afraid to speak, and they were afraid to protest. They were afraid of drawing attention to themselves, as they had already been made to feel that their presence in factories was somehow illegitimate. They were afraid to protest because they knew they could not count on support from male unions.

PIONEERS OR SCHOOLMISTRESSES

A girl with some education or from a well-to-do family did not become a factory worker or servant. Most of these girls stayed with their parents until they got married. Nevertheless, an increasing number decided, willingly or unwillingly, to look for a job with some social standing.

Most liberal professions were not open to women because they required a university education – which women often could not get – or because professional associations refused to accept women as members. Consequently, only about ten Anglophone women who studied medicine at Bishop's University after 1899 became doctors. McGill University admitted women only into its teacher-training college and its Faculty of Arts; more than a hundred girls went there to obtain qualifications, from a bachelor's degree to a Ph.D., in various arts or scientific disciplines, but the only profession open to them was teaching. The other faculties of the university were closed to women. For Francophones, the situation was even more disastrous; they were admitted to university, but they could only audit lectures. Only two teacher-training colleges, opened in 1857 and 1899, a few nursing schools, founded at the end of the century, and a number of private secretarial schools were open to girls. Many convents offered a musical education, so there was a large number of piano teachers.

A few women pioneers came to the fore: journalists, pharmacists, university professors, dentists, publishers, shopkeepers and civil servants. But they were the exceptions, and they sometimes had to fight furiously for the right to practise their trade or profession.

Among traditional professions, only journalism was open to Francophone women. By the end of the century, a proliferation of convents had produced many women with an education but no profession. A good number of them turned to writing for a living. They wrote quietly at home and sent off their manuscripts to the publishers; some contributed to magazines and newspapers. By the end of the century, some had succeeded in finding an avenue for their literary expression, and were making a living from it. The important newspapers of the last decade of the century had women's columns and women columnists but the woman columnist generally used a pseudonym: at *La Presse* it was "Gäetane de Montreuil"; at *La Patrie,* "Françoise"; at *Le Temps,* "Madeleine"; at the *Montreal Star,* "The Hostess"; at *Le Journal,* "Colette." In 1900, a survey of thirty-two Quebec newspapers revealed that there were forty-nine women correspondents and contributors. Thus, the first small inroad by women into the "male" professions was achieved by women columnists.

Teaching remained the principal career open to educated women. A teaching certificate was obtained by attending a convent and passing examinations set by the Board of Catholic Examiners, or by studying at a teachers' training college and obtaining its more prestigious diploma. The table below shows that teachers' training colleges produced twice as many female as male graduates. Most women students received the elementary diploma, but not one Francophone woman was awarded an academic diploma.

The majority of graduates were women, and the majority of teachers were women. At the beginning of 1856, they constituted 68 percent of the teachers in the public-school system. By 1878, 78 percent of teachers were women. After the 1850s, throughout North America, male teachers were replaced by female teachers.

Historian Alison Prentice found that great numbers of women were accepted into the profession because women generally occupied subordinate positions. As more women worked in the school system, a hierarchy developed: the women were concentrated in the primary grades and looked after the youngest pupils; the men taught the higher grades and were school inspectors.

Women also received much lower salaries than men. Estimates of typical salaries in 1853 suggest that a woman teacher earned 40 percent of a man

TABLE 5

Diplomas Granted by Teachers' Training Colleges, 1857-1888

| | Female Teachers | | Male Teachers | | |
	Laval	McGill	Jacques-Cartier	McGill	Laval
Academy diploma	-	110	109	88	118
Model school diploma	588	540	269	101	319
Elementary diploma	697	1112	204	52	305
Total	1285	1762	582	241	742
Total by Sex	3047		1565		

Source: Report of the Superintendent of Public Instruction, 1888.

teacher's salary. The differential still existed at the end of the century, but by then there were also considerable salary differences amongst women teachers: while the average woman teacher's salary in 1899 was ninety-nine dollars a year, women teachers in Montreal high schools were sometimes paid more than three hundred dollars. The least well-paid were rural women. Their salaries reflected the avarice of the school commissioners. In many cases, they were comparable to a servant's wages, but from time to time a teacher would be obliged to accept payment in agricultural produce and some had to purchase firewood for the school out of their own pockets.

Many qualified women teachers were unable to find employment. A female teacher was often the only woman in the village or surrounding area to be paid out of community taxes; her position was often highly sought after, and her deeds and conduct were carefully scrutinized by the community. Unusual behaviour, even outside the classroom, could bring dismissal. In 1871, the school commissioners of the village of Saint-Hermas attempted to expel the schoolmistress because she "was alleged to have had very intimate relations with her lover, now her husband," and to have given birth to a son three months after her marriage. The Saint-Hermas schoolmistress had used her lodgings to indulge in liberties not permitted at the time. However, women who lived alone in a country school must have experienced considerable anxiety. Historian Normand Séguin reports that the Hébertville schoolmistress received a visit one winter's night from a man whose face was covered; he attempted to rape her and her female companion. Not suprisingly a sizable number of women teachers preferred to board with pupils' parents.

The low salaries paid to women teachers were denounced at the beginning of 1864. The teachers' newspaper *La Semaine* demanded "that no distinction should be made between institutions at which men teach and institutions at which women teach and that their salaries should be the same." It is not known whether the demand indicates that male teachers were afraid of competition from low-paid women, or that women teachers had realized the injustice of their situation.

At the end of the century, some women teachers in Montreal signed a petition stating that their annual salary was insufficient for anyone who had to pay for board and lodging, and they demanded a salary increase. In 1893, Miss Binmore wrote an article in the Quebec *Educational Record* in which she described the salaries paid to women teachers in North American cities. While emphasizing that there was less salary discrimination in most cities, she noted:

> In Montreal the distinction is retained; but let us not, therefore feel discouraged. It can only be a question of time, when the difference shall be removed.[2]

Miss Binmore's article is evidence of a new attitude on the part of women workers, who had become aware of the social importance of their work. It is also evidence of an awareness that times were changing: "It is no longer absolutely necessary that every woman in the family should be dependent upon the men – to be reduced to unknown straits and intolerable suffering on the death of the latter."

The struggle for financial independence and equal salaries was considerably hampered because, in many villages, women teachers were less in demand than men teachers. In Hébertville, parishioners claimed that they

---

TEACHING AND SELLING AT SEEDING TIME ...

St. Arsène, 31 December 1858
The Hon P. J. O. Chauveau
S. E.
Montreal

Sir,

For several years now the school commissioners of St-Arsène have compelled the women teachers of this municipality to take half their salary in agricultural produce for which they fix a price higher than the going rate, so that in addition to the inconvenience of having to go around to the markets to get rid of it, we are forced to sell it at a loss. This year, for example, wheat is selling for between five and six shillings, rye for four shillings; the school commissioners have fixed the price for wheat at eight shillings and rye at five shillings and have done the same thing for other produce.

You will understand, Superintendent, that in the final analysis, the commissioners are only paying us part of our salary, on the pretext that the education laws allow them to do so.

I would be happy if you could tell me whether the education laws are as arbitrary as this and how I can deal with the commissioners on this matter. Please note that all the commissioners are farmers.

I have the honour to remain,
Sir,
Your Obediant[sic] Servant

Adeline Roy
Teacher

Further to your letter of the 20 January 1859 in which you informed us that Melle A. Roy had complained that we were forcing her to accept agricultural produce at inflated prices, we are pleased to provide the following explanations ... if she lost money by selling the produce unnecessarily too early, then that is her fault, because she would have probably made a profit if she had waited until seeding time, this would have been easy for her since she has a good loft for storage.

I have the honour to remain, Superintendent, your very humble and obliging servant.

Romain Dubé
President of the E.C. St-Arsène.

Your letter of the 31 January, in response to my letter of the 20th of the same month, has convinced me that Miss Adeline Roy has indeed a right to complain of the price that you charge her for the produce that you force her to take as payment. In such a case, you must charge the going rate and not the price that could be obtained at a later date. The teacher is not in a position to wait, he must sell immediately, and when in an exceptional case, he delays, it should not be the commission who should profit from it but the teacher himself.

J. O. Chauveau[3]
Reference: ANQ no 48 – 1899.

were unable to send their sons to school because the teacher was a person "of the female sex." They wanted a school run by nuns. (Nuns are, of course, sexless.) In 1852, in Saint-Grégoire de Nicolet, the parishioners, at the suggestion of their priest, tried to persuade the nuns of the Congrégation Notre-Dame to come to their village. At the time, the academy of Saint-Grégoire was run by a woman teacher, the mother of five children. The clergy, in the absence of a better solution, founded a new community, the nuns of the Assomption de la Sainte-Vierge, in the parish.

Each village and school commission tried to hire teaching nuns: their vow of poverty cost the community less than did school graduates. In 1830, there were only two teaching communities; in 1900, there were twenty, ten of which ran boarding schools. In 1853, one woman teacher in ten was a nun; thirty years later, half were. The educated girl who wanted to teach could choose between teaching as a member of the laity or teaching as a nun. In spite of the vow of poverty taken by the nuns, their material existence was probably less difficult than that of the lay teacher: nuns had security of employment, the certainty of finding a position, and a lifetime guarantee of board and lodging. By the end of the century, the religious life had become the best way to enter the teaching profession.

PROSTITUTES

But how could a woman survive if the factories were not hiring, or if they were hiring at such low wages that people refused to work? What could a

---

FROM SATANIC LITERATURE TO PROSTITUTION

In 1835, a book written by Maria Monk entitled *An Exposé of The Horrible Crimes Committed at the Hôtel-Dieu de Montréal* appeared in New York. The book informed its readers that, among other crimes, the nuns executed their mother superiors as soon as they reached the age of forty, that the acceptance of a new sister was accompanied by the assassination of an older sister, and that the nuns killed between thirty and forty newborn children every year. The publication of the book provoked considerable response not only in the Hôtel-Dieu, but also in Lower Canada and New England. Newspapers of the time unanimously leaped to the defence of the nuns. The Anglophone and Protestant newspapers were the most zealous in their defence. In 1836, visits to the Hôtel-Dieu were organized, and a Boston newspaper demonstrated conclusively that the calumnies had been copied from a Portuguese book published in 1781.

With the obvious aim of making money, Maria Monk and her agents published even more sensational "revelations." As late as 1849, people were still publishing rebuttals and analyses of the lies put out by Monk.

Monk was a young Irish girl who had been a servant in the Montreal region, in Sorel, Saint-Ours, Saint-Denis and Varennes between 1831 and 1835. She was imprisoned several times for theft and vagrancy; in all likelihood, she spent some time at the Montreal Home for Fallen Women, where nuns were trying to rehabilitate prostitutes. In 1836, Monk was in New York, where she used a pseudonym to write for the scandal sheet *Awful Disclosures*. She died in a New York prison, in 1849, at the age of thirty-two. Monk's life is evidence of the existence of an unstable, parallel society, which had no respect for institutions and their order.

---

woman of little education do? What if she could not stand being a servant supervised all day long by an overbearing mistress?

For a number of women, prostitution was the answer. Despite societal disapproval, the job generally provided a better income than women could earn elsewhere.

In Montreal brothels prospered. According to statistics compiled by Jacques Bernier, there were forty-one brothels in 1871 and, in 1891, 102, employing 390 prostitutes. These figures, from the Montreal chief of police, include only full-time prostitutes. There is no knowing how many women worked occasionally or part-time in order to survive after being fired or to tide things over. In 1875, the chief of police added about fifty vagabonds of no fixed address and a hundred kept women to the list of 245 women working in brothels; this, according to him, brought the total number of prostitutes to around four hundred. Slightly more than half of them were French Canadians; the others were mostly Irish or Scottish immigrants.

WOMEN AND WORK

A good husband could not always protect a woman from life's woes: economic crises, dismissal, accidents at work, sickness, death and natural calamities disturbed the daily routine and left thousands of families destitute. In Canadian towns, about half the population were chronically classified as "poor." Poverty did not mean an absence of luxury, but rather the absence of a decent place to live, firewood, coal, clothing and food. Most women spent their lives trying to survive.

Natural disasters, such as fire and epidemic, were especially cruel, since they left thousands of people in need of help at the same time. In 1845, in the town of Quebec, two fires ravaged the Saint-Roch and part of the Saint-Jean district, leaving twenty thousand people homeless; in 1866, fifteen hundred dwellings were razed. In Montreal, in 1852, one-sixth of the population found itself out on the street. At one stroke, women lost both their homes and their places of work. Housewives and home workers also lost their work tools. Huge epidemics were similarly disruptive. The cholera outbreak of 1832 killed a tenth of the population of Montreal, and large numbers of orphans and widows had to turn to charity:

> A vast field of endeavour awaits the attentions of the Association [des dames de la Charité]. One hundred and seventy two widows and five hundred and twenty orphans are going to find themselves in the most desperate straits during the harsh season, which is now approaching.

The charity of citizens will no doubt help the Ladies of the society to clothe them and to get them through the winter.[4]

In the face of natural disasters and the social problems produced by the influx of people into towns, traditional structures of mutual assistance were no longer sufficient. As a result two orphanages were built at the same time: the Catholic Orphanage of Montreal, by the dames de la Charité, and the anglo-protestant orphanage of the Ladies Benevolent Society. A widow, Emilie Tavernier-Gamelin, spent her assets and time organizing shelters and hostels for poor, aged or sick women. The widow Rosalie Cadron-Jetté took in single women who were pregnant and who had nowhere to go. The Conférence de Saint-Vincent-de Paul de Québec set up a shelter for women ex-prisoners and placed Marie Fitzbach-Roy in charge.

Charitable endeavors were becoming increasingly organized. Widow Gamelin circulated a number of petitions to obtain government money for her home for aged women. She lobbied the wives of *députés* Viger and Papineau and Julie Bruneau spoke to her husband on the matter:

> She has beseeched me to intercede with you. I warned her that nothing would come of it that I knew you were opposed to overburdening the House with such requests, which ought to be obtained through voluntary individual contributions. But everybody is in financial difficulties and she says that these poor old ladies are going to die of want.[5]

It was difficult to attract voluntary donations during economic crises, but the charities had to rely on private contributions. Church collections, fund raising and bazaars helped affluent bourgeois Anglophone and Francophone women keep the organizations going. Rich businessmen and wealthy widows gave houses and land or contributed money. Bazaars, which were as much social as money-raising events, were very much in fashion and sometimes brought in substantial sums.

Widows seemed particularly inclined to devote themselves to charitable work, but their charity alone could not guarantee the survival of their institutions. The State rarely intervened, leaving the field to the Church. Monseigneur Bourget, Bishop of Montreal, personally collected money from his diocese to provide new lodgings for Madame Gamelin's elderly women in the Asile de la Providence, and approached a French religious community about taking over Gamelin's work.

Problems of finance, organization and continuity were solved when religious orders took over charities. The great French-Canadian communities that history has attributed to the enthusiasm and breadth of vision of Monseigneur Bourget were, in fact, founded by charitable women from the laity, and

---

WHAT PRISONS ARE FOR ...

In 1852, Dr. Wilfred Nelson produced a report on prison conditions in Lower Canada. The report stated that women constituted 47 percent of those incarcerated in Montreal's prison at that time. According to the sheriff of Montreal, "it is very often the case that people who are simply homeless or devoid of funds are incarcerated. The old, the sick, the infirm and the mad are often sent to prison on the very vague charge of being idle and debauched and for having disturbed the peace."

The doctor in the Montreal prison gave it as his opinion that "The Montreal prison is improperly referred to as simply a prison ... one could almost call it a maternity hospital, because so many of the women who go there are pregnant and give birth there.... One could call it a children's home since very large numbers of very young children are taken in there...." The children were in prison because their parents had been imprisoned and because they had nowhere else to go.[6]

---

only later taken over by the Church. When French sisters refused to take over the Asile de la Providence in 1840, Emilie Gamelin founded the Soeurs de la Providence to ensure that her work would be continued. In 1848, Monseigneur Bourget persuaded Rosalie Cadron-Jetté to open the hospice Sainte-Pélagie "to rescue fallen girls, to return them to a better life, to guarantee their children baptism and a Christian education." Three years later, Madame Jetté's colleagues became the Soeurs de la Miséricorde. In Quebec City, the director of the Asile du Bon-Pasteur, the widow Fitzbach-Roy, founded the Soeurs du Bon-Pasteur in 1865. The traditional orders expanded and they, too, entered the social services. After five years of lay management, the Catholic Orphanage of Montreal was handed over to the Grey Nuns.

Between 1840 and 1902, twenty-one new communities were founded. In education and in social services, nuns responded to needs produced by the economic and social situation. Teachers from the laity were replaced by nuns, and women who organized charities were relegated to giving religious communities financial support. In both cases, women laity were replaced by women but the latter had taken a vow of obedience to the ecclesiastical authority.

Amongst Anglo-Protestants, the laity continued to organize charity. Charitable associations, homes, and orphanages were often launched by women's groups organized on confessional lines.

Between 1870 and 1880, the Anglophone laity, unlike the Francophone laity, had the opportunity to take part in lay philanthropic organizations, which tended to become interdenominational and involved in a variety of areas. The Young Women's Christian Association, formed in Montreal in 1874 and in Quebec City in 1875, devoted itself to the problems of poor city girls. The YWCA and other women's organizations slowly moved from work that was strictly religious to areas they considered appropriate and to activities that went beyond the strict definition of charity.

BRIDES OF CHRIST

In 1870, there were ten times as many nuns as in 1830. By 1900, about one woman in a hundred over the age of twenty-one took final vows in Quebec. There were also all those who were novices for a number of months or years but left the religious life when they realized they did not have the vocation. According to Marta Danylewycz, the number of nuns enumerated in each decade should be multiplied two or three times to approximate the number of women who experienced the religious life. Sixty percent of the sisters of La Miséricorde and 35 percent of the nuns from the Congrégation Notre-Dame, for example, gave up the religious life before taking their final vows. For several thousand Quebec women, life as a novice was a form of community work undertaken before marriage.

The religious life offered a very interesting alternative to exile in a newly settled area or the United States, and to domestic or married life. A life of celibacy meant a woman had a life far removed from constant pregnancies, sleepless nights looking after sick children, heavy work on the farm and sewing in the home. It was a life free from material insecurity (although those starting new communities often had financial problems). The guarantee of a roof over one's head in old age and a bed to oneself attracted more than one recruit.

Because they exchanged their sexual and personal lives for the veil, nuns enjoyed the respect and esteem of their community, and a number of them were able to become "career women." Many professions were open to those with the ability to succeed: mother superior, administrator, bursar, musician, painter, teacher, nurse, pharmacist, and historian among others. For a number of women, the religious life was the way to achieve personal, social, intellectual or artistic success. In the outside world, such a career was forbidden or inaccessible.

But, of course, for every bursar occupied with the finances of her community, there were ten or twenty sisters who changed sickbeds or worked in hospital kitchens. The work directed by communities, in refuges, hostels,

---

THEY GIVE THEIR SERVICES FOR NOTHING ...

By collecting money the Sisters are doing our work. They look after us for nothing. They are our traveling salesmen, they represent us in Christ's work with his suffering brethren. Many Canadians do not seem to know that society is required, under natural law, to take care of its poor, its abandoned sick, its old, its orphans, its rejects of every kind. As society does not know of its obligation, it forgets to thank those women who relieve it of this obligation. The Sisters perform our duties without charge.... Those who are too tired to give or who turn down a request for one pennyworth of charity from these collectors for the Good Lord will later pay the government a dollar to do the work that the Sisters could do for a penny.[7]

---

nurseries, homes, lunatic asylums, hospitals, orphanages, and shelters, required an abundant supply of labour. Even if the communities recruited lay help or put their orphan girls, prisoners and reformed girls to work, a large number of the cooks, laundry women and housekeepers responsible for the smooth running of the institutions wore *cornettes* (headdresses). Housekeepers like their mothers, sisters and grandmothers, nuns nevertheless enjoyed the respect of society.

The clergy also profited from the great wave of religious charity. If nuns could serve God as convent housekeepers, why could they not practise their vocation in the seminaries? Historian Sister Marguerite Jean tells of ecclesiastics who persuaded young girls to found communities devoted entirely to looking after the clergy. In the nineteenth century, two auxiliary communities were founded.

The sisters of Sainte-Marthe de Saint-Hyacinthe were a small community of "domestic nuns" who worked in the seminary of Saint-Hyacinthe. Their constitution clearly described their vocation as brides of Christ, and established a dependency on the seminary. "Our principal aim," said the Abbé Gendron of the Saint-Hyacinthe seminary, "has been to make them absolutely dependent on us so as to force them to have no other interests but ours." And he added: "In practice, the Sisters retain many of the strengths and many of the weaknesses of their sex, and they do not like this dependence very much." [8]

In the auxiliary communities, the religious life was surprisingly similar to that of thousands of housewives. But the traditional division of labour between women and men was absent in other religious communities, where manual and intellectual work were not separated according to gender. In the religious communities there was a hierarchical structure, but all positions – from the most menial to the most elevated – were occupied by women.

The absence of men in the daily lives of the nuns did not mean that there was an absence of patriarchal power over the community. According to Marguerite Jean, Monseigneur Bourget proclaimed himself the first Superior of the congregations which were founded with his consent, and took care to establish the new communities under his own "dependence" and "jurisdiction." He had the right to oversee admission of novices, daily routines and appointments.

Indeed, the real power did not belong to the mother superior or to the founder of the community, but to the bishop or his representative. Mother Marie-Anne, the founder of the sisters of Sainte-Anne, learned this to her cost. She found herself saddled with a young, ambitious chaplain, the Abbé Maréchal, with whom she did not get on. The chaplain removed certain

---

BECOMING TRUE BRIDES ...

According to the first article of their constitution, the sisters of Sainte-Marthe must become true brides of Christ:

> The first aim of the sisters of Sainte-Marthe, who have come together to live under one rule, is to help one another in their holy work and to become true brides of Jesus Christ. This is why they assume the name of sisters. They are also aware at every moment that they are all members of one family with the invisible Jesus Christ as its head; he alone must they seek to please.

According to an article in the canonical decree that established them, the sisters of Sainte-Marthe also had to become good housekeepers:

> The sisters of Sainte-Marthe have dedicated themselves to maintaining and working in the diocesan seminary with which they have identified themselves in perpetuity and under whose authority they will remain as long as they live. They will never have to take on work other than that they agreed to perform upon entry into the institute, and it is Our wish that they never stray from this principal aim of their foundation.[9]

---

articles from the constitution she had drawn up for her community. The conflict between Mother Marie-Anne and Abbé Maréchal became so great that she had to abdicate as mother superior of her own community. To ensure that Mother Marie-Anne would no longer influence the vocation of the community, she was sent to Saint-Ambroise, where she became sexton and looked after the sisters' robes.

Given the lack of higher education, religious life in the nineteenth century was probably the only way for Francophone women to avoid becoming a mother of a large family or a spinster who had to board with relatives. In the short term, the religious life was an effective strategy for women to remove themselves from the direct control of men. It was also a means of formally maintaining their legal status, as nuns were, in effect, unmarried, and unmarried women enjoyed full legal rights. The religious life was, for most, insurance against misery and poverty; for some, it offered a means of refusing inevitable childbearing. For others, it was a means of making a career.

But, in the long term, the strategy proved disadvantageous for women. First, the activities undertaken by religious communities reinforced the popular belief that women could play a role in society only if they were involved in a life of devotion or in charitable work.

Second, the religious life offered an easy way out for women who wanted a different life from that of their mothers. They could achieve their aim without having to fight opposition to higher education for girls and the concept of working women. At the turn of the century, when women throughout the western world were forcing their way into universities and professional organizations, Catholic women in Quebec were entering religious communities.

SPEAKING OUT

Women may have spoken out about their suffering and their hopes, but they have left hardly any written record. When did women find time to write about their lives? Although she had servants, Julie Bruneau wrote to her husband:

> as for myself, I cannot write you in more detail. I am busy and because I cannot write at my leisure I cannot gather my thoughts and I am doing nothing worthwhile. When one is not in the habit of writing it takes time to produce something acceptable and since I expect to see you soon I will be able to tell you face to face what I know and what I think. I merely wanted to give you news of the children.
>
> Your friend and affectionate wife
>
> Julie Bruneau Papineau[10]

Only educated and well-off women had sufficient time to write. Several became *épistolières* and wrote of daily events to relatives and friends. But their letters, which were probably women's most frequent means of expression, were rarely kept. Julie Bruneau's correspondence survives and was considered worthy of publication in 1959 primarily because she was the wife of Louis-Joseph Papineau. A number of other families also kept their letters, intimate diaries or family mémoires, but these are only now being considered for publication.

Nineteenth-century Quebec literature did not concern itself with daily life, for this was the glorious period of "good" literature – antiseptic, sterile and removed from life – which awarded pride of place to works inspired by history or to those celebrating traditional customs and patriotism. Those who did not write within these noble confines stood little chance of being published.

However, at the beginning of 1832, Madame Gosselin founded the *Museum of Montreal* (also called the *Journal de littérature et des arts* and the *Ladies Museum*). This Montreal-based magazine, which was aimed at women, was an educational and cultural publication devoid of political and religious debate. Only the first issue was published entirely in French; later issues would be bilingual. It was not a feminist publication: the women portrayed in the *Museum of Montreal* were typical wives and mothers. Nevertheless, the existence of the magazine was evidence of an awareness that a woman's world was wider than the household.

After the demise of the *Museum of Montreal*, women writers were published in literary magazines in Lower Canada. Before 1880, the most prolific women writers were Anglophones. One, Eliza Cushing-Foster, published numerous novels, short stories and poems; she became the manager of a literary magazine and then, in 1847, founded a children's magazine.

Rosanna Mullins-Leprohon was read by English and French Canadians. The daughter of an Irishman, she studied in French with the nuns and began, at a very early age, to write novels. Her literary career was interrupted by her marriage to a Francophone, by whom she had thirteen children, but continued several decades later. Her biographer, John C. Stockdale, does not appear to consider her a great writer but grants her a certain talent, especially in her descriptions of domestic quarrels, in which the dialogue is particularly incisive and the emotions authentic. Rosanna Leprohon was able to publish five novels between 1860 and 1873, probably because she published them first in English, then in French. The fact that she belonged, in part, to Anglophone society perhaps helped her to blaze a path forbidden to others. Francophone women did their writing at home and for their own enjoyment, and seemed to be almost entirely absent from formal literature.

In 1880, the most beautiful female voice in the world came to Canada. In

---

THE MUSEUM OF MONTREAL

In 1832 in Montreal, Madame L. Gosselin published the first number of the *Museum of Montreal*. The magazine was published until 1834. In their list of Quebec publications, historians Beaulieu and Hamelin describe the magazine:

> The editor stated that her magazine would be a definitive response to those foreigners who had made disparaging remarks about the lack of literary education displayed by Canadians; the magazine would serve as a means of acquainting people with "the creative Canadian genius" (December issue, 1832). Madame Gosselin went on to say that women in every country played an important role in literary life. In Canada, the few rare attempts to produce literary magazines had ended in failure: political discussions and religious controversies had destroyed the first attempts to establish literary magazines.
>
> The *Ladies Museum* would avoid past pitfalls by banning politics and religion from its pages. "Education, the refinement of the heart, cultivating the mind, promoting right conduct, these will be our principal aims." The magazine had been assured of contributions from women in Montreal, Quebec and Upper Canada, and its pages would be enriched by extracts from English and French literature and recent work by American women.[11]

---

nineteenth-century newspapers, where women were rarely talked about, suddenly there was talk of an actress from overseas – Sarah Bernhardt. Her visit to Montreal was a delirious occasion. She was greeted at the station by the mayor, various notables, a crowd of students, and the poet Louis Fréchette, who composed *Ode à la Diva* in her honour. People scrambled for tickets to her performance. Sarah Bernhardt was not just a star: she was a legend. Her private life – free, risqué and eccentric – was reported in the newspapers. Some people saw her visit as a patriotic as well as a theatrical event. It may have created a new female myth: the free and scandalous woman, admired all the more because she was remote from the daily lives of Québecois.

The singer Albani, born in Chambly as Emma Lajeunesse, had the same electrifying effect on Montreal crowds. In 1883, ten thousand people greeted her at the station and Fréchette recited one of his most beautiful poems. The love of Québecois for the "diva Albani" was an expression of their immense pride at seeing "one of our little girls" (though she was raised in the United States) become a great international star. Quebec women also loved Albani because, for the first time, one of their own was famous and admired. Albani was the only nineteenth-century woman to be recognized in the formal history of Quebec for anything other than her devotion to good works.

The visits of these two great artists coincided with the publication of the first book that departed from the typical nineteenth-century style of Quebec literature. In 1882, Laure Conan, born Félicité Angers in La Malbaie, wrote a book called *Angéline de Montbrun*. The novel is a cornerstone of Quebec literature; it was also the first work in Quebec to describe the pain of a woman's lost love.

Pressured by the Abbé Casgrain, Laure Conan was forced to give up writing psychological novels and devote herself to the historical novel. But she twisted the historical genre and wrote analytical novels with historical themes. Her heroes were those unknowns ignored by historians. Conan's work also describes the suffering of women: her heroines have everything they could want, but they are never happy.

After the 1880s, more women began to write. Anne-Marie Duval-Thibeault, a Franco-American, published in Montreal a collection of poems, full of fantasy and love, entitled *Les Fleurs du printemps* (1892): her poetry was different because it was not inspired by patriotic enthusiasm. Adèle Bibaud wrote two novels; "Françoise" (Robertine Barry) published a collection of articles and another of stories; and Josephine Dandurand wrote stories and plays.

Women began to write and to talk. Outside the literary tradition of the century, their writing described the sufferings of love, domestic quarrels, the bitter fights between lovers, the sorrows caused by children and the world around them.

Women's literature did not escape the criticism of the clergy. Laure Conan was called to order by the Abbé Casgrain. Duval-Thibeault, the only recognized woman poet of the century, lived abroad, far from the attacks of the clergy. Jules Tardivel, the Ultramontane, criticized Françoise's collection of stories *Les Fleurs champêtres* (1895), for its naturalist inspiration and its lack of religious content. Françoise replied that she had no intention of writing a popular book. But Françoise was a free-thinking journalist, one of the rare feminists in the 1900s who dared to criticize the clergy; she was a woman who belonged to another century.

In 1893, Josephine Dandurand founded *Le Coin du feu,* a literary magazine. Its object was to raise the intellectual level of French-Canadian women. The magazine became a literary forum for the great writers of the period and for the first texts of feminist writers. Sixty years after the demise of the *Museum of*

Montreal, Josephine Dandurand revived women's literary journalism. Dandurand's magazine recognized the female sphere of activity, but it also contained new ideas popular with the Francophone bourgeoisie. Josephine Dandurand and a number of contributors to her magazine, including Marie Gérin-Lajoie, were members of the Montreal Local Council of Women, a feminist organization founded in 1893.

A TINY LITTLE PLACE FOR WOMEN

The nineteenth century seemed to be one great migration: thousands of women packed their bags and left, with their children, for the United States, for northern Quebec for western Canada or for town.

Life as a mother, as a servant or a factory worker was hard. Women's every act symbolized submission, but their protests were muffled. The only way out of the hardships was to take the veil. But in the convents, a woman's life was restricted to the service of God.

Everything seemed to be as it should be. There were no demonstrations, no poems, few associations making demands of the government. It was as if a century of upheaval had passed women by, causing neither tears, rage, hope nor despair. There were, instead, thousands of nuns silently caring for, consoling and nourishing the victims of the miseries of the century. History reports only the bucolic images of an unchanging, rural Quebec. Paradoxically, the nineteenth century is identified as "the good old days."

And yet, during the nineteenth century the place of women in society changed. They lost their traditional rights, and political and economic life became resolutely male. The importance of women in the family economy declined; many became housewives, dependent on a husband-provider. Men defined the newly emerging society in terms of what they were doing; women were excluded from it. Men also defined what women should and should not do. Men reserved a tiny little place for women, where they were queens and prisoners: the domestic sphere.

During the twentieth century, the century of the electric light and the automobile, the changes that began in the nineteenth century continued and accelerated. Women had no choice: every day, the reality of their lives contradicted *the* ideal female image; and every day, they suffered injustices at the hands of a society whose norms were defined by men, for men.

On the other hand, there would be a redefinition by feminists of what women were and what they wanted to be. The domestic image of women, as defined in the nineteenth century, would be ceaselessly contradicted in the daily lives of twentieth-century women.

NOTES

1 Fadette, *Journal d'Henriette Dessaulles 1874-1880* (Montreal: Editions Hurtubise HMH, 1971), p. 82.

2 Miss E. Binmore, "Financial Outlook of the Woman Teachers of Montreal, Quebec, March 1893," quoted in R. Cook and W. Mitchinson, *The Proper Sphere, Woman's Place in Canadian Society* (Toronto: Oxford University Press, 1976).

3 *Education Quebec,* vol. 11, no. 1, p. 30.

4 *La Minerve,* 29 October 1832, quoted in E. Nadeau, *La Femme au coeur attentif Mère Gamelin* (Montreal: Editions Providence, 1969).

5 Letter from Julie Bruneau to L.-J. Papineau, November 1835, in *Rapport de l'Archiviste de la Province de Québec,* nos. 38-39.

6 Raymond Boyer, *Les Crimes et les Châtiments au Canada français* (Montreal: Le Cercle du livre de France, 1966), pp. 477, 482.

7 *Entre Amis,* Letters of P. Louis Lalande s.j. to His Friend Arthur Prévost (Montreal: Imprimerie du Sacré-Coeur, 1907), p. 273.

8 Letter from the Abbé Gendron, 6 June 1887, quoted in Marguerite Jean, *L'Evolution des communautés religieuses de femmes au Canada de 1639 à nos jours* (Montreal: Fides, 1978), note 23, pp. 136-137.

9 Marguerite Jean, *L'Evolution des communautés religieuses de femmes au Canada de 1639 à nos jours* (Montreal: Fides, 1978), p. 136.

10 Letter from Julie Bruneau to L.-J. Papineau, 9 March 1829, op. cit.

11 A. Beaulieu and J. Hamelin, *Les Journaux du Québec de 1764 à 1964* (Quebec: P.U.L., 1965), p. 75.

FURTHER READING

Bradbury, Bettina. "The Family Economy and Work in an Industrializing City; Montreal in the 1870s" in *H.P./Ch.* Ottawa: CHA, 1979, pp. 71-96.

Cleverdon, C. L. *The Woman Suffrage Movement in Canada.* Toronto: University of Toronto Press, 1950, 1974.

Cross, Suzanne D. "La majorité oubliée: le rôle des femmes à Montreal au XIXe siècle" in Marie Lavigne et Yolande Pinard, *Les Femmes dans la société québécoise, aspects historiques.* Montreal: Boréal-Express, 1977.

Dumont-Johnson, Micheline. "Des garderies au XIXe siècle: les salles d'asile des Soeurs Grises à Montréal" in *R.H.A.F.,* 34.1, 1980, pp. 27-56.

Danylewycz, Marta. "Changing Relationships: Nuns and Feminists in Montreal, 1890-1925" in *Social History*, XIV, 28, 1981, pp. 413-434.

Falardeau, J. C. and P. Garigue, eds. *Léon Gérin et l'Habitant de Saint-Justin*. Montreal: Presses de l'Université de Montréal, 1968.

Gaffield, Chad M. "Canadian Families in Cultural Context: Hypotheses from Midnineteenth Century" in *H.P./Ch.* Ottawa: CHA, 1979, pp. 48-70.

Hamelin, Jean and Yves Roby. *Histoire économique du Quebec 1851-1896*. Montreal: Fides, 1971.

Henripin, Jacques. *Tendances et facteurs de la fécondité au Canada*. Ottawa: B.F.S., 1968.

Jean, Marguerite. *L'Evolution des communautés religieuses de femmes au Canada de 1639 à nos jours*. Montreal: Fides, 1978.

Lacelle, Claudette. "Les Domestiques dans les villes canadiennes au X1Xe siècle: effectifs et conditions de vie" in *Social History*, XV, 29, 1982, pp. 181-208.

Linteau, Paul André, René Durocher and Jean Claude-Robert, *Histoire du Quebec contemporain, De la Confédération à la Crise*. Montreal: Boréal-Express, 1979, parts 1 and 2.

McLaren, Angus. "Birth Control and Abortion in Canada 1870-1920" in *Canadian Historical Review*, IX, 3, 1978.

Ouellet, Fernand. *Histoire économique et sociale du Québec 1760-1850*. Ottawa: Fides, 1966.

Prentice, Alison. "The Feminization of Teaching" in S. Mann Trofimenkoff and Alison Prentice, *The Neglected Majority. Essays in Canadian Women's History*. Toronto: McClelland and Stewart, 1977.

Reeves-Morache, Marcelle. *Les Québecoises de 1837-1838*. Montreal: Editions Coopératives Albert Saint-Martin, 1975.

Séguin, Normand. *La Conquête du sol au X1Xe siècle*. Montreal: Boréal-Express, 1977.

Stoddart, Jennifer and Veronica Strong-Boag. "And Things Were Going Wrong at Home" in *Atlantis*, 1, 1, 1975, pp. 38-44.

Trofimenkoff, Susan Mann. "One Hundred and Two Muffled Voices: Canada's Industrial Women in the 1880s" in *Atlantis*, 3, 1, 1977, pp. 66-83.

Women of Canada, Their Life and Work. Compiled by National Council of Women of Canada for the Paris International Exhibition, 1900; reissued 1975.

IV
CONTRADICTIONS
1900-1940

THE FIRST DECADES of the twentieth century were the golden age of capitalism, punctuated by World War One and the devastation of middle-class dreams in the crash of 1929. During these years, North America experienced unprecedented industrial growth. In Quebec, there were various reactions to the changes. One ideological faction favoured development; another opposed it.

Exploitation of natural resources brought about the growth of new industrial sectors. There was massive development in the hydroelectric and pulp-and-paper industries. Textiles, clothing and food continued to dominate the manufacturing industry. Business mergers transformed financial structures and led to the creation of huge production and sales conglomerates, such as Dominion Textile in 1905 and Wabasso in 1907; the construction of the dam at Shawinigan around 1900; and the first electric paper mill in Saguenay-Lac-Saint-Jean, founded by William Price. Workers unionized in an attempt to gain greater collective strength.

The Depression, which was triggered by the stock-market crash of 24 October 1929, put the brakes on growth by severely reducing exports and curtailing business and industrial activity. At the end of 1929, the unemployment rate in Quebec was around 15 percent. By 1931, it had reached nearly 20 percent and at the beginning of 1933, it was more than 30 percent.

There was considerable change in the demography of Quebec during this time. The population grew by 107 percent, from 1,560,000 in 1896 to 3,230,000 in 1939. This was due in part to natural growth but also reflected increased immigration.

Rapid urbanization was changing the face of Quebec: at the turn of the century, one Québécois in three lived in the countryside; In 1931, nearly 60 percent of Québécois were living in urban centres. Montreal, where more than half the urban population lived, and Quebec City were the most populous centres; but several new towns sprang up as well, particularly in northern Quebec. The urbanization of the north was closely linked to the exploitation of natural resources: new towns grew up around pulp-and-paper mills and chemical and electrometalurgical plants in regions such as Mauricie and Saguenay-Lac-Saint-Jean.

Emigration to urban centres changed family life and created new social needs: the urban poor and elderly had to be looked after. The need for a better-trained work force for the new industries brought about educational reforms. Unemployment caused by the Depression exacerbated social problems.

Settlement of new areas in Quebec continued. At the turn of the century, regions such as Lac-Saint-Jean, the Outaouais, Témiscaming, the Lower St. Lawrence and the Gaspé Peninsula experienced considerable growth. During the Depression, attempts at large-scale settlement in the Abitibi region had been made; however, during the Thirties, the creation of new settlements became more intensive and systematic, with greater government involvement than in previous decades. More than two hundred thousand people moved from towns and cities to the countryside or were given aid to stay on the land. But the movement, which had been instigated by the clergy and the government, was largely articificial and many families soon returned to their cities or villages.

Textile mills in New England continued to attract men, women and children. At the beginning of the twentieth century, many people were still leaving Quebec, but they comprised a smaller percentage of the total population than those who emigrated at the end of the nineteenth century. The exodus ended in October 1930, when only those with visas were permitted to enter the United States.

At the beginning of the century, Jews from eastern Europe, Italians and Germans arrived en masse in Quebec: between 1901 and 1931, the non-French, non-British population of Quebec increased by 500 percent. Nearly all these new immigrants settled in Montreal, as had the British, who remained the largest non-French ethnic group, even though between 1901 and 1931 Quebeckers of British heritage fell from 17.6 percent to 15 percent of the total population.

At the turn of the century, the Quebec government began to take on aspects of its present structure. It became more interventionist and began to regulate economic and social life. As a result, the fears of the clergy were awakened. The administrative structure of the government was put in place during the long tenure of Premier Louis-Alexandre Taschereau. Maurice Duplessis, leader of the Conservative Party, made an alliance with the Action libérale nationale to found the Union nationale which was elected in 1936.

However, Duplessis was defeated in 1939 and the Liberal Party, led by Adélard Godbout, came to power.

In documents of the period, Francophone Quebec still depicted itself as "eternally beseiged," writes historian Richard Jones. "However," he adds, "we must not forget that it was a small élite, largely made up of clergy and men from the liberal professions who had been educated in the classical colleges run by the Church who produced this literature." But was this élite representative of men and women? It is doubtful. Nevertheless, attacks by these intellectuals against the English, Protestants, Americans, Jews, Bolsheviks and feminists did influence the masses. Fearing "threats" to traditional social order – agriculture, Catholicism, and the French language, the very bases of Francophone Quebec identity – some Québécois hesitated between choosing a different social structure and keeping their traditions.

Nevertheless, one element of the Francophone élite and the majority of Anglophones did not accept the views of this reactionary group; hence, tensions and contradictions emerged in the nationalist movement.

The conflict between the forces of change and the forces of established order affected the lives and thinking of women. In a Quebec that was modernizing, the early 1900s were rife with contradiction, and some conservatives were rapidly losing touch with reality. The role of women became the subject of considerable discussion; no doubt, society was ambivalent about changes in the lives of women, dubbed the *gardiennes de la race* (guardians of the race).

Industrialization had been growing in Quebec since the mid-nineteenth century. It continued to demand cheap female labour, which was exploited mostly in sectors where capitalism was thriving – clothing, textiles, tobacco, offices, the retail business and the food industry – and in those sectors dominated by the clergy – education, health care and social work.

In a society that viewed poverty as the fault of the victim and in which people were led to believe that if they wanted something badly enough they would get it, hundreds of women were called upon to alleviate the misery caused by the growth of capitalism and its sudden decline during the Depression. Urged on by the clergy and doctors, women signed up by the thousands to "fight poverty." Many were bourgeois women, imbued with a reformist and liberal ideology and encouraged by the teachings of the papal encyclicals *Rerum novarum* (1891), *Casti connubbi* (1930) and *Quadragesimo anno* (1931), or nuns, who found in their work a means to express their altruism and intellectual potential.

During the early twentieth century, workers, owners and women all over the industrialized world attempted to organize. By organizing, and making demands as a group they achieved some success. Women workers, bourgeois women and farm women united. Some fought for better working conditions, thereby starting the process of determining their status in society; others committed themselves to the struggle for basic rights, particularly the right to vote. In addressing these issues, they joined other feminists who were already fighting in other countries.

CHAPTER EIGHT

MODERN WOMEN

EMULATING MOMMY AND GRANDMA

DURING THE EARLY TWENTIETH century, every little girl learned from her mother her role as a woman – the basics of housework. In this respect, life had not changed since the beginning of New France.

As school attendance was not compulsory, it was not uncommon for urban working-class girls of ten to fourteen years to be responsible for looking after younger siblings while their mother was at work. How many such girls there were is difficult to estimate, because there are no statistics on these invisible working women. In addition, the sickness or death of a mother often left quite young girls to head up a family.

When a young woman had to make a decision about her future, there were only two acceptable choices: marriage or the convent. Women who chose neither were ridiculed and criticized by society for being selfish. But these women often had no choice but to look after their families and help support them.

There is very little period documentation on courtship and women's sexuality; however, we do know that in rural Quebec practical concerns were still as important as romance. A man would look for a girl who would be a capable housekeeper; a girl was often advised by her parents to marry a fine, respectable, hard-working young man.

The recruitment of spouses for isolated settlers harks back, in some ways, to the King's Daughters. A monograph describing life in the village of Guérin explains how arranged courtships were undertaken: "The priests who recruited the settlers were also responsible for recruiting young spouses. In Témiscamingue, they provided spouses by recruiting female teachers." The teachers often discovered on their arrival in newly settled areas that they had

"Oh! ... don't be silly! Romantic love ... will it put bread on the table? In any case, as for me, I have given up on romantic love! If I weren't shut up in here all year long I might meet a fine fellow from around here who is hardworking and not a drinker. If I did I would be tempted to spend the rest of my days with him. Everything else, like romantic love, is nothing but codswallop. What we women need is a man who can give us something to put in the pot. The rest we'll take care of, bringing up children, cooking, keeping the house clean."[1]

been tricked; they had been recruited to marry a settler rather than to teach.

In cities, it was becoming increasingly common for young women to marry for love and to reject unappealing suitors. One unmarried woman who was born in 1890 and worked in textile mills all her life recounts: "Away from home and here, I have suitors; but if I am to get married, it must be for love, but those I love don't approach me and those who approach me don't interest me; that's why I am still unmarried. You can tell the young girls today that you can't make me believe that in my day all the girls stayed at home with their parents and waited for their prince charming. There were some like me who had some independence." No one was going to force this woman into marriage with a man she did not like!

The modernization of Quebec society was gaining momentum. The invasion of the radio, the development of retail commerce and the availability of ready-to-wear clothes, the arrival of capital investment in Quebec, together with American fashions and the increased mobility that came with the automobile, put women in contact with new ideas and new trends.

Whether they were middle class, working class or armed-forces personnel, women were influenced by what was happening in the United States and aspired to a more modern way of life. The clergy and civil authorities, scandalized by women's preoccupation with change, condemned the new ideas but were unable to curb the enthusiasm the ideas aroused. Girls were criticized for wearing nail polish, plucking their eyebrows, wearing lipstick, smoking cigarettes and drinking cocktails – all accessible to those with some income.

World War One brought about important changes in women's clothing. Dresses became straighter and shorter. Clothes were standardized and fashion was dominated by styles from London, Paris and New York, especially during the Twenties. Silk stockings, wavy hair, shorts, knickers and beach pajamas were hot topics in fashion magazines: women had to look sexy. American women invented the word "flapper" to describe the new style, and many women thought female emancipation had peaked. Indeed, the flappers paved the way for the achievement of the feminist objective of liberating women from the cumbersome clothing of the nineteenth century in favour of comfortable clothes that were attractive and allowed for freedom of movement. However, many such changes simply established a new set of norms for women to follow: women who had been expected to look pure, were now invited to look sexy. Cosmetics sales boomed.

Quebec women were enjoying themselves immensely on the beaches, at dances and on Sunday outings. The conservative Catholic clergy appealed to French-Canadian mothers, warning them, for example, that it was unsuitable and even dangerous for male instructors to teach swimming to females. But the clergy's authority carried less and less weight.

This Anglo-Americanism is also attempting to create a kind of standardized woman in French Canada. The cinema, magazines, newspapers, and even the music borrowed from the Americans are influencing the soul of the French-Canadian woman and go against her hereditary traits. The passionate interest of our sisters in the thrill of new experiences, their habit of eating hot-dogs, tomato sandwiches and tinned food, their predilection for the excitement of jazz music, cocktails and emotionally-charged films, their often reckless undertakings, their fascination with the larger than life and the fake, as well as their way of looking like emancipated women are the consequences of American influences that are slowly changing their ethnic character.[2]

Sports became an increasingly large part of women's lives. Tennis, skiing, canoeing and swimming were practised especially by young, middle-class women, who had the time and the money for such activities. However, there were few team sports for Francophone girls.

The precarious financial situation of many families, the rapid dissemination of new ideas through developments in communications, and the influx of immigrants shook up established ways of life and undermined traditional models for women. Even though the roles of wife and mother, and even of nun, would be dominant for a long time, women had new aspirations. In the decades to come, political activism and speeches by women would be marked by ambivalence and contradictions – the clash between old and new roles for women in Quebec society. Céline Beaudet has made a study of the newspaper *Radio-Monde,* which first appeared in January 1939. The newspaper dealt with artistic life in Quebec and conceded to women "the right to have a professional life and to show ambition in their work, as long as they preserve the attributes of the ordinary woman i.e. those of housewife and mother. A woman's sphere of activity is love, marriage and the home, a man's is the work place."

LARGE FAMILIES: A DISAPPEARING SPECIES

The birthrate had begun to fall off in the second half of the nineteenth century, and the trend continued into the twentieth century. In fact, by around 1940, Quebec women would have an average of three children.

But the myth of the large family would persist for several decades. Many people would continue to think all Quebec women had ten or twelve children. Of married women born around 1887, 20.5 percent gave birth to more than ten children – more than half the children born to Quebec women of this 1887 generation came from large families, but producing these large families would be the fate of only one Quebec woman in five.

Of married women born between 1916 and 1921, only 7.6 percent would have more than ten children. These children made up 24.3 percent of all children born in the period. In the next generation, women born between 1922 and 1926, only 3.5 percent of married women would have more than ten children and 19.2 percent more than six. A very high percentage of Quebec children were born to rural women. Of married women in Quebec, 40 percent had only one or two children, or none at all. Coitus interruptus was generally used to limit the size of families, but the use of condoms and diaphragms was becoming widespread.

When a baby was due, the children in the family were told that a gypsy known as *le sauvage* would bring a baby to their mother and try to give it to her. If she refused it, he would force her to take the child and would break her leg, which explained why she was bedridden. Sociologist Horace Miner interprets the mother's refusal to take the child as women's fear of the long-lasting aftereffects of pregnancy, adding that it was mostly husbands who wanted large families.

During the Thirties, the presence of women in the work force was often attributed to Americanization and birth control. In 1935, Dr. Joseph Gauvreau wrote: "Propaganda about free and barren unions was spread the most actively amongst women factory workers. Surreptitiously but systematically, campaigns for sterility and sterilization by artificial rays were launched. And something unheard of until now, we have seen in our homeland a considerable drop in the birthrate."

In *Trente Arpents* (Thirty Acres), by Ringuet, a Quebec farmer receives a visit from his American cousin, who has only two children. The farmer asks his cousin if his wife is sick. When the cousin says no, that he quite simply does not want a large family, the farmer replies: "But you can't do just what you want in these matters." The American retorts: "Damn it! My wife and I decided to put the brakes on...." The farmer concludes that it must be "one of those monstrous practices that the priest had spoken of at the retreat for men, the aim of which is to prevent God's will from being carried out." "Women will not be able to give themselves over to the pursuit of pleasure and take on the responsibilities of motherhood at the same time."

The Eastview trial (1936) provides some interesting information on the practice of birth control. Eastview, now called Vanier, was a French-Canadian suburb of Ottawa. In 1936, 17.6 percent of the town's families lived on social assistance and 71 percent of the population was Catholic. Dorothea A. Palmer, a nurse who worked for the Parents' Information Bureau of Kitchener, visited large families to distribute contraceptive devices and a brochure, which described a dozen contraceptive methods. In 1936, she was arrested for violation of the Criminal Code, which forbade sale or promotion of contraceptive devices.

The trial opened with the evidence of twenty-one women visited by nurse Palmer, all except one, Francophone and Catholic. They had received in the mail from the Parents' Information Bureau a box containing three condoms and a tube of contraceptive jelly, as well as a brochure in French entitled *Le contrôle de la natalité et quelques-unes de ses méthodes les plus simples* (Birth Control and a Few of the Simplest Methods). They were told that they could continue to obtain these products, but that those who could afford it had to pay. When questioned by the Crown Prosecutor, with two or three exceptions, witnesses answered that they saw nothing wrong with contraception.

The trial also put French-Canadian men in the witness box. Of these, only a social worker said that he was in favour of contraception. Doctor J. E. Haître, who was opposed to contraception, admitted, when cross-examined by the defence, that the abortion rate was high and that abortion could be avoided if contraceptives were used.

The star witness for the Crown was Doctor Léon Gérin-Lajoie, professor of gynaecology at the Université de Montréal and son of feminist Marie Gérin-Lajoie. He believed that too much medical information was given to the public, and stated that no contraceptive method should be practised without medical supervision. The Church's rules concerning contraception were strict and the encyclical *Casti connubii,* which was published in 1930, explicitly forbade contraception. This notwithstanding, during the trial doctors admitted that the Catholic ideal was not always easy to uphold. Under cross-examination, Doctor Gérin-Lajoie agreed.

Q: Do you think the mother should wait until doctors study this out to get unanimous ... and when doctors have established it, a clinic can come along, is that your idea?
A: No.
Q: What will the poor mother do in the meantime?
A: See her doctor.
Q: Not you?
A: Yes, on the contrary; you would be surprised.

Dorothea Palmer, who could have been sent to prison for two years, was acquitted on the grounds that her work in promoting contraception had the public interest at heart.

Shortly after the trial, a nurse with the Parents' Information Bureau began working in Montreal. Léa Roback, who was organizing dressmakers in Montreal, took the nurse to visit working-class families she knew. According to Roback, "the nurse was very conscientious. She explained to the women how to put in the diaphragm. But most of the husbands gave us a very poor reception. We visited 15 families and succeeded only three times in giving the demonstration. The nurse was very surprised that the husbands had so much authority and that they were so determined to prevent their wives from limiting the size of the family. She decided to discontinue her visits because she did not want to cause trouble, especially since the Eastview trial had been very controversial."

In the countryside, it was still common practice for women to give birth at home with the help of a doctor or midwife. Doctors were often far away and roads impassable in winter, but there was always a female neighbour who could help deliver the baby. A woman from the Lower St. Lawrence area wrote: "Not all women were qualified to practise this profession. The essential quality was the ability to remain calm.... A woman from the family or a neighbour would have to assist the midwife. The husband was almost always away working at logging camps or elsewhere; in any case, he felt that he didn't belong there, as delivering babies was women's business." But this women's business, which was unpaid, had already become almost exclusively men's business in the towns, where women giving birth were attended by male doctors.

Hélène Laforce, who has studied the history of midwifery, shows that medical intervention gradually excluded women from the profession that had belonged to them. For doctors in the towns, the financial advantage of delivering babies was long-term: each baby was a potential patient. The public resisted the doctors and, in 1919, a petition by the inhabitants of the village of Sacré-Coeur, in the Saguenay region, defended midwives who had been taken to court by the Professional Corporation of Physicians. Laforce notes that a small number of midwives continued to practise but that with the introduction of medical insurance women began having their babies in hospitals.

1914-1918: WORLD WAR ONE
AND THE GROWTH OF NEW ATTITUDES

World War One did not drastically change the role of women in the work force. The increased number of women in the job market during the war was part of a trend that had begun at the turn of the century and would continue to the present day. Nevertheless, World War One did bring about a sudden if temporary increase in women workers, some occupational changes, and some changes in attitudes toward young women in the work force.

Conscription was not introduced until the end of the war, so there was no great demand for female labour. Historian Ceta Ramkhalawasingh points out that unmarried women occupied most of the new jobs. At this time, there was an important, fundamental change in attitude toward "working girls." It became acceptable for women to work before marriage, especially as their wages were needed by their families to buy consumer goods that had formerly been produced at home. It was also recognized that women could take on certain jobs for which they had previously been considered physically incapable.

In 1919, Enid Price published a study of the effects of World War One on women's work in Montreal. She visited munitions factories, railway-related industries, wholesalers, stores and so on, and concluded that women who worked in industry were given heavier jobs during the war than before it. For example, in the railway industry, during the war women were given the traditionally male jobs of building and repairing locomotives and cars. In 1918, in Montreal, 2,315 women were employed by the railway, steel and cement industries in jobs that had been previously filled by men. At the height of the war, there were thirty-five thousand women in the munitions industry in Montreal and in Ontario; most of them had come from other manufacturing sectors. Although there was little change in the make-up of the work force in factories not involved in the war effort, the war did provide more opportunities for women to replace men in office jobs and clerical positions.

Ramkhalawasingh notes that a woman in the arms industry received between 50 and 80 percent of a man's wages. Price says that, between 1914 and 1918, salaries paid to female office clerks ranged from 10 to 60 percent of that of men. During the war, the wage gap shrank, reducing the enormous inequities, if not eliminating them.

At the end of the war, many women faced unemployment as a result of a reduction in war production and the return of men to sectors which had hired women to replace them. The increase in female unemployment confirms the theory that women form a reservoir of cheap labour to be manipulated as economic crises come and go.

PULLING THROUGH IN BAD TIMES

In October 1929, the New York Stock Market collapsed, plunging the world into a recession that was to last until the end of the Thirties.

The Depression profoundly affected women's lives. High unemployment, wage cuts, the difficulties of getting married and of finding food, shelter and clothing forced many women to take on extra domestic work.

Unemployment in Quebec rose from 15 percent at the end of 1929 to 20 percent in 1931 and 30 percent at the beginning of 1933. Many women had to find work to make ends meet and to compensate for their husband's lack of work. Ruth Milkman states that the theory that women constitute a reserve labour force does not hold, particularly in a period of recession. She notes that the effect of a division of labour by gender, at least in the United States during the Depression, was that women lost their jobs less quickly than did men because men's jobs were more greatly affected by the recession. However, as the recession grew worse, women also lost their jobs. Moreover, as more women had entered the work force, the official rate of female unemployment increased. Milkman's research demonstrates that, contrary to popular belief, women did not occupy jobs that could have been filled by men.

In spite of attempts at the turn of the century to redefine the role of women in Quebec society, attitudes regressed during the postwar period and the Depression. Demands by the labour movement to protect working women – a guaranteed minimum wage, mother's allowances, regular working hours and increased security were resolutions passed at annual meetings of union centrals – were rejected, particularly by the new Canadian Catholic Confederation of Labour. Instead women workers were denounced for taking jobs away from "poor fathers with families to feed." Such antipathy peaked with the introduction of the Francoeur Bill in the provincial legislature in 1935. It decreed "that women and girls looking for a job will have to prove they really need one." The bill proposed that women be restricted to working on farms or as cooks and domestic servants. The bill was defeated by a vote of forty-seven to sixteen, but it illustrates the state of mind of a society split between conservative Catholic and liberal ideologies.

When describing the work they did during the Depression, women list cleaning houses, taking in boarders, serving meals and searching for inexpensive lodgings.

"I noticed I had mended my husband's pants seven times. People better off than us passed along their children's clothes to us. For two years, I would take the clothes off the children's backs, wash them and put them back on," said a housewife who lived through the Depression.

Another noted: "We ate a lot of baloney.... We made baked beans, we got to the point where we were just surviving."[3]

WHEN SCIENCE GETS INVOLVED: HEALTH AND CHARITY

The systematic organization of health and charitable services continued in the wake of the urban-reform movement. Those sectors in which the medical profession was gaining a firmer grip were rapidly invaded by the scientific approach. Women still played a major role in providing social services, either as lay reformists in goodwill associations or as nuns working in institutions. The goodwill associations were comprised mostly of bourgeois women and were created to relieve urban poverty. They were formed by individuals or at the suggestion of a church, religious community, or *médecins-hygiénistes* (public health doctors), whose power increased considerably during this time.

Women were working zealously in many areas: orphanages, homes, nurseries, hospitals, hostels, shelters, youth clubs, sewing rooms, libraries, parish halls and devotional groups. Nevertheless, Catholic organizations remained under the control of the clergy through its chaplains or religious counselors, whose approval or disapproval could affect the success of an initiative. The charitable activities of Protestant women were also strongly influenced by religion and the women worked in close consultation with the churches. However, the organizations were less hierarchical than those under the auspices of the Catholic Church. Protestant women had more autonomy as the pastor, unlike the Catholic chaplain, did not assume direct control of the women's activities.

There were many social problems, and, despite a more systematic organization of charity, measures were insufficient to combat effectively the misery caused by urban squalor and the polluted environment, and the low wages of most people who lived in the cities.

Montreal had the highest death rate of any big city in the West, and there would be no significant improvement until after the war. Between 1900 and 1929, infant mortality was responsible for 12.6 to 17 percent of all deaths in Quebec. Infant mortality was highest in poor urban areas: from 1910 to 1915, 78,000 children under one year old died in Quebec.

Poor quality milk and water was the major cause of death from what was known as "infantile diarrhoea." A water-purification plant was opened in Montreal in 1914 but pasteurization of milk did not become widespread until 1926; in 1914, only 25 percent of the milk consumed in Montreal was pasteurized. (Large dairies distributed it to well-to-do areas in the west end of the city.)

This situation alarmed doctors concerned about hygiene; they urged mothers to breast-feed their babies rather than feed them contaminated milk.

According to historian Claudine Pierre-Deschênes, doctors belonging to the Conseil d'hygiène de la province de Québec, founded in 1887, launched a popular-education campaign. Between 1895 and 1914, their crusades reinforced the power of the medical profession. To overcome the difficulty of reaching working-class women, doctors recruited bourgeois women convinced of the merit of their positon. A leaflet prepared by the Conseil d'hygiène entitled *Sauvons nos petits enfants. Appel aux mères* (Let's Save Our Children. Appeal to Mothers) was given to every new mother when she registered the birth of her child. It promoted breast-feeding and infant hygiene, and included advice on growth, teething, washing, clothing and diet.

A number of organizations were devoted to *les Veillées des berceaux* (Watching over the Cradle): the Gouttes de lait (Drops of Milk), the Ligue des petites mères (Young Mothers' League), the Garderie de nourrissons (Infant Nursery), the Day Nursery, the Baby Welfare Committee and the Fédération nationale Saint-Jean-Baptiste. Prenatal work, which was being practised in the United States, was introduced into Quebec. Usually doctors directed the organizations, while women did the work, usually unpaid. In the Twenties, the campaign against infant mortality began to produce results. As science developed, formalized information about childbirth, infant hygiene and breast-feeding no longer came from women: men produced the knowledge and women applied it.

As hygiene and charity were professionalized, patriarchal control over women's activities in these two sectors increased. At the turn of the century, according to Pierre Dechênes, we see the beginnings of the growth of biopower – the control and exploitation of the human body. Hygiene became an important socio-political issue, a means of control and of influencing behaviour. Women did not speak about looking after their own health and taking posssession of their bodies until the Seventies.

The Charities Organization Society, organized in Montreal in 1900, and the Montreal Council of Social Agencies, created in 1919, attempted to coordinate work done by charitable organizations and give them a more scientific and professional image. However, the Charities Organization Society did not become an umbrella for the Francophone groups; the Saint-Vincent-de-Paul continued to work independently. Moreover, the program was only superficial. The new organizations did not attack the roots of poverty, which they continued to see as a problem of individuals rather than as a social phenomenon resulting from unemployment and low wages.

Women and men believed they should approach their good works more scientifically. The very nature of charity was changing. Women realized that, if they wanted to be taken seriously, they would have to meet scientific criteria for personnel training, hygiene and record keeping.

Their concerns led to the creation of a new profession in Quebec and North America: social work. Two women who led very different lives were pioneers in the profession early in the century: an Anglophone, Bella Hall-Gould, and a Francophone, Marie Gérin-Lajoie (daughter of the feminist of the same name). Born in Ontario in 1878, Hall-Gould moved to Manitoba in 1882. She studied music at the turn of the century in Germany, where she was exposed to the gulf between the poverty of the masses and the wealth of the privileged class. When she returned to Canada, she worked with immigrants and went to Winnipeg to work with J. S. Woodsworth, a Protestant minister who founded the Co-operative Commonwealth Federation (CCF). Hall-Gould realized that she needed special training to work with immigrants and, in 1912, she enrolled in the social-science program at the University of Toronto. Around 1915, on the recommendation of Woodsworth, she accepted the position of director of the Montreal University Settlement, established by women graduates of McGill University. The settlement was a social project that provided women from poor neighbourhoods with a place to have a cup of tea and a snack, to rest and relax. Hall-Gould gradually dissociated herself from this kind of charitable work, however, and concentrated on Marxism and Marxist activism (praxis) among male and female workers and the unemployed.

Marie Gérin-Lajoie convinced her mother that she should remain single so she would be free of family responsibilities and able to devote herself to social work. According to historian Marcienne Proulx, her spiritual adviser encouraged her to found a community that would enable her to organize social work in Montreal. In 1923, the Institut des soeurs Notre-Dame-du-Bon-Conseil de Montréal was set up. Gérin-Lajoie found it difficult to found an institute outside a religious context, and it was difficult for Francophone women, no matter how educated, to step beyond the role of volunteer worker and make a career in social action.

The government was encouraged by doctors and charitable organizations to increase its involvement, to regulate sanitary conditions and to assist the most destitute. In spite of several initiatives at the beginning of the century, such as the introduction of compulsory smallpox vaccination in 1903, it was not until the Thirties that government intervention became significant.

A number of organizations were founded by middle-class women concerned about the poverty of mothers in working-class neighbourhoods. Wives of business or professional men participated in industrial and financial development. Caroline Béique, Marie Gérin-Lajoie and many others used the free time afforded them by their wealth to help other women. In 1912, seeing that there was no help for mothers in need, Caroline Leclerc Hamilton founded the Assistance maternelle, to help mothers of poor families. "Sickly, heavily burdened with children and responsibilities, they bring into the world, into destitution and anguish, other children who will only have the effect of once again bringing about this whole existence of misery and poverty."

The activities of the Assistance maternelle exemplify how charitable work enabled women to put their organizational skills to use under the watchful eye of the Church and the medical profession. They tried to assist poor mothers before, during and after giving birth. Parish committees were organized, made up of volunteers and supervised by doctors and nurses. They provided medical advice, layettes, clothing, bedding, food and fuel. The Assistance maternelle was affiliated with the Saint-Vincent-de-Paul and the Sainte-Justine hospital. In 1936, the organization assisted 4,294 women and their babies.

In 1897, Georgiane and Léontine Généreux and Aglaée Laberge founded the Sacré-Coeur hospital for the disabled and for people with cancer. In 1908, Justine Lacoste-Beaubien, wife of lawyer and banker Louis de Gaspé Beaubien, founded the Sainte-Justine hospital. Appalled by the high rate of infant mortality amongst French-Canadians and by the lack of space in Catholic hospitals – where children under five were refused admittance – Doctor Irma Levasseur, the first woman doctor in Quebec, requested that a committee be formed to discuss the Sainte-Justine project. On the first honorary committee were some well-known women from the upper classes of Montreal: Caroline Béique, wife of Frédéric Liguori Béique, who was reported by the *Montreal Star* in 1911 to be a millionaire; Josephine Dandurand, wife of Senator Raoul

Dandurand; Marie Thibaudeau, wife of Rosaire Thibaudeau, a senator and businessman involved in commerce, finance and the railways; Madame Leman, wife of Beaudry Leman, general manager of the Banque Canadienne Nationale; and Marie Gérin-Lajoie, wife of lawyer Henri Gérin-Lajoie.

The hospital clinic was set up in January 1908 and its dispensaries were opened in March. Nurses' training courses and maternity courses began shortly afterward. Like their predecessors, who had founded hostels fifty years earlier, the women had to petition the Quebec legislature to waive their legal incapacity to control the hospital. With governmental dispensation, they could form a corporation. Following their legal battles, according to Thaïs Lacoste, secretary to the hospital, they "emerged victorious from a little campaign which had been mounted against us women, who wanted the greatest freedom to work as efficiently as possible at our beloved charity and by the gentlemen who, jealously guarding their rights, were not prepared unless they were begged a little, to share them with us ... even for charity."

Assistance for mothers was traditionally provided by other mothers, especially during delivery and the first months of the child's life. Women have always shown concern for and helped other women in childbirth. However, even bourgeois women often had very little money to fund their charitable work. Most of the time, they found it difficult to continue projects they had launched, and the projects were eventually taken over by religious communities or by the State.

The history of the Gouttes de lait is a good example. These pediatric centres, which were set up to provide information to mothers and to distribute good-quality milk, were not supported by a government grant until 1922. In 1935, Dr. Joseph Gauvreau addressed a conference held to celebrate the twenty-fifth anniversary of the founding of the Gouttes de lait. In his address, he praised Monseigneur Le Pailleur, who had founded the organization in the parish of Saint-Enfant-Jésus in 1910. He recalled "that a similar attempt had been made on Ontario Street between 5 July and 24 November 1901, under the patronage of the newspaper *La Patrie,* which had been prompted by its women contributors, Madeleine (Madame Huguenin) and Madame L.-G. Beaubien (Justine Lacoste). Therefore, the true founders of the Gouttes de lait were women!" Dr. Gauvreau described the work done by Monseigneur Le Pailleur and stressed the indispensable role played by the doctors; he also praised the secondary but very effective, "even indispensable" role of the mothers themselves, the patronesses and the nurses.

In Gauvreau's opinion, nurses and patronesses were effective educators, but training required more than "the charms of seduction. There has to be confidence." Clearly only doctors could instil such confidence. Women were "signed up" by Monseigneur Le Pailleur to help organize services for the physically and morally destitute and the monseigneur attended "society events" to seek support for these services.

Who were the women who founded the Gouttes de lait? We know very little about them. Dr. Gauvreau mentioned only a few of the volunteer nurses. We do know, however, that the first and most dedicated was Madame Labelle, the sexton's wife. She was probably responsible for the success of the organization, but she received very little recognition for her work.

Those who had worked long and hard to bring about a new sharing of responsibilities in health and charitable work in Quebec saw their efforts rewarded when the Quebec Public Charities Act was passed in 1921 and the Quebec Old Age Pensions Act was adopted in 1936. (The Old-age Pensions Act had been passed in 1927 by the federal government.) According to historian Terry Copp, the two laws represented a compromise that enabled the Quebec government to regulate and plan while taking full advantage of the existing network of charitable organizations. Women who had worked in charitable organizations moved from a religious structure to a state-run structure. In the transition, they lost the power that had been theirs when they had administered the religious communities. The shift from religious to state control in the Thirties and Forties anticipated the Quiet Revolution, when health and girls' education would be taken out of the control of nuns.

The Quebec state did not begin to take over charitable work until 1937, when it passed a law providing assistance to needy mothers; until then, charitable work had been left to private individuals. Early in the Thirties, the Quebec Social Insurance Commission (the Montpetit Commission) recommended that the Quebec government adopt a law for needy mothers, as seven provinces had done at the request of doctors, feminists and social workers, who believed that such a law would help reinforce family unity and prevent infant mortality and juvenile delinquency. Feminists held that a mother could run a family even if she were alone, although more conservative elements in society maintained that a woman could not be independent and must be given help if her husband died. The commission pointed out that a mother in need could not count on the income provided by a job or on the social assistance provided by institutions; nor could she survive solely on private charity. The commission urged the government to help mothers with at least one child under sixteen, mothers whose husbands were dead, interned in an institution or disabled, needy mothers with good morals, British subjects and resident in Quebec for at least three years. Separated and divorced mothers, women whose husbands were in prison and new immigrants were to be excluded.

Quebec was one of the last provinces to adopt such a law. (A similar law had existed in the United States since 1911 and in Manitoba since 1916.) The legislation, which provided a form of salary for mothers, marked the beginning of social security in Canada. According to historian Veronica Strong-Boag, it was a major turning point for child welfare in Canada. The supporters of the law emphasized the importance of the family unit as the best environment in which to raise a child. This marked a break with past practice, which had emphasized orphanages and hostels.

Introduced by Premier Maurice Duplessis in 1937, the Quebec law was even more restrictive than that proposed by the Montpetit Commission. It stipulated that, to receive assistance, a mother had to have at least two children under sixteen, be married, to have been a British subject for at least fifteen years, and to have lived in Quebec for at least seven years. Moreover, a woman had to provide reasonable proof of being capable of giving her children good, motherly care, which raised the question of a mother's morals. Two certificates had to be provided: one from a minister of religion, the other from an impartial person. A woman also had to be able to demonstrate need. We can well imagine a woman's humiliation and anxiety in the face of these requirements. In 1938, the law enabled the government of Quebec to spend two million dollars to help five thousand women heads of family; in the same year, the Ontario government came to the aid of twelve thousand women and spent five million dollars. The law was a turning point in the history of social policy in Quebec: it reached many needy people outside the walls of social-service institutions; it was also a departure from the popular ideology of private charity. But a strong sexist bias and a narrow-minded view of the role of women in society determined eligibility.

NOTES

1 Marielle-Brown Désy, *Marie-Ange ou Augustine* (Montreal: Parti Pris, 1979), p. 35.

2 *Almanach de la langue française* (Editions Albert Lévesque, 1936), p. 12.

3 La Fédération des femmes canadiennes-françaises, *La part des femmes, il faut la dire* (Kaic-Tec Reproduction Ltée, June 1981), p. 35.

CHAPTER NINE

PULLING THROUGH

THE PERFECT HOMEMAKER

BY THE TURN OF THE century, many women were learning to live in the city, where 80 percent of the population were tenants. Rent and food absorbed three-quarters of their income and most working-class people lived below the poverty line: to make ends meet, women had to be creative, energetic and intelligent.

At the beginning of the century, the middle classes began to move to the suburbs. The houses they left empty would be subdivided into several poorly designed units that would, in some cases, be occupied by a number of families. In Montreal, the number of available apartments diminished rapidly and new ones were hastily constructed. Usually, a two-storey house was divided into three flats; a three-storey house became five flats. Both featured an outside staircase and were very long and narrow. The rooms of each flat gave onto a common hallway. These poorly ventilated, badly lit flats often had outside toilets. Landlords could do as they pleased, as the city had no building code and its few sanitation regulations were rarely complied with. In working-class neighbourhoods, there were clearly not enough trees or green space, and factories polluted the atmosphere. Public utilities were totally inadequate. Streets were very dusty and as a result women opened their windows as little as possible.

The meagre wages obviously did not enable people to buy much furniture. In 1928, the Fraternité canadienne des cheminots carried out a survey on the cost of living in several locations in Canada. The purpose of the survey was to find out how much money was required to maintain an acceptable standard of living. Based on an average budget of two thousand dollars a year, the minimum considered necessary for a decent life, it was suggested that workers buy the following furniture for a family of five:

a. For the living room: oak furniture, leather armchairs with matching sofa bed, which can also be used as an extra bed, an oak table and an inexpensive, standard-size carpet.

b. For the dining room: a reasonably priced oak table with six chairs, an extra leaf for the table, a sideboard and linoleum on the floor.

c. For the kitchen: a coal stove, a 48-inch pine table, two chairs and moderately priced pots and pans (for example, grey enamel).

d. For the bedroom: modern steel beds, simple but durable, oak furniture, rag mats, standard quality, durable, inexpensive, bed linen.

It is understood that these articles should be bought when the family takes possession of its flat. They constitute the necessary possessions for a family of five to ensure health and a good life. The budget provides for a maintenance cost of only 7%.

It should be noted that there is no credit for various articles such as curtains, blinds etc. These articles must be bought directly from the family savings.[1]

In 1931, the average wage of an adult male was $1,200; this was sometimes supplemented by $200 from the wife and children. Needless to say, most families did not have much furniture.

Whatever a city woman's civil and economic status, she was a second-class citizen. Deprived of a number of legal and political rights, she had little access to education and was a prisoner of the reproductive function. During the Depression, women were *bricoleuses du quotidien* (day-to-day survivors), as historian Pascale Werner puts it. "When surviving meant being inventive and ingenious, knowing what to do and how to do it, through the ages, women wove the finest mesh of social fabric from which history was made and unmade."

We know very little about the daily life of a housewife, and large areas of women's lives remain obscure; but we do know that in the cities, women often did the same work as men and were subject to the same socio-economic instability. However, the similarity between female and male work was a superficial one: a woman's relation to her work could not be separated from her role in the family. A woman worker had two jobs; husbands did not do housework. When they finished work at the factory, men often went to taverns or gambling houses where, according to Léa Roback, many a week's wages were swallowed up. On payday, women often had to wait for their men at the factory gates to make sure that they got some money.

In some ways, the family network was perpetuated in the city, where the

TABLE 6
Budget for a man, woman and three children – 1926[2]
(one thirteen-year-old girl, two boys nine and eleven)

Commodity	Weekly Budget	Unit Price	Total
Milk and Cheese	14 Pints of milk	$0.14	$1.96
	1/2 pound of cheese	.25	.12 1/2
Eggs & Meat	3 pounds of rumpsteak	.20	.60
	3 pounds of salt beef	.22	.66
	2 pounds of haddock	.12 1/2	.25
	1 pound of liver	.30	.30
	1 dozen eggs	.45	.45
Vegetables	4 pounds of carrots	.03	.12
	2 pounds of rape cabbage	.03	.06
	2 pounds of onions	.05	.10
	12 pounds of potatoes	.02 1/2	.30
	2 tins of tomatoes	.10	.20
Fruits	6 oranges	.30	.15
	18 apples	.30	.30
	1 pound of plums	.12 1/2	.12 1/2
	1 pound of figs	.12 1/2	.12 1/2
	1/4 pound of grapes		
	or gooseberries	.16	.04
Cereals	14 pounds of bread	.12	1.68
	2 pounds of flour	.07	.14
	1 pound of macaroni	.08	.08
	1 pound of rice	.09	.09
	1/2 pound of corn meal	.06	.03
	3 1/2 pounds of oatmeal	.06	.21
	1/4 pound of sago	.10	.02 1/2
	1/4 pound of tapioca	.10	.02 1/2
	1/4 pound of barley	.10	.02 1/2
	1/2 pound of split peas	.10	.05
	1/4 pound of beans	.09	.02 1/2
Desserts	1 pound of jelly	.12 1/2	.12 1/2
	1/2 pound of corn syrup	.09	.0
Fats	1 1/2 pounds of butter	.46	.69
	1 pound of fat	.21	.21
	1/2 pound of suet	.18	.09
	1 jar of peanut butter	.25	.25
	1/4 package of starch	.12	.03
Miscellaneous	1/2 pound of cocoa	.16	.08
	1/4 pound of tea	.60	.15
	1/4 package of baking powder	.32	.04
	1/4 tin of pepper	.09	.02 1/4
	1/4 sack of salt	.10	.02 1/4
	4 pounds of sugar	.07	.14

nuclear family often lived within an extended-family structure. Many families continued to live in close proximity, and family members would frequently find jobs for their kin who came to the city and were lodged in the family home.

In 1926, the daughter of a Montreal family, one of four children in 1926, described the tiny wage brought home by their father, a tinsmith. One daughter was a domestic servant in a doctor's house and contributed her wages to the family income; another daughter lived at home to help her mother and to look after her grandfather. A third daughter was married and lived upstairs. Her husband was an alcoholic, and her parents and sisters looked after her children most of the time.

As in other eras, women were responsible for feeding the family and had to bring in extra income.

EARNING A LIVING: SERVING
CAPITAL AND PATRIARCHY

As big industry killed off cottage industries and removed spinning wheels and looms to the factory, hungry women and children took the factory road and indeed, are there still.[3]

Women continued to work in manufacturing jobs. They were both exploited as a reserve work force and told by religious and civil authorities that they must not work – a sanction that suited employers' purposes. It was argued that it was sinful for young women to be working, that mothers who worked were neglecting their children, and that women were taking jobs from men during a recession. These principles were used to justify many types of discrimination. Women received low wages, were stuck in job ghettos, and had poor working conditions. Historian Terry Copp remarks that factory inspectors in Montreal in 1921 attached little importance to working conditions for girls, assuming that they would soon get married.

Jennifer Stoddart and Marie Lavigne have studied conditions for women workers in Montreal in the Twenties. The garment, textile and tobacco sectors continued to require a great deal of female labour. The food and service industries (offices, banks and retail business) were developing rapidly and employers were happy to hire women willing to work for long hours and pathetically low wages.

Working conditions for women in Montreal, the industrial centre of Quebec, give us a good idea of a woman worker's life between 1900 and 1940. The number of women in the work force grew steadily, and neither the war nor the Depression interrupted this trend. In 1941, women formed 27 percent of the Montreal work force. Most of these women workers were unmarried. In 1921, more than 25 percent of working women in Montreal were under twenty-one; 51 percent were under twenty-five. Some lived alone; some provided extra income for their working-class families. Over the years, there was a slight increase in the number of married women working in Quebec. In 1921, 1.8 percent of married women worked; in 1931, 2.8 percent; and in 1941, 3.3 percent. The range of their jobs was still quite limited; most worked in factories, in service industries or in offices.

TABLE 7

Percentage Distribution of Female Work Force
by Main Occupational Group
Montreal, 1911-1941

Occupational Group	1911	1921	1931	1941
Factories	40.1	33.5	23.4	29.6
Personal Services	32.6	20.2	29.3	26.9
Office Clerks	-	18.5	18.9	19.9
Specialized Trades	9.6	14.2	11.6	10.0
Business	13.9	8.8	8.4	10.0
Transport	2.7	3.6	4.4	1.5
Percentage of Women in Work Force	21.6	25.2	25.4	27.4

Source: M. Lavigne, J. Stoddart, "Ouvrières et travailleuses montréalaises, 1900-1940" in M. Lavigne, Y. Pinard, Les femmes dans la société québécoise, Montreal, Boréal Express, 1977, p. 127.

TABLE 8

Differences in Wages by Sex and Age, Montreal, 1930-1931

	Yearly Average	Average Number of Weeks Worked	Weekly Wage
Men (over 20)	$1083	41.3	$26.23
Women (over 20)	$629	45.4	$13.53
Boys (under 20)	$406	41.1	$9.88
Girls (under 20)	$368	43.8	$8.40

Source: T. Copp, Classe ouvrière et pauvreté, Montreal, Boréal Express, 1978, p. 39.

Women earned about half the amount men earned. In Montreal, women received 53.6 percent of a male wage in 1911, 56.1 percent in 1921; 56.1 percent in 1931 and 51 percent in 1941.

The number of hours worked was also discriminatory: women worked longer hours than men and girls worked longer hours than boys.

FACTORIES

Most working women were employed in the manufacturing sector. In 1911, 63 percent of Quebec's women workers worked in the textile and garment industries, 6 percent in leather and rubber products and 7 percent in tobacco. This distribution remained virtually constant until 1941. In 1911, 27 percent of factory workers were women; in 1941, 30 percent. The industrial structure of Quebec, which was based on light industry, required cheap labour in large numbers. French-Canadian, Polish, Italian and Syrian women were confined to those industries that paid the lowest wages. The exploitation of women workers was, in fact, an important element in the structure of the Quebec economy.

The garment industry needed little capital investment. Most owners opened small workshops and subcontracted work. Most of the employees in the garment industry, which was dominated by Jews, were women. They worked all day long making coats, hats, ties and dresses, and often took home unfinished work to do in the evening with the help of children and grand-mothers.

In 1919, the government of Quebec introduced a minimum wage for women. The law was not implemented until a commission established work-ing hours and wages for women in various manufacturing industries. The commission was set up in 1925. At first, it covered two sectors: laundry, dyeing and dry cleaning; and printing, binding, lithography and envelope produc-tion. In 1930, its terms of reference were extended to women working in com-mercial establishments and, in 1935, to those who worked in hotels, clubs and restaurants.

The commission first attempted to establish a basic budget for a working woman. It fixed the weekly cost of living for an unmarried woman at between $10.35 and $19.81, and set $12.20 a week – $634.40 a year – as the minimum wage. The commission's figures seem to have been influenced by the mini-mum wage paid by big business. The chairman explained that a woman could pay her rent and eat on $7 a week. Clothing would cost $11.50 a month and $11 was reserved for incidental expenses. After the cost of transport was deducted, 25¢ a day could be saved for emergencies such as a work slowdown. The first commission ruling came into force in 1928. It applied to 10,189 women working in thirty-nine textile mills. An experienced employee with more than twenty-four months seniority was to be paid at least $12 for a fifty-five-hour work week.

In the shoe industry, which employed 2,304 women, the minimum wage was fixed at $12.50 after two years. In the garment industry, which hired 9,510 women in 1929, nearly half the workers were classified as unskilled labour and were paid an average weekly wage of $8.50. The 5,431 "experienced" women earned the fixed minimum of $12.50 a week. The situation in the tobacco industry was the same.

All sorts of tactics were used to deceive inspectors: experienced workers were classified as apprentices; and two or three women from the same family were forced to punch the same card, so that a single wage could be paid for the work done by all of them.

In the long run, the various minimum-wage regulations for women prevented the most flagrant abuses. However, the law did not question the gap between wages paid to women and men. On the contrary, the laws enshrined women as "different" workers and also enshrined the principle of unequal wages according to gender. Although low wages often pushed girls into prostitution, the civil and religious authorities who were quick to denounce them, did nothing to improve women's wages. It was common practice in the garment industry for work to be done in homes or in small, illegal workshops. Such work was poorly paid. In spite of protests, these exploitative conditions continued throughout the period. In 1935, a federal commission on prices reported that a seamstress working at home earned 25¢ for a dozen pairs of short pants, while the same work done in a unionized factory was worth $1.50. Yet, because the home work system enabled women to earn money while caring for their children, housewives supported it, even though they knew it was illegal. The feminist position was ambivalent: while against the exploitation of women in their homes, they, too, saw the system as a way for women to have a job and look after their children.

Society frowned upon women who earned a living outside the home and encouraged women to work in an environment protected from subversive ideas. The Fédération nationale Saint-Jean-Baptiste, a feminist organization founded in 1907, encouraged women to make ends meet by accepting sewing jobs at home during World War One and the Depression. Those who protested the poor pay were told that a woman working at home had fewer expenses and saved on clothes. Moreover, such work enabled her to look after her children.

Lack of sanitation in factories was denounced by all investigations. In 1938, the Turgeon Commission on the textile industry recorded complaints by

A WOMAN WORKER'S BUDGET

December, 1925

Item   *Annual Cost*

Room and Board (calculate on basis of shared accommodation)

CLOTHING

Shoes and repairs (... pairs at ...)
   slippers ... pairs at ... ; rubbers ... pairs at ...
Stockings ... pairs at ...
Underclothes ... at ...
Night dresses ... at ...
Petticoats and bloomers
Corsets (...) camisoles (...)
Kimono
Hats
Suits (divide cost by number of years in use – two years or more)
Winter coats
Winter dresses
Housedresses
Wool sweater (cardigan)
Aprons
Handkerchiefs
Gloves
Scarves
Umbrella (divide the cost by the number of years in use)
   Total Amount for clothing

OTHER EXPENSES

Laundry
Doctor, dentist, optician
Streetcar tickets (... per week)
Newspapers etc
Stamps and stationery
Leisure activities and recreation (concerts, theatre etc.)
Church and charity
Insurance (life and medical)
Toiletries (combs, brushes, soap, tooth powder, talcum,
   wax and polish, needles, pins, thread and laces)
   Total for other Expenses

Total Expenses for the year
Room and Board for the week
Clothing per week
Other expenses per week
   Total per week
   Name of person or Association[4]

women workers of bad ventilation, dust, dampness and dirt, noise and lack of sanitary facilities. But improvements were a long time coming.

The relationship between life cycles and women's work has been studied by historian Gail Cuthbert-Brandt. According to Brandt, young unmarried women workers had little independence and had to make regular contributions to the family income. Such financial obligations delayed their marriage; before 1940, the average age at which women married was twenty-five.

DOMESTIC SERVICE

In spite of the poor working conditions, girls often preferred factory work to domestic service. Around 1920, a seventeen-year-old textile worker who had gone to work in a factory in the United States at the age of fourteen returned to Quebec. "The only work I can find is with a family ... I have been doing this job for so long at home and wages are so low that a future in domestic service does not look good to me. I am returning to the textile mills with my sister who is five years older than me, first in Trois Rivières, then from there to Massachusetts."

In 1891, servants constituted 41 percent of the female work force in Canada. In 1921, the figure had dropped to 18 percent, but domestic service was still the second largest employer of women. Historian Geneviève Leslie notes that many women continued to work in domestic service until World War Two; however, in the period 1880-1920 a considerable number of women left domestic service: industrialization moved production out of the home and created new jobs. Once women were able to make choices, the household and the nature of domestic work were transformed.

Under the new conditions, working women were able to organize and make collective demands for improved wages and working hours, which servants were unable to do. Domestic work was not considered to be an integral part of the economy with economic and political importance. It was merely "nonproductive" work that took place in the home and involved a personal relationship between employer and employee. As society became organized around production of profit-making goods and less production was done in the home, the value of domestic work decreased.

The lives of domestic servants resembled the lives of wives, little girls, "old maids" and poor cousins, who provided poorly paid or free domestic service to help families make ends meet.

Servants had no legal protection and little job security. They could be laid off without notice during summer holidays or economic recessions.

A survey carried out in Toronto in 1913 found that nearly half of all prostitutes were former domestic servants. Historian Lori Rotenburg maintains that a servant who lost her job suffered greater insecurity than did an unemployed woman factory worker, because the servant lost her home as well as her job. Rotenburg notes that the isolation of domestic work made it difficult for immigrant women or women from the countryside to create a network of friends who could help them. Finally, she points out that, given the low prestige of domestic servants, their descent into prostitution was not seen to be as shameful as it might be for other women.

But not every domestic servant was a potential prostitute. Servants were more likely to become factory workers or mothers.

Between 1900 and 1940, most servants in Montreal were recent arrivals from the countryside or Europe who had been hired by families in the Saint-Antoine district or the new suburbs of Outremont and Westmount. According to Léa Roback, Irish, Russian and Czech girls were paid a dollar a day. Some of the women who hired them gave them clothes and food for their families; others fed them poorly and did not pay them at all or threw their wages on the ground, forcing them to to scramble for them. The newly arrived girls were of peasant stock, not used to the big city, mostly illiterate and incapable of working in factories.

Country girls served established Francophone or Anglophone families in Trois-Rivières, Grand-Mère, Chicoutimi, Jonquière and Quebec City. They left their homes to work for a family in the town who, the parents hoped, would protect them against the moral dangers of urban life. However, women *were* subject to sexual harassment. According to Roback, girls were constantly bothered by the husbands and sons of the family they worked for, ("I knew some who fled without being paid their wages.") Many girls from the Saguenay and Gaspé regions were raped by their masters. In general, servants did not stay long with the same family, at least in Montreal, and the middle class complained about this.

Domestic servants were at the mercy of their mistresses, who considered subservience a very important quality in a domestic servant. Orders were to be obeyed; and recruiters from the Ministry of Immigration were told to find girls who knew what was required of them. Any act of rebellion meant dismissal. In Quebec, the clergy exercised strict control over the lives of girls in their parishes and servants, like teachers, could lose their jobs if the priest complained of their behaviour.

We have very few personal accounts from servants, but as far as we know, the job was not attractive: witness the numerous recruitment campaigns for servants supported by village priests and the Ministry of Immigration. The "instability" of servants was probably a sign of their discontent. The wages of servants were never fixed by the Women's Minimum Wage Act; and even bourgeois women who took an interest in conditions for working women were not concerned about the long hours worked by their own servants.

Another factor in the decline of domestic service was its low social status. Women factory workers and saleswomen were respected more than servants. Young women said men preferred to marry factory workers and saleswomen "even if they hardly knew anything about housekeeping."

Rose-Marie Dumais, who was a housekeeper in a presbytery, paints a clear picture of domestic service.

> A housekeeper in a presbytery is like the mistress of a house, with one difference – she does not have the advantages. She sees to everything, she is responsible for everything, the kitchen, the upkeep of the house, the shopping, supplies; she is responsible for the well-being of those who live under the same roof, but she must remain discreet and invisible; her presence is felt, but she must never be seen.... Priests competed for the best housekeepers. They all wanted to have the best and for the lowest wage.... Thus wages could vary from $8 a month to $25 a month. I remember once hearing one priest say to another: "You are paying your housekeeper too much, you are going to drive the prices up." In the presbyteries, it was like working for a family: the more you were capable of, the more they asked of you.... You had to look after the garden, put up vegetables and jams and, quite often, you were also left with looking after church ornaments: washing robes, surplices and altar cloths.... If I were to give advice, I would say it is not always a good idea to show how capable you are, if you want to avoid being taken advantage of.[5]

World War One caused a great demand for labour, and fewer women had to work as servants. During the Depression, in Montreal the number of domestics swelled again when employment opportunities in manufacturing decreased. Servants, cooks and cleaning women constituted a reserve labour force for the manufacturing sector.

In Quebec, a priest's housekeeper was special: she had a "consecrated" man as a master. Men were not created for domestic work – a woman was needed, to run the house and to sometimes help the priest in his religious duties. The woman should not be visible. To be hired, she had to be at least forty and above reproach. She could not allow the priest's reputation to be sullied by her presence. A priest's housekeeper served a man without the economic advantages or security of marriage.

As soon as they could find other jobs, women gave up domestic service, and responsibility for all the housework fell to the wife.

The coming of modern household technology did not abolish housework, but it did alter the way the work was done. Middle-class housewives were told that domestic science was as important as any other science. Historians Strong-Boag and Stoddart have noted that this domestic ideology, which glorified the housewife as an efficient shopper and competent operator of household appliances, was not without its appeal for many women. Ironically, however, housewives discovered the same drawbacks complained of by their former employees: loneliness, endless hours of work, lack of independence, insufficient rewards, lack of status, health problems and lack of motivation.

IN THE SHOPS AND OFFICES

Office work, a rapidly growing profession, required little training and was accessible to girls from better-off working-class and lower-middle-class families. In 1916, when the O'Sullivan Business College was founded in Montreal, four other business colleges were already teaching typing, shorthand, office practice and English.

Correspondence Translation Copies and Circulars
Special courses in preparation for office work
Mme. E. Bouthillier
SHORTHAND-TYPIST
Qualified employees provided upon request
We specialize in mimeographing
474 Dorchester Street East
Tel EST 5859
Montreal[6]

Women did not enter the clerical professions unimpeded, for they were invading a sector that had been strictly male. Opponents raised the spectre of moral corruption: at the turn of the century, they attempted to prevent women from becoming stenographers; later, from entering the public service. During the Thirties, a white-collar association conducted a survey of jobs occupied by women, with the aim of gradually replacing women with men. As in other sectors, women in office jobs were paid less than men, but the wage gap was not as great as elsewhere. For example, in 1931, women office workers earned 73 percent of male wages.

It was federal and provincial government agencies that effectively created the job of secretary as we know it today. Village girls such as Mme. Eugène Martin (Jeanne Guérin) attended specialized institutions and took bilingual courses to enable them to hold fairly well-paid positions. Society strongly disapproved of these young, smart women who dared enter the male world to work in responsible positions.[7]

Working conditions for saleswomen were barely tolerable. They often spent twelve hours a day on their feet serving customers, and shops were often drafty. The conditions attracted the attention of women reformers, who founded the Association des demoiselles de magasin (Shop Girls' Association). From 1900 to 1920, the Fédération nationale Saint-Jean-Baptiste and the Conseil local des femmes de Montréal organized campaigns to close stores early in the evening and enforce the Loi des sièges (Chair Law). (The chair law decreed that chairs had to be provided for the use of saleswomen when there were no customers, but a 1927 investigation revealed that it was rarely observed.)

Part-time workers were employed mostly by department stores. Up to 40 percent of women employed by Woolworths were hired part-time. The Commission sur les écarts de prix (Commission on Price Differences) found that part-time work prevented women from obtaining full-time jobs elsewhere.

A JOB TO MAKE ENDS MEET

Servants, factory workers and salesgirls were easy prey for pimps. According to Roback, "prostitution flourished in the hotels, brothels and massage parlours of Montreal. The pimps, female or male, would often deduct the cost of the girls' silk underwear from the money they brought in. Saint Lawrence, Saint Dominique and Guilbault streets were full of brothels."

We know little about these prostitutes. Many were destitute, had terrible childhoods and found themselves, at an early age, in need of a job but without a trade or skills. Maimie Pinzer was one of these women. She was born in Philadelphia in 1885 and lived in Montreal around 1913. Her prolific letters describe the life of a prostitute at the turn of the century.

There were many illegitimate births. Girls who had their babies in homes run by nuns (such as La Miséricorde) were treated as sinners, although Anglophone institutions were less repressive. Some nurseries had as many as five hundred illegitimate babies to care for with very limited resources. "Anyway," said the nuns, "they will become angels!"

According to Roback, women workers were cheerful and courageous in spite of everything. They laughed together and leaned on one another for support. "I remember," Roback said, "a resourceful young woman who would go to work at Old Orchard as a waitress when she was out of work in the summer. She used to make a lot of money by insisting on an extra tip if a customer lifted up her skirt or pinched her bottom. She was an excellent seamstress and her Jewish employers wanted to keep her. If they intimidated a shy young girl, she would tell them to stop bothering her and they often listened."

IN THE SERVICE OF GOD:
RELIGIOUS CELIBACY

Between 1900 and 1960, eighteen new religious communities were added to the twenty-three already in existence in Quebec. The women in the religious communities worked in Quebec or in overseas missions. In 1901, there were 6,628 nuns in Quebec; there were 25,488 in 1941. Demographers have shown that the number of young women entering the convent peaked during the Depression.

The location of these new religious communities reflected fundamental changes in Quebec society. The growing towns and the social problems caused by the exodus from the countryside – poverty, social and cultural disintegration and the isolation of ethnic groups – prompted religious communities to intensify their activities in urban centres. Most new communities did social work or provided services to ethnic groups. Their work was important, as providing aid to the needy was still mostly left to private initiative.

The Quebec Public Charities Act of 1921 gave a special status and statutory subsidies to private charitable institutions, in recognition of their provision of

THE LITANY OF THE OLD MAIDS

Kyrie	I would like
Christé	To be married
Kyrie	I pray to all the saints
Christé	May it happen tomorrow
Ste-Marie	Make it so that I will marry
St-Joseph	Very soon
Ste-Claire	His honour the mayor
St-Gervais	Or the justice of the peace
St-Mucaire	Or the notary
St-Clément	Or the registrar
St-Didier	The brigadier
St-Anatole	The school master
St-Lucien	Or the pharmacist
St-Alexandre	Don't keep me waiting
St-Oreste	Must I be left behind
St-Irénée	I am the oldest
St-Padoux	I must have a husband
St-Léon	May he be a bachelor
St-Barthelémy	May he be handsome
St-Julien	May he be healthy
St-Adrien	May he be a man of means
St-Antoine	May he have some family property
St-Cyprien	May he be a good Christian
St-Leu	May he not be a gambler
St-Jean	May he love me tenderly
Ste-Eloi	May he love no one but me
Ste-Félicité	May he do my bidding
Ste-Charlotte	May I wear the pants
Ste-Isabelle	May he be faithful to me
St-Lazare	May he not be miserly
St-Loup	May he not be jealous
Ste-Marguerite	Send him quickly
Ste-Madeleine	Release me from my sorrow
Grand St-Nicholas	Don't forget me.[8]

a public service. This in turn enabled the Church to maintain control over these institutions.

In 1936, there were approximately 150 institutions, with 30,000 beds, operated by nuns. They took in orphans, the sick and the homeless. Many of the institutions were those started by lay women in the nineteenth century, which were later transferred to religious communities; the nuns, controlled their day-to-day administration, although lay women continued to provide some services.

In the 1900s, unmarried lay women were accused of selfishness. However, a woman who entered the religious life could remain unmarried, have a career and fulfil her potential. According to a preacher in Notre-Dame in 1925, "Unmarried women are a scourge on humanity." His sister, Marie Gérin-Lajoie, however, wrote: "Obviously, all women are not called to make a home or participate directly in family activities. The Church encourages celibacy for spiritual reasons, and entrusts its nuns with maternal responsibilities."

FEMALE AND MALE PROFESSIONS

Throughout the Western world, women had to fight their way into the liberal professions. First, they gained access to higher education; then they confronted prejudice in the universities and professional associations. In 1918, McGill University opened its Faculty of Medicine to women; the Université de Montréal followed in the Thirties. Women were permitted to practise law in 1941, and to work as notaries in 1956.

The French-Canadian élite jealously guarded access to the most prestigious professions so that women would either stay at home or choose other professions, such as nursing and teaching.

The professionalization of nursing took place at the turn of the century. Until that time people did without hospital care if they could because hospitals were overcrowded and dirty, and spread disease. The development of medical science created a demand for hospital workers with good basic training. Medical knowledge became the monopoly of those trained in medical schools, and medical care was centralized in hospitals. The introduction of health services contributed to the disappearance of the independent woman practitioner; and, as it was almost impossible for women to get training as doctors, they became nurses.

In 1875, the Montreal General Hospital decided to provide training for nurses and sought advice from the founder of the profession, Florence Nightingale. Her representative was a graduate of the school she had founded in 1860. According to Judi Coburn, the young woman was horrified by the lack of sanitation in the hospital and resigned, as did the three nurses who succeeded her. (Hospital money was used to buy, amongst other things, champagne to fortify patients for operations and nurses lived in an old leaky building.) The school opened in 1890 instilling middle-class, puritanical morals in working-class girls.

By 1909, there were seventy schools of nursing in Canada. Hospitals soon realized they could save money by training nurses. Training courses were extended to three years, thus allowing greater exploitation, as nurses in training earned little or nothing.

The institute in which I have the honour of being a student [L'Hôpital Notre-Dame] has sent me here as a delegate today. Our motto is "O.B.I."[obey]; and I have come here to tell you that hospital training admirably prepares a woman for her duties in the family and in society....

After three years of work and struggle, when the student has completed her professional training, especially when she has learned how, according to the great law of duty, a woman can repress all her inclinations to be repelled, all impetuosity and all the desires of her heart, when she is ready for the suffering world, she is called a graduate.[9]

It was difficult for lay Francophone women to become nurses because they had to compete with nuns; it was not until 1897 that a nursing course was offered in French to lay women at the Hôpital Notre-Dame.

There were long battles for legislation to control access to the profession. By 1922, laws had been passed in all provinces, but they still permitted numerous abuses in the work place and it was still extremely difficult for women to study nursing in a university. Although McGill University offered a basic nursing diploma around 1920, working conditions remained difficult for many years.

The schoolteacher was the perfect stereotype of the early-twentieth century working woman. Schoolteachers had a mission, linked to the maternal role of women and carried out under difficult conditions, both material and psychological.

Before 1960, fewer than 10 percent of lay Catholic women teachers taught in Montreal and Quebec. By the mid-nineteenth century, teaching had become a predominantly female profession. The trend continued until, by 1950, between 80 and 88 percent of lay and religious teachers were women.

This disturbed school authorities, who tried to encourage men to accept teaching positions by offering them grants, because "it takes a man to educate a man."

Rural women teachers, the majority of lay and Catholic teaching personnel, were poorly paid, poorly housed and poorly fed. They were closely supervised by school boards, parents and priests, who did not hesitate to dismiss them if they were found to have a young man in their classroom after working hours, drank a glass of beer at a hotel or were considered to have been too strict with a child.

Rural teachers were paid less than teachers in the towns. They were responsible for the upkeep of the classroom, stoking the stove and clearing snow in winter, and sometimes had to share their lunch with the children. As they rarely had opportunities to improve their qualifications or to retrain, and often had only a basic education, lay Catholic women teachers taught mostly at the elementary level. Protestant women often had a wider choice of jobs, as they did not have to compete with nuns.

According to historian Maryse Thivierge, teachers in Quebec were the lowest paid in the country between 1900 and 1960. In 1924, of the 7,262 lay Catholic women teachers in the province, 73 percent earned less than $350 a year. Of jobs held mainly by women, teaching was the lowest paid. During summer holidays, teachers had to supplement their incomes. They went into domestic service, sold fruit to tourists or worked on their fathers' farms. During the Depression, many experienced women teachers were fired, replaced by teachers hired at lower salaries.

Women teachers' salaries began to increase after 1937. In 1936, the Superintendent of Public Instruction denounced

> the unjustifiable tendency of some municipalities to unduly lower the salaries of rural women teachers. For five years before 1931-32, not one woman teacher received a salary under $150 a year. In 1931-32, reports mentioned five whose salary was lower than $150 and in 1932-33, there were nearly 400, of whom 135 were earning only $80-$125. While Protestant women teachers earned, on the average, $1,140, Catholic women teachers earned $394.

"All forms of disparity in the salaries of teachers derived from the general attitude that it was exceptional for a woman to take on a paid job, because her real vocation was domestic. As long as women teachers subscribed to this view, no organization could change their economic conditions," concludes Thivierge, who adds that bosses and unions had a vested interest in maintaining the status quo.

In his novel *La Scouine,* published in 1918, Albert Laberge describes how a teacher was fired for strapping – three times – a little girl who had exasperated her.

> She told her alarmed mother that the mistress had strapped her 12 times on each hand. Mâço [the mother] left immediately. She arrived in a fury and, in front of all the other pupils, created a terrible scene and heaped insults on the teacher.... In the evening, all the families on the road talked about nothing else but the drama that had unfolded at the school. On Saturday, one of the commissioners went to see Mlle Léveillé and told her that such a thing could not be tolerated.... He added that all the parents were up in arms and were demanding her resignation. On Sunday, before mass, the teacher went to see the priest and told him her side of the story. The priest patiently heard her out. He seemed to recognize that justice was on her side, but when Mlle Léveillé asked him to speak to the commission on her behalf, he declared that although he really wanted to help her, he could not get involved in the affair because it would be an abuse of his authority. The school commission had to be left free to do as it saw fit.
>
> Mlle Léveillé, a slim, blond young woman, who looked so nice in her blue dress, had to leave after teaching for one week.

Before 1943, parents could decide whether their children stayed in school. (After 1943, attendance was compulsory until the age of fourteen.) The rural woman teacher often had to confront parents who wanted to send their daughter or son to work at an early age. Many children left school after their first communion, around ten or eleven, and very few went beyond grade six. A teacher who worked in Abitibi recalled the reaction of a mother upon being told that her son was having trouble with his school work: "When I married his father, he didn't know how to make the sign of the cross and it was all the same to me."

Such working conditions did not encourage rural women teachers to stay in the profession for long. Between 1900 and 1964, close to 80 percent taught for ten years or less, according to Maryse Thivierge. Rural women teachers taught for the shortest period of time (an average of 5.84 years), while urban women teachers taught for an average of 13.4 years. "In rural Quebec, few women teachers could withstand the pressures brought upon them year after year; in addition, there was the insecurity of the future." Although the law did not formally prohibit married women from teaching, tradition and the prevailing mentality virtually excluded them from the job market. Nonetheless, in the countryside, some married women taught in schools that could find no other teacher.

PRESENT BUT ABSENT IN
WRITING AND THE ARTS

It is said that women have always written because paper is inexpensive and because they can fit writing in between daily chores.

In the 1900s the number of women journalists increased. Women continued to make a place for themselves as columnists, but some wanted to leave the women's pages and start their own publications, as Josephine Dandurand had done in the nineteenth century. Robertine Barry was the editor of *Le Journal de Françoise,* which was published between 1901 and 1908; Gaétane de Montreuil was editor of *Pour vous Mesdames* from 1913 to 1915; and Madeleine Huguenin founded *La Revue moderne* in 1919.

Women wrote many of the novels, children's stories and poetical and theatrical works published between 1900 and 1940; Réginald Hamel has cited more than eighty novels or collections of poetry written by women. The mores of the time restricted women's subject matter: they were forbidden to be aggressively feminist or to express strong opinions. As a result, women often wrote children's books or melodramatic stories that reflected their imprisonment in domestic life.

Writers – Marie-Claire Daveluy, Michelle Le Normand, Gaétane de Montreuil, Jovette Bernier – were well-known in literary circles. Women poets wrote about their roots, patriotism, nature and maternal love. Jovette Bernier wrote about love even though it had "deceived her ten times, twenty times." In her novel *La Chair décevante* (The Betraying Flesh), her theme was maternal love.

Many women writers used pen names, hiding their identities so they could indulge in more personal expression than society would accept from a female. Women were therefore present in literature, but absent. There were a few exceptions. Gaétane de Montreuil "lets the words speak for themselves, the meaning escape and, in the most total abandon, all trace of herself vanishes," wrote Gabrielle Frémont. Women journalists supported feminists' demands for greater participation of women in society, but novels, children's stories and poetry hardly reflected these preoccupations. The female imagination was still focused on "feminine" values.

CLEMENT LUCIE
En marge de la vie (1934) ... 0.60
(Prix d'action intellectuelle, 1934). Simple, rapid style with little action. Strong tone, which is surprising from a female pen. Very modern message about mixed marriages, but no development of point of view.

TASSE, MME HENRIETTE
Quebec
Niece of humourist Hector Berthelot. Mme Tassé is an avowed though not aggressive feminist. Secretary of various women's clubs.
La Vie et le rêve. De Tout un peu. La Femme et la civilization. Les Salons français. La Vie Humoristique d'Hector Berthelot.
In Preparation: *L'Art culinaire.*
Montréal[10]

The arts allowed women to express themselves. Many women musicians followed in the footsteps of Albani. Pianists, violinists and singers won the prestigious "Prix d'Europe" and most pursued their careers abroad. A catalogue published in 1935 included fifty-five Francophone women musicians who had gained international reputations. Pianist Germaine Malepart, violinist Annette Lasalle and singers Béatrice Lapalme, Eva Gauthier and Victoria Cantin contributed to the musical reputation of Quebec.

Actresses Mimi d'Estée, Marthe Thierry, Antoinette Giroux and Camille Bernard delighted crowds who went to theatres such as the *Stella* and *His Majesty*. When radio was invented, these women became stars in Quebec.

PAULINE DONALDA (1882-1970)

Pauline Donalda, a Montreal Jew, had a brilliant opera career that lasted eighteen years, from 1904 to 1922. She then taught singing in Paris and trained many award-winning singers. She returned to Montreal in 1937 where she continued her career as a professor. In 1942, she founded the Opera Guild, and remained its artistic director until 1969.

Though most students attending fine-arts schools were girls, there were few women painters and sculptors – Sylvia Daoust and Simone Hudon were exceptions. However, Anglophone women Lilias Torrance Newton, Mabel Lockerby, Kathleen Morris, Annie Savage, Sarah Robertson and Prudence Heward dominated the Beaver Hall Hill Group, formed during the Twenties with painter A.Y. Jackson. Women artists were almost always unmarried. The following biography of a singer is perhaps true of many women artists: "Hortense Mazurette could have had a brilliant musical career. However, she chose family life over the theatre."

WOMEN UNIONISTS AND STRIKERS

From the beginning of the century, the trade-union movement grew rapidly in Quebec until the Depression caused a rapid decline in union membership. International unions formed the Trades and Labour Congress of Canada (TLCC). The TLCC formed a Quebec wing in 1937. It was called the Fédération provinciale du travail du Québec. The TLCC was part of the Congress of Industrial Organizations (CIO). Catholic and provincial unions were grouped together in the Canadian Catholic Confederation of Labour (CCCL), founded in 1921. All the unions tried to reach out to women.

Before 1920, women workers had been helped and protected by a number of associations. For example, associations affiliated with the Fédération nationale Saint-Jean-Baptiste brought together women workers who wanted to improve their lot. The associations tried to protect members by ensuring that existing laws concerning the rights of women workers were respected. Members were encouraged to seek personal promotion through education, in order to create an élite of women workers in the working class. Women working in stores, factories and Catholic institutions in Montreal, domestics and nurses came together in these associations. (The associations declined after World War One, when the Church threw its support behind the newly formed Catholic unions.)

Once they were organized into unions, women workers were less inclined to submit to exploitation. Although only a small percentage of women were organized in unions by 1937 (2.6 percent in 1923 and 5.6 percent in 1937), they were active and contributed directly to the success of worker agitation.

The textile industry, where women constituted 58 percent of employees, and the garment industry, where they made up 60 percent of employees, were, after the transport industry, the sectors most affected by strikes or lockouts between 1901 and 1915.

Newspapers reported that, during the Dominion Textile strike of 1908, women went to union meetings dressed in their Sunday best and comprised the majority of the members present, showing courage and solidarity. Furthermore, two-thirds of the membership of the union running the strike (the Federation of Textile Workers) were women. They participated fully in the union's administrative structure; indeed, most local vice-presidents were women.

Numerous strikes broke out after 1930. Some were limited to one shop and were called for very specific reasons. In Montreal, for example, fourteen presswomen in a blouse factory "walked off the job after three women were laid off because of changes in the piecework system." The strike lasted seven days.

On 21 August 1934, a general strike was called in the garment industry. Four thousand male and female workers demonstrated in the streets. The Workers' Unity League, a union central founded with the help of the Communist Party in 1929, ran the general strike through the Needleworkers' Industrial Union. It was the first big strike in the women's garment industry and women played an important role. Mounted municipal and provincial police dispersed the strikers; and women defended themselves by striking pins in the horses. At a demonstration on 28 August, ten women and two men were arrested.

The union refused arbitration but was defeated. Only a few companies continued to recognize it. However, according to the Ministry of Labour, male workers received a wage increase of 20 percent. The Workers' Unity League was dissolved in 1935.

The International Ladies Garment Workers Union (ILGWU), which had links with the CIO, revived militancy amongst Quebec shopgirls. Bernard Shane ran the union, assisted by Rose Pesotta, a talented organizer and passionate unionist who had been raised on libertarian doctrines. According to journalist Evelyn Dumas, in 1934, Pesotta broadcast a bilingual program on the radio, prepared leaflets and went door-to-door talking to shopgirls.

There were numerous strikes in Quebec in 1937, a year of crisis. Five thousand shopgirls, mostly French-Canadian and Jewish, stopped work for three weeks and won some basic rights: union recognition, better working conditions and higher wages. This *grève dans la guenille* (strike in the rag trade) was followed by another in 1940, which ended with a 5 percent wage increase.

Unions generally defended women but continued to consider women workers to be different from male workers: there were few demands for equal wages, and discrimination was inherent in all collective bargaining. For example, in the collective agreement of the ILGWU, which came into force on 30 April 1940, the minimum wage for pressmen was 54 1/2¢ an hour; presswomen were to get 36 1/4¢ an hour.

Some demands were met. The *Gazette du travail* reported that, in one factory, male workers were not allowed to use the elevators because they harassed the women. Women workers requested female rather than male supervisors and that they work in all-female departments or be allowed to leave five minutes earlier than men at lunch time and in the evening. They hoped this would curtail the persistent sexual harassment of their co-workers.

Yvette Charpentier was involved in organizing women in the ILGWU in the Thirties. In 1967, she was asked, "Do women participate in union life?" She answered: "Their reasons for not participating are obvious, they do not have the time because their work day does not end when the shop closes. Women who, as they say, belong to the weaker sex, have another day ahead of them when they get home." She added that married women were permitted work as long as no one in the family was inconvenienced by it. Thus unmarried women and widows were the most militant members of newly formed unions.

Between 1900 and 1940, the unionization of women became a reality; but there was still opposition to women workers. Paternalism, protectionism, division of male and female activities, lack of shared decision-making and the perception of a working woman as a non-permanent worker still existed. The Syndicat des allumettières (Matchgirls Union) went on strike in Hull between 1919 and 1924. (The story has been told by Michelle Lapointe.) The Association syndicale féminine catholique, of which the matchgirls were members, was affiliated with the union central, which did the actual negotiating. The association was involved in two major conflicts, one in 1919 and one in 1924. The matchgirls quickly mobilized during the two conflicts but, in 1924, "throughout the lock-out, several of the men who were called in to help showed paternalistic attitudes towards the matchgirls and excluded women

---

Women workers' unions are very different from male workers' unions because, generally speaking, women do not remain members very long as they enter more or less quickly into the state of marriage.

Everybody knows that every young woman who does not become a nun will naturally want to get married one day. There might be exceptions to this rule, but as the exceptions constitute only a few people, we will not dwell on them. Furthermore, the majority of these exceptions have only decided or only decide to remain old maids so that they can continue bringing up a family abandoned by a mother when death took her away from her loved ones or so that they can support aging parents.[11]

---

from decision-making. In this way, agents more or less external to the conflict took control during the counter-strike." Lapointe notes that it was women who raised the money but men who explained union activities to the public; the negotiators were male union workers and chaplains. Lapointe concludes that unionization was a double bind for women: women were not able "to develop the class consciousness that would have prompted them to defend themselves as workers and as women and, partially or completely, step outside of the narrow confines of their traditional role."

In Quebec, there had been teachers' associations since 1845. But, until World War One ended, most of the associations were under the direct control of school commissions and the Department of Public Instruction. After the war, the teaching profession in Quebec began to organize.

The instigator was an energetic young woman, Laure Gaudreault, who said: "Your best advocate is yourself." In 1906, when she was sixteen, she began teaching in Les Eboulements for $125 a year. Until 1937, she taught in

---

LEA ROBACK

Léa Roback was born on Guilbault Street near St. Lawrence Street in Montreal. Her father, a Polish immigrant, was a tailor. As the family did not have enough money to support itself, the Robacks moved to Beauport, near Quebec City, where Léa's mother opened a shop, which she ran until 1919. Life was difficult in this Catholic village, where they were the only Jewish family. Most of the men in the village were poorly paid public servants, and the women worked at night as cleaners. When she was 18, Léa went back to Montreal and worked at a cleaner's from 8.30 to 4.30 every day, for $8.00 a week. In 1925, she used the money she had earned working evenings as a theatre ticketseller to go to France to study. In 1929, in Berlin, she witnessed the growth of anti-semitism. When she came back to Montreal, she opened its first Marxist bookshop and, in 1935, she worked for Fred Rose, a militant Communist candidate in the general election. She then began organizing women garment workers. In 1937, we find her in Rosemont working as a community organizer, going from door-to-door and inviting parents to send their children to the art studio where she taught drawing. In 1942, she returned to union organizing and worked at R.C.A Victor in Saint-Henri, where she became very involved in community life.[12]

Chicoutimi and Charlevoix counties, and contributed to the women's column in *Le Progrès du Saguenay*. She introduced the idea of a teachers' association for rural women in her column and launched her project in 1936, when the government decided not to provide the salary increases promised to women schoolteachers. At a teachers' conference, Gaudreault launched and collected twenty-nine signatures to found the Association catholique des institutrices rurales.

Between November 1936 and February 1937, Gaudreault traveled all over the diocese of Chicoutimi and founded three other associations, in Jonquière, Saint-Joseph d'Alma and Chicoutimi. On 19 February 1937, the Association catholique des institutrices rurales was formed with its head office in La Malbaie and annual fees of one dollar. Gaudreault became the union's full-time official at a salary of $450 a year. For the next twelve years, the union newsletter, *La Petite Feuille,* defended the interests of women schoolteachers. Until 1943, the struggle was focused on increasing and regulating salaries.

Many people believed that women should be only wives and mothers; such attitudes did not change for a number of years. This perception of the role of women – which unions also shared – rationalized the most flagrant discrimination against women.

NOTES

1 T. Copp, *Classe ouvrière et pauvreté* (Montreal: Boréal-Express, 1978), p. 177.

2 Ibid. p. 169.

3 Marie Gérin-Lajoie, "Le travail des femmes et des enfants dans la province de Québec" in *La Bonne Parole,* October 1920, pp. 5-6.

4 Commission du Salaire minimum des Femmes.

5 Jeanne D'Arc Lévesque-Martin and Liliane Greven-Raymond, *Les reconnaissez-vous?* (La Pocatière, 1980), pp. 142-145.

6 1907, *Premier congrès de la Fédération Nationale Saint-Jean-Baptiste.* Montreal, May 1907.

7 Jeanne D'Arc Lévesque-Martin and Liliane Greven-Raymond, op. cit. pp. 168-169.

8 Song manuscript by Florence Proulx, grandmother of Lucie Charlebois, circa World War One, in Montreal.

9 P. Williams, "La carrière d'infirmière pour les femmes," *Premier congrès de la Fédération Saint-Jean-Baptiste* (Montreal, 1909), pp. 20-21.

10 *La Femme canadienne-française, Almanach de la langue française* (Montreal: Editions Albert Lévesque, 1936).

11 Thomas Poulin, *Le Droit,* 29 October 1919, quoted by Michelle Lapointe in "Le syndicat catholique des allumettières de Hull, 1919-1924," R.H.A.F., vol. 32 no. 4, March 1979, p. 611.

12 Lucie Lebeuf, "Léa Roback ou comment l'organization syndicale est indissociable de la vie de quartier" in *Vie ouvrière,* no. 128, October 1978, pp. 461-470.

CHAPTER TEN

WOMEN WORKERS: INVISIBLE, OR ALMOST

SPREADING THE RURAL IDEA

DURING THE EARLY YEARS of the century, agriculture in Quebec had not yet entered the technological age, and the family still played an important role in agricultural production. Less hired labour was used in Quebec than in Ontario: until 1931, an average of 17.1 percent of Ontario farm labourers worked for wages; in Quebec, the average was only 10 percent. The father of a Quebec family counted on his children to provide the labour needed on the farm.

At this time, civil and religious authorities panicked and tried to counter urbanization; but they had little success, although writings of the period regularly sang the praises of rural life.

Rural women lived hard lives, which followed the seasons, birth and death, in a daily round of heavy chores. Near the towns, market farming was on the increase; the produce was sold by the husband. Domestic work, which was done by the wife, was perceived by the farmer to be an essential contribution to the farm; however, for society, the work remained invisible and because it was unpaid it had no value.

The formation of groups for farm women may be attributable to their awareness of losing their traditional economic role. As in the cities, life on the land was being modernized and the world outside the parish was finding its way into parish homes. Rural women bought from the Eaton's and Dupuis Frères catalogues, and cars were seen in the countryside. Radio and electricity were slowly making an appearance.

DOMESTIC CHORES: "DEAR GOD, SEND ME TO HEAVEN WITH A BROOM IN MY HAND"

Rural women were responsible for the kitchen, the vegetable garden, for clothing the family, making hay, making bread and soap and, once a year, canning. The Depression forced many women in both town and countryside to work at night making sweaters, clothes and blankets – sold to supplement the meagre family income – and to stop buying ready-made clothing from the catalogues. Although, as historian Geneviève Leslie points out, most early domestic appliances were invented around 1920, they were not widely available, particularly in the countryside and in urban, working-class areas. Catalogues provide a picture of what was on the market: the first Eaton's catalogue came out in 1885. As the years went by, new stoves and cleaning brushes appeared. Wood- and coal-burning stoves were still being used, but there were also a few oil furnaces. Gas stoves first appeared in 1919, but cooking remained a messy activity.

Electric refrigerators did not appear in the catalogues before 1920. In the 1909 edition, two electric vacuum cleaners were illustrated. Middle-class women in the towns had access to some of these modern appliances before 1940, but rural women and working-class families continued traditional methods. Leslie concludes that many Canadian women cooked on wood stoves, washed diapers by hand and cleaned their houses without a vacuum cleaner until 1940 – and, in several regions of Quebec, until 1950.

RECIPE FOR HOUSEHOLD SOAP

15 jugs of water (12 quarts)
20 pounds of fat (to be melted and poured in molds)
5 pounds of caustic soda
5 pounds of resin

Boil for an hour, stirring constantly with a wooden spatula; then add 5 pounds of coarse salt. Let it settle until the next day and cut into squares.

This recipe makes a nice golden-coloured soap.[1]

Although these innovations made housework less tiring, they did not eliminate its repetition and boredom, for women who had the new machines cleaned more thoroughly and more frequently.

WOMEN COLONISTS

The wife of a frontier settler ostensibly led the same life as the wife of a farmer, but she was farther away from civilization. Farmers near cities could sell their produce in the cities, but others practised subsistence farming.

In 1916, promoters of colonization organized the Ligue nationale de la colonisation to keep people in the countryside and to bring back the "sons of the soil." In 1923, the bishops published a pastoral letter supporting colonization. The Union catholique des cultivateurs, founded in 1924, demanded that the Taschereau government take the matter in hand. There was little response from the government until the Depression, when an audacious colonization policy led to a small revival of colonization. However, many of those who returned to the land quickly went back to the cities, proving that the colonization movement was essentially artificial.

In 1932, the government of Quebec formed the Comité de retour à la terre. The committee drew up a list of criteria for new colonists, included the following: a would-be colonist had to have a legal marriage certificate; settle on his plot of land with only his family; possess winter clothing, a stove, a sewing machine and kitchen equipment; and have a wife who knew how to sew, knit, perform all household duties, and make bread. A colonist who had made a bad marriage could not survive.

The emphasis placed on the colonist's marriage recognizes the great importance of the wife's work. Yet our history books talk about men who logged and cleared the land, but never about their wives. These women, often widowed in their forties and left alone with a large family, continued to clear the land.

Measures designed to counter unemployment and the exodus from the countryside had only limited success. The role of the colonist's wife was seen to be so important that women were singled out in writings and in speeches as the cause of the abandonment of family lands and the exodus to urban centres.

Nevertheless, the contribution of women was recognized. Criteria for evaluation in a farming competition between 1920 and 1940 included a landowner's assets, his agricultural production, his work methods, the number of animals he had – and his wife. (Farmers who were married were given extra points).

STOPPING THE EXODUS
FROM THE LAND

The concern of civil and religious authorities about the exodus from the land led to the organization of the Cercles de fermières (Farm Women's Circles). Since the beginning of the twentieth century, there had been talk of introducing a domestic-economy organization in the countryside. There were already several models in existence: Homemakers Clubs, founded in English Canada in 1897, were introduced to Anglophone Quebec (the Eastern Townships) by Mrs. G. Beach in 1911; they worked in close collaboration with Macdonald College. In 1920, the Homemakers Clubs became the Women's Institute. The objectives, constitution and structure of a Belgian farm women's association were eventually adopted as a model for Francophone Quebec. Alphonse Désilets and Georges Bouchard, agronomists with the Ministry of Agriculture, spearheaded the movement. In 1915, they helped found the first Cercle de fermières in the Chicoutimi region.

The Cercles were intended to instill women with a desire to stay at home and use their housekeeping skills to keep "our sons on the land and stop our daughters from deserting the rural parish."

In five years, the number of Cercles grew from five to thirty-nine and the number of members increased tenfold. The first presidents were the wives of local *petit bourgeois.* In October 1919, their first convention brought together in Quebec City the presidents and secretaries of the Cercles, and a general organization of all the Cercles was undertaken. A provincial council, responsible for liaison with the Ministry of Agriculture, was elected and *La Bonne Fermière,* a magazine to be published three times a year, was launched. In addition, there was an exhibition of home crafts and "female" agricultural work: beekeeping, poultry farming, horticulture, floriculture, canning, flax cultivation, spinning, and growing medicinal plants. After the Cercles de fermières became affiliated with the Fédération nationale Saint-Jean-Baptiste and the Women's Institute of Canada, it was decided that public education courses, subsidized by the government, should be made widely available. According to the brochure put out by the Ecole sociale populaire, there had been a general improvement in housekeeping, gardening, poultry farming, beekeeping and interior decoration, and young people were increasingly attached to country life. This overall progress was, in its view, attributable to the Cercles.

In 1937, Françoise Gaudet-Smet founded the magazine *Paysana.* In it, she stated: "Organizations such as the Cercles de fermières seemed to be vital if we were to keep our 'agricultural vocation'." In a way, the Cercles were born out of interests common to women, the clergy and the government.

WHAT IS A CERCLE DE FERMIERES?

It is an organization that brings together women and girls from our rural centres, helps them to get to know one another, understand one another, exchange ideas, help one another out, makes them more interested in thinking about their problems and helps them train together to do more and better things for the improvement of living conditions on the farm.

It provides an opportunity for members to meet and discuss their work or duties and share their common experiences to improve their individual worth and personality.

In a parish, a Cercle de fermières is a veritable public school for domestic and agricultural teaching. It is also a milieu that encourages charity; the Cercle provides its members with the opportunity to develop ideals and convictions which will enable them to better fulfill their role.

The Cercle de fermières is a rural education group that encompasses many other activities such as charity, social service, the Action catholique, hygiene, domestic arts, interior decoration, recreation and library work.[2]

They enabled the government to tie women to domestic and rural work at a time when women had little say in whether Quebec should be a rural or urban society. The groups gave many women the opportunity to learn how to organize and function as a group, and to work with other women towards common objectives. They also allowed rural women to preserve their way of life and to avoid becoming dependent housewives.

MORE THAN HOUSEWIVES: WOMEN AS ACTIVE PARTICIPANTS

From 1900 to 1940, rural women often took on the extra duties of pharmacist, nurse and midwife, and they were frequently called upon to lay out the dead. As mail service, radio, telephones, office work and retail business developed, women worked for the post office as telephone operators, and with their husbands in grocery shops and small businesses. But "their name never appeared anywhere on any document," says Jeanne d'Arc Lévesque-Martin, who collected several accounts from women.

237

Juliette Richard, a rural telephone operator in La Pocatière, recounts that, in 1921, telephones were becoming more numerous and calls more urgent. She was hired by Lucienne Dion, who

> managed the telephone exchange for the Kamouraska Co. The Centrale, as the exchange was known at the time, was in a private residence. A space had been made in a room in the house and a switchboard installed.... The exchange opened at seven o'clock and I often had to work in the evenings. When I started working, I earned $5 a month.

By 1923, she was earning fifteen dollars a month. On this modest wage, the young woman was forced to live with her parents and had barely enough money to buy clothes.

> Although men invented the telephone, once they had installed the equipment, it was women who were called upon to operate the apparatus.... I think that, at first, because of the wages that were offered, men were not interested; it was often only a supplement to the family income, which a woman brought in while she continued to bring up her family. Another reason women were used as telephone operators was that they were more patient, more intuitive and had a softer voice than men.

Richard also mentions that the operators had to be discreet because they were privy to such secrets as the names of pregnant girls.

The rural postal service expanded between 1900 and 1940. Postmasters were appointed in the countryside and their names form part of local history. Post offices were meeting places, where people from the community exchanged news, but the postmasters did not do their work alone. "It was wives and daughters who discreetly got the job done after doing their housework and looking after the children," said one observer. The work began at five o'clock in the morning and finished at six in the evening, when the train left. Women participated actively in the work. Some women, for example, helped their husbands deliver mail to rural boxes.

The new roles assumed by rural women underlined their importance in rural life. They took on extra jobs to support the family or help their husbands or fathers, often without pay or for a pathetically low wage, cheerfully and with dedication, even though most of the time they were closely supervised by men. A close look at these jobs reveals that they were often exhausting, requiring long hours, patience and energy.

In the cities and in the countryside, modern life increasingly required a formal education, and women began to demand access to knowledge.

NOTES

1 Jeanne d'Arc Lévesque-Martin and Liliane Greven-Raymond, *Les reconnaissez-vous?* (La Pocatière, 1980), p. 86.

2 Constitution of the Cercles de Fermières, 1928.

CHAPTER ELEVEN

GETTING AN EDUCATION
AND ORGANIZING

ACCESS TO EDUCATION:
THE LONG HAUL

HISTORICALLY, EDUCATION FOR GIRLS has reflected societal attitudes to the role of women. Studies of nursing, of the entrance of women into the professions and of the growth of office work show that certain fields of knowledge were reserved for men, and that men tended to foster those improvements in girls' education that best served men.

Contradictory concerns regarding the role of women produced numerous ambiguities in educational models developed for women particularly in the Catholic school system. Both the Catholic and Protestant systems were poorly coordinated and poorly defined. Anglophone girls had access to public high schools (grades nine to eleven); from there they could go to university; for Francophone girls, anything above a primary education was available only in private schools run by nuns. In 1917, there were at least thirty-two teaching communities running 586 boarding schools.

The number of years of Francophone public schooling was increasing. In 1923, a pupil spent six years in primary school, and then a two-year complementary course was added. In 1929, the three-year superior primary course was introduced for a total of twelve grades. But there were no public high schools for girls. They could continue their education beyond primary school only at private institutions offering complementary and superior primary courses. The number of girls at the postsecondary level was not included in the official statistics for the first half of the twentieth century, so it is difficult to calculate how many girls reached that level. The popular belief in Quebec is that girls were more educated than boys, but this remains to be proved.

Research carried out by sociologist Thérèse Hamel shows that, in the country-side, girls went to school a little longer than boys did, but that in the towns the opposite was true: the urbanization of Quebec seems to have had a negative effect on girls' school attendance.

Private schools developed a number of programs specifically designed for females; between 1899 and 1920, several such programs were introduced. They were devised, structured, and supervised by the Department of Public Instruction (teachers'-training colleges), the Ministry of Agriculture (domestic-science courses) and the universities (superior-primary courses, arts and science courses and the classical course).

The network of private secondary schools came about as a result of pressure from nuns. Since the beginning of the twentieth century, they had been demanding that girls be given secondary education and granted a recognized diploma. Three great avenues were thus opened to women.

The first avenue was the *école normale* (teachers'-training college). In 1898, there was only one Quebec teachers' training college for girls; but by 1940, there were twenty-two; the increase was due to the efforts of bishops and religious communities. But there were few graduates (112 in 1901 and 907 in 1939) because girls could obtain a teaching certificate from the Catholic Board of Examiners without attending a teachers'-training college. Until 1952, there was only one teachers'-training college in Montreal. (It was run by the Congrégation Notre-Dame for those with religious vocations.) As a result, lay teachers remained in the countryside while nuns undertook urban teaching. The teachers'-training colleges were criticized particularly because most students aimed only for the elementary certificate, which took the least time to obtain.

In 1910, the teaching communities discussed giving formal recognition to those courses which were being given to girls who had obtained the elementary certificate. (What they really wanted was a Francophone high school.) Their efforts resulted in the creation of the arts-and-science course in Montreal and the superior-primary course in Quebec City. These prestigious four-year programs were referred to as university courses, although graduates had completed only eleven years of schooling. The four-year course was attended mostly by girls from the upper classes, and then only a minority. However, this minority consisted of six times as many girls as attended the regional domestic-science schools.

For more than a century, the teaching of domestic science in Quebec propagated the ideology of woman as wife and mother. The first domestic-science course was taught at the Ecole ménagère de Roberval, founded in 1882. According to Nicole Thivierge, the Roberval school supported the colonization movement: women were educated to keep their husbands on the farm. In 1905, another domestic-science school opened its doors in Saint-Pascal de Kamouraska; its program was widely recognized.

The growth of these two important domestic-science schools prompted the Department of Public Instruction to establish the *cours ménager agricole* (agricultural domestic-science course). After 1905, most convents in the province were transformed into domestic-science schools, which offered eight years of training. There were more than 160 domestic-science schools in 1930, but it was difficult to recruit students for the advanced program: parents were reluctant to pay to have their daughters trained to be housewives. In 1937, only 230 girls studied domestic science at the secondary level.

The domestic-science movement spread to the towns and throughout Quebec. Housekeeping was to be approached as rationally and as scientifically as medicine or charitable work. Domestic work was a profession and urban housewives had to be efficient housekeepers; housekeeping principles had to be instilled in girls from childhood and wouldn't be acquired by working outside the home.

During the Thirties, a group of middle-class women decided to set up a school where other women would be given general training in domestic science. The Ecole ménagère provinciale was founded in 1904 under the auspices of the women's section of the Société Saint-Jean-Baptiste, aided by a citizen's committee. Such lay initiatives in the Francophone community were rare, indeed. The school – unique in the Francophone community – offered day and evening classes for girls in Montreal, courses in cooking, pattern-cutting, sewing and hat making. Classes, taught in French and in English, were designed to train women to be good housekeepers and to provide factory employees with professional training that would enable them to find better jobs. Feminist Marie Gérin-Lajoie took a great interest in the school; she taught law courses there and gave lectures on various subjects, including marriage contracts.

At the suggestion of Adelaide Hoodless, domestic-science courses were also offered to Anglophone women. In 1902, James Robertson and Sir William McDonald had expressed an interest in creating domestic-economy and domestic-science courses for girls. In 1907, McDonald College founded the School of Household Science, offering three types of courses: a three-month survey course, a one-year course in housekeeping and a two-year course in domestic science.

The courses concentrated on preparing girls for married life. However, during World War One, there was a demand for dietitians to supervise food supplies for the army. As a result, the study of domestic science became more scientific and less domestic.

Graduates from the school (all women until the 1970s) worked as dietitians in hospitals, department stores, public services and, during World War Two, in the armed forces. Their advanced professional training as experts in food chemistry was recognized. In 1919, a four-year diploma in domestic science was begun. The first two courses offered training in housekeeping; the two- and four-year courses trained girls to become specialists: teachers, dietitians in hospitals or restaurants, lecturers or dedicated community workers.

By the end of the Thirties, domestic science was an important part of a girl's education, from primary school to university. Domestic-science instruction provided a forum for discussions on girls' education, a subject very much in vogue at a time when women were beginning to question traditional models.

It was easy to convince much of society that domestic science studies were useful: the subject seemed to be the perfect way to train housewives and ser- vants to go to heaven "with a broom in their hands." However, secondary and post-secondary education were still not available to all women. Anglophone women had been admitted to the McGill Faculty of Arts since 1884, but they had to sit at the back of the lecture hall with their chaperones. Women were not allowed into most other university faculties at all, and strict segregation of the sexes was still considered desirable.

The Royal Victoria College owes its existence to the generosity of one of the great Canadian Pacific Railroad barons, Donald Smith (Lord Strathcona), who gave almost a million dollars for the creation of the college. The build- ing, across from the McGill campus at the corner of Sherbrooke and Univer- sity streets, was completed in 1889.

Named for the ruling British Queen, the college was a social, academic and administrative centre for resident and nonresident female students. There were lecture halls, a library, several large auditoriums and private accommo- dation for students. There was a well-equipped gymnasium in the basement and tennis courts behind the building.

The students, known as "Donaldas," took first- and second-year university courses at the college. They attended most advanced courses and laboratory work alongside male students on the McGill campus, although Lord Strathcona's grant was conditional on separate education being maintained within McGill.

Ethel Hurlbatt, principal of the college until 1929, was an ardent defender of women's suffrage. During World War One, McGill became a rallying point for women who wanted to change their situation. The Dean of the Faculty of Law supported the admission of women to the Bar, and a few radical feminists taught at McGill: Carrie Derrick in the biology department and, later, Idola Saint-Jean in the French department.

In 1917, there were more women than men in the McGill Faculty of Arts. Because of the growing female enrollment, it became necessary to offer more

WHAT SHOULD GIRLS LEARN IN SCHOOL?

An education, to be complete, should include everything that makes for good housekeeping.... What makes a strong woman useful to her family is her ability to make them totally happy, which comes from a clear conscience and good spirits, which are usually the fruit of maternal devotion; a mother should know how to provide clothing and food to all members of her family in a home where the housekeeping is impeccable. Although the world will be able to excuse a woman her ignorance of many things, it will always be grateful to the convents and have complete confidence in them because they train excellent housewives. History, arithmetic, French and the social graces are treated as complementary subjects and this will be of service to those who live in a house with a woman who has been trained not to become a *femme savante* (learned woman) whose ridiculous vanity would only take her away from her vocation and the duties which are appropriate to her sex.... There is absolutely no comparison to be made with, and no similarities to be found in, boys' education....[1]

courses on campus, and the principle of separate education dwindled. Gradually, the professional schools at McGill were opened to women – Law in 1911 (Annie Macdonald Langstaff, the first woman graduate, could not practise her profession because the Bar refused to admit women until 1941), Medicine in 1918 and Dentistry in 1922. Most faculties however long remained male bastions.

After 1880, McGill women were encouraged to take physical-education courses. Funding for women's athletic activities was ludicrously small in comparison to that for male activities, and equipment was poor, nevertheless, athletic activities became an integral part of a woman's studies. While North Americans were still debating whether it was possible for a young woman to retain her femininity and child-bearing capacity if she engaged in rigorous physical exercise, a few women professors at McGill championed the need for physical training for female students. Students played hockey, tennis and basketball, and did gymnastics, and the McGill women's teams entered inter-university sports competitions.

Francophone women had access to a university education only after it became possible for them to take the four-year classical course; authorization was not granted until 1908.

According to Lucienne Plante, Québécois, like people everywhere, were afraid to let women out of the home because they believed that "any initiative on the part of a woman to have access to humanist culture is seen as a rejection of the female role, as a desire to imitate men."

Sister Sainte-Anne-Marie, a Congrégation nun and teacher at the Mont-Sainte-Marie convent, was aware of the needs and deficiencies of the girls she taught. In 1897, she met the Abbé Georges Gauthier, chaplain and teacher at the convent who thought like her that the girls should be allowed to do classical studies. As teachers were needed, the Abbé Gauthier set up a program of classical studies, which was followed by Sister Sainte-Anne-Marie and other nuns at the Mont-Sainte-Marie convent. Around the same time, the Université de Montréal (at this time a branch of the Université Laval) introduced literature courses for the general public. But nuns could not take the courses, as nuns did not attend university. When Sister Sainte-Anne-Marie became mother superior in 1903, she brought in professors to teach at her convent.

In April 1904, community authorities began to negotiate affiliation with the rector of the Université Laval. The director of studies and her assistant, armed with a letter from Monseigneur Bruchési, were sent to Quebec City. They were well received by the rector, who encouraged them "to present the Congrégation's academic program to the Council of Public Instruction and, following that, to make an official request for affiliation with the university." In September, the Catholic Committee of Public Instruction refused the Congrégation sisters' request, stating that "the request seemed premature, that it was not the right time to introduce higher education for girls." Not even all the convent superiors within the community were of one opinion: several preferred girls to enrol in the Ecole normale Jacques-Cartier, which had been run by the Congrégation since 1889.

Some feminists tried to obtain an education for their daughters. Marie Gérin-Lajoie, a member of the Fédération nationale Saint-Jean-Baptiste, wrote to Mother Sainte-Anne-Marie pointing out that French-Canadian women had to go to McGill, the United States or Europe to complete their studies. The sisters of the Congrégation must open an institute of higher education she said, or a lay group would do it.

On 25 April 1908, *La Patrie* announced the opening of a girls' high school with compulsory Greek and Latin. The institution was nondenominational, which caused some concern amongst Catholics. Mother Sainte-Anne-Marie urged her superiors to take action. They were not enthusiastic, but sent her to see Monseigneur Bruchési. She revealed to him her plans to found an "école supérieure" (secondary school) at the mother convent on Sherbrooke Street. Monseigneur Bruchési was won over and promised to speak to the vice-rector of the Université Laval à Montréal. The mothers general of the community formally approached the archbishop, who approved the project immediately.

However, some nuns feared that the school might make their community an object of ridicule. Others saw the school, which was near the novitiate, as "an insidious and dangerous threat to spirituality and monastic discipline." Members of the clergy were also divided: some approved of the project; many more declared it to be outrageous modernism. Priests thought it dangerous to make scholars of women – they might refuse to marry and have a family when they finished their studies. The Sulpiciens refused their written approval, and the public seemed to think that a classical education for girls was extravagant and irrelevant.

Faced with these diverse reactions, Monseigneur Bruchési thought it best to wait a few years, especially as the other bishops had not been consulted. Mother Sainte-Anne-Marie consulted her friend Abbé Georges Gauthier, who had supported her from the beginning and who had become a canon and priest of the cathedral, while remaining chaplain to Mont-Sainte-Marie. He told her to pursue her project. Mother Sainte-Anne-Marie went back to Monseigneur Bruchési, who capitulated, advising the nuns to announce their plans in *La Semaine religieuse* and to include his letter of response to the director of studies. The article, which appeared on 20 June 1908, announced the foundation of a college to be called "Ecole d'enseignement supérieure." (The name "collège féminin" was considered too daring.) The Ecole supérieure opened its doors on 8 October, offering the last four years of the classical course, in English and French. The first graduate was Marie Gérin-Lajoie (1916), who placed first in the baccalauréat exams, ahead of all the students enrolled at the Université de Montréal. However, her success was not recognized, as it did not seem appropriate for a girl to be placed ahead of boys.

By 1938 there were eleven classical colleges for girls, but very few students attended them. Little was heard of these institutions until the Fifties, because society did not favour higher education for girls. The government did not subsidize the colleges until 1961, although boys' colleges had been subsidized since 1922.

Anglophone and Francophone students complemented their academic studies by joining clubs. The first women students at McGill were automatically excluded from male clubs and therefore founded their own associations. In 1885, they founded the Delta Sigma Society, which sponsored debates and discussions on such topics of public interest as women's suffrage, capital and labour, equal salaries for equal work and cooperative housekeeping. The group was one of the earliest feminist groups in Quebec and its debates often focused on the status of women. Other philanthropic societies founded around this time took an interest in missionary work, French culture, music, science and so on. There were Protestant, Jewish and Catholic women at McGill. Some women formed separate clubs, such as the Menorah Society for Jewish women (1915); others were admitted to male societies, such as the Newman Society for Catholics (1925). However, women did not have status at McGill: they could not hold executive positions in the Students' Council until 1931, for example.

At the Ecole d'enseignement supérieur, girls participated in study groups, attended lectures and did charitable work.

Study groups were formed around 1910 in schools and student associations. In these groups, students worked together to gain the intellectual and social training that would enable them to influence the world around them.

CONTINUING EDUCATION

Women workers, housewives and teachers had access to different types of continuing education. Hundreds of associations and groups offered courses and lectures to women from all walks of life. Thousands of women took introductory or advanced courses in sewing, food preparation, hygiene, elocution and domestic science.

The Ecole des arts domestiques was founded in 1930. The school encouraged women to dust off their looms and spinning wheels. In 1935, twenty thousand farm women were enrolled in these courses. Many of the women who took courses in crafts and trades were encouraged to go into business.

In some Montreal parishes, the Fédération nationale Saint-Jean-Baptiste organized courses in cooking, dressmaking, hat making and pattern-cutting. Around ten thousand women enrolled each year.

Ready-to-wear clothing was widely available, but women who could sew saved a lot of money by making their own clothes. As they became more skillful, they could make the elegant dresses they could not afford to buy. A number of seamstresses worked for middle-class families, revamping old clothes or making new ones.

Schoolteachers could upgrade their skills through conferences, lectures and study groups, according to Maryse Thivierge. The first public lecture for teachers was held in 1886, the first teachers' conference in Montreal in 1901. However, it was difficult for poor teachers and those who lived far away to attend these events.

Study groups, however, were quite accessible. In Montreal, they had existed since 1924. In 1934, regional inspectors organized parish study groups in their districts. The groups were successful in the large towns and in places where rural teachers' associations had been founded.

Left-wing groups were also training their members, and women such as Bella Hall Gould, Léa Roback, Bernadette Lebrun and Annie Buller helped develop new approaches to political activism.

Bella Hall Gould, the director of Montreal University Settlement, quickly discovered that the solution to poverty did not lie in helping individuals. She studied Marxism in New York, then came back to Montreal to found the Labour College with Annie Buller, a militant who organized women workers in the garment industry. The college offered courses in Marxist economics, the history of the workers' movement and current affairs; classes were taken mostly by union members. Internal strife closed the Labour College doors in 1924 and its members went their separate ways; some upheld the ideas of the British Labour Party; others supported the Communist Party of Canada, founded in 1922.

In 1925, Albert Saint-Martin organized a workers' university on Craig Street to educate the Francophone masses. According to historian Marcel Fournier, the university held Sunday lectures on Communism, Russia, the history of France, Canadian literature, religion, geography and astronomy. Militants acquired a basic education: reading, teamwork, elocution and principles of philosophy and political science. A number of women attended the university, but they felt uncomfortable being there: "I saw the movement as being so right and necessary ... on the other hand, I still held certain beliefs, it was three years before I could give up those beliefs."

Right-wing or left-wing, women were confronted by resistance, but opposition did not stop these first feminists from organizing to obtain their rights and to broaden their activities.

THE WOMEN'S MOVEMENT: SOCIAL FEMINISM AND CHRISTIAN FEMINISM

Since the end of the nineteenth century, middle-class women had been participating in the urban-reform movement through their charitable associations.

As lay women's activities expanded, the experience women gained in organization and in collective action would help them organize in the struggle for fundamental rights: the vote, higher education and a legal status in keeping with modern times. The women endorsed feminist ideology, to the great displeasure of civil and religious authorities, who could see female-male relations were changing profoundly. These men saw most clearly what allowing women to work, get an education and vote would lead to. Women were seeking the source of their oppression; they were looking for remedies for its most glaring manifestations.

A women's movement emerged in Montreal aimed at the reorganization of charitable work, equality for women in the work place and the promotion of women's rights. Initially, Quebec women worked within the Montreal Local Council of Women, the Montreal affiliate of the National Council of Women, founded in 1893 by Lady Aberdeen, wife of the then Governor-General. The national council hoped to unify women's associations, to secularize the women's movement, and to stay away from partisan politics. The formation of the Council was the culmination of a general unification movement. In the years preceding the formation of the Council, a series of women's associations had sprung up: the Women's Christian Temperance Union, the YWCA, the Girls' Friendly Society and so on. These associations consisted of women mainly from the bourgeoisie and the petite bourgeoisie.

According to Yolande Pinard, the National Council was very conservative; it wanted to save the family from the perils of industrialization and to protect the traditional vocation of mother and wife. Like many people, the Council thought that the "maternal instinct," was unique to women and made women different from men.

The council wanted women to have the vote, legal equality and higher education, but very few council women argued in favour of equality between women and men. Most, especially Quebec Francophones, based their demands on the gender differences between women and men and the complementarity of roles.

In 1888, American women founded the Washington International Council of Women. Canadians Bessie Star and Emily Howard Stowe attended their founding conference; Lady Aberdeen participated in several women's groups in Great Britain. Women increasingly believed that, by organizing they could adequately deal with industrialization, urbanization, immigration and the growth of the working class.

Quebec middle-class women wanted to play a larger role in society and to reorganize charitable work. The increase in the number of Anglophone charitable institutions controlled by lay women led to the foundation of the Montreal Local Council of Women (MLCW) in 1893. Francophone women, on the other hand, saw several lay Catholic associations – as well as associations controlled by doctors and social workers – transferred to nuns and the clergy. The lay women relegated to supporting roles had difficulty overcoming the poor image that resulted from their ancillary role especially in the face of virulent antifeminism.

Defined as spouses, mothers and housewives and held up as the guardians of the language and the faith, Catholic Francophone women did not enjoy the freedom of action of Anglophone women, who did not have to deal with a hostile clergy. Nevertheless, a small number of Francophone women espoused the ideas of reformist liberalism, enabling French and English women's groups to come to an understanding. Solidarity between Francophone and Anglophone women in Montreal was essential to the development of a feminist movement for social change and to a feminist movement for equal rights.

These feminists believed that their activism would give rise to a better social order and to a higher morality. They pursued their objectives through the Montreal Local Council of Women, a mainly Protestant organization whose first president was Lady Julia Drummond, wife of the president of the Bank of Montreal. The organization attracted feminists Carrie Derrick, Grace Ritchie England, Elizabeth Monk, Marie Gérin-Lajoie, Joséphine Marchand-Dandurand, Caroline Béique and Marie Thibaudeau. Women doctors, journalists and professors and women involved in social work met through the council. It was in the council, too, that Marie Gérin-Lajoie first assumed her major role in the feminist movement.

The council chose its causes carefully; but many people, particularly in the Francophone community, were reluctant to support it. The council involved itself in projects designed to reduce the social problems in metropolitan Montreal. It also supported the suffrage movement, access to higher education for women and improvements in the legal status of women.

But Catholicism and the nationalist question sidetracked Francophone liberal reformists, who were torn between their religious and nationalist beliefs and their reformism. The Christian-feminist movement, which began in France, provided a means of reconciling religion with demands for women's rights. The Fédération nationale Saint-Jean Baptiste, founded in 1907 by Marie Gérin-Lajoie and Caroline Béique, adopted the Christian-feminist ideology but did not give up feminist demands for equal rights.

The federation brought together diverse women's associations and centred its activities on charitable work, work projects and education. But because of its ideological ambivalence, the federation vacillated between calling for fundamental changes in the status of women and the Catholicism that would keep women in their traditional role. Moreover, the federation's lack of contact with the more progressive Anglophone movement increased its ideological isolation.

Nevertheless, the federation opened the way to the political and legal liberation of women. It took an interest in all traditional female activities and established close ties with the Sainte-Justine children's hospital and the Gouttes de Lait. It led temperance battles, demanded that prisoners' wives receive their husbands' wages, and furthered such causes as assistance for the unemployed, workers' housing and the creation of juvenile courts.

There were several reasons for the decline of the federation during the

Twenties: reduced activity of professional organizations, which were being replaced by unions; the conflict between reformism and traditional conservative ideology; and the difficulties middle-class women had in reaching women of other classes. Yet, in spite of the inevitable stumbling blocks, the first generation of feminists made important contributions to the liberation of women.

GETTING THE LAW CHANGED

At the beginning of the century, unmarried women and widows enjoyed full rights. Married women did not. In fact, Marie Gérin-Lajoie described marriage as the legal death of women.

The legal incapacity of the married woman was the basis of the whole family structure. The husband was the uncontested head of the family; he totally controlled the administration of the family's assets. A married woman's legal rights were subject to her husband's authorization. At the beginning of the century, a jurist stated that this requirement derived

> from simple logic: in all partnerships, the person the least apt at business should be supervised by the more capable person. This requirement is based on the common interests of the husband and the wife, and the former would be jeopardized if the fate of their partnership were left to the lack of foresight and thoughtlessness of the member of the association who is the least competent to be in charge and whose very nature impels her to be subordinate.

The legal strictures on a married woman did not stem from weakness or inferiority, it was said, but from the obedience and respect she owed to the authority of her husband. As most women married very young, they rarely had the chance to enjoy independence. Moreover, no woman could hold public office.

Reforms to the Civil Code became the major target for feminists at the turn of the century. The Fédération nationale Saint-Jean-Baptiste, founded in 1907, included reform of the Civil Code in its platform, and drew the attention of legislators to loopholes in the laws. Marie Gérin-Lajoie published a booklet called *Traité de droit usuel* (Practical Guide to Law), a primer of civil and constitutional law. The book was aimed at a wide audience, but the author hoped it would reach women in particular. Because of her knowledge of the law, she was recognized as the legal resource person for feminists and she was active in the legal struggles that preceded the Homestead Act and the Pérodeau Act.

Since 1897, the Homestead Act had provided minimal protection to wives in certain colonized regions. The act prevented a husband from disposing of any portion of his wife's assets designated as family property without his wife's consent. (This generally consisted of the house and part of the land.) It was not easy for creditors to evict a mother and children from the family home. But in 1909, the Charbonneau Bill, designed to remove such protection, was introduced in the Legislative Assembly. The bill's supporters said that creditors were being victimized and that the law made it difficult for a colonist to obtain credit. The Fédération nationale Saint-Jean-Baptiste and the Montreal Local Council of Women opposed the Charbonneau Bill. Doctor Grace Ritchie England, Marie Gérin-Lajoie and Caroline Béique went to Quebec City to present a petition; but in spite of their protests, the Charbonneau Bill became law. Wives of colonists no longer had protection against creditors or husbands who acted in bad faith.

In 1913, Marie Gérin-Lajoie published a series of articles on the status of women in *La Bonne Parole* (The Good Word). She wanted to prepare public opinion for the matrimonial law reforms that the federation intended to put forward. In 1914, the federation sent a delegation to Sir Lomer Gouin to press for reforms in the Civil Code. The federation also suggested that the government set up a commission of enquiry and demanded that the Civil Code be reformed to entitle married women to exercise control over their wages, to be appointed as guardians for children who were minors, and to be members of the family council. They also wanted to prevent husbands from unilaterally disposing of family assets. With the onset of war, however, the proposals were forgotten.

The Pérodeau Act was adopted in 1915. Before it was passed, a married woman whose husband died without leaving a will was thirteenth in line to inherit. The act decreed that a woman who married separate as to property could inherit from her husband if her husband died without leaving a will in the absence of other close heirs (father, mother, brother, sister, nephew, niece), or could share the inheritance with existing heirs.

The Bank Act, a federal law, allowed women who married in community of property to deposit five hundred dollars and those who married separate as to property to deposit two thousand dollars. The federation and the Catholic Women's League asked the government to raise the amount from five hundred to two thousand dollars for women in community of property. They also requested that the provincial legislature protect the deposits, so only the women could withdraw the money. Only the federal government complied with these requests. Gérin-Lajoie thought this change no improvement: there was no law expressly permitting or forbidding the husband to withdraw the money, yet judicial precedent case law gave him the right to do so.

TABLE 9

Legal Status of Married Women
as Defined in the Quebec Civil Code, 1866-1915
(numbers in parentheses indicate relevant Civil Code articles)

A. *As a Person*

1. General incapacity (akin to minors and interdicated persons). She has, however, the right to make a will (184).
   a. Legally incapable of contracting (986).
   b. Legally incapable of offering a defence or suing before the courts(986).
2. Denied right to tutorship (282).
3. Denied right to be appointed curator (337a).

B. *Personal Relationship with Husband*

1. Submission to the husband. In return, the husband owes protection (174).
2. Nationality determined by the husband's (23).
3. Choice of domicile rests with the husband (83).
4. Choice of places of residence rests with the husband (175).
5. Exercise of civil rights in husband's name (customary law).
6. Double Standard principle: the husband is free to seek a separation on grounds of adultery; the wife can do so only if the husband keeps his concubine in the common household (187,188).

C. *Financial Relationship with Husband*

1. Wife may not engage in a calling distinct from that of her husband (181).
2. Wife may not engage in commerce without her husband's consent (179).
3. In cases of legal community or property:
   a. The husband alone administers the property of the community (1292).
   b. The wife is responsible for her husband's debts. The contrary is not the case (1294).
4. In cases of separation of property:
   a. The wife cannot dispose of her property. She can, however, administer her property with the authorization of her husband or, failing the latter, that of a judge (1422).
   b. The husband cannot grant general authority to his wife: a special authorization is required for each to act (1424).
   c. The wife cannot dispose of her professional earnings (1425).

5. Cannot accept a succession alone (643).

6. Cannot make or accept a gift *inter vivos* (763). The husband can, however, make his wife the beneficiary of insurance on his life (1265).

7. Cannot alone accept testamentary executorship (906).

8. Cannot inherit from her intestate husband until after the twelve successoral degrees (637).

D. *Family Status*

1. Cannot alone consent to marriage of a minor child (119).

2. Cannot allow an unemancipated minor to leave the house (244).

3. Does not have the right of correction of children (245). The wife has, however, the right of supervision over the children (customary law).

4. Cannot exercise alone the right to tutorship of her minor children (282).

Source: Paul André Lintreau, René Durocher and Jean-Claude Robert, *Quebec: A History 1867-1929*, trans. Robert Chodos, Toronto, James Lorimer, 1983. p.187.

A FIRST COMMISSION OF ENQUIRY INTO THE STATUS OF WOMEN

At the end of the Twenties, feminists in Quebec, lay women, intellectuals and Anglophone women were growing impatient with restrictions imposed by a legal tradition that had changed little since the sixteenth century. The inferior status of married women had become humiliating.

Although the Fédération nationale Saint-Jean-Baptiste had been asking the provincial government for a commission of enquiry into women's rights since 1914, the government continually found excuses to avoid appointing one. Nationalist élites, influenced by the clergy, thought the French-Canadian identity was enshrined in the Civil Code and in the traditional family: questioning the way the family functioned could threaten the very foundations of society.

Nevertheless, at the end of the Twenties, Premier Taschereau realized that he had to do something to appease the feminists, whom he had denied the right to vote. How better to channel feminist energies than to create a commission on women's civil rights? After all, the government was in no way obliged to adopt its recommendations. Moreover, such a commission might silence progressive critics, especially Anglophones.

The Dorion Commission, named after the devout Catholic judge who presided over it, comprised four male Francophone jurists, despite pressure that a woman be included. The commission held two public hearings, one in Montreal and one in Quebec City, and received written submissions.

Five women's associations presented briefs: the Fédération nationale Saint-Jean-Baptiste (represented by Marie Gérin-Lajoie); the Association des femmes propriétaires; the Alliance canadienne pour le vote des femmes au Québec (represented by Idola Saint-Jean); the League for Women's Rights (represented by Thérèse Casgrain); and the Montreal Local Council of Women. Their demands were modest: they wanted married women to control their own incomes. Although fewer than 10 percent of wives worked outside the home, those who did so were often those who needed the money most. Under the Civil Code, the wife's income was common property unless the couple had a notarized marriage contract providing otherwise; the husband was free to dispose of her income as he wished. He could even demand that the bank manager hand over his wife's savings to him. The Dorion Commission estimated that, in 1930, 80 percent of couples were married in community of property.

The groups also wanted limits placed on the husband's freedom to squander or to give away family assets without his wife's consent. They also demanded that women have the right to be guardians of minors and trustees for those without legal capacity. Traditionally, a mother or grandmother could take on these responsibilities after the death of the father. If they remarried, they were ineligible unless their new husband was willing to assume the responsibility for them.

The groups proposed that some of a wife's moveable property be excluded from a couple's common property. Most women brought only a few pieces of furniture, a trousseau and their meagre savings into the marriage. Yet everything fell under the husband's control: he was not even accountable to his wife for his management of her assets.

The feminists also wanted to simplify separation procedures and to make them less expensive. The Association des femmes propiétaires, supported by Thaïs Lacoste-Frémont, sister of Marie Gérin-Lajoie, even dared suggest that the need for a husband's permission be abolished. The Montreal Local Council of Women and the Alliance canadienne suggested that it should become easier for women to obtain a separation from an adulterous husband. (The Civil Code stipulated that a husband could ask for a separation on the grounds of adultery; a wife could do so only if the husband brought his concubine to live in the family home.)

In addition, they asked that a fixed proportion of a husband's estate go to the wife and that separated women have freedom to manage their own property. There were also proposals to raise the marriage age for girls and to make a mother's consent obligatory.

No one suggested that laws relating to community of property or a wife's duty of obedience be abolished. Few questioned the man's venerated position as head of the family, and no one suggested that both spouses share leadership of the family.

The commissioners listened with respect to the rather conservative representations made by Gérin-Lajoie, but reacted with contempt to some of the more radical women, whom they called *bourgeoises intellectuelles*.

The Dorion Commission report was published in three volumes. In the first volume the commissioners justified the retention of the status quo for women in Quebec and stated that, if social order was to be preserved, the Civil Code had to be left intact: "The theory of equal rights is absurd because women play a special role which is different from that of men. Women have to sacrifice themselves for the general good of the family." The commissioners recognized that the Civil Code could sometimes put women at a disadvantage, but they thought this happened only in exceptional cases. They did not see merit in the women's arguments.

No doubt, there are women who are unhappy in their marriage (and men also), they are unhappy because they made a bad marriage, not because the law protects the husband more than the wife.[2]

And if the law had hardly changed for centuries, it was because women had not changed, according to the commissioners.

With such an outlook, radical change was impossible – the commission recommended only those reforms that left the family hierarchy intact. Radical change might bring on the worst possible catastrophe – divorce. The commission used the powerful position of men in the legal profession to silence feminists and critics of the Civil Code. The commissioners did, however, recommend a number of reforms, but only those that were already included in the French Napoleonic Code. For example, the commission created a category of assets reserved for married women. All in all, the recommendations of the Dorion Commission were not very innovative: and as such, most of them were acceptable to the legislators.

A woman married in community of property was given exclusive access to the money she earned and exclusive right to administer and dispose of any assets she bought with that money. But a woman who worked in the home still had no say in the administration of family assets.

The commission also recommended that a woman have a veto over her husband giving away certain assets belonging to the community property. (If she was married separate as to property, she was free to dispose of her moveable property.) A woman who had obtained a legal separation was given the same legal status as a widow, and did not need her husband's or a judge's authorization. All unmarried women and widows were eligible to become guardians and trustees; married women were also eligible, if they were appointed jointly with their husbands. Finally, women could witness wills before a notary.

The commission did not question the principle of a husband authorizing legal transactions made by his wife. They also rejected the idea of giving a mother the same family powers as a father; the inequality of spouses was also maintained in cases of adultery.

The Dorion Commission found no need to change the laws as in their view most women did not feel them to be injust. They were probably not far wrong: unmarried women enjoyed the same rights as men; most wives were busy with housework and bringing up their children, and were happy to leave the finances to their husbands, knowing that half the assets accumulated during the marriage belonged to them.

A few Francophone women, no doubt encouraged by the clergy, openly proclaimed their disapproval of even the small changes made by the Dorion Commission. For example, Rolande S. Desilets, representing the Cercles de fermières, which had eight thousand rural women members, took the following position:

> It is our belief that the great majority of French Canadian mothers and wives will disapprove of this feminist movement. Even more to the point, they will ask the competent authorities to put an end to the agitation which is troubling the peace of certain homes. There have been some ridiculous scenes between husbands and wives as a result of recent lectures given by feminists in Quebec City and in Montreal, where young wives who had been perfectly happy until then imagined, to the great astonishment of their husbands, that they had been persecuted without knowing it.[3]

To Marie Gérin-Lajoie, the changes in the Civil Code were a reward for all the years of fighting for improvements in the legal status of women, although she was disappointed that the code did not punish the adulterous husband, except when there was a veritable ménage à trois. But Thérèse Casgrain was more critical of the commission in her autobiography, published in 1971:

> The Dorion Report, although it brought about a few changes in the Civil Code, did not go very far. If you read between the lines, it becomes obvious that our male élite has a contemptuous and arrogant attitude toward women, whom they do not hesitate to treat as inferior, even within the family. A few years later, I met Judge Ferinand Roy [one of the commissioners] and naturally, I told him that the Commission Report on

women's civil rights had disappointed us. The learned magistrate admitted that the jurists who had put it together had not gone far enough in the reforms that should have been made to the Civil Code.[4]

THE DORION COMMISSION'S VIEW OF WOMEN

When A Woman Marries

When a woman marries, she leaves her family to make a new family and takes her husband's name; her identity, without disappearing, is defined by the father of her children, and this complies with the inescapable law of nature and our Christian morals, our laws take into account this fact that governs the situation of women, who are naturally dependent and the laws do nothing else but legally sanction the commitments of natural law and divine law that are freely made by both spouses. And this is why a woman who marries sacrifices, quite simply, her freedom, her name and her identity, and at the same time and as a consequence, sacrifices a part, not as they say, of her legal rights but of the exercise of these rights.[5]

The Principle of the Legal Incapacity of the Married Woman

In truth, what it protects is not the rights of men to the detriment of those of women, but the conjugal relationship and the family, by using the power of civil authority to strengthen a pre-established hierarchy, by recognizing the husband as head of the family, which he already was according to natural law and by giving him only the powers necessary to exercise this responsibility.[6]

Eternal Femininity

A woman's activity has taken on new forms, she is exploring new areas of education, her attitudes which seem new, only show that although some things have changed in the milieux where she is evolving, women themselves have not really evolved. Created to be the companion of a man, a woman is still, above all, a wife and a mother.[7]

Private and Public Life

The emancipation of women is a word which is associated both with the question of the civil rights and the question of the political rights of women. But the private and public situations of women are two separate domains: and it happens too often, and we have seen this ourselves – that they are confused and that one impinges on the other.[8]

Feminists Who Are Too Critical of the Existing Laws

Neither has it escaped our attention that the zeal displayed by certain women in pointing out the powerlessness of the law when dealing with certain cases, which are as exceptional as they are contemptible, derives from a kind of resentment; it appears, then, that women here are beginning to echo the voices of women abroad, who override the so-called male laws and rail against them.[9]

The Dangers of Public Life

The main question here is only to find out if it would be good or bad for society to bring into public life those who, by their very nature, are, without exception, called to play a role in the family and in society, a role which is delicate and already keeps them busy, and this role seems for many, both men and women, to be incompatible with the exercise of governing the people and the hard demands it makes. But, in this matter also, there are those who wonder if it is not at the expense of the family that the community as a whole will benefit from the direct participation of women who choose to become public figures.[10]

Adultery

Whatever we say, everyone knows that in fact, the wound to the heart of the wife is not usually as severe as the wound to the husband who has been deceived by his wife.... [in] a woman's heart, forgiveness is naturally easier; also, in her mind, the wound to her self-esteem is not as cruel. People around her pity her and are kind to her; the betrayed husband, however, can suffer just as much, but receives no sympathy from others for the injury done to his family furthermore; the infidelity of his wife exposes him to the pain of ridicule....

Practically speaking, the husband cannot disavow any child born to his wife during their marriage.

Are the children he is rearing his own? He is the only one of the two who can be caused anguish by this question. And the child of doubtful parentage, once the husband is aware of his wife's mistake, is a constant reminder of the blow he received and prevents the wound from healing with time. No doubt, the husband can have children outside the marriage; the wife does not rear them.[11]

WOMEN'S SOLIDARITY

In response to problems that emerged during the Depression, the government set up a welfare system and a number of public-works programs. The money provided by the programs was to pay for food, clothing, heating and housing. Most of the money went to the unemployed through Saint-Vincent-de-Paul and the Montreal Council of Social Agencies. Charitable organizations distributed funds and their volunteers worked in shelters and public soup kitchens.

The aid was insufficient and often poorly distributed. In 1932, Blanche Gélinas, Bernadette Lebrun, Angéline Dubé and other militant Communists formed the Solidarité féminine. They worked with the Association humanitaire and other groups organized to defend the interests of the unemployed. The Solidarité féminine comprised only women. Its purpose was "to focus particularly on the situation of women who are usually neglected (unmarried mothers, mothers in need) and to convince them that they should get involved directly in the struggles." In 1937, the Solidarité féminine organized several big demonstrations in Montreal. In March, a delegation asked the municipal executive committee for a 25 percent increase in assistance and protested increased rents. In May, several hundred women demonstrated in front of the MacDonald Tobacco factory. On 25 June, four hundred women gathered in front of the Unemployment Commission in the Champ-de-Mars. They all rode the streetcar, without paying, to protest in front of City Hall. The executive committee refused to meet the delegation, which was treated brutally by the police. Five women were arrested.

Fournier notes that women were poorly represented in the Communist Party, and that the Solidarité féminine was set up to give direct help to the unemployed and to increase the participation of women in the Party. The group collected clothing, money and food, and protested evictions and the sale of furniture belonging to tenants who were unable to pay their rent. Bernadette Lebrun reports:

> When we knew that a bailiff was going to come, we formed a group of 15 people and at five in the morning we filled up the house. Now, according to the law, the bailiff had to conduct the sale of contents on site. We would buy the contents of the house, a table for five cents, a kitchen chair for a cent. The bailiff would get very angry and try to reason with people. He would often collect two or three dollars, which he would pass over to the landlord. And the group would give the furniture back to the tenant.

The Solidarité féminine also explained how to use electricity and gas without paying. The movement survived until 1939.

SUFFRAGETTES AND THE STRUGGLE FOR EQUALITY

Civil and political rights for women became the primary goal of the Montreal Local Council of Women and for a number of feminists from the Fédération nationale Saint-Jean-Baptiste.

In 1893, when the Montreal Local Council of Women was founded, women did not have the right to vote in provincial or federal elections. In Quebec municipal elections, only widows and unmarried women who paid taxes could vote. In 1902, the municipal council tried to revoke the vote of women tenants. Marie Gérin-Lajoie represented the Montreal Local Council of Women in its battle to retain the vote, which was especially important to women in the urban-reform movement. The council won its fight, but failed in its bid to have a woman appointed to the Protestant Board of School Commissioners.

For several decades, votes for women had been widely discussed in literary circles, temperance societies and rural organizations; but progress was slow. Around 1880, there were numerous campaigns in support of the vote in Canada. Because they could not go out alone in public, women met and exchanged ideas in their kitchens and living rooms. They believed that if they could vote, they could pose a sufficient electoral threat to persuade authorities to implement desired reforms.

Western women won the right to vote in 1916. By 1919, women could vote in provincial elections and become members of the legislature of all provinces except Quebec and Prince Edward Island.

In Quebec, the Montreal Suffrage Association, led by Carrie Derrick, was founded in 1912 and struggled for the right to vote in federal elections. In 1917 the vote was given to women with relatives who had served or were serving in the armed forces. In 1918, it was extended to all Canadian women.

The Provincial Franchise Committee, founded by Marie Gérin-Lajoie and Mrs. Walter Lyman, continued the work of the Montreal Suffrage Association. The suffragettes encountered opposition from civil and religious authorities who, for different reasons, were trying to keep women out of politics.

Religious authorities were afraid that women's suffrage would emancipate women too rapidly and weaken religious faith in families. Civil authorities were convinced that women would support the opposition Conservative Party. It was recruiting many supporters among the clergy, and French-Canadian women were believed susceptible to clerical influence.

Antifeminist forces delayed the victory until 1940, and the virulence of their attacks kept many women from fighting to win the vote. The movement, according to its opponents, wanted women to become involved in political intrigue and to work as election organizers, members of the legislature, senators and lawyers – in short, to do the things men did. Such women wanted to destroy the "woman-mother" and the "feminine" woman. Respected politician and journalist Henri Bourassa virulently opposed the vote. Why would such an intelligent man react so violently? Susan Mann Trofimenkoff explains that Bourassa's vision of women was based on a particular vision of men. For Bourassa, a man was a reasonable and logical being and the natural leader of society. But a man could also be brutal, and needed a woman to be a peace-maker, to moderate and reconcile opposing views. Like many men of his generation, Bourassa thought that it was very important to keep the roles played by the two sexes separate. In 1922, feminists decided to seek a meeting with Premier Louis-Alexandre Taschereau and to press for the right to vote. The first women's pilgrimage to Quebec City set the tone for other marches, and provoked the clergy, politicians, journalists and other women.

On Friday, 10 February 1922, *Le Devoir* reported the march on the front page: "The statement by feminist delegations in the Quebec Parliament produced considerable agitation. If this is what happens when women ask for their political rights, what will it be like when they exercise them?"

Taschereau announced that he opposed the vote for women, declaring: "It is precisely because men want women to fully carry out their mission in life that they want to keep them out of politics; women have a ministry of love and charity to fulfill and this role is totally inappropriate for men." Idola Saint-Jean countered that the feminist movement was worldwide and there was no stopping it. She believed that women would not give their utmost to society until they obtained their full rights as citizens.

Chauvinist articles about the feminist delegation to Quebec City were full of ridiculing physical descriptions that transformed the women into a tasteless spectacle. On 17 February, *Le Devoir* published an article entitled "Contre le suffrage féminin" (Against Women's Suffrage), stating: "The women who are organizing the campaign for women's suffrage are apparently meeting with a great deal of opposition to their movement, in spite of the fact that the premier told their delegation that he wished them every success."

Some women organized a countercampaign against women's suffrage. Many Quebec women opposed the suffragettes because they believed that, if women voted, they would lose their authority and the power conferred on them by their noble mission.

Françoise Gaudet-Smet, whose influence on rural women was considerable, opposed women's suffrage. In an article published to celebrate the twenty-fifth anniversary of the right to vote, she explained:

I was not against it in principle, but Quebec women, especially in the countryside, were not ready for it. They were not interested in the power of the vote. They looked after their homes, yes, but society kept them out of public life. Politics at that time was a vote-getting racket, a chance to have drinking bouts, contentious meetings and battles, it was no place for women.... Women knew where their strength and their influence lay; this was not only evident on election day but 364 days a year.

Gaudet-Smet's was a popular argument: women had so much power in the home they did not need any more.

Because of the virulence of the campaign against suffrage, the struggle died down. However, it picked up again in 1927, when Idola Saint-Jean founded the Alliance canadienne pour le vote des femmes du Québec. In 1930, Saint-Jean ran in the federal election and won three thousand votes in the Dorion-Saint-Denis riding. In 1928, Thérèse Casgrain became president of the Provincial Committee. In 1929, she changed the group's name to the Ligue des droits de la femme (League for Women's Rights). Feminists from the two associations traveled to Quebec City year after year to press for the right to vote.

In June 1938, women were invited to the Liberal Party convention. Thérèse Casgrain, wife of the Speaker of the House of Commons, was vice-president of the Women's Liberal Federation of Canada. She had forty women selected as delegates to the convention and they ensured that women's suffrage was added to the agenda. The convention endorsed women's suffrage. Adélard Godbout was chosen to be party leader and an election was called in 1939. During the campaign, Godbout promised women the vote and after his victory, feminist associations reminded him of his promise. The speech from the throne in 1940 stated that the promise would be honoured.

Opposition from the clergy was virulent. On 1 March 1940, Cardinal Villeneuve issued a communiqué:

We do not favour political suffrage for women;

1. Because it goes against the unity and hierarchy of the family;

2. Because voting exposes women to all the passions and machinations of electioneering;

3. Because, in fact, it seems to us, that the majority of women in the province do not want it;

4. Because the social, economic and hygienic reforms that are being brought forward to justify women's suffrage could just as well be obtained through the influence of nonpolitical organizations.

We believe that we are expressing the general sentiment of the bishops of the province.

Adélard Godbout was in a difficult position. He solved the dilemma by threatening to resign, to be replaced by the anticlerical T. D. Bouchard. Opposition from the clergy was stifled, and the law was passed on 25 April 1940.

But women did not gain their share of power when they got the vote. It was not until the Sixties that feminists could begin to expose the sexism and misogyny of the political system.

ALMOST EQUAL BUT STILL ON THE SIDELINES

Men had defined women in terms of their domestic role and created a special status for them; the first feminists showed how offensive the definition was. Many injustices had disappeared by 1940: women had gained the right to vote, access to education and the right to work in certain professions.

But men still defined women's place in society: women won the right to vote not because they were equal to men, but because their role as mothers made them important enough to be given a voice in public affairs. Middle-class women had gained access to the classical course and were breaking through the barriers to university faculties one after another. Many Quebec women took advantage of their right to an education, but followed traditional female courses, in which women were educated not to compete with men but to be better mothers.

By the beginning of the twentieth century, men controlled domestic-science courses in the schools and had discredited women's traditional knowledge. In the past, women had looked after, brought up and fed their children the way their mothers had taught them; now doctors, educators and priests explained that such things were scientific. Teaching programs and clinics, such as the Gouttes de lait, were founded. Women could continue to be mothers and educators but had to apply male knowledge to do so.

Overzealous ideologues denounced wages for women, while increasing numbers of women needed to earn a living. Because women were so often told that their place was in the home and not in the work place, some women felt that they were taking jobs away from men and accepted being left on the periphery of the job market.

World War Two upset the fragile balance between the forces of the past and the forces of change. Women were asked to abandon the role of mother and work in war factories. After the war, they retired from the job market, but only temporarily, because the postwar economy demanded greater and more regular participation of women in paid work. The situation created a deadlock: women were expected to stay at home and have babies, but they were needed in the work place.

NOTES

1 Pastoral letter from the Bishop of Valleyfield, 1915, to the teaching nuns in his diocese.

2 "Premier rapport de la Commission des Droits civils de la femme" in *Revue du Notariat, vol. 32, 1929-1930, p. 249.*

3 "Nos droits et nos devoirs" in *La Bonne Fermière,* January 1930.

4 Thérèse Casgrain, *A Woman in a Man's World* (Toronto: McClelland and Stewart, 1972).

5 "Premier rapport de la Commission des droits civils de la femme," op. cit., pp. 234-235.

6 Ibid., p. 241.

7 Ibid., p. 243.

8 Ibid., pp. 273-274.

9 Ibid., p. 273.

10 Ibid., p. 274.

11 "Deuxième rapport de la Commission des droits civils de la femme" in *Revue du Notariat,* vol. 32, 1929-1930, pp. 365-366.

FURTHER READING

Beaudet, Céline, "Radio-Monde ou la vie revée" in Michèle Jean, *Québécoises du 20 siècle*. Montréal, Quinze, 1977, p. 287-294.

Brandt, Gaile Cuthbert, "Weaving it Together: Life Cycle and the Industrial Experience of Female Cotton Workers in Quebec, 1910-1950" in *Labour/Le Travailleur*, Spring 1981, p. 113-126.

Casgrain, Thérèse, *A Woman in a Man's World*. Translated by Joyce Marshall. Foreword by Frank R. Scott. Toronto: McClelland and Stewart, 1972.

Cleverdon, Catherine L., *The Woman Suffrage Movement in Canada*, second edition, Toronto, University of Toronto Press, 1974, 324 pages.

Coburn, Judi, "I See and am Silent: A Short History of Nursing in Ontario" in *Women at Work, Ontario, 1850-1930*, Toronto, Women's Press, 1974, p. 127-163.

Copp, Terry, *Anatomy of Poverty: The Condition of the Working Class in Montreal, 1897-1929. Toronto: McClelland and Stewart*.

Pierre-Deschenes, Claudine, "Santé publique et organisation de la profession médicale au Québec, 1870-1918" in Revue d'Histoire d'Amérique française, vol. 35, no 3 (December 1981), p. 355-375.

Dodd, Diane "Women, Functionalism and Reproduction: The Birth Control Movement in Canada", Ottawa, 1981, 39 pages.(unpublished manuscript).

Dumas Evelyn, *Dans le sommeil de nos os*, Montreal, Leméac, 1971, 170 pages.

Dumont-Johnson, Micheline, "Histoire de la condition de la femme dans la province de Québec" in *Tradition cuturelle et histoire politique de la femme au Canada*, Study no 8 prepared for the Royal Commission on the Status of Women in Canada, Ottawa, Information Canada, 1971, 57 pages.

Fournier, Louis, *Communisme et anticommunisme au Québec (1920-1950)*, Montréal, Editions coopearatives Albert Saint-Martin, 1979, 165 pages.

Hamel, Thérèse, *L'Oblibation scolaire au Québec: objet de la lutte des classes*, thése de doctorat 3e cycle, U. E. R. des sciences de l'éducation, université René-Descartes, Paris, 1981.

Hamel, Réginald, *Bibliographie sommaire sur l'histoire de lécriture féminine au Canada 1769-1961*, Université de Montréal, 1974, 134 pages (unpublished manuscript).

Jean, Michèle, *Québécoises du 20 siècle*, Montreal, Editions du Jour, 1974, 303 pages.

Jean, Michèle "Histoire de luttes féministes au Québec" in *Possibles*, vol. 4, no 1, Autumn 1979, p. 17-32.

Lapointe, Michelle, "Le syndicat catholique des allumettières de Hull, 1919-1924" in *R.H.A.F.*, vol. 32 no 4, March 1979, p. 603-627.

Laforce, Hélène, "La sage-femme québécoise" in Bulletin de la Fédération des femmes du Québec, no 2, May 1982, p. 12.

Lavigne, Marie, and Yolande Pinard, ed., *Les Femmes dans la sociéété québécoise.* Montreal, Boréal Express, 1977, 214 pages.

Lavigne, Marie, Yolande Pinard and Jennifer Stoddart, "La Fédération Nationale Saint-Jean-Baptiste et les revendications féministes au début du 20 siécle" in Marie Lavigne and Yolande Pinard, op. cit., p. 90-108.

Lavigne, Marie and Jennifer Stoddart, *Analyse du travail féminin à Montréal entre les deux guerres*, M.A. Thesis (History), Université du Québec à Montréal, 1974, 268 pages.

Linteau, Paul-André, René Durocher and Jean-Claude Robert, *Histoire du Québec contemporain*, Montreal, Boréal Express, 1979, 660 pages.

Miner, Horace, *St. Denis, a French-Canadian Parish*, Chicago, Phoenix Books, 1963, 299 pages.

Monet-Chartrand, Simone, *Ma vie comme une rivière*, Montreal, Editions du Remue-Ménage, 1981.

Pinard, Yolande, "Les débuts du mouvement des femmes" in Marie Lavigne and Yolande Pinard, op. cit., p. 61-87.

Plante, Lucienne, *La Fondation de l'enseignement classique féminin au Québec*, 1908-1916, thèse de D.E.S. (Histoire), Université Laval, 1968, 187 pages.

Stoddart, Jennifer, "The Dorion Commission, 1926-1931: Quebec's Legal Elites Look at Women's Rights" in David Flaherty, *Essays in Canadian Legal History*, vol. 1, Toronto, University of Toronto Press, 1981, p. 323-337.

Strong-Boag, Veronica, "Wages for Housework: Mother's Allowances and the Beginnings of Social Security in Canada" in *Journal of Canadian Studies – Revue d'Etudes canadiennes*, vol. 14, no 1, Spring 1979, p. 24-34.

Strong-Boag, Veronica, *The Parliament of Women: The National Council of Women of Canada 1893-1929*, National Museums of Canada, "History" section, document no 18, Ottawa, 491 pages.

Thivierge, Maryse, *Les Institutrices laiques à l'école primaire catholique au Québec, de 1900 à 1964*, Ph.D thesis (History), université Laval, 1981, 437 pages.

Thivierge, Nicole, *L'Enseignement ménager-familial au Québec 1880-1970*, Ph.D thesis (History), université Laval, 1981, 562 pages.

Trofimenkoff, Susan Mann and Alison Prentice, *The Neglected Majority*, Toronto, McClelland and Stewart, 1977, 192 pages.

Trofimenkoff, Susan Mann, "Henri Bourassa et la question des femmes" in Marie Lavigne and Yolande Pinard, op. cit., p. 109-124.

————, *Women at Work, Ontario 1850-1930*, Toronto, Women's Press, 1974, 405 pages.

V
THE IMPASSE
1940-1969

WOMEN IN QUEBEC WERE finally granted the right to vote in provincial elections during World War Two. This symbolic women's entry into public life had little effect on their status, but women were too preoccupied with the effects of a world war to notice.

The Depression had increased friction among the great powers. After the invasion of Poland by Hitler in September 1939, France and England declared war. Several days later, the Canadian parliament followed suit. Two years later, the United States joined the Allies against Japan, Germany and Italy.

For almost six years, Quebeckers were totally caught up by the war. Its outbreak provoked a national crisis. Canadian Anglophones were determined to spare no effort to aid England, but French-speaking Canadians were less enthusiastic. A controversy developed over conscription and Canada's participation in the war with nationalists denouncing the growing power of Ottawa. By the end of the war, Quebec had lost power federally.

After the war, the economic situation did not favour working people. Shortages and rationing were followed by inflation; industrial unrest was suppressed. The economy was severely disrupted by war and it took some time to produce new models for prosperity and development.

Postwar Quebec was utterly dominated by its premier, Maurice Duplessis. His party, the Union Nationale, was reelected in 1944, and its leader held the province in an iron grip. "The bishops," he maintained, "are eating out of my hand," and he fed them grants and subsidies for their large seminaries, hospitals, convents and colleges. "The best medical insurance is good health," he said, but he rejected numerous attempts to modify the province's social legislation. His battle cry of provincial autonomy served him as shield, sword, javelin and armour.

However, Duplessis' adversaries were legion. They could be found among the publishers of magazines and newspapers, in the Action catholique movements, in the unions, in the universities and colleges, and in literary and artistic circles. The Automatistes, a group of artists, signed a manifesto, *Le Refus global,* a symbol of opposition to traditional Quebec values and to societies that inhibit creative spontaneity. Duplessis was openly contemptuous. He insulted them and countered their attacks with ridicule. Numerous commissions of enquiry into social problems produced some innovative reports, but they were discreetly buried.

While Duplessis was in power, concrete was poured into schools, hospitals, expressways and hydroelectric dams. Quebec underwent rapid economic expansion: electricity, radio and television transmitted to the most remote village advertising for the latest modern conveniences, *The Plouffe Family,* and a dubbed version of the popular American program, *Father Knows Best.* Duplessis opened the North Shore to resource development and accepted enormous amounts of American capital. The first post-war bedroom communities appeared, followed by the first shopping plazas. Quebec was becoming a consumer society.

The death of Duplessis in the autumn of 1959 was followed by Paul Sauvé's brief period in office and the stir caused by the publication of *Les Insolences du Frère Untel* (The Impertinences of Brother Anonymous), a book which attacked the traditional education system. Reform had arrived. On 18 June 1960, the *équipe du tonnerre* (thunder team), the Liberals of Jean Lesage, assumed power in Quebec. Lesage introduced a new economic vision and new legislation, and a new class of civil-servant-cum-manager-cum-technocrat took over key positions. The Lesage government devoted its efforts to transforming the State. Powers hitherto entrusted to the Church or to private enterprise were taken back, and goods and services were redistributed. Lesage's bold measures were made possible by the post-1962 upswing in the economy. The "Quiet Revolution" coincided with a period of expansion in the capitalist economy. After 1964, the pace of modernization quickened. The State provided increasing support to the economy, whose prosperity was largely assured by monopolies and large corporations. Many of these companies were multinationals, and it was they who effectively imposed the economic principle of the survival of the fittest. All this brought profound changes in the work force and, as a result, in union organization. The manufacturing sector shrank, and Quebec ceased to be a ready supplier of cheap labour. There was also a massive increase in public consumption and consumer credit; the level of personal debt rose. It was at this time that the Ministry of Education popularized the slogan *Qui s'instruit s'enrichit* (Get educated, get rich).

The period was characterized by growing nationalist sentiment. The

Duplessis government had been defensively nationalist; the Lesage government was aggressively nationalist. The Lesage government's policies ensured that the 1966 transition to the Johnson Union Nationale government was a smooth one. Nationalism took many forms of expression; from the bombs of the FLQ to the separatist parties by way of the Marxist demands of the journal, *Parti pris*.

In 1965, Trudeau, Pelletier and Marchand were elected to Parliament, and Quebec's nationalist position was strengthened. At the same time, the Laurendeau-Dunton report concluded that two solitudes existed in Canada. The period that started with an expansion of the Quebec state ended with the demise of traditional ideologies. "Equality or Independence," demanded Daniel Johnson. René Lévesque, a star of the Liberal Party, quit to found the Parti québécois.

During the 1960s, Quebec society changed radically. As education and health services became available to everyone, the traditional social structure was destroyed; many people began to leave the Church. A new labour code was adopted and the public services were unionized; these changes transformed employer-employee relations.

Around this time, Quebeckers became aware of a truly Québécois culture: "québécois" replaced the timeworn "canadien-français." And, ironically, Canadian pride, created by the success of Expo 67, bolstered Quebec pride. Music, architecture, poetry, crafts, cooking, painting, television, the cinema: all aspects of culture blossomed in a new Québécois identity. Québécois listened to the songs of Pauline Julien, Gilles Vigneault, and Robert Charlebois.

The 1960s were a decade of worldwide protest, and Quebec was no exception. There were FLQ bombs, massive demonstrations, Saint-Jean-Baptiste day marches, a police strike, imprisonment of militants, and unrest in the colleges and universities. The press and television gave the unrest unprecedented attention.

The Quiet Revolution was not a spontaneous development, and 1960 was not a turning point for women: like other groups, they had begun the "quiet" revolution long before it was heard. Moreover, despite its egalitarian ideology, the Quiet Revolution created institutions with a new double standard. Women may have had a new and different role, but they were still inferior.

Between 1940 and 1969, women's lives changed fundamentally – initially because of the war, later from the aspirations of women themselves. Ultimately, however, women realized that these changes did not go far enough and that they had reached an impasse. Women began to organize once more.

CHAPTER TWELVE

YOUR COUNTRY NEEDS YOU: FROM BOMBS TO BABIES

THE WAR: A DECISIVE EXPERIENCE

FOR CANADIAN WOMEN, World War Two was an extraordinary experience. Mothers lost their sons, wives their husbands, sisters their brothers; some girls did not recognize their fathers. Many a wounded soldier returned to his family unable to resume his former life. For the mothers and sweethearts of soldiers sent to the front, the war was a long waiting period. When letters stopped coming, families feared the worst. Sometimes these fears were confirmed by an official telegram coldly announcing the death or disappearance of a loved one. Yet many men stayed in Canada and were not in danger; most others returned safe and sound at the end of hostilities.

For many young women, the war was an adventure. For the first time, Canada called on all women, and women wanted to play a part. For the first time in their lives, young single women could choose among the jobs left vacant by the exodus of young men into the armed forces. War production created thousands of new jobs, which were often filled by women with no work experience. If their friends or their fiancés had gone to war, there were other men in uniform: every Canadian city had its barracks where young, bored soldiers waited to be sent to the front. To keep morale high, single women were encouraged to go to dances and other social activities organized by the military or by volunteer groups.

Canada called on married women as well. In Quebec, only a few agreed to work outside the home to help the war effort. But all housewives did their part, as food rationing forced them to plan menus carefully and to keep a tight rein on budgets. No material useful to the war effort was wasted; housewives saved metal, fat and wool, which were recycled to make arms, explosives and uniforms. Charitable work was encouraged and women's groups offered their services to the authorities.

Many women realized that without them, the war economy could not keep going. Their new-found awareness had a profound effect, although it would be felt only fifteen or twenty years later. When their children grew up women looked for a life outside the home. They took up their abandoned careers. They encouraged their daughters to get an education and to obtain professional training. After 1965, women began to question traditional female values in Quebec. Living through the war played a part in this reevaluation: women had become aware of their potential.

WAR: MEN'S BUSINESS

Despite the involvement of women, World War Two remained essentially a male domain. For six years, the country anxiously followed every move of the Canadian forces. More than ever, the individual and collective fate of women depended on men.

When war broke out in 1939, women began to worry. Would their boyfriends or sons have to fight? For many young men, war offered adventure and stable, worthwhile work after the unemployment of the Thirties. But others did not wish to risk their necks in a war that did not seem to affect Canada directly and tried to avoid military service.

Thousands of women spent six years waiting for their men to return. Some never did come back; others returned home seriously wounded. Throughout Canada, but especially in Quebec, men who refused to go to war had to hide when pressured to enlist. At the end of 1944, when preparations were being made to send the first conscripts to Europe, a number of soldiers did not return from embarkation leave: they were hidden by their families until the general amnesty at the end of the war.

As married men were the last to be called up for military service, marriage became a way to avoid the army. When it was announced, on 12 July 1940, that single men would be mobilized on 15 July, there was a country-wide stampede to get married. (There were line-ups at church doors; some people got married in groups to save time.) Between 1938 and 1940, the number of marriages in Canada tripled, and many Canadians saw their youth come to an abrupt end.

Many women who had become engaged during the Depression and who had been waiting for better economic times found a reason to get married earlier, despite the austerity. Food and fabrics were strictly rationed, so brides simply put on their best dresses, and guests often brought their own rations to the reception. Women who married hastily to save men from the war sometimes came to regret their generous acts – particularly Catholic women in Quebec. During the Forties, divorce was available only to those with both financial resources and the courage to brave ecclesiastical disapproval. For divorce required an act of Parliament.

Military authorities discovered that the best way to keep troop morale high was through parcels and letters from Canada. Volunteer women were assigned young soldiers who received little mail; throughout the war, they wrote comforting letters to reassure young soldiers that the people back home supported and appreciated what they were doing.

Women in Europe and Great Britain greeted the Canadian soldiers with enthusiasm. The soldiers courted the young single women and were generally considered good matches – the number of prospective European husbands had been reduced by the war. A life in Canada, free from invasion and bombardment, where almost everybody had enough to eat was a tempting prospect. In Quebec, the Church and the more nationalist groups disapproved of marriages between Catholic Francophones and Anglophone Protestant women. But most war brides were British who married Anglophone men.

MILITARY SERVICE

The war effort required so many men that the authorities considered having women perform auxiliary functions, especially within Canada, to free up men for active combat.

The Women's Division of the Royal Canadian Air Force, the Women's Corps of the Canadian Army and the Women's Corps of the Royal Canadian Navy were founded in 1941-42. They were popularly referred to, even by Francophones, as the WDs, the CWACs and the WRENs. At the beginning of the war, although there were thousands of women in the reserve corps, there was an intensive campaign to recruit more. Madeleine Saint-Laurent (whose father became prime minister) was a captain and later a major in the Women's Army Corps. She traveled throughout Quebec urging young Francophone women to join the army.

A woman wishing to become an officer in one of the women's divisions required a university degree or equivalent. Other recruits needed only seven to ten years of education. They had to be between eighteen and forty-five, single or childless, have a good reputation, and be in good health.

In 1942, more than seventeen thousand women from across Canada were in the armed forces; at the end of the war, there were forty-five thousand. Some women joined the army to stay close to their husbands or fiancés; others joined so they could leave home to learn a trade and do a little traveling.

The recruits had to wear uniforms and keep their hair regulation length. (To boost their morale, recruits were allowed to wear jewelry and make-up.) They underwent basic training – physical training, military regulations, first aid, cartography and so on. Then they were put to work. They led a military-style life and slept in barracks on military bases, but they did traditional women's work as cooks, switchboard operators, laundresses, waitresses and housekeepers. Some acted as chauffeurs, but none carried arms. Toward the end of the war, as more men were sent to the front, women were trained to replace them as mechanics, telegraph operators or technicians. According to historians Geneviève Auger and Raymonde Lamothe, many women who had signed up in the hope of adventure were disappointed to find themselves waiting on tables in officers' messes, earning lower wages than the men did. Wage discrimination was easily justified, however. After all, women's civilian jobs were almost identical, and women had to make sacrifices for the war effort.

There was a double standard in the army. Women had almost no power. Women officers commanded only women; yet women's divisions were always under the authority of a man. A controversy broke out over whether men should salute women of a higher rank. (There were such few women to salute, however, as promotions for women were almost nonexistent.)

According to Auger and Lamothe, the armed forces women who enjoyed the most professional independence were nurses. They were essential because they assisted the doctors and, of course, their "feminine" sweetness and patience with wounded and convalescent soldiers was "just what the doctor ordered."

Nurses automatically became officers and received the same salary as men of their rank. (This was more than three times what Quebec nurses received in civilian hospitals.) The salary and the prospect of adventure were powerful attractions. More than eight thousand Canadian women applied to be military nurses; more than four thousand were accepted. Other health professionals, such as physiotherapists and dietitians, enjoyed similar status.

One-third of the nurses remained in Canada, working in military hospitals, convalescent homes and air and naval bases. Most were sent to England, where the Canadian forces were preparing to invade Europe and North Africa. The nurses looked after soldiers wounded at the front. The large military hospitals were uncomfortable and often in dangerous positions, but the nurses were rewarded by the gratitude of the soldiers. Life for thousands of men was dangerous and monotonous, and nurses, often the only women around, were the objects of continual male attention.

Relations between women and men in the armed forces was a concern for military authorities. At the beginning of the war, army women had a bad reputation, which adversely affected the recruitment of women. Young army women were separated from their families; they lived near soldiers who sometimes behaved imprudently and their lives were harsh. Many people thought army women were women of easy virtue. Historian Ruth Pierson explains that the Francophone population of Quebec, many of whom were strongly opposed to the war, found it difficult to accept a young single woman living far from parental supervision. At the beginning of the war, young male soldiers did not accept the presence of women in their world and reacted with obscene jokes about *filles à soldats* (soldiers' girls). The Minister of Defence appealed to the National Council of Women for assistance; the Council's president assured Canadian mothers that their daughters would be supervised as they would be at home.

In fact, military life was harsh and dating was tightly controlled. Women who became pregnant were dismissed from the service. The most urgent problem for the military was a serious outbreak of venereal disease, which threatened the number of men fit for combat. (Until 1944, no effective cure existed.)

The authorities launched a campaign to educate the soldiers. Pamphlets which explained the dangers of syphilis and gonorrhoea were distributed and films showed horrifying scenes of the effects of venereal disease. As men could not be expected to restrain themselves, they were given condoms and prophylactic kits. According to Pierson, women were portrayed to soldiers as the embodiment of the disease: all "easy" women who had sexual relations outside marriage were potential carriers.

The authorities relied on the chastity of the CWACs, the WRENs and the WDs, and gave them neither contraceptives nor prophylactic kits. It was hoped that the pamphlets put out by the armed forces would convince the women to refrain from sexual relations. Nowhere in the educational material prepared for women were men depicted as the source of infection. If women were infected, they had only themselves to blame. Once again, the double standard made women the sole guardians of morality and, thus, primarily responsible for the transmission of sexual diseases.

EACH WOMAN WORKER COUNTS

Canada made great contributions to the Allied war effort by providing food and military equipment. The whole economy of the country was reorganized to maintain production levels: all industries and services functioned strictly within an overall plan. The unemployment of the Depression years was quickly forgotten with the onset of war. In Quebec, explosives, planes, tanks, aluminum and uniforms were made. These industries absorbed the male work force that was not in the army, but by 1941 the war industries were short of workers. The solution: call in the women.

Starting in 1942, a few women were trained to be mechanics, electricians and welders in war factories. Most women did monotonous, routine and sometimes dangerous jobs. Producing munitions, for example, was boring, but the slightest inattention could blow up the factory.

Despite health problems and work hazards, the war factories attracted women in large numbers. Money was in short supply and wages in the war industries were high, even though women's wages were never as high as those of men. Unions recognized the injustice, but did nothing to fight it.

The work week was long: a shift was often twelve hours. During the war, women were allowed to work at night. Sometimes they worked seven days a week for months at a time. The hours and the difficult, unhealthy nature of the work – toxic fumes, dangerous materials, heavy and loud machinery – resulted in health problems for women workers. (There were numerous serious accidents, but the government hushed these up.) But the wages were good, and incessant government propaganda encouraged women to do their part to hasten the war's end.

Women left other professions to work in the war industries; in 1942, for example there was a shortage of women teachers. During the school year, teachers were forbidden to move to other jobs, but during summer, they were encouraged to work in war factories or to go to the country to help the farmers. The service sector – hospitals, schools, institutions, hotels, transport and communications – began to feel the shortage of cheap labour. Accordingly, in 1943, the government began the next phase of its campaign and encouraged housewives to accept part-time employment.

Given such opportunities, many refused domestic service; they could earn more money and have more free time in other jobs. Women, especially those who had always had servants, were panic-stricken at not being able to keep their maids.

Women, particularly young students, were encouraged to help with the harvest and to spend their summers on the farm; farmers were encouraged to work in war factories during the winter.

As new workers entered the job market, the unions hurried to sign them up. Between 1939 and 1943, union membership in Quebec increased considerably. Many women had their first experience of unions, but most did not have much time for union activities – there was still the housework.

However, some women did become full-fledged union leaders: Léa Roback at RCA Victor; Madeleine Parent in the textile industry; and Yvette Charpentier, who organized women in the garment industry, for example.

Despite a wage and price freeze, the cost of living rose more rapidly than wages. As well, increased production was stressful for the workers. Union organization had strengthened since the outbreak of war, and employees demanded union recognition. In spite of harsh legislation aimed at reducing expensive work stoppages, there were many strikes. In Quebec, the textile, shoe, garment and tobacco industries were particularly hard hit by industrial strife.

During the war, employers were making large profits and did not want to risk having their factories closed down by strikes. Union and worker demands led to important gains for women. Quebec and Ottawa introduced new guidelines, which eventually became the labour codes of today.

WOMEN HOSTAGES IN A POLITICAL GUERRILLA WAR

Quebec's participation in the war was a major issue for more than six years. Most Anglophones and some Francophones were ready to make any sacrifice. Other Francophones had reservations about participating. Anti-British sentiment, the alienation they experienced within the mainly English-speaking military, a philosophy of isolationism, sympathy for Catholic and ultraconservative France symbolized by Maréchal Pétain, the Nazi collaborator, and a distrust of Ottawa's centralized policies were all factors. Some clergymen were critical of federal leadership and the war effort, as were Quebec's more nationalist intellectuals and politicians, including Maurice Duplessis, Leader of the Opposition; Jean Drapeau, future Mayor of Montreal; and André Laurendeau, who would eventually become editor-in-chief of *Le Devoir*.

These three men led a crusade against Ottawa and the war effort. Women were their easiest targets. Women who worked outside the home were accused of deserting their families, of fostering juvenile delinquency and of sacrificing the interests of the French-Canadian nation. One of the features of Quebec's collective identity was the traditional family: a mother in the house, a male head of the family and numerous children. Women working outside the home were a threat to this model. The Canadian Catholic Confederation of Labour (CCCL), an umbrella group for Catholic unions had long been denouncing working women. It joined in the crusade, as did the Ligue ouvrière catholique (Catholic Workers' League) and the Jeunesse ouvrière catholique (Young Catholic Workers).

Women who worked in the war industries were told that they were jeopardizing the lives of future generations. There had been relatively little concern about the health and security of women workers before the war (and there would be little afterward); but during the war, factory work was suddenly too dangerous for women. Sexual harassment, a subject not discussed in any other context, became one more reason for keeping young women at home. Domestic service in a good Catholic home was a better alternative than factory work. The more conservative women's groups, such as the Fédération nationale Saint-Jean-Baptiste, agreed.

The campaign against married women working outside the home was partly successful, but it failed to convince young working women that domestic service was preferable to factory work.

The federal government anticipated that mothers would be needed for the war industries and instituted day nurseries for their children. At the beginning of 1942, Quebec agreed with the federal government to share the costs of these day nurseries. In Ontario, by the end of the war, there were twenty-eight day nurseries not including overnight nurseries and summer camps. In Quebec, there were only six; all were in Montreal and four of them were for Anglophone Protestants, Irish Catholics and Jews. One of the two nurseries for Francophone Catholic children closed for lack of business: mothers had been repeatedly told that the nurseries were a form of state interference in family life, and that they were the result of Communist inspired ideology. Women who preferred not to offend the local priest left their children with a neighbour or a relative; or the eldest daughter might be pulled out of school to look after the smaller children. Some children were placed in private nurseries, which were more acceptable than government nurseries. Doubtless, however, many mothers simply stopped working rather than brave the wrath of the priest.

FAMILY ALLOWANCES

After World War One, the federal government granted women the right to vote; after World War Two, it gave them family allowances. Apparently, there had to be a catastrophe before women were granted their fundamental civil rights and minimal financial aid – paid out of their taxes – for the education of their children.

A number of feminists in Canada struggled for a long time to obtain family allowances; most women's organizations had been demanding them for years. In Quebec, Thérèse Casgrain, Florence Martel and journalist Laure Hurteau promoted the idea of a basic allowance to be paid to all mothers, regardless of their financial or matrimonial status.

THERESE CASGRAIN 1896-1981

From 1928, when she became president of the League for Women's Rights, to 1966, when she founded the Quebec Federation of Women, Thérèse Casgrain dominated the feminist movement in Quebec.

Thérèse Casgrain (née Forget), was born into one of the great bourgeois families of Montreal. She received a convent education; and, when she was very young, married a liberal lawyer and raised four children. But she lived in an environment in which industrial magnates rubbed shoulders with distinguished politicians; and in the early 1920s, she became involved in social and political issues. She was charming, intelligent, witty, and inexhaustible; she was also very self-assured and had a vast network of acquaintances in almost every walk of life. In 1921, when the Provincial Suffrage Committee was founded, the young Thérèse Casgrain became one of the pillars of the feminist movement, taking over from Marie Gérin-Lajoie, Professor Carrie Derrick and Dr. Grace Ritchie-England.

During the 1920s and 1930s, she fought relentlessly to improve the legal status of Quebec women and to gain for them the right to vote in provincial elections. Her program on Radio-Canada, *Fémina,* made her known throughout French Canada. In 1926, she founded the Ligue de la jeunesse féminine (Young Women's League), a volunteer organization for social work; she showed great independence by refusing to have a chaplain for the organization.

During the war, Thérèse Casgrain was responsible for administering half of Canada at the Consumer Branch of the Wartime Prices and Trade Board. In 1945, the Canadian government approved the family-allowance program. In Quebec, legal experts, priests and nationalists insisted that the allowance be given to the father as head of the family. Casgrain led a successful counter attack – her friendship with Prime Minister Mackenzie King helped – and, at the last minute, it was decided that the cheques would go to the women of Quebec.

Thérèse Casgrain was more than a feminist; she was a great humanist, always ready to work for civil liberties and individual rights. Her political convictions led her to join the Cooperative Commonwealth Federation (a socialist party, from which the New Democratic Party was formed). She stood several times as a candidate for the CCF in Quebec, but was never elected. In the 1950s, she concentrated on organizing the CCF in Canada; she attended international meetings of socialist parties and joined with intellectuals and trade-unionists in the struggle against Duplessis.

The threat of nuclear war drove her to organize, in 1961, the Quebec chapter of the Voice of Women, a vast organization of women opposed to nuclear armaments throughout the Western world. In 1963 and 1964, she stood as a peace candidate in the federal elections. In 1966, she founded the Quebec Federation of Women to bring together several feminist organizations; but the Fédération nationale Saint-Jean-Baptiste refused to join, wanting to remain a Catholic organization.

The causes to which Thérèse Casgrain devoted her energies were numerous: adult education; the Montreal Symphony Orchestra; Vietnam war victims; and the status of Native Indian women. She founded the Fédération des oeuvres de charité canadienne-française and, many years later, became a founder of the League for Human Rights.

In 1970, she was appointed to the Senate, but served for only one year before the mandatory retirement age of seventy-five. She remained active until her death and received many honours from across Canada. In her autobiography, she defined her vision of the future:

> The true liberation of women cannot take place without the liberation of men. Basically, the women's liberation movement is not only feminist in inspiration, it is also humanist. Let men and women look at one another honestly and try together to give society a new set of values. The challenge which we, both men and women, must meet is that of living for a peaceful revolution and not dying for a revolution that would be cruel and, ultimately, illusory.[1]

Hundreds of people attended Casgrain's funeral. Jeanne Sauvé, then Speaker of the House of Commons, gave the televised eulogy. Thérèse Casgrain, feminist and humanist, ended her life as she had lived it – at the centre of events.

When Prime Minister Mackenzie King announced the introduction of mothers' allowances, or "baby bonuses" a number of people panicked. The government of Maurice Duplessis, which had been returned to power at the end of 1944, saw the move as a federal encroachment on provincial jurisdiction. Duplessis commissioned studies by eminent jurists, who declared the new law unconstitutional because it limited the rights of the father, who was the head of the family and sole administrator of a couple's common property.

The federal government had dared to make out cheques in the mother's name!

The clergy, who had fought proposed public nurseries, also attacked the new measure as a threat to male authority within the family. However, some young intellectuals and nationalists supported it. In her autobiography, Thérèse Casgrain describes the extent of the hostility. Monseigneur Charbonneau, Archbishop of Montreal, Gérard Filion, a militant member of the Action catholique and future director of *Le Devoir,* Daniel Johnson, premier of Quebec from 1966 to 1968 and François Albert Angers, a well-known economist, all declared that they were opposed to mothers' allowances. Some women's groups, such as the Union des fermières catholiques (Union of Catholic Farm Women), shared the clerical and nationalist ideology and joined the opposition. The Confédération des travailleurs catholiques du Canada (Canadian and Catholic Confederation of Labour), the Union catholique des cultivateurs (Union of Catholic Farmers) and the Fédération des travailleurs du Québec (Quebec Federation of Labour) supported payment to mothers.

In the face of such criticism, the federal government made an exception of Quebec, and addressed the cheques to fathers. Thérèse Casgrain used her considerable influence with Mackenzie King to try to change his mind while leading an unceasing press campaign in Quebec that explained women's point of view. Finally, a loophole was found: according to the Civil Code, a married woman had a "domestic mandate" to buy the necessary day-to-day needs of the household. Therefore, she could cash the mother's allowance cheques. The printing plates, already cast in the fathers' names, were changed. Quebec women one month later than other Canadian women finally received their mother's allowances.

THE "FERMIERES" DISPUTE

The war demonstrated to the clergy and to its allies, the nationalist and conservative forces that their control over women was weakening. Despite them, the Godbout government had given women the right to vote, and had forced the Bar to accept women into the legal profession in 1941. In the countryside, too, the clergy was losing control; the Cercles de fermières, an organization of rural women, was undergoing considerable expansion.

The Cercles de fermières channeled the activities of rural women into the war effort. The Cercles were looked upon favourably by the Godbout government, whose educational reforms threatened, in the eyes of the clergy, to turn Quebec over to the laity. In 1940, the Cercles de fermières, which had approximately thirty thousand members, established a province-wide network. By 1944, they had forty-nine thousand members.

According to historian Robert Rumilly, in 1941, Monseigneur Charbonneau began to encourage the Union des cultivateurs catholiques, which was dominated by its chaplains, to form a women's organization, in order to break the alliance between the provincial government and rural women. In 1944, with the support of senior clergy, the chaplains created the Union des fermières catholiques (Union of Catholic Farm Women). In each parish the word went out that the bishop wanted women to join the new association.

The Cercles de fermières were disturbed. What had they done wrong? Didn't they have chaplains? Weren't they good Christians? In the diocese of Trois Rivières, the entire Cercle obeyed the bishops; in Valleyfield, there was so little Church pressure that the new movement passed unnoticed. In Sherbrooke, Nicolet, Saint-Jean, Quebec City and Joliette the parishes split into factions. Some priests closed the parish halls where they met, others ignored the bishops' orders. Some leaders were subjected to subtle pressures – "It will be impossible to ordain your son" – or were denied communion. Pamphlets claimed that the Cercles de fermières were created by the State and therefore a threat to the Catholic religion. Nearly ten thousand Cercle members obeyed their bishops and joined the rival association.

During the next twenty years, the rift grew between the two associations. The constitution of the Catholic movement stipulated that members must come from the countryside; the Cercles de fermières gained in the towns members they lost in the rural areas. Then, in 1946, the bishops attempted to set up Syndicats d'économie domestique. The matter was referred to Monseigneur Desranleau, a specialist in union matters. The bishop was extremely embarrassed: in his view, "Married women do not really have a place in professional unions as they are presently constituted; in this respect, they marry their husband's profession."

In 1952, a new association for urban women (the Cercles d'économie domestique) was created by the bishops and a skillful propagandist, Madame Savard from Kenogami. The Cercles de fermières further declined in membership; some priests associated the Cercles with "the spectre of Communism." A short pamphlet issued in 1945 by the UCC, *L'Etat et Les Associations professionelles* (The State and Professional Associations), declared: "Since women were granted the right to vote, they have organized themselves into groups dependent on the State. This has introduced the risk that governments with their backs to the wall or unscrupulous politicians may be tempted to profit from the situation to unduly influence their votes." In its attempt to dominate society, the Church did not hesitate to exert its power over rural women and to accuse the State of the very "crimes" that the Church itself committed without the slightest remorse. The affair would have curious repercussions in the years to come.

WARTIME RESTRAINT

The war suddenly opened the eyes of governments to the importance of housewives: women decided what the family would buy. The government began to recruit housewives for the war effort. A barrage of advertising stressed the new importance of women's daily tasks to the nation's economy.

For six years, the country's resources were committed to the war. Armaments had to be manufactured; the troops and allied populations had to be fed; and the soldiers had to be adequately housed before the civil population could be indulged.

Speculation and increased demand for food supplies led the government to introduce rationing of staples. To guarantee access to staple foods and to prevent the very rich from buying up products at the expense of the poor, coupons were distributed to everyone across the country. These had to be given to the grocer to obtain butter, milk, sugar, meat and tea or coffee. They had no monetary value; they simply ensured that people got their fair share. (The sick and people on special diets were given extra coupons.) The coupon system forced housewives to plan family meals very carefully. Historians Auger and Lamothe describe how people adapted. For example, sugar was one of the first foods to be rationed; weekly consumption was fixed below the level to which people had grown accustomed, and making jams or pickles became almost impossible. It was difficult to find sugar substitutes, as honey, syrup and molasses were also rationed. In contrast, meat was readily available. Butter and cheese were sent to war-ravaged England, thus butter became scarce in Canada and cream disappeared.

Housewives displayed patience and ingenuity: they exchanged recipes adapted for wartime, made cakes requiring hardly any butter or sugar, regularly renewed the family's ration books, traded coupons with neighbours and found new resources to feed the family (for example, a garden could provide variety for the family diet).

Despite the threat of severe penalties, the black market boomed; many merchants made a fortune during the war. There were many ways ordinary people could beat the system: falsifying ration books, stealing coupons, taking over the ration books of the dead and arranging for relatives to send food from the farm.

Inflation challenged housewives as much as rationing. In theory, prices and wages were strictly controlled; in reality, prices, especially those of consumer goods climbed. Wages had risen since the Depression, but the supply of consumer goods had hardly improved. There was a scarcity of accommodation, especially near new war factories. Once more, the government put its trust in the housewife and appealed to women to take in lodgers. Tax regulations were altered and rental income became largely tax-exempt: rent could be claimed as income by the woman rather than by her husband, and women frequently did not make enough money to pay tax. After 1943, the Wartime Prices and Trade Board took charge of flats and rooms for rent. It fixed rent prices and tried to find accommodation for everyone; but, according to Auger and Lamothe, demand outstripped supply.

Boarding houses met only part of the need for accommodation, so the authorities created an organization that would later become the Canada Mortgage and Housing Corporation. It arranged for the construction of thousands of small, flimsily built houses, intended to last only as long as the war. Several families lived together in one house. Many marriages were postponed for want of available space.

Housewives were encouraged to reduce their consumption of electricity to keep the war factories going, and to lower the temperature of their houses to save fuel. They also learned to recycle household wastes.

According to Auger and Lamothe, the National Salvage Office orchestrated an education campaign aimed particularly at housewives. Garbage was to be sorted and put in piles for collection. Metal, vital to the manufacture of arms, was recycled: housewives were asked to bring old saucepans, cans and other metal containers to receptacles set up in the town square. Rags and worn-out clothes were picked up and used to make uniforms or military equipment. Fat, carefully purified in the home, was used in the production of explosives, medicines and soap. Even bones were collected, to be used in the production of glycerine, an essential in explosives. Paper was recycled into containers for transporting military equipment. (Old magazines and books were also sent to homesick soldiers in military barracks.)

The war also dictated fashion. In 1942, almost all fabric was being appropriated to make uniforms. To make sure the military received enough fabric, the Wartime Prices and Trade Board regulated the length of dresses. Styles that demanded too much material were forbidden: fringes, cuffs and even unnecessary pockets disappeared. Volunteers taught women how to recycle clothes; for example, men's suits could become children's outfits. (Fortunately, women were used to such recycling: the Depression had taught many how to make dresses out of flour sacks.) The Consumer Branch of the Wartime Prices and Trade Board organized fashion shows across Canada to demonstrate the elegant clothes to be made from recycled materials.

WOMEN'S ORGANIZATIONS
IN TIME OF WAR

During the war, volunteerism amongst women reached its peak. All the women's associations, from the most conservative to the most militant, adjusted to the wartime way of life. The government found an unexpected supply of free labour: accustomed to devoting themselves to the needs of others, Canadian women were easily convinced to give up their leisure time for work.

From the beginning of the war, the government used the resources of volunteer organizations. In 1940, a new Department of National War Services was created; in 1941, a division called Women's Voluntary Services (WVS) was set up to oversee the work done by volunteer women. The WVS operated in more than thirty centres and kept on file the names of all the women who offered their services; the volunteers were given the job that best suited their talents.

Civil defence relied heavily on women. It was not known whether enemy bombs would reach Canada; the country, therefore, had to prepare for the worst. The St. John's Ambulance Brigade taught first aid. Their volunteers had to be single, so the participants were mainly nuns and women students. In Montreal, a women's section of voluntary firefighters was started. All housewives were taught how to black out their homes and how to smother incendiary bombs.

The Red Cross relied mainly on women to collect clothing, toiletries and food, which were sent to England and to the troops at the front. Women sewed and knitted clothes to be sent overseas, working in the evenings or on Sundays, around the radio or on the front porch. In 1942, thirty-five thousand Quebec women sewed and knitted for the Red Cross; 80 percent were Francophones. The Quebec clergy who opposed women working outside the home blessed work done in the home. In the Fédération nationale Saint-Jean Baptiste, women who in 1910 would have been embroidering altar clothes, now knitted socks for the soldiers. Other women worked for the Red Cross, driving ambulances or running blood-donor clinics.

Across Canada, the National Council of Women, the Catholic Women's League, the Young Women's Christian Association (YWCA), the Imperial Order of the Daughters of the Empire and the National Council of Jewish Women threw themselves into the war effort. In Quebec, the FNSJB and the Cercles de fermières also contributed, and Quebec religious communities donated personnel and space.

Mothers, wives and sisters of officers formed volunteer committees to look after the families of soldiers who had left for the war. They distributed baskets of provisions, fuel and clothing, and raised money through card parties, receptions and raffles.

The population's savings were channeled into the war effort through "victory bonds," savings bonds issued by the Government of Canada to finance military expenditures. The bonds earned 3 percent interest, an exceptionally high return at the time. Many people feared another Depression when the war ended, and so put money aside. To make it easy to buy bonds, twenty-five-cent savings stamps were put on the market. The Comité consultatif féminin des finances de guerre (The Women's War Finance Committee), headed by Madeleine Perreault and Germaine Parizeau, launched a bond-buying campaign aimed at women's organizations. The FNSJB was especially generous in its response.

The cooperation of women was indispensable for price controls and rationing to succeed. After 1941, the Wartime Prices and Trade Board became a huge machine that regulated the entire consumer market. It relied heavily on volunteers from different women's associations to join the board's consumer branch. Charlotte Whitton, later the Mayor of Ottawa, and Thérèse Casgrain supervised the work of the volunteers, who were formed into local committees. The volunteers – three thousand in Quebec by 1944 – kept an eye on prices in their districts, checked the quality of products sold and exposed merchants who did not respect the law. They also made suggestions to help the battle against inflation. The Cercles de fermières were especially active in the rural areas. Other volunteers supervised by the Consumer Branch were responsible for the weekly distribution of food-ration books. The books were not sent in the mail but were collected at distribution centres, where thousands of volunteers ensured the ration system ran smoothly. In recognition of the work done by women, Mariana Jodoin, head of the Comité consultatif féminin de Montréal, Madeleine Perreault and Germaine Parizeau were made members of the Order of the British Empire, one of the country's highest civil awards. Thérèse Casgrain became an officer in the same order.

The end of the war came as a relief to the entire Canadian population. Men returned from the front; war restrictions were relaxed and industries were converted back to peacetime needs. As the country's needs became less pressing, the family's needs became a priority for women.

Even after the war had ended, life was not easy: demand for almost all consumer goods was high because the needs of the population had been a low priority during the war. The housing shortage was especially trying for young families. Inflation remained almost as high as it had been during the war; it peaked, in 1948, at 12 percent. As men returned to the work force, wives returned to the home or to jobs that did not pay high wartime wages.

RETURNING TO THE HOME

After the war, people began to fear the return of the unemployment of the Thirties. During the war, the government had made every effort to recruit women into the work force; it now spent as much energy trying to get women to return to the home: husbands whose wives worked were penalized through taxation and nurseries were dismantled. A new propaganda campaign extolled the advantages of staying at home. In Quebec, the Jeunesse ouvrière catholique launched a campaign for better regulation of domestic service to make it more attractive to women.

For the authorities, women obviously had to return to their "proper place." Before demobilization, the armed forces gave certain servicewomen courses preparing them for domestic life. Army women wanting salaried positions were hired over civilian women, for employers were required to grant preference to former soldiers; however, even these women were not allowed to take "men's" jobs. Women who had driven military vehicles during the war did not become truck drivers; they were forced into traditional employment areas. The government undertook to pay for the education of veterans. This gave a sizeable number of young people access to higher education, although fewer than one hundred and fifty women veterans studied in Quebec universities. Veterans were lent money to buy land, start a farm or build a house; but the program was based on the needs of men. Few women benefitted.

After the war, most women were busy getting married and having children: the baby boom was on. During the Depression, people who could practise contraception had limited their families; many more people postponed their marriages. The war reduced unemployment, and people could once again afford to get married. Catholics had children soon after marriage and the birthrate rose beginning in the 1940s. Women's magazines glorified this rediscovery of domestic life. Wartime mechanics now had to be perfect mothers.

The housing crisis was made worse by demobilization and the population explosion. A number of families remained in "war housing"; others lived in tiny flats, overcrowded with children.

Despite the inconveniences, women were sold on the joys of domestic life and femininity. Christian Dior, the Parisian couturier, introduced his impractical "New Look" in 1948, featuring high heels, fitted bodices, slim waists and long, voluminous skirts, all of which emphasized female sexuality. But women were unconcerned about practicality: after years of deprivation, they were only too happy to follow Dior's lead.

WORKING WOMEN PROTEST

In spite of the housewife's new status, not all working women could afford to go back to the home. In fact, the number of women in the paid work force continued to grow after the war; between 1941 and 1951, the number of working women in Quebec increased by almost a third.

Many priests, nationalists and intellectuals were hostile to working women, but their hostility did not keep all women at home. Historian Francine Barry notes that, in 1941, 8 percent of working women were married; in 1951, the rate was more than 17 percent. The increase was most noticeable in the manufacturing sector, not surprisingly, as the working class is the most vulnerable to price increases. A working-class family could not survive without two breadwinners. Gail Cuthbert-Brandt notes that, in 1940, working women began to marry earlier and that many returned to work after the birth of their children. One-third of those who married after 1940 tried to limit their families by using the Ogino-Knauss "rhythm" method, the only form of contraception sanctioned by the Catholic Church.

In 1944, the Godbout government introduced the first Quebec Labour Code, which placed severe restraints on public-sector workers' right to strike. Duplessis' coming to power at the end of 1944 signaled the beginning of repression of the unions. He did not hesitate to invoke the Padlock Law against union activists. He used it to decertify unions he judged to be too radical, and to prevent legal strikes. In addition, a hunt began for Communists and Communist sympathizers in the workers' movement.

The textile industry in Quebec was one of the largest employers of women. Yet in the 1940s, only 32 percent of textile workers were women. In 1911, half had been women. Mechanization had transformed many jobs, and owners preferred to give the new jobs to men. Women were relegated to unskilled, badly paid work.

In 1946, the six thousand workers at the Dominion Textile plants in Montreal and Valleyfield went on strike for one hundred days. They were led by Madeleine Parent and her husband, Kent Rowley, leaders of the United Textile Workers of America. Duplessis sent provincial police to intimidate the strikers, and the union leaders were arrested a number of times: Kent Rowley served six months in prison for "seditious conspiracy." However, the strikers emerged victorious, winning certification of the union, their first collective agreement, and an eight-hour working day. In 1947, seven hundred employees of the Ayers textile factories in Lachute stopped work. The strike lasted more than five months and ended in defeat. Madeleine Parent and the president of the union were found guilty of seditious conspiracy by a jury, and were sentenced to two years in prison. However, they did not serve their sentences; their conviction was quashed because of problems with the court record. Five years later, Madeleine Parent and Kent Rowley were expelled from the union.

But Parent's persecution did not frighten factory workers at Ayers. In 1947, they joined with workers from Dominion Textile – six thousand people in all – and launched a strike in factories at Montmorency, Sherbrooke, Drummondville and Magog. This time, the strikers carried the day.

The tobacco industry also employed large numbers of women. In 1951, the three thousand women employees of Imperial Tobacco went out on strike and their demands were met. But, in 1952, the women employees of a textile factory in Louiseville laid down their tools: Duplessis sent in the police to help break the strike. After eleven months, the women went back to work, still without a union or collective agreement.

In 1952, a strike at Dupuis Frères, a Montreal department store, brought out eight hundred women. Their victory, several months later, was of particular significance, as it showed that women retail workers could be mobilized against their employers, even employers who were Francophone and Catholic. After the Dupuis collective agreement was signed, other Montreal department stores paid their employees better wages and improved working conditions.

In the 1940s, teachers became secularized and unionized. It is difficult to say how long the secularization took, as the existence of private schools distorts the picture. Private education was completely dominated by female religious communities; public education in the cities was also dominated by nuns. The least rewarding and lucrative positions were still in the country schools, where all the teachers were lay women.

Between 1940 and 1950, the number of women teachers in the public schools went from 9,846 to 11,957; the number of teaching nuns declined from 7,184 to 6,064. Women teachers' wages – barely six hundred dollars a year – explain the rapid increase in unionization during the decade. The first teachers' union – of rural women teachers – became, in 1946, the Corporation des instituteurs et institutrices catholiques de la province du Québec (the CIC). Its membership, all lay teachers, was estimated at more than ten thousand; 85 percent were women. The most important union in the CIC was the Alliance des professeurs de Montréal, led by Léo Guindon. There were three women on the executive, including Marianna Marsan and Fabiola Gauthier. In 1949, the union demanded a modest wage increase; the Montreal Catholic School Board rejected their demand. The Montreal teachers decided to launch a strike, although strikes were illegal in the public sector.

The women teachers of Montreal paid dearly for their disobedience. After six days on strike, the Bishop of Montreal "counseled" them to return to work.

The union lost its accreditation. (It would get it back only in 1959.) The teachers'-union movement broke into numerous factions, and it was some time before unity was restored. When the movement started up again, it was totally dominated by male teachers.

MADELEINE PARENT

Madeleine Parent was no ordinary woman. She was educated at the Sacré-Coeur convent in Montreal and studied at McGill, where she met a number of socialists and developed an interest in improving working-class conditions. On completion of her studies in 1940, she did volunteer union work and became secretary to a committee organizing the war effort. She helped to organize workers in the war industries and then did union organizing in the textile industry, which employed large numbers of women and paid particularly low wages.

She was unsurpassed as an organizer and signed up thousands of women and men to the United Textile Workers of America. Her tactical skills and her gift of leadership place her amongst the great union leaders of the Forties.

Duplessis wanted Madeleine Parent and her husband Kent Rowley discredited at any price. He brought charges of illegal activity against her. During her trial for seditious conspiracy in 1948, the judge who conducted the investigation told the jury:

> You are twelve gallant and generous men, perhaps there are some fathers, some husbands among you. It is sometimes difficult to teach a lesson to one of your peers, especially when the accused is a young woman, with a fine education, from an excellent family, but who has been led astray into a milieu where she does not belong and where she invariably succumbs to the bad influence of those around her.[2]

This was the period of anti-communist witch hunts. In 1952, Madeleine Parent and Kent Rowley, who was affiliated with the Communist Party of Canada, were expelled by their union's American bosses. They moved to Ontario and continued to organize textile workers; eventually, they founded a new Canada-wide federation, the Council of Canadian Unions.

THE EDUCATION OF WOMEN:
DISHPANS OR DIPLOMAS

From 1940 to 1950, the clergy's iron grip on education was challenged. In 1943, the Liberal government of Adélard Godbout passed the Compulsory School Attendance Act. The clergy became resigned to the intrusion of the State into education but retained total control of the content of the new programs. During the decade, the clergy's control over women's education peaked and aroused serious, even bitter questioning of the Church's role in education.

Young girls in Quebec were still victims of an ideology which refused to admit that women could fulfill themselves outside the home. In 1941, 46 percent of Montreal women between the ages of fifteen and twenty-four were part of the labour force; another 16 percent were at school; 16 percent were married. What were the remaining 22 percent doing? We can only conclude that they remained at home assisting their mothers with the housework, or looking after siblings or elderly parents. Yet in Ontario, the neighbouring province, only 3 percent of women were neither married, in school or in the labour force.

Opportunities for women were further restricted, during the Forties, by an increase in the number of domestic-science schools. Cardinal Villeneuve, an opponent of women's suffrage, arranged for the dynamic Abbé Albert Tessier to run the domestic-science schools. A personal friend of Maurice Duplessis, Abbé Tessier completely reorganized the teaching of domestic science. Until the 1940s, teaching had emphasized domestic and agricultural skills; but under the Abbé, femininity and the family were stressed. Technical and academic subjects replaced exclusively "educational" material. The course was lengthened by two years (up to thirteen) but the purely academic component of the curriculum was cut back. As a result, graduates had difficulty passing the standard grade-eleven examinations. In 1940, there were twenty domestic-science schools and about forty *écoles moyennes familiales* (intermediate family schools). The two systems provided the equivalent of a regular grade-nine education. In 1950, there were thirty-eight domestic-science schools and seventy *écoles moyennes*. After 1942, graduates could attain university level if they attended the Ecole supérieure de pédagogie familiale in Outrement, an affiliate of the University of Montreal that granted a diploma in family studies. In Quebec City, the nuns of the Congrégation Notre-Dame founded an advanced domestic-science school within the Université Laval; the school granted a diploma in domestic science.

There was pride in the fact that a complete range of specifically female-oriented courses was available in Quebec. Abbé Tessier was a skillful propagandist for the cause. He was a man of action and a good teacher; some of his

---

ABBE TESSIER BELIEVES HE HAS TAMED
THERESE CASGRAIN

Thérèse Casgrain publicly criticized the choice of a man, Abbé Albert Tessier, to head the domestic-science school system. An extract from Tessier's autobiography shows that Casgrain was a force to be reckoned with in the struggle against traditional male élites. Her wit and charm – and her influential friends – disarmed her opponents.

A mutual friend, Jean-Marie Gauvreau, advised Madame Casgrain to meet the new administrator, assuring her that she would change her mind. She was kind enough to invite me to dinner. I replied that I would accept on condition that it was a simple meal, since I didn't want to be embarrassed. I also asked her not to serve any cake, as I didn't like this type of dessert, even when it was well made.

The dinner was very pleasant. For dessert she served *madeleines* as a sign of her contrition.[3]

---

reforms scandalized the nuns who taught domestic-science education. The black uniforms worn by students disappeared; drab schools were decorated in lively colours; the personal mail of students was no longer opened by school authorities; bursaries were easy to qualify for and plentiful. There was no shortage of students. Tessier did not want the course to be preparation for the work place, but the nuns convinced him that this was what parents demanded. In 1941, the Abbé agreed that "his" graduates be awarded a "superior" diploma, which qualified them to teach primary level domestic arts. People from a number of countries came to study Quebec's innovative system, which reinforced the concept of the uniqueness of women who were called upon to "rebuild, perfect and defend family life." The convents were nicknamed *écoles de bonheur* (schools of happiness). Women students were isolated from the world and given an idyllic picture of "real" life. The *institut familial* perfectly reflected the image the Francophone élite entertained of women and their place in society.

However, the growth of domestic-science teaching between 1940 and 1950 was accompanied by an expansion in the number of teachers'-training colleges. During the war, more than 75 percent of Catholic women teachers had never attended a teachers'-training college; they merely possessed a certificate issued by the Board of Catholic Examiners when they left the convent. (The Board of Examiners was abolished in 1939.) The Compulsory

---

TRAINING COURSES IN PAEDIATRIC NURSING
AT THE INSTITUT DE PEDAGOGIE FAMILIALE

Student trainees were responsible for a child two to three years old and a baby several weeks old for a period of ten days. They spared no effort to provide their two charges with proper hygiene and cleanliness; they prepared and distributed food; they also learned how to treat minor illnesses. They were supervised in their work by nurses and doctors. Students returned from this exposure to reality more mature and more realistic. They were also highly moved by the experience.

A training period as a housewife also, in its own way, contributed to their maturity. Women students in their third and fourth year had to take this part of the course. For one week, the student housewife assumed full responsibility for running a small household. When this domestic apprenticeship was first introduced, the household consisted of one room, more or less equipped, but it subsequently became a real house with a kitchen, a dining room, two bedrooms and all the equipment of a modern home.

Each student trainee was given a fixed sum, which varied according to the cost of living and which had to feed four or five people for a week. In addition to everyday meals, students had to prepare a special meal for parents, the priest or invited guests.

The nun in charge of the "Petit Foyer" (Little Home) had to hand over all responsibility to the mother of the week. She set up her schedule for the week, organized economic and well-balanced menus and could ask for comment on her overall plan, but the nun only intervened to prevent serious errors in budgeting or meal planning. The "mother" had to go to the market herself, assisted by a classmate rather than a nun. At the end of the training period, the "supervisor" gave a critical analysis and provided each student with a detailed assessment. In addition to providing meals, the mother of the week had to do the normal chores of a well-kept house: housework, laundry, sewing and darning, ironing, etc. All students agreed that this week of practical experience was worth dozens of theoretical courses. When we arrived unexpectedly, the mistress of the house had to serve a meal. I remember a supper at the end of a training course when we had to eat left-overs.... The young mother was short of butter, but she had more than enough bread. She went to the grocer's and succeeded in negotiating an exchange. She recounted this incident with humour and concluded: "In any case, if I get married I am going to try to find a husband who earns more than $30 a week."[4]

School Attendance Act caused an increase in teachers'-training colleges – twenty-three for Catholic and Francophone girls were opened between 1940 and 1950. The average number of diplomas granted in a year rose from 712 to 1,636. (Most candidates received the elementary diploma.) But there was a growing movement to improve teacher training. Anglophones, Catholic and Protestant, continued to attend the School for Teachers at Macdonald College of McGill University.

Francophones realized that to get work, a woman needed a diploma. But domestic-science education was giving women traditional training, without the benefits of a general education. Feminists and non-feminists alike criticized the system publicly. In addition, the Francophone bourgeoisie became aware that, if their daughters wanted to marry a professional, they would need at least some classical education. Finally, the last barriers to women entering certain liberal professions were broken down: notably, the law in 1941 and the notarial profession in 1956. In 1946, McGill University awarded an engineering degree to the first woman admitted to the engineering faculty.

A woman's classical college began a public debate: *"Vadrouille vs Baccalaureat"* (The Mop vs The Diploma). In 1946, a girls' school, the Collège Marie-Anne, walked off with almost all the prizes in a competition held by the Association de la jeunesse catholique. The college was far ahead of its greatest rival, the prestigious Collège Jean-de-Brébeuf, which was open only to boys. The presence of women in classical colleges was hotly debated in the student newspapers of Francophone universities. Quite clearly, by the time the *instituts familiaux* were created, education for girls was already a major issue.

NOTES

1 Thérèse Casgrain, *A Woman in a Man's World.* Translated by Joyce Marshall. Foreword by Frank R. Scott (Toronto: McClelland and Stewart, 1972), p. 190.

2 Charge of the Honourable Judge Philémon Cousineau to the jury, *La Reine Contre Madeleine Parent et Azélus Beaucage,* Queen's Bench, district of Terrebonne, no. 522, 6 February 1948. Bernard Mergler Papers, Archives of the Université du Québec à Montréal.

3 Albert Tessier, *Souvenirs en vrac* (Montreal: Boréal-Express, 1974), p. 199.

4 Albert Tessier, *Souvenirs en vrac, op. cit.,* pp. 255-256.

CONTEMPORARY WOMEN

THE FEMININE MYSTIQUE

BY THE 1940s, A MINORITY of educated and professional women in the United States had created a new image of women: the career woman. The "Roaring Twenties" had popularized the image of the young, emancipated, sexually aware woman – the "flapper." Birth control had become a statistically significant force in almost all sectors of society, and World War Two mobilized women into the work force.

After the war, people in the United States saw marriage and the family as the greatest bulwark against life's problems. There was severe inflation, and memories of the Depression were still fresh. Experts held that the job market could not absorb war veterans and maintain female employment levels. The desire to return to "normal" helped maintain a very conservative social climate. Feminist demands were toned down; the proportion of girls in the student population began to decline; the average age of marriage for girls went down to nineteen; the number of children per family increased (this was the famous baby boom); and millions of families moved to the suburbs. Political, economic and social authorities attempted to persuade American women that a career as a good homemaker offered security and was the key to happiness for all women. The "feminine mystique," denounced later by Betty Friedan, was spreading across America.

The Quebec media spread the ideology across the province. The war had radically changed the roles of Anglophones and Francophones. The postwar period and the propagation of the feminine mystique returned traditional values to both communities and this new climate brought them closer. However, the ideal of the wife and mother, the woman who found fulfilment in motherhood and in the thousands of available household gadgets (which often did not reduce the time spent on domestic chores) was everywhere: in magazines, advertisements, on television, in the supermarkets, in the movies. Priests could gradually tone down their traditional admonitions that women stay at home; for strange as it may seem, Quebec women modified their self-image. Housekeeping, once a traditional occupation, became a very sophisticated job.

Cooking was no longer enough. Menus had to be varied; nutritional principles had to be followed; and the freezer, blender, pressure cooker and Corning ware had to be utilized to their utmost. Women had to shop for bargains and know how to sew. Sewing machines made pleats, buttonholes, fancy stitches and a thousand other things. Women moved from Simplicity patterns to Butterick to the prestigious designs of Vogue. Cleaning became more sophisticated and soap was sold in fancy cans and bottles. Housework had become a business, and bringing up children was a formidable job. The Ecole des parents was never short on advice. There were dilemmas: Should one permit or forbid? Which educational toys should be bought? How can parents become their children's friends? Should toilet training be taught at age one or two? At what age should dating be allowed? The house had to be nicely decorated, ideally by the woman herself, right down to the curtains, bedspreads, wallpaper and flower arrangements. A woman had to be pretty, well groomed and perfectly made up, especially at six o'clock when her husband returned from work. She had to know how to entertain, prepare buffets and organize parties, while leaving her husband the delicate task of mixing cocktails. In her spare time she had to attend school meetings, help out at the local library and scout fund-raising campaigns, go to Action catholique meetings and help her husband keep his books.

Moreover, it became increasingly difficult to get servants. Bourgeois women who hoped that the end of the war would bring women back into service were disappointed, and turned to a new type of domestic help: the cleaning lady. Most women, however, including the wealthy, gradually became servants to their own families. Advocates of the feminine mystique proclaimed that, in a house with "all the modern conveniences," such easy work could be creative and fulfilling.

Working-class women had neither the time nor the money to conform to the pervasive image of the feminine mystique. They became defensive and uncomfortable as traditional models became unsatisfactory.

Women's magazines offered working-class women a different image, one that placed less emphasis on consumerism and more on fantasy. The ordinary woman's concept of the feminine mystique was based on popular romance stories, movie magazines and magazines such as *True Stories*. These publications presented an ideal universe where love conquers all, and were designed·

to prevent women from becoming aware of social inequalities and injustice.

But reality was very different. Women were dependent economically; they knew they would have to find jobs when their husbands were temporarily out of work. Yet working-class women thought paid work was a grind, as they could get only the least interesting and worst paid jobs. In their households, the authority of the head of the family was rarely questioned.

Working-class women could not develop the "feminine" refinements of middle-class women, so they drew their self-worth from their children. However, their inability to offer their children the educational or economic advantages of the upper classes, increased their frustration, which they had difficulty expressing.

We know very little about the daily lives of working-class women during the 1950s. (The subject was not researched until the early Seventies.) Moreover, studies of the working class have ignored workers' wives, who were not part of the work force. What happened in the middle classes was not characteristic of the daily lives of all Quebec women; but the middle classes were given the attention and would determine the collective future of women.

After 1950, women quietly gained access to what seemed to be equality. They saw a number of doors, hitherto firmly closed, opened on condition that they remained "real women" with a respect for their maternal and family vocations. They could become involved in socio-political issues and artistic and cultural matters, so long as they remained *anges du foyer* (angels of the home). They could become active in any number of associations, provided that their children and husbands were not inconvenienced.

AN EDITORIAL
FROM CHATELAINE MAGAZINE IN 1960

It is important for a woman to cultivate, with ever-increasing perfection, elegance and beauty as well as the various household arts which, in our daily lives, carry on the finest French traditions. However, the fine arts, politics, education, science or social problems are today no longer the special preserve of the stronger sex; the accomplished woman should also know a little about everything, since her destiny and that of her children are tied to the fate of the world.[1]

FAMILY PLANNING

At the beginning of the 1950s, the birthrate in Quebec was up. Thanks to the war, it had regained its pre-Depression level. But the baby boom was a statistical illusion. In Quebec, the birthrate had been slowly declining for more than a century. Women were not having more children; more women were having children. Moreover, during the war, many couples had put off having a family. Large families became less common. In his commentary on statistics in the 1961 census, Jacques Henripin states: "Families without children and families with six or more children tended to disappear; most families consisted of from two to four children." In Quebec, the birthrate dropped spectacularly, by ten points between 1956 and 1966. In other societies, such a decline had taken a century. The trend started in the towns, amongst women of higher education, and spread gradually to the less-educated classes and to the country.

In part, the decline in the Quebec birthrate was tied to contraception. Information on contraception, which had long been prohibited, had become more accessible. Since 1944, the Church had been providing husbands with a *Cours de Préparation au mariage*. Three of its chapters contained a solemn warning within a black border: "You must not, in all conscience, communicate the contents of these chapters to others. Guard the text carefully." The chapters were:

10 – Male and Female Anatomy
11 – Relations Between Spouses, Pregnancy, Birth and Breast Feeding
13 – What Is Allowed, What Is Forbidden in Marriage[2]

Chapter thirteen contained a section on birth control. The text was riddled with the concept of sin. "Planned parenthood" was satanic. However, future spouses were told of the Ogino-Knauss method ("rhythm" method) method and were given a list of situations in which it could be used without sin.

The limitations imposed by the handbook were severe. But the fact that the information was disseminated indicated enormous progress.

Catholic associations, such as the Service d'orientation des foyers, the Foyers Notre-Dame and the Ligue ouvrière catholique gave premarital classes; more couples began to discuss contraception openly. Another innovation was introduced in the diocese of Mont-Laurier: retreats for married couples. Husband and wife spent their annual vacation at these retreats, without the children, and they shared the same bedroom. After 1955, the church heard about a new contraceptive method, which had been written up in French medical journals. The method was disseminated amongst Catholic associations by a Lachine couple, Rita Henry and Gilles Brault. It was called

---

PREMARITAL COURSE

The wife who wants to have children and who is opposed by a masturbating husband may be severely troubled in her conscience. What should she do? Turning to her confessor will often be a great help in her attempts to quiet her conscience.

1. *When the husband uses contraceptives* the wife may not seek sexual relations. Nor may she acquiesce in them, unless she is afraid of the very grave consequences that may attend her refusal, and provided that she totally rejects all attempts to give her total satisfaction.

2. *If the wife knows that the husband* is going to withdraw and ejaculate outside the vagina:

a) Agreement to Relations by The Wife:

i. The wife must first of all inform her husband that she is opposed to this way of acting;

ii. After which, if she fears grave consequences attendant upon her refusal, she may agree to sex and accept the satisfaction, even total satisfaction produced all the time that sexual activity continues. But she may not seek or have her husband seek excitement for her if she has not experienced it.

b) Request for Relations by The Wife:

i. The wife who anticipates that her husband will not be able to perform the act of marriage as he should will not have sinned if she asks for sexual relations.

ii. Concerning sexual excitement: she may enjoy sexual excitement, even total satisfaction, that occurs during the whole time that sexual activity continues. But she may not seek or have her husband seek excitement for her if she has not experienced it.[3]

---

the sympto-thermic method, more commonly known as the basal temperature method. Also in 1955, the first official Francophone family-planning association was started. The association, called Serena, advocated natural methods. From 1955 to 1960, it was the only official association involved in family planning, and it helped to spread new information. Like many new ideas of the time, it emerged from within Action catholique circles.

The medical community was as reticent as the Church toward contraception. In the Fifties, women exchanged the names of "good doctors" and "good confessors."

After 1960, contraception became a subject of general interest. Controversial articles appeared in *Time, La Patrie, Actualité,* and *Marie Claire,* which spread the general impression that Quebec women did not practise contraception before 1960. However, the real innovation of 1960 was widespread access to information. In defiance of the criminal code, Serge Mongeau opened the first family-planning clinic. The Editions du jour published *Pouvez-vous empêcher la famille?* (Can You Practice Family Planning?) The pill was introduced and "good doctors" grew in number, as did the "good confessors." But women still needed a man's permission to control their fertility; and the movement did not get beyond urban areas. In 1963, *La Revue Populaire* published an article by Renée Rowan called "La régulation des naissances; la joie d'avoir un enfant quand nous l'avons voulu" (Birth Control: The Joy of Having a Baby When We Want It). The article had considerable impact. Huge sacks of mail from every region in the province arrived at *La Revue,* asking for further information. Many Quebec women had decided to have fewer children.

There is no unanimity in hypotheses for explaining the decline in the birthrate. The first explanation is economic: in Quebec between 1950 and 1965, tastes and needs developed more rapidly than available resources; this imbalance had a negative effect on the birthrate. The second explanation is social: structural changes in education, technology and work made Quebec women less interested in having children and gave them the social power and technical means to ensure their wishes were respected. The third explanation is cultural – the astonishing speed with which Quebec women abandoned traditional family values would indicate those values were not deeply internalized. The three explanations share a common demominator: women. Quebec women were becoming aware of the technical aspects of contraception, and were freed from the taboos surrounding contraception. They could now control their own fertility, despite official pronouncements to the contrary. Before it became a feminist issue, contraception was a reality for every couple in Quebec.

Changes in childbirth practices, which had been ongoing for a century, were now institutionalized. Having a child at home became a dangerous anomaly. Childbirth became the exclusive preserve of doctors. A general anaesthetic was systematically administered to mothers giving birth, except to unmarried mothers who, it was felt, should be punished for their sin. (In 1956, pain-free births had made a timid entry onto the medical scene, but they were ridiculed and derided by doctors, who discouraged women from requesting anaesthetics.) After 1960, local anaesthetics began to be used: the epidural, the pudendal bloc and the paracervical bloc. But these techniques remained experimental, and the side effects were little understood. In the mid-Sixties, there was great confusion surrounding the whole subject of childbirth. Doctors, not mothers, controlled childbirth: women had the means to control pregnancy, but they were losing their control over how their children were born.

THE SCHOOLS OPEN UP

Generations of Quebec girls had asked themselves the same questions: Should I become a nun, get married or will I end up an old maid? Each of the three choices meant a life of hard work. Nuns could do work in a convent or hospital, where they might find opportunities for social and personal advancement. Mothers could work at home, keeping house and raising the children without a wage (although, after 1945, they received a family allowance). Or, if they were single, they could work in a family business or in an office, store or factory for a low wage. But a working woman derived no status from her work. In fact, male rhetoric generally portrayed her as somewhat improper. Women were not seen as people who actually worked.

As Quebec began to modernize, secondary education became more accessible to women. Public schools, which were free, extended their curricula to the eleventh grade; fee-paying boarding schools were closing down. With the passing of the Compulsory School Attendance Act in the Forties, educational reforms revitalized the structures and programs of secondary education. Many people view the educational reform of 1964, the Parent Report, as the beginning of the revolution in girls' education. In fact, however, the revolution began with the introduction of a full-fledged public secondary-education system, between 1954 and 1959.

After 1954, the teachers'-training program was transformed. New diplomas were introduced; courses were better structured, required more extensive study and led to a baccalauréat. After 1959, female and male teachers'-training colleges in the Montreal region formed a "common market" with a complete range of options. Women and men attended the same Montreal institutions and took the same courses. In 1961, the number of women graduating from teachers'-training colleges in Quebec rose to 5,600.

After 1956, the network of domestic-science schools (which went up to grade nine) disintegrated as enrollment declined. Parents were reluctant to pay for two years' useless study; commercial studies at the secondary level became much more attractive, as more links were established between education and the job market. The number of girls attending *instituts familiaux* went up, but it represented an increasingly small proportion of girls in secondary education.

In addition, the "Lettres-Sciences" program was abolished. Science and Latin departments were set up in public schools for the increasing numbers of young girls who wanted to get a classical education. The public school

---

THE PARENT REPORT
AND THE EDUCATION OF GIRLS

1019. Preparing young girls for life must not be limited to domestic training, understood here in a narrow sense: cooking, housekeeping, etc., or in a wider sense: budget keeping, buying and purchasing expertise, etc. On the one hand, all young girls should be interested in these occupations and in the role of housekeeper, those who are going to become doctors, teachers, technicians as well as those who will marry as soon as they leave school; on the other hand, to a certain extent they should all be prepared to become women aware of the major problems of married life and mothers capable of caring for and educating their children fittingly. Finally, every young girl should receive some practical training so that she can earn a livelihood before or during her married life or after her children have been raised. Being trained to hold a position and filling it will make a woman into a more developed and interesting individual, often happier and more poised and more secure in the knowledge that, in the case of need, she could bring financial aid to her husband, or earn the family living should he become incapacitated. The number of women over thirty who return to school or to work is constantly increasing; for a certain number of women, this is indicative of a profound need to combat boredom, to feel alive in a less restricted world, after the several years spent in the duties of motherhood.

1020. Domestic science should be included in the curriculum for young girls, who will thus learn to enjoy housekeeping for its human and aesthetic qualities.

1024. Without wishing, of course, to transform future men into charwomen or to subject them to a form of domestic tyranny, the school can try to facilitate their participation in home life through a certain preparation. It should in particular introduce them to child psychology, to family budgeting, to an understanding of the problems their wives have to face in this regard.

---

offered four options: classics, science, commercial and general studies. In order to keep up their enrollments, boarding schools converted to day schools. After 1955, the university welcomed into its senior-matriculation classes girls from grade twelve or from the Lettres-Sciences program who wished to study medical technology, rehabilitation and dietetics. Between 1954 and 1962, fifteen classical colleges for women were set up, two administered by the laity. In 1964, the Parent Report proposed structural reforms that would bring uniformity to school boards. It also recommended that girls have the right to the same education as boys, that classes be mixed and that education be free. Two women, one a nun, were invited to sit on the Parent Commission.

At first, it seemed that the report would change the school system in Quebec. According to Francine Descarries-Bélanger:

> a closer reading of certain passages in the Parent Report, however, reveals that at no time did the fathers of educational reform truly call into question the traditional allocation of tasks and roles that were the basis of the arbitrary pedagogical practice that saw the two groups as distinct. In actual fact, they persisted in seeing the education of women as marginal to their primary "vocation."

The idea of a specifically female education persisted. The aim was to develop in a woman predispositions or qualifications for her role as mistress of the house, wife and mother. Some women still worked, but their work was viewed as an antidote for boredom or a source of extra income: a woman should, after all, live entirely for her family. The new "experts" on the female condition conceded that a woman had the right to join society, but only when the house was tidy, the children safely off to school and the happiness of the household guaranteed by her devotion and diligence – or if all hope of marriage was gone.

Boys, on the other hand, were advised "to be useful in society" (article 1023) and "to understand better how much work it takes to maintain a house" (article 1022).[4] In the final analysis, the school reformers had not risen above traditional stereotypes of woman and mother.

MARRIAGE OR WORK

The secularization of Quebec society helped to alter patterns of entry into the work force, especially for women. Two areas of employment were affected: nursing and teaching.

After 1950, girls could become nurses or teachers without being pressured to enter the religious life. From 1950 to 1960, the number of new novices stayed at around 1,990 per year; about 63 percent took their final vows. From 1960 to 1964, the number of new novices went down by 31.5 percent, at a time when the number of women eligible to enter the convent was increasing. Demographers have calculated that, in fact, the real decline was 50 percent.

There was also a drastic decline in the birthrate as free, universal, secondary education was introduced in Quebec. Girls no longer chose the religious life, because society offered alternatives to marriage and the prospect of numerous pregnancies. Once it was possible for a nurse or teacher to attain a position of responsibility without becoming a nun, a nun's life seemed less attractive. As a result, the two professions were freed from a vocational ethic based on sacrifice, devotion and charity, and working conditions improved. The working world for women was thrown into turmoil.

After 1956, girls in Quebec were confronted by a dilemma. No longer forced to choose between getting married, becoming a nun or being an old maid, they chose between marriage and remaining single. A young girl who pursued her studies could opt for both a career and marriage. Women were still getting married, and most interrupted their "careers" for a number of years to raise children. For even in 1960, marriage meant children. For many women, marriage put an end to a routine job without prospects. Such women undertook their "career" as wife and mother with enthusiasm. But an increasing number of women found their job interesting. They faced an agonizing decision when they married: Should they give up their work? For how long? Could they combine the two? Society expected them to make a choice, but many women wanted both.

According to Francine Barry, the rate of increase in the female work force has always been much higher than amongst male workers. The gap between the two rates has increased from one census to the next: in 1951, the difference was ten; it rose to twenty-six in 1961 and climbed to forty-two in 1971.

In 1951, when married women entered the job market, they represented only 17 percent of working women. The percentage had risen to 48 percent in 1971. If widows and divorcees are added to this number, single women constituted no more than 45 percent of the female work force. (Moreover, these figures do not take into account the thousands of women who worked without pay in family businesses.)

The education of working women underwent a number of changes. Women with little education (three years or less) remained at about 3.5 percent between 1951 and 1971; the number of women with high-school diplomas also remained stable at about 42 percent. But the number of women with only a primary education declined considerably, from 42 percent to 24 percent, while the number of women with a college or university education rose from 8 percent to 31 percent. Clearly, universal secondary education for girls

TABLE 10
Increase in the Labour Force
in Quebec, 1941-1971

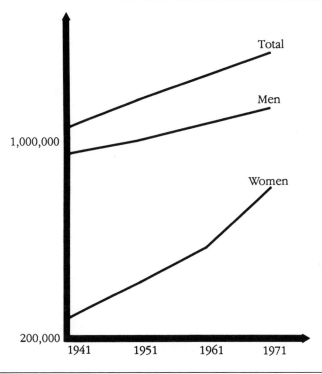

Source: Francine Barry, *Le travail de la femme au Québec,* Montreal, Presses de l'Université du Québec, 1977, p. 6 (according to *Census of Canada,* 1971, vol. III part. I, cat. 94-702 Table I).

had a direct impact on the presence of women in the job market. A good education was a virtual guarantee of a better-paid job, and a married woman might well decide to remain in an interesting job.

These changes can best be explained by the concurrent increase in services and by the increasing bureaucratization of private and public concerns. At the same time, the proportion of women factory workers declined as they were, made redundant by the technological change and mechanization that had begun at the turn of the century. Office jobs, however, expanded rapidly:

311

one-quarter of all working women worked in offices. Although female office jobs increased, the lives of "pink-collar workers" remained fundamentally the same. Women were still directed toward specifically female jobs. We shall confine ourselves to just one example – nursing.

Between 1941 and 1971, women fifteen years and over in Quebec multiplied by 1.9, almost a twofold increase. During the same period, the increase in working women was 2.9, an almost threefold increase. The number of nurses multiplied by 9.42, almost tenfold. If there was a female job ghetto, it was nursing. (However, before 1940, there were too few nurses to be noticeable in the overall work force.) A women-teachers' ghetto had formed between 1850 and 1880; a women textile-workers' ghetto developed between 1880 and 1920; between 1920 and 1940, it was the turn of secretaries and telephone operators. The nurses' ghetto was formed at the height of the postindustrial age, during the technological and bureaucratic revolution, when Quebec society was being secularized and when the work force was experimenting with flexible working hours.

TABLE 11

Nurses in Quebec, 1941-1971

	1941	1971	Increase
Number of women 15 years and over*	1,132,172	2,157,785	90%
Number of women working*	260,191	754,745	190%
Number of nurses**	4167	39,252	842%

Source: *Census of Canada, 1971, vol.III. part. I.
     **Nursing Québec, Nov-Dec. 1980

From 1950 to 1970, the term "female ghetto" was hardly used. Instead, "firsts" were emphasized: the first woman accountant, the first woman engineer, the first woman notary. People did not realize that these professionals were "token women." There was no public interest in maternity leave or in day-care centres, or in the question of the double work day. Society was still concerned with the incompatability of private and public life: a woman could not work and raise children. Motherhood was not recognized as a social act.

The years between 1950 to 1964 were a transitional period, during which society began to accept the working woman. However, there was little public discussion of the concept. Indeed, the subject was typically ignored by the press and rarely studied. The conservative viewpoint, as exemplified by the magazine *Relations,* continued to make itself felt, but a more realistic, resigned attitude was also developing, an attitude that accepted, with some reservations, the idea of the working woman. It was still not appropriate, however, for mothers with young children to go out to work.

Unions, formerly hostile to working women, changed their attitude. "We are not opposed to the working woman; moreover, we believe that opposition from us would be useless in the face of the powerful forces that are prompting women to work," declared the president of the CSN. But there was often a huge gap between theory and practice.

Nevertheless, some women were being elected to union executives. The vice-president of the CTCC (later called the CSN) was Jeanne Duval, who held the office from 1953 to 1964. Huguette Plamondon was with the FTQ and Laure Gaudreault, a pioneer of the Thirties, was on the executive of the teachers' unions. But unions were still largely protectionist. "We want the 'nature' of women to be respected," wrote Jean Marchand in 1964. "Women who work have a right to a status that protects them not only as individual wage earners, but also takes into account their special needs as women with family responsibilities."[5]

In 1963, a strike broke out at the Sainte-Justine Hospital for Children. A scandalized public looked on as nurses picketed for better working conditions. It was the first strike in the social-services sector and had symbolic significance. Would unionized women be like other workers? In the unions, it was generally felt that they would.

Many unions had women's committees to discuss the situation of women. In 1966, however, the women's committees were disbanded on the grounds that women members were not fundamentally different from male members, and that they should be integrated into the unions, which were, after all, seeking wage parity for women and men. It is true that the division of jobs and tasks by gender enabled everybody – employers and unions – to avoid the consequences of applying this principle, but before 1965, wage parity had rarely been debated publicly. In fact, employers and unions sometimes conspired against the hiring of women in certain job sectors.

In the Sixties, there were fewer women than men in unions. Women's jobs were the least unionized, and the most difficult to unionize. Wherever working conditions have allowed (sufficient numbers of employees, precise objectives, role of militants), women have responded to unionization in the same way as men. If there were fewer women than men in unions, the reasons must be sought in the jobs women had and in the structure of the companies that hired them.

Moreover, the militants of the Forties – Laure Gaudreault, Yvette Charpentier, Léa Roback (all single women) – had no successors in the Fifties and Sixties, perhaps because of the persecution of the first women union militants.

COMMITTED WOMEN

From 1950 to 1965, there were no feminist groups. Women had the right to vote and feminist associations lacked precise objectives. The deaths of Idola Saint-Jean (in 1945) and Marie Gérin-Lajoie (in 1945) helped to dampen feminist aspirations. Thérèse Casgrain took a new approach. She chose to fight within political associations, the Voice of Women – an international organization dedicated to world peace – and the New Democratic Party – the principal voice of the left in Quebec.

At the end of the 1950s, the Voice of Women played a key role in mobilizing women's energies. It was a Canadian movement, and its national president was Laura Sabia. Like all movements aimed at disarmament, the association was linked with left-wing movements; members were mobilized on several fronts. The association was a training school in political activism for women, and Anglophone and Francophone women learned to work together. Its leaders, Laura Sabia and Thérèse Casgrain, formulated the demands that gave birth, after 1965, to neo-feminism.

Other movements that mobilized women included the Mouvement laïc de la langue française and groups within the Action catholique. Small political and social circles also had their committed women. Women signed the *Refus global* with Borduas. Others signed articles in *Cité libre*. Louise Lorrain ran Action de la jeunesse canadienne, the only nationalist group in the Fifties. Groups from within the Action catholique had as many women as men amongst their leaders. Alec Leduc worked beside Gérard Pelletier, whom she married; Fernand Cadieux worked with Rita Racette; Claude Ryan shared the objectives of Madeleine Guay. In such organizations, where women spoke up and participated in decision-making, new relationships between women and men were formed. The values of the couple were placed ahead of traditional family values and women became less passive. They rejected the image of the sweet, tolerant, loving woman who took all the knocks only to break down after a couple of years. Although the number of wives who typed their husbands' theses was greater than the number of men who did the spring cleaning, the bourgeois image of the family was changing.

It was tacitly assumed that "the women's question" had been resolved: women could get whatever jobs they wanted, and could participate in the causes of their choice while raising their families. The publication of *The Second Sex* by Simone de Beauvoir passed almost unnoticed.

Feminists of an earlier era, though small in number, could be found in the University Women's Club. At the beginning of the Fifties, the club took part in public discussions on education for girls. By a happy accident, the visit of

Cardinal Tisserant, a Roman prelate, to the Institut familial de Saint-Jacques, in 1950, caused a public controversy. The Cardinal cast doubt on the merits of domestic-science education for girls. Albert Tessier, the champion of domestic-science education, responded that the more women who received a university education, the fewer "real women" there would be. A lively debate followed, in which an academic psychologist, Monique Béchard, defended higher education for girls and claimed that, far from changing their true nature, education helped to provide more opportunities for self-fulfillment. Supporters of domestic-science education went to great lengths to defend the schools, but their arguments were unconvincing. The question simply did not effect the thousands of adolescents in school at the time. Eventually, the association's influence declined and, during the Fifties, it became, to all intents and purposes, a social club.

Only one feminist organization, the Ligue des femmes du Québec, founded by Laurette Sloane in 1958, existed in Quebec at that time. The group was small and consisted primarily of women unionists and militants whose influence was limited, largely because of its espousal of Communism. The league did not take part in collective action during its first years and was virtually unknown to the public at large. Cracks were slowly developing in the cohesion of Quebec society and the very existence of the league illustrates this process. But, the league kept the flame of the feminist cause alive at the end of the Fifties – no mean feat.

Although there was only one feminist organization, women's associations abounded. The conflict in rural Quebec that had surfaced after the war among the Cercles de fermières broke out again with increased virulence. As mentioned previously, the Church orchestrated an artificial schism in the association. On one side were the Cercles de fermières, organized by the Ministry of Agriculture; on the other was the Union catholique des fermières (UCF), set up at the instigation of the bishops. In spite of attempts to unite the two groups in 1945 and 1952, the Fermières still existed in 1957. A new offensive against them was launched. The UCF changed its name to Union catholique des femmes rurales (UCFR), to avoid any confusion with the Cercles de fermières. New directives were issued by the bishops, who denounced state-controlled associations. Pamphlets, distributed to local priests, explained how to change the Cercles de fermières into UCFR circles. But the Fermières held their ground.

The bishops eventually tired of the struggle and, in 1963, proposed that the three women's organizations – the Cercles de fermières, the Cercles d'économie domestique and the UCFR – amalgamate. The Fermières politely and diplomatically dissociated themselves from the proposed union. Their official reason was that they wished to devote their energies to organizing their fiftieth anniversary celebrations; however, the following anonymous account seems closer to the mark:

> It would be unjust for us "Fermières" who were the pioneers and did the spade work to hand over the "plats tout cuits" (food already cooked) to the ladies of the UCFR who, in the final analysis, are the product of a small attempt at revenge by the clergy at a time when they had the power of life and death over women, whom they sought to terrorize into supporting them. And I can prove to you what I am saying. If only you knew of all the intrigue and the injustice accompanying their attempts to swallow us up.[6]

The bishops did, however, achieve a union between the Cercles d'économie domestique and the UCFR in 1966. The new organization was called the Association féminine pour l'éducation et l'action sociale (AFEAS).

The Cercles de fermières and the UCFR had a great deal in common. They had the similar mottoes: *Pour la terre et le foyer* (For Country and Home) (Fermières); and *Pour la terre et la famille* (For Country and Family) (UCFR). They had the same objectives and discussed the same topics: the rural way of life, the happiness of the family, household budgeting, work, the place of women in society, and so on.

Inexplicably, the Cercle de fermières was denied the official support of the Church. In their desire to obtain the backing of the bishops, the Cercles de fermières vigorously supported the clergy's views on the sacred mission of women. In their magazine, *La Terre et le Foyer,* they published articles on the themes of motherhood, housekeeping, the family and Christian values. More than half the magazine's articles concerned arts and crafts, the real attraction of the association. In order to maintain its reputation and moral standing, the magazine adhered to a traditional ideological line, dictated, to some extent, by the Church. Teachers also became officially answerable to the Church for the content of their courses, and if they did not follow the Church's line, they were denied absolution for, amongst other things, the Montreal teachers' strike of 1949 and the continuing unionization of their profession. Similarly, proposed reforms for the secularization of teaching had to be submitted to the Church for approval.

The Union catholique des femmes rurales initially discussed unionization, but abandoned the idea. In addition, the association ceased to be known for the quality of its arts and crafts. (The Church contended that professional associations should be independent of the State. The association therefore did not accept government assistance, which was vital to the promotion and practice of arts and crafts.) The UCFR concentrated on study groups. Its magazines, conferences and directives centred on church-influenced themes. However, by the end of the Fifties, women's discussions were taking on a different tone. Discussions became increasingly concrete, increasingly related to Quebec's social transformation (especially after 1957), and began to touch the daily lives of women. Even contraception was discussed.

The direction taken by the association fostered the continued development of a collective women's consciousness. Its traditionalist stance was deceptive: the increasing social involvement of women in study groups must have been decisive in the transformation of Quebec society. Remarkably, the women affected by this evolution were not confined to a closed circle. More than thirty thousand members were influenced by the association. The discussions generated by the UCFR profoundly changed the social behaviour of its traditionally conservative members. Suddenly, women had opinions that they were stating publicly.

In the towns, and in Montreal especially, women were influenced by a new form of public persuasion – the media. The real platform for women was television, radio and the press. Suddenly, actresses and singers were joined by women commentators, journalists and radio and television hosts, who discussed topics that had previously been the province of men: politics, psychology, philosophy and literature. (Recipes, make-up and interior decoration were still discussed; after all, the "feminine mystique" was at its height!) When journalist Judith Jasmin explained the latest international crisis or interviewed Pierre Mendès-France, thousands of young Quebec women looked at her and thought, "Why not me?" There were regular television programs about women, and the radio serials, which for more than fifteen years had been almost the only "product" offered to women in their homes, began to be replaced by news programs, which brought women into literary and political events.

Newspapers underwent similar changes. Women's pages, gossip and social columns dealing with gala events and forthcoming marriages, were abandoned. The *Nouveau Journal,* launched in 1961, introduced new ideas and new images. It contained political columns signed by women, a new kind of woman's page and romantic, passionate cartoons that broke with the American tradition of hypocritical modesty.

Newspapers hired entire teams of women journalists, and women were assigned to many departments (except, or course, that inviolable bastion, the sports section). Renaude Lapointe became editorial writer for *La Presse.* Even the women's advice columns changed their image. During the Fifties, the most famous was Janette Bertrand's, in *Le Petit Journal,* which published letters and replies in full. Every Sunday, the column commented on such topics as marriage, domination, battered women, sexuality, courtship, drunkenness and contraception. There were no veiled allusions, and Bertrand did not counsel resignation. The column contained clear, direct and provocative language; it invited women to react, to respond and to make demands.

In the universities women students were becoming visible, and were found on all committees. Although women were concentrated in the "female" disciplines, they were also elected to the executives of the powerful student associations.

In 1958, universities in Quebec declared that they were in a state of financial crisis. Duplessis refused to allow them to draw on federal subsidies. Three students, one of them Francine Laurendeau, held a sit-in at Duplessis' office, to make him change his mind.

Female creativity made headlines. Gabrielle Roy won the Prix Fémina in 1947. The number of women novelists, poets and playwrights grew. Marie-Claire Blais, Suzanne Paradis, Anne Hébert, Charlotte Savary, Françoise Loranger, Rina Lasnier – the list is endless. There was similar ferment in the other arts. Theatre troupes were directed by women; Ludmilla Cheriaeff founded Les Grands Ballets Canadiens; the best-known art galleries were run by women.

In short, after 1950 there was no limit to the causes women embraced: the patriotic and religious causes of the Fifties gave way to cultural, social and political causes as the Sixties and the Quiet Revolution approached. Women had grown up without questioning their right to advanced education, equal wages and contraception, and their right to participate in political and social life. In this transformed society, women could dream more about doing things, and less about demanding things. Women no longer saw the need to be feminists as dozens of "token" women could be found to testify to their personal success: "Anyone can do what I have done." There was no better diversion from the fight for equality.

THE FABRICATED WOMAN

After the war, and especially after 1950, the State attempted to persuade women to stay at home and to devote themselves to their children and their husbands. Betty Friedan called this ideology "the feminine mystique." But, during the Fifties, the women of Quebec used effective contraceptive methods; the women in the job market increased rapidly, and their presence became permanent. Women stopped becoming nuns and, increasingly, took up public causes. In the Voice of Women, in the Fermières, in the associations that gave birth to the AFEAS, on the radio, on television, in the newspapers and magazines, in literature and the arts, thousands of women reconciled their public and family lives. Nicole Germain knitted, Janette Bertrand cooked and

Simonne Chartrand raised seven children. Women could become public figures only if they were superwomen.

While many structural and social changes were taking place, female rhetoric remained almost unchanged. The women's press was regarded as a consumer product, and had to avoid controversy. The best-selling magazines of the period, *La Revue Moderne, La Revue Populaire, Le Samedi,* and *Le Film* published love stories that kept women in a state of sugary euphoria.

TABLE 12

Novels Published in Women's Magazines

La Revue Moderne (1951)		*% of pages*
Toi que j'aimais	Suzanne Mercey	26%
La Duchesse aux jasmins	Magali	37%
Le Droit au bonheur	Marguerite Rivoire	27%
A la conquête du bonheur	C. et L. Droze	45%
En cherchant l'oubli	A.P. Hot	30%
L'Amoureuse cantilène	Maurice Danyl	30%
L'Amour en exil	Claude Langel	51%
Le Val aux fées	Claude Virmonne	50%
Tendre imposture	Mireille Brocey	47%
Son sourire	Léo Dartey	42%
La Gardienne	Suzanne Mercey	30%
	Average	38%

La Revue populaire (1954)		*% of pages*
Son trop jeune papa	Nancy Assy	40%
L'Ennemie	Alix André	51%
Saison sèche	Daniel Gray	50%
Un seul amour	Ruby M. Ayres	55%
Le Maître de Floreya	Claude Virmonne	50%
L'Amour sans fard	Louis Derthral	50%
La Haine aux yeux tendres	Magda Contiro	51%
Chérie	Magali	55%
Les loups hurlent	Alix Abdré	55%
Le Sacrifice Sylvetti	Guy de Novel	57%
La nuit qui chante	Magda Contiro	53%
	Average	52%

A taste for the exotic was carefully cultivated. Between 1946 and 1956, *La Revue populaire* published 114 articles on Paris. The so-called "women's pages" discussed make-up, sewing and cooking: there was not one article a year on the situation of women. The magazines of the rural associations, *La Terre et le Foyer* and *Femmes rurales,* toed the clerical line on the role of women, though they were read for their practical advice on arts and crafts. (More than half the pages in *La Terre et Le Foyer* were devoted to arts and crafts.) The magazine denounced working women, although its average reader worked twelve hours a day on the farm and in the house. Religious magazines tried to update their image, and *Idéal féminin*, a "magazine of culture and fashion," was launched to compete with *Marie-Claire* and *Elle.*

But the woman portrayed in all these magazines was a fabrication. She was no doubt charming and comforting, but she was not real. She was never a mother with generous hips, but always a slim and intelligent young woman. The National Film Board produced two films that typified this vision of women: *La Beauté même* and *La Femme-image.* Between the script and the reality of a woman's life was a chasm.

A generation after Anglophone women had heard about new theories on female sexuality and psychology, Quebec women were confronted by the theories of Sigmund Freud. The Jansenism of the preceding decades had denied women the right of sexual expression; but the popularity of Freud's theories made sexuality fashionable. Henceforth, people spoke openly about sexuality – a real innovation in Quebec society. However, Freud's writings were distorted by his "disciples," whose popular ideas enclosed women in a new corset of passivity. Each month, *Readers Digest Selections* published articles that increased women's guilt and confusion.

Women were responsible for the emotional problems of their children; women were sexually passive; women were doomed to frigidity; menstrual periods were "the tears of a disappointed uterus"; menopause was an expression of women's regret at being no longer able to bear children. These myths appeared in the popular writings of the Fifties, in the almanacs and in the women's pages of the newspapers. Most women did not identify with these theories, but to question them was evidence of an unconscious desire to be a man!

After 1960, two magazines changed the female image. In January 1961, *Châtelaine* took over from *La Revue moderne* and inaugurated a new era in women's publications. *Châtelaine* published editorials and articles that described the lives of an increasing number of women, and fostered the views of educated women who had decided to have fewer children and to combine career and family.

The ambiguity was far from resolved, however. Every year, *Châtelaine* chose its "woman of the year," always a family woman who had taken up a particular cause. And the word "feminism" never appeared on its pages.

The same ambivalence was to be found in a new publication, *Maintenant*. No subject was taboo for the editors of *Maintenant*, – contraception, abortion, the role of women in the Church and changes in the convents. But the magazine was uneasy about its positions. On the one hand, there was a very obvious desire for change; on the other hand, there was a comfortable security in the image of the woman who stays at home. Freed from large families and the need to earn a living, many women supported the feminine mystique. The collective voice of women was developing, but it was still silent.

AND POLITICS

As of 1940, Quebec women had the right to vote, but they limited their political participation to casting that vote. The few daring women who stood as candidates represented marginal parties with no chance of being elected. Thérèse Casgrain, a militant supporter of the CCF and the New Democratic Party, failed to win a seat in Parliament.

Maurice Duplessis died in 1959, and an election was called. The provincial election of 1960 marked the official beginning of the Quiet Revolution, yet there were no women candidates, for the first time since 1940.

In 1961, the member for Jacques-Cartier, Doctor Kirkland, died, and a by-election was called. His daughter, Claire Kirkland-Casgrain, stood as the Liberal Party candidate and won easily. The first woman MNA in Quebec was immediately made a minister.

Kirkland-Casgrain combined her maternal and her ministerial responsibilities admirably. This fact was emphasized in the media, which stressed the importance of this fine victory for women. She was given her own column in *Châtelaine*, "Ce que J'en pense" (As I see it). Unknown one moment, she was a prominent public figure the next. But Kirkland-Casgrain was more than the first Quebec woman MNA: she was the first token woman in Quebec politics. The Liberal Party needed a new image – what could be better than to elect a woman? Kirkland-Casgrain's abilities are not in question, for she had the makings of an effective politician. What is being questioned is tokenism, which misled women to believe that they had a voice in political decision-making.

Claire Kirkland-Casgrain began her political career with a brilliant initiative: she introduced a bill that drastically changed the legal status of married women. On 1 July 1964, the Quebec Assembly passed Bill 16, whose principal clause ended the legal incapacity of married women. A woman no longer needed her husband's signature to transact daily business; she assumed legal rights previously denied her, such as launching a lawsuit or acting as the exec-

TABLE 13

Women in a Male Domain

Number of Candidates in Provincial and Federal Elections

Since 1945 (Quebec only)

Election	Female Candidates	Elected	Male Candidates	Elected
Ottawa 1945	2	–	282	65
Quebec 1948	–	–	311	92
Ottawa 1949	3	–	250	73
Quebec 1952	3	–	233	92
Ottawa 1953	11	–	217	75
Quebec 1956	7	–	265	92
Ottawa 1957	3	–	210	75
Ottawa 1958	2	–	217	75
Quebec 1960	–	–	253	95
Ottawa 1962	4	–	279	75
Quebec 1962	3	1	221	94
Ottawa 1963	7	–	288	75
Ottawa 1965	6	–	321	75
Quebec 1966	11	1	407	107
Ottawa 1968	9	–	314	74
Quebec 1970	9	1	457	107
Ottawa 1972	29	3	314	71
Quebec 1973	25	1	454	109
Ottawa 1974	43	3	327	71
Quebec 1976	47	5	509	105
Ottawa 1979	78	4	440	71
Ottawa 1980	90	6	428	69
Quebec 1981	82	9	444	115
Federal by-elections 1945-1980	10	–	196	52
Provincial by-elections 1945-1979	6	2	160	51
Total	490	36	7797	2,139
	5.9%	1.6%	94.1%	98.4%

Source: Pierre Drouilly, "Les femmes et les élections," in Le Devoir, 17th December, 1980, p. 9.

Note: 1981 election results have been included in the table and the percentages adjusted. The adjustment is less than 1%.

utrix of a will. Her independence within marriage was legally recognized. (Nonetheless, bank managers, notaries and department store credit departments took their time in recognizing a woman's rights, and continued to demand a husband's signature.)

Bill 16 provoked considerable criticism from experts: some considered it too conservative; others thought it biased. But many women were ahead of the law – all those who had not waited until 1964, when the law was changed, to "undertake a profession different from that of their husband."

TABLE 14
Changes Brought About by Bill 16

1. Equality of spouses in marriage.

2. A woman may choose another residence if the residence chosen by her husband exposes the family to danger.

3. A married woman has full legal capacity as to her civil rights, subject only to such restrictions as arise from her matrimonial régime:
   a. A married woman can represent her husband;
   b. A married woman may engage in a calling distinct from that of her husband;
   c. A judge can provide authorization, in the absence of the husband's authorization.

4. In cases of separation of property, a married woman:
   a. can be appointed to a tutorship;
   b. can be appointed as curator;
   c. can make or accept a gift inter-vivos;
   d. is legally capable of contracting;
   e. is legally capable of offering a defence or suing before the courts;
   f. can accept a succession alone;
   g. can alone accept testamentary executorship;
   h. can administer and dispose of her own property.

5. In cases of legal community of property, the married woman:
   a. can exercise the same rights as a woman separate as to estate, with the authorization of her husband;
   b. is responsible for her husband's debts. The contrary is also the case;
   c. can administer her own property with certain restrictions.

6. Broadened definition of reserved property.[7]

Women expressed very little interest in the laws that concerned them – perhaps because they had no direct power at the federal level. They were especially powerless during the Sixties, when there was no women's association to defend their rights.

The laws that concerned women were based on the concept of "natural law," and women had been badly served by natural law. Indeed, the *cultural* models that defined the lives, roles, rights and duties of women were so old that society considered them to be *natural.* The long list of attributes women allegedly possessed "naturally" is astonishing: devotion, forgiveness, faithfulness and sensitivity are but a few. Some activities were thought to come to women "naturally" – embroidery, mending, looking after children and infants, housework and laundry. Legal systems based on such presumptions imprisoned women, but women felt powerless to argue against these cultural models.

In 1964, the collective silence of women was remarkable. However, the upheavals of the next five years would lead to the emergence of a collective female consciousness. This would be a period of quiet feminism.

NOTES

1 Fernande Saint-Martin, *Châtelaine,* vol. I, no. 1, October 1960, p. 3.

2 *Cours de Préparation au mariage,* Action catholique canadienne, Service de préparation au marriage du diocèse de Montréal (Ottawa, 1944).

3 *Cours de Préparation au Mariage,* Ch. 13, p. 10, Action catholique canadienne, Service de préparation au mariage du diocèse de Montréal, Ottawa, *Le Droit,* 1944.

4 *Parent Report,* Report of the Quebec Royal Commission of Enquiry on Education, vol. 3. (Quebec, 1964), pp. 227-228.

5 Archives of the C.S.N., *Procès verbal du Congrès de 1964,* President's Report, p. 8.

6 Anonymous account quoted in Soeur Marie-Thérèse-du-Carmel, SNJM. *Les Cercles de fermières et l'action sociale,* paper given to the Institut de pédagogie familiale, Outrement, 1967, p. 37.

7 Micheline D. Johnson, *Histoire de la situation de la femme dans la province de Québec* (Ottawa, 1971), p. 47.

CHAPTER FOURTEEN

QUIET FEMINISM

WOMEN'S ABILITIES GO UNRECOGNIZED

FOR MORE THAN A CENTURY, Quebec had relied on the work and the skills of women to keep its basic services going. Religious communities maintained many institutions, among them nurseries, hospitals, homes and hospices.

In 1965, the 43,265 Quebec nuns who worked in these institutions were almost entirely responsible for the secondary and college education of girls. In isolated areas of the province, almost all medical services were provided by lay nurses. Social service was seen as an essentially female occupation, and the many urban services were usually introduced by a woman. The structure of these institutions was simple, with little hierarchy; but the top of almost every pyramid was occupied by a doctor or a priest, often the only male presence in an otherwise female organization. Management and bursar positions were occupied by an army of qualified nuns who, after the Thirties and especially after 1950, took diploma courses qualifying them for these positions. In 1962, nuns in Quebec held seventy-one doctorates, 1,165 undergraduate degrees and 285 master's degrees. Between 1964 and 1968, thousands of women students from various religious communities appeared on university and college campuses for advanced educations, either as full-time (1,453) or part-time (5,645) students. Lay graduates were in a minority.

After the creation of the ministries of Education and Social Affairs in 1964, the great upheavals of the Quiet Revolution began: secularization, co-educational schools, mixed institutions and hospitals, bureaucratization, a multitude of new professions, and tremendous growth of unionization, especially in the public service. With these changes came a reevaluation of the competence of women in the work place.

As we have seen, until the nineteenth century, teaching was dominated by men. Gradually, women were admitted into the profession; but they were given inferior positions, while men assumed positions of authority. In the mid-twentieth century, there was a new version of the same phenomenon: a hierarchical structure developed within the "female" professions – library science, social and paramedical services, mixed secondary education and continuing education (into which nuns had made considerable inroads) – and men were quick to rise in these professions.

A hierarchical structure became the norm in the work place. Bureaucratization propelled men into the upper levels; women occupied the lower levels. The position of general manager was essentially a male position. For decades, women had run libraries, schools and hospitals, but they failed to maintain their hold on managerial positions. A number of female and male institutions – in Rosemount, Saint-Laurent, Saint-Hyacinthe and Sherbrooke – were transformed into CEGEPs. Initially, some women, nuns and lay women, were appointed to executive positions; however, they did not hold them long – for reasons that are still unclear. Young bureaucrats, fresh from university, were telling respected teachers with years of valuable experience and hospitalers well-versed in health-service administration how to do their jobs.

It was probably no coincidence that nuns began to leave the convents during this period. The secularization of Quebec society happened at the same time as the upheavals in the Church following Vatican II. There were desertions from the clergy and from various religious communities, but departures from women's communities were most remarkable. It is estimated that, between 1968 and 1978, ten nuns left the convent every week. Their decisions had one specific significance: they had entered a religious community because society refused them their chosen profession except in the guise of a religious vocation; they left because they no longer needed to be nuns to have a profession. The one institution that had offered career opportunities for women suddenly became a dead end.

In 1970, psychologist Jacqueline Bouchard studied women's reasons for leaving the convent. Her conclusions are interesting: women left primarily because the religious communities did not respect human values. They left out of an unsatisfied desire for freedom and independence. And they left because nuns had lost their high social status. These decisions, however, were not taken without soul-searching: religious vows are not broken casually. Yet, the clumsiness with which various religious orders dealt with changes in the Church must have contributed to nuns' anguish. "When I returned from the field," reported one ex-nun, "where I had been deeply involved for five years in problems of development, injustice and poverty, and found myself involved in the empty and petty debates over our dress and our status, I felt stifled. How could we still be involved in such things, at a time when there were so many important things to do and to think about?"[1]

The sisters were not the only ones to leave; priests and monks also left the Church. But ex-clerics had a ready-made male network to welcome them into the world. Through these networks, men obtained positions, often at the top. No such network existed for nuns. When they entered the laity they became isolated. The new professional hierarchies were now career paths for men. As long as work done by women was invisible, anonymous and free, it was easily tolerated. But society would not match a woman's skills with a managerial salary. The few token women who held good positions and became public figures led people to believe that society was well intentioned and egalitarian, and to place the reponsibility for the inequalities that existed on individual women. The ability of these women is not in doubt: they had to have impeccable qualifications to get top positions. But what effect did they have? The token woman unknowingly reinforced the rigidity of the social structure.

The situation did not change with the arrival, in the job market, of the new women graduates of the Quiet Revolution. In 1979, women made up one-third of Quebec's huge public service. Two percent of these women held upper-echelon positions. (Even these worked primarily as executive assistants.) Fifteen percent held middle-management positions; of these, nearly half were in administrative-support positions. Sixteen percent held professional positions – information officers, researchers and administrative assistants. But 56 percent of Quebec's women public servants were office workers: administrative officers, secretaries, telephone operators, inspectors, administrative secretaries. Only 2 percent did manual labour, working, of course, as charwomen. Discrimination in the public service mirrored Quebec society as a whole.

The Quiet Revolution reproduced the traditional double standard, though in a new guise.

FROM NURSERY SCHOOL
TO UNIVERSITY

After the Ministry of Education was created in 1964, the educational structures we know today were gradually put in place. Three objectives were pursued: mixed schools, free education and universal accessibility. The goals caused considerable upheaval: a decrease in private schools, the appearance of *polyvalentes* (composite secondary schools), the abolition of domestic-science schools, the creation of CEGEPs, the founding of the multi-campus Université du Québec, the integration of teacher training into the university system. The sciences became accessible when the CEGEPs offered a choice of courses: pure sciences, health sciences, administrative sciences, human sciences, and so on.

Girls enthusiastically entered the various levels of the restructured educational system, for the State was finally offering opportunities to all women, opportunities that, in the past, only a privileged few had been able to benefit from. Gone were the domestic-science schools; school uniforms became obsolete; the old-fashioned supervision of the nuns was no more. Even nurses did their training in CEGEPs.

Schools offered a wide range of courses; the calendars of the *polyvalentes*, CEGEPs and universities were inviting. Finally, girls could think of pursuing a career. Women professionals – seventeen engineers, one hundred and fifty lawyers, seven architects, two psychoanalysts, and six town planners employed in Quebec in 1968 could rejoice: women were about to take their rightful place in society.

A generation later, scepticism was the order of the day. The *polyvalentes* had inundated the job market with hairdressers, typists, beauticians and nurses' aides.

Colleges were as accessible to girls as they were to boys (in 1976, college enrollment was 51.3 percent boys, 48.7 percent girls). But 54 percent of the girls were in vocational studies; only 44 percent were in general studies. As a result, many more boys qualified for university. The CEGEPs offered more than one hundred different vocational programs, but girls and boys did not take the same courses. Table 15 provides statistics on the most popular programs.

The areas of specialization chosen by women students paralleled the job sectors traditionally occupied by women. Women had little success overcoming cultural and social constraints on moving in new career directions. In the bureaucratic structures where they did find employment, they were placed in the lower ranks.

Was the situation the same for women who studied at university? University women were also subject to socio-cultural constraints. First, the proportion of women decreased as the level of education rose. In 1976, 44 percent of BA graduates, 33 percent of MA graduates and 19 percent of Ph.D.s were women. Most female students were enrolled in the teachers'-training programs, previously offered in normal schools. Most attended the Université du Québec, where more than half the degrees awarded were in education. In dietetics, 96 percent of students were women, but they made up only 3 percent of engineering students.

But changes were taking place. Women students invaded the field of optometry and veterinary medicine. (There had been only ten pioneers in 1968.) They doubled their numbers in law, in medicine and in business and

TABLE 15
Subjects Chosen by Female Cégep Students
in 1976-77 (for programs of more than 900 students)

Subject	Number of Students	% of female students in the program
Electronics	20	1.4
Electronic Technology	41	1.6
Civil Engineering	11	3.6
Police Technology	149	12.8
Architectural Technology	157	17.3
Marketing	286	31.6
Administration	2,761	48.2
Finance	1,248	48.6
Computer Science	1,093	49.3
Recreation	563	55.1
Special Education	1,492	83.4
Social Work	958	86.2
Laboratory	920	88.8
Nursing	8,007	94.6
Secretarial	2,826	99.9

Source: Francine Descarries-Bélanger, L'Ecole rose ... et les Cols roses, Montreal, Editions coopératives Albert Saint-Martin – Centrale de l'enseignement du Québec (C.E.Q.), 1980, p. 82-84.

overtook the number of male graduates in pharmacy. It is still too soon, however, to analyze the results of these changes.

It is easy to explain why girls continued in "female" sectors although no structural obstacle prevented them from taking new subjects. First, the images in school textbooks, literature and the media conveyed the sexist prejudices of society: mothers had slimmer waists, men had new work tools, but nothing fundamental had changed. It might be thought that, by introducing co-educational schools, all those "girl's" books the religious communities had used would have become obsolete. In a 1975 study of school texts, Lise Dunnigan found that 71 percent of the texts contained male characters. At least in the old-fashioned girl's books, characters had been predominantly women – traditional role models, to be sure, but *female* role models.

Another impediment to change was the make-up of the teaching profession.

Simply by going to school, children learned that nursery and primary teachers were women, that men held administrative positions and that the few women at the university and CEGEP level taught "female" subjects. A woman studying business or chemistry never had a woman teacher as a model. But a woman studying literature or education would encounter many women teachers. A woman student was more likely to become a literature or education teacher than a chemistry teacher.

TABLE 16

Percentage Distribution of Women Teaching
in the School System, by Level, 1977-78

Level	Number of Women	Percentage
Pre-School	2,169	99.7%
Elementary	23,251	89.1%
Secondary	13,868	40.6%
College	3,500	37.2%
University	1,029	14.4%

Source: Francine Descarries-Bélanger, *L'Ecole rose et
... les Cols roses,* op. cit., p. 79.

To entrench the status quo, guidance counselors steered girls into "female" programs and dissuaded them from exploring new job opportunities. Studies show that adolescent girls do not think of their future as boys do. They are less informed about opportunities, and think that status is obtained through marriage, not through work. Girls and young women believe that, to be accepted, they must conform to the traditional female stereotype. They learn their roles early, and society – parents, educators, books and even career-guidance literature – conspires to reinforce those roles. Girls choose careers that will not interfere with family responsibilities. Guidance counselors may not be solely responsible for the socialization process, but neither are they totally free of responsibility as they provide different information to girls and boys.

Despite these attitudes, after 1965, hundreds of women decided to return to school to obtain professional and academic training in the numerous continuing-education programs. One woman who returned says:

The days I left home in the late afternoon to go to class, nobody could accuse me of having neglected my family. I had made everything easy for them: all the food for the evening meal had been precooked and all they needed to do was warm it up for a few minutes in the oven before serving it; the garbage had been put out on the sidewalk, if that was the evening they were picking it up; I marked the interesting programs in the TV guide in case my family wanted to consult it. When the children were young, I bathed them and put them in their pajamas before I left. My family could relax and enjoy themselves while I was away, and it seemed to me that I had done everything to guarantee that they were comfortable. Then, worn out, I would make a dash for the subway, become an irresponsible pedestrian and cross against a red light and finally arrive at the university. I would sit down at my desk, trying to get my strength back, while the professor totally confused me with the intricacies of structuralism. I wouldn't catch my breath until after the break; then I would become my old self and the green light in my brain would go on and allow the information to filter through. I had just changed identities.[2]

Students often got married before they finished their studies. The young wife supported the couple while her husband finished his undergraduate degree or his master's degree with the tacit understanding that it would be her turn after he had finished. How many nurses subsidized their husbands' studies and kept house for them? How many women were deceived? No studies have been done on the subject, but we know that their turn never came. Many women found themselves alone, divorced after "his lordship" finished his studies.

In education, the Quiet Revolution had truly been achieved on the backs of women. It is true that the real achievement of educational reform was the removal of inequalities. Everyone could go to secondary school, but students made the same choices as they always had; there were as many girls as boys in the CEGEPs, but they were enrolled in traditional subject areas; almost as many girls as boys went to university, but the girls' studies were shorter and very "feminine." There had been an increase in the number of adult students, but a very different fate awaited women and men.

THE PINK-COLLAR WORKERS

Educational reform had little effect on women's opportunities to get different vocational training. The job market influenced the way girls were trained; girls could penetrate only those job areas where they were already in a majority. Women made the very choices that led to the growth of female ghettoes in the work place and in education. But society was not changing. According to

Francine Descarries-Bélanger, "the existence of a divided job market, based on the social division of the sexes, had a considerable effect upon the job sectors where women worked. Such a division brought about a higher concentration of women within certain specific occupations that were predominantly female and their restriction to jobs that were often merely an extension of their activities as housewives and mothers." Nearly two-thirds of all working women were employed in only twenty occupations including shorthand typists, saleswomen, elementary teachers, waitresses, cashiers, agricultural workers, nurses and nurses' aides, office workers, sewing-machine operators, hairdressers, cleaners and receptionists. (More than 90 percent of the workers in several of these occupations were women.)

TABLE 17
Female Occupations

Occupation	Proportion in 1961	Proportion in 1971
Secretaries, stenographers	96.8%	97.4%
Saleswomen	53.6%	66%
Cashiers	62.6%	79.4%
Elementary teachers	70.7%	82.3%
Waitresses	70.5%	82.9%
Nurses	96.2%	95.8%

Source: Francine Descarries-Bélanger, L'Ecole rose et ... les Cols roses, op. cit., p. 49.

TABLE 18
Inequality in Male and Female Wage

	Men in $	Women in $
Grocery clerk	5.09	2.91
Knitting machine operator	3.98	3.07
Packer	3.50	2.85
Receptionist	5.78	4.53
Power press set-up operator	5.19	3.60
Bindery worker	6.44	4.05

Source: Conseil du statut de la femme, Pour les Québécoises égalité et indépendance, Québec, 1978, p. 239.

The gap between female and male salaries continued to widen; women and men were paid different rates for identical work. Illegal work and the "sweating" system we associate with the industrial revolution still existed, and thousands of women were still being exploited. Immigrant women – particularly Italians, Portuguese, West Indians, Greeks and Vietnamese – were the most exploited, and worked under inhuman conditions.

Female and male work was never considered to be comparable. Women were employed when there were not enough male workers, to keep wage levels down, and to compensate for the absence of men during wartime.

The institutionalization of female unemployment was useful in liberal economies such as Quebec's. The reserve labour source – women – formed an integral part of the capitalist production forces outside the work place. Thus, female work was always seen as optional. Advertisements and the media consistently ignored the productive aspects of women's work, or presented women's work in a distorted, idealized or erotic way. Relations between the sexes became most stereotyped in the work place. Some of the blame certainly lay with women, but how many waitresses, secretaries and cashiers were obliged to look sexy? Job advertisements demanded that women be young and attractive. Moreover, on any day in factories, shops and offices, there were hundreds of examples of sexual harassment, which indirectly told women: "You are out of place here."

The economic expansion of the postwar period did not lead to expansion of the female labour force. It did, however produce a greater compartmentalization of the work done by women and created an increasingly rigid separation between "female" and "male" work. The proportion of working women did not increase, but the number of "female" jobs did, jobs that reproduced all the "natural" female functions – sewing, cooking, nursing, teaching, washing, and so on.

Many employers hired part-time workers, and this led to new problems. Women made up the great majority of the part-time work force. In 1971, there were three times as many women as men in part-time jobs; the proportion continued to increase, particularly in the service sector, where the great majority of working women were found. Work was organized so that part-timers were excluded from fringe benefits – pensions, sick leave, paid holidays, seniority, insurance and so on. Unions were often opposed to part-time work, an opposition that caused strife amongst workers. Many women sought part-time employment because it enabled them to combine paid work with family responsibilities.

Quebec's social structure was based on an illusion that "real" women raised families, looked after the house and prepared the meals while "real" men supported the family. This ideal had never really existed, yet people pretended they believed in it.

Today, people seem more interested in the working woman, but she is hardly a recent phenomenon. Women have always worked, within the home or outside it. The working woman has become a topic of discussion for two reasons.

First, men became alarmed by the presence albeit small, of women in certain traditionally male sectors. The first woman taxi driver caused quite a stir. Fear was the typical male reaction: fear of so-called male drives, fear of seeing women free themselves from the protection of men, fear of losing privileges and fear of seeing their professions decline in status. And indeed, the entry of women into a given job sector did result in a decline in status and wages.

But the main reason people questioned the presence of women in the work force was because they believed that women, especially married women, made an important contribution to society by staying at home. Domestic chores were still their lot, even if they had typed a hundred words a minute for seven hours, even if they had punched four thousand computer cards, even if they had served seven hundred cafeteria meals or disinfected six thousand face cloths in a hospital laundry. Most working women had a double workday, and most of them could not give up their jobs. Their wages were needed to pay the rent and the car bills or pay for the children's education and the groceries.

THE PSYCHOLOGY OF DAILY LIFE
THEO CHENTRIER

What I admire most about a woman is the opportunity she has for doing chores, that is, for doing tedious and selfless work. That there exist in this world beings, known as wives and mothers, capable of doing the housework, the cooking, the dishes, and the laundry every day of the year (even with the assistance of machines) has always been for me a source of amazement. However, I know now where the woman gets her strength to do such chores, day in day out: from her love for her husband and her children! What I admire the most, then, is the power of love to conquer boredom. What I also admire is the touch of beauty and greatness that it gives to things, even the most insignificant. The woman is also proud and this leads her to look after her house as if it were a palace. This is true even of the poorest home.[3]

Society did not provide help for working women with children. Before maternity leave was ever discussed in companies, institutions or collective agreements, thousands of women had accepted compromises: loss of wages, loss of a job, extra work before and after the child was born and terrible hours.

Before day-care centres existed, thousands of women used their ingenuity, tolerated being overworked and did everything possible to find babysitters. Thousands of grandmothers worked as babysitters for their children's children.

Female heads of families – divorcées, separated women, single mothers and widows who did not go out to work – received social assistance. (Perhaps society could not imagine a world in which one could both work for a living and raise children.)

One group of women was especially vulnerable: the nearly 150,000 (according to the 1966 census) who worked in profit-making businesses alongside their husbands. They were not paid, and their work experience was not recognized; therefore they were ineligible for the social-security plans guaranteed other working women. If their marriages fell apart, they had no legal protection. In Ontario, the Murdoch case sparked enormous interest in the question of legal rights for the wife / business partner. Ontario law, like that of Quebec, allowed for separate property. When her marriage broke down, Mrs. Murdoch claimed part of the value of the farm on which she had worked for many years. The Supreme Court declared that she was not entitled to any share of the farm "since she only did her duty as a farmer's wife." Her work was taken for granted, and she had no claim to material compensation.

What is to be said of all the other women who, according to Yvon Deschamps, "didn't work because they had too much work"? These prisoners of housework often suffered from boredom, especially once the children were at school. When a woman no longer had her children to keep her busy, life at home seemed empty. Women were aware of their imprisonment but rarely articulated that awareness. They were almost ashamed to do so, as it is not easy to speak out against a condition that people proclaim to be natural and universal. Psychologists in their articles, priests in their retreats and broadcasters on their radio programs told women to overcome their boredom and adjust to the role society expected of them. Men explained what women were feeling: one radio program aimed at women was called "Un homme vous écoute" ("A Man Is Listening To You").

Today, women define their own problems. They have groups, associations and places where they can meet. They have opportunities to discuss their problems and to search for solutions. They even have government bodies to pursue their demands politically. All this did not come about by chance. In

1965, such talk was unheard of; such consciousness had not yet surfaced. Far-seeing women set up associations, demanded enquiries, commissions and strategies for action. The word "feminism," which had seemed as antiquated as a suffragette, again became part of our language.

THE REBIRTH OF ORGANIZED FEMINISM

At the beginning of 1965, a number of women realized that Quebec women had had the vote for twenty-five years, yet the franchise had not been celebrated collectively. Thérèse Casgrain initiated the idea, and she asked representatives from women's associations to organize the celebration.

In associations such as the Union catholique des femmes rurales, the Voice of Women, the Unions de famille and the University Women's Club, women began to analyze the female condition.

The anniversary of the right to vote would be celebrated with a two-day conference in Montreal, called *La Femme du Québec. Hier et aujourd'hui* (Women in Quebec. Past and Present). Committees studied the legal status of women, the participation of women in the Quebec economy and in society. Claire Kirkland-Casgrain, Quebec's first female MNA, gave the keynote address and Mariana Jodoin, Quebec's only woman senator, was honorary chair.

At the closing session, the conference voted unanimously to found the Quebec Federation of Women. The federation would include representatives

---

ORGANIZING COMMITTEE FOR CELEBRATIONS TO MARK THE TWENTY-FIFTH ANNIVERSARY OF THE RIGHT TO VOTE FOR WOMEN

Thérèse Casgrain, ex-president of the League for Women's Rights

Colette Beauchamp, Anne Postans and Raymonde Roy of the Voice of Women

Maire-Ange Madore, of the Fédération nationale Saint-Jean- Baptiste

Lise Trudeau and Cécile Labelle, from the Anciennes de Pédagogie familiale

Dorothée Lorrain, from the University Women's Club[4]

SIGNATORIES TO THE CONSTITUTION
OF THE QUEBEC FEDERATION OF WOMEN,
1 MARCH 1966

Colette Beauchamp, journalist

Monique Bégin, sociologist

Fernande Cantero, homemaker

Thérèse Casgrain, politician

Réjane Colas, lawyer

Alice Desjardins, lawyer

Jeanne Duval, union official

Madeleine Favreau, homemaker

Cécile Labelle, businesswoman

Dorothée Lorrain, biologist

Denise Payeur, homemaker

Huguette Plamondon, union official

Louise Rousseau, secretary

Raymonde Roy, real estate agent

Fernande Saint-Martin, journalist

Lise Trudeau, homemaker[5]

from all the women's associations as well as having individual members; its first objective would be to coordinate all activities aimed at promoting the interests and rights of women. Participants adopted the organizational structure chosen by the National Council of Women in 1893 and in 1907 by the Fédération national Saint-Jean-Baptiste.

The press greeted the proposed federation with enthusiasm. According to Renaude Lapointe of *La Presse,* the federation would be a new strike force. In *Le Devoir* the demands of the federation were front-page news: a government enquiry into working conditions for women; the introduction of a law requiring equal pay for work of equal value; the immediate creation of state-run day-care centres; the recognition of parental authority; the creation of a divorce court, and the abolition of the terms "housewife" and "needy mother." The federation knew that, amidst the enthusiasm of the Quiet Revolution, women were once again being left on the sidelines. The feminism that people believed to be dead was very much alive, even if the word "feminism" was rarely used.

A campaign was launched under the leadership of Thérèse Casgrain. Her living room became headquarters for the committee preparing for the founding convention; the committee drawing up the constitution; the committee liaising with regional groups; the committee sounding out opinion in the various women's associations; and the committee liaising with unions and professional associations. On 1 March 1966, a group of women requested and obtained the official constitution of the federation. (The constitution would be ratified at the founding convention.)

Nearly four hundred women came to the convention, held on 23 and 24 April 1966. Thirty-six associations sent delegates, thirty-eight sent observers and one hundred and thirty individual women came from all parts of the province.

This was the first time women from all regions, from all social groups and from all religious denominations had come together. There were Francophones and Anglophones, women from the country and women from the cities. Quite obviously, a new solidarity had to be forged. However, not all the women were on the same wavelength. Some were disturbed to see such words as "divorce" and "abortion" in federation documents. Delegates objected to certain procedures; they wanted to help write the constitution and regulations and were unwilling to endorse the proposals of the organizing committee. Despite these problems, the association got off the ground. Delegates and several members from the organizing committees were elected to the first executive committee. The committee's first act was to appoint Thérèse Casgrain honorary president of the federation in recognition of her crucial founding role. Women now had a political platform to support their demands.

In the face of the inevitable disagreements caused by the two days of debate, journalists wondered if unity would be possible in a federation in which there were so many different constituencies. Discussion during the convention had raised disagreements between women who worked and those who "didn't" (sic); between women from the towns and those from the country; between university graduates and those without fancy titles; between women with babies and women with diplomas. Réjane Laberge-Colas, the first president, responded to the objections of the press by stating that unity would be possible, since "women would concern themselves with questions that were primarily of interest to all women. And when they took an

---

PRESIDENTS OF THE QUEBEC FEDERATION OF WOMEN

1966-67	Réjane Laberge-Colas – lawyer
1967-69	Rita Cadieux – social worker
1969-70	Marie-Paule Dandois – social worker
1970-74	Yvette Rousseau – trade-unionist
1974-77	Ghislaine Patry-Buisson – *animatrice*
1977-80	Sheila Abby-Finestone – *animatrice*
1980-81	Gabrielle Hotte – trade-unionist
1981-	Huguette Lapointe-Roy – historian[6]

PRESIDENTS OF THE CERCLES DE FERMIERES

1960-64 Madame Charles Gosselin
1964-68 Madame Adélard Jolin
1968-74 Madame Fredeline Caron
1974-80 Madame Marielle Primeau
1980-   Madame Marie Tremblay[7]

---

interest in a particular class, it would be because their problems were of importance to the whole community."

The federation was multiethnic. The constitution stated that the federation would not have a chaplain, which was hardly surprising given the prevailing atmosphere of pluralism and secularism. Autonomy from religious and national power was vital to the emergence of an independent woman's voice, as the activities of the Quebec Federation of Women proved.

In 1966, the new organization did not get the affiliation of all the women's associations in Quebec. Its nondenominationalism was enough to dissuade the powerful Cercles de fermières. Strongly reproved by the bishops in the past, the Cercles would not risk another dispute, particularly since they had celebrated their fiftieth anniversary in great style. In the future, the Cercles provided a platform for those conservative voices that wished to influence women.

Quebec's other rural women's organization, the Union catholique des femmes rurales, took a different stance. Provincial president Germaine Gaudreau was a member of the first executive committee of the Quebec Federation of Women. The UCFR was in the process of reorganizing: it had been discussing amalgamation with the Cercles d'économie domestique for three years. Amalgamation took place in August 1966, with the creation of the AFEAS.

PRESIDENTS OF THE AFEAS

1966-1970 Germaine Gaudreau – partner in a family business
1970-1975 Azilda Marchand – community worker
1975-1980 Solange Gervais – partner in a family business
1980-   Christine Gagné – project leader[8]

The members of the first executive committee of the AFEAS felt that the new association should be properly organized and established before affiliating with the Quebec Federation of Women. A premature move in this direction could create tremendous confusion and harm recruitment. In 1966, the AFEAS was describing itself as a new association. Its membership was primarily rural. Fifteen years earlier, its members had been introduced to discussions of social issues and to direct participation in public life. Reacting to pressure from dynamic and astute women to subsidize numerous projects involving "ordinary" women, the AFEAS became a forum for social action. Discussions of

---

ASSOCIATIONS AFFILIATED TO
THE QUEBEC FEDERATION OF WOMEN – 1980

Association d'économie familiale du Québec • Association de familles monoparentales bas-Saguenay "La Ruche" • Association de familles monoparentales de l'Estrie Inc. • Association des cadres et professionels de l'Université de Montréal • Quebec Native Women's Group • University Women's Club (Montreal) • University Women's Club (Quebec) • Association des puériculturices de la province de Québec • Association des veuves de Montréal • Au bas de l'Echelle • B'nai B'rith Women's Council • Centre bénévole de Mieux-être de Jonquière • Centre d'information et de référence pour femmes • Cercle des femmes journalistes • Cercle des rencontres du mercredi inc. • Club culturel humanitaire Châtelaine • Club Wilfrid-Laurier des femmes libérales • Communauté sépharade du Québec • National Council of Jewish Women • Fédération québecoise des infirmières et infirmiers • Junior League of Montreal Inc. • Les auxiliaires bénévoles de l'hôpital de Jonquière • Ligue des citoyennes de Jonquière • Montreal Lakeshore University Women's Club • Mouvement des femmes chrétiennes • Mouvement: services à la communauté; Cap Rouge • Regroupement des garderies, région six C • Réseau d'action et d'information pour femmes (Saguenay) • Sherbrooke and District University Women's Club • Société d'étude et de conférences (Quebec) • Voice of Women • West Island Shelter • West Island Woman's Centre • YWCA

women's work produced severe criticism of working women, who had a "sacred" and "natural" role to play in the family. Azilda Marchand, an early militant in the AFEAS, was one of the first women to refute these criticisms, as all women worked; it was more important to study the problems arising from the work they were doing, in the family or in the family business. Marchand denounced the invisible nature of women's work. Her observation would lead, in 1976, to the birth of the Association des femmes collaboratrices and, in 1978, to the publication of *Pendant que les hommes travaillent, les femmes elles* ... ("While the Men Work, the Women ...").

The Quebec Federation of Women became the operations central for most Quebec's women's associations. Many important groups joined as affiliates. Today, the federation represents more than a hundred thousand members and is made up of representatives from associations, regional councils and individual members.

THE BIRD COMMISSION

The question of the status of women became a public issue in Quebec. Newspapers wrote editorials about it; editorials in *Châtelaine* magazine, under the editorship of Fernande Saint-Martin, informed its readers about demands made by women. On the radio, a series entitled *Fémina,* produced by Louise Simard, discussed the status of women; on television, *Femmes d'aujourd'hui* (Today's Women) confronted the most controversial problems head-on. Participants at family-planning conferences discovered that Quebec, hitherto so conservative, had caught up with, and sometimes surpassed, Protestant and Anglophone associations when it came to getting people involved in women's issues. In 1964, the Quebec delegation of the Voice of Women had abstained from voting on the issue of abortion; in 1966, a Quebec woman, the vice-president of the VOW, explained the fundamental techniques of contraception to a committee of the House of Commons, which was examining the decriminalization of contraception. The president of the Canadian Federation of University Women's Clubs, Laura Sabia, took part in the enthusiastic preparations for the founding convention of the Quebec Federation of Women. Cooperation between Anglophones and Francophones, especially in the VOW, led people to predict that solidarity amongst all Canadian women was finally possible. (In 1964, a Canadian delegation from the VOW to NATO in Paris was arrested and imprisoned during a demonstration against nuclear arms. Toronto women disapproved of the demonstration, but Thérèse Casgrain, one of the delegates, was welcomed as a heroine in Quebec and warmly embraced by the premier.) The idea of a commission of enquiry into the status of women gained ground: Jeanne Sauvé demanded such a commission in March 1966.

In English Canada, women were inspired by the example of American feminism. Laura Sabia introduced the idea of a new political platform for women, and a new organization was created: the Committee for the Equality of Women in Canada. A number of Quebec associations joined, and one of the first achievements of the committee was an agreement, in May 1966, to demand a royal commission into the status of women. Thirty-two women's associations endorsed the initiative. On 19 November 1966, a delegation arrived in Ottawa to demand a federal enquiry.

The timing was absolutely perfect. The Canadian economy was booming. In the cabinet, Judy Lamarsh, the only female minister, spoke forcibly on the need to deal with the status of women. Western nations had carried out, or were in the process of carrying out, enquiries and studies in this very area. The minority Liberal government was obliged to place greater emphasis on the basic rights of individuals, as they depended on the NDP for a majority in the House.

International peace movements, opposition to the war in Vietnam and discussions on racial segregation had focused on "the rights of man," and provided a valuable theoretical framework in which to place the question of the status of women.

The government did not immediately agree to the demand for a commission. During an interview, Laura Sabia spoke of a possible women's march on Ottawa; the next day a Toronto daily newspaper headline read "Three Million Women to March on Ottawa."

OFFICIAL ENQUIRIES INTO THE STATUS OF WOMEN AT THE BEGINNING OF THE SIXTIES

Country	
U.S.A.	1961-1963
West Germany	1962-1966
Denmark	1965
France	1966
United Kingdom	1966
Finland	1966
Holland	1966
Austria	1966[9]

MEMBERS OF THE ROYAL COMMISSION OF ENQUIRY
ON THE STATUS OF WOMEN IN CANADA,
16 FEBRUARY 1967 – 28 SEPTEMBER 1970

Florence Bird – journalist, Ontario
Jacques Henripin – demographer, Quebec
John P. Humphrey – lawyer, Quebec
Lola M. Lange – farmer, Alberta
Jeanne Lapointe – professor, Quebec
Elsie Gregory McGill – engineer, Ontario
Doris Ogilvie – lawyer, New Brunswick
Monique Bégin – sociologist, Quebec – Executive Secretary
of the Commission and Director of Research [10]

In February 1967, the government of Canada set up a Royal Commission of Enquiry on the Status of Women in Canada. The commission – named the Bird Commission, after its chair – would be of considerable importance for women. The response from women confounded all predictions: in less than two years, the status of women became a major social problem. The long-unbroken tradition of women's social commitment was revealed in all its dimensions. A link was formed between the feminists of the turn of the century and a new feminism, the reformist feminism whose objective was equality for all in society.

In Quebec, the formation of the commission received a lukewarm reception. People feared that there would be jurisdictional conflicts between the federal and provincial governments. Thérèse Casgrain stated that the enquiry ought not to encroach upon provincial rights; she also held that women had to be educated before they could become aware of their problems.

The Bird Commission got through an enormous amount of work: it received 469 briefs and more than 1,000 letters; held public meetings for 37 days in 14 cities, at which more than 890 people voiced their complaints; commissioned 34 studies on particular points; and published, on 28 September 1970, a 540-page report that included 167 recommendations.

The Bird Commission recommended that priority be given to the establishment of absolute equality between women and men, both institutionally and in daily life. It saw economic independence as the basis of this equality and, therefore, demanded equal pay, equal employment opportunities and equal opportunities for promotion, particularly in the public service and in the army. It also demanded that all educational avenues, programs, professional training and so on be open equally to women and men. Family responsibilities, which fell to women and were primarily responsible for keeping women in a state of dependence, were discussed: the commission recommended complete equality between spouses, and proposed changes in the divorce law. It demanded that the minimum marriage age be fixed at eighteen years and that day-care centres be made available to all women. It proclaimed the importance of birth-control clinics and advocated free abortion on demand for all women less than twelve weeks pregnant.

On this particular point, however, three commissioners wrote dissenting reports: two because they opposed the proposal and one because she thought the commission had not gone far enough. Disagreement among the commissioners on other points – day-care centres, compensation for working women – shows the extent to which the problems raised by the Bird Commission challenged Canadian society.

THE BIRD REPORT: A BOMBSHELL

At 2:11 PM in the House of Commons Monday, the Prime Minister rose, bowed politely to the Speaker, and tabled a bomb, already primed and ticking.

The bomb is called the Report of the Royal Commission on the Status of Women in Canada, and it is packed with more explosive potential than any device manufactured by terrorists.

As a call to revolution, hopefully a quiet one, it is more persuasive than any FLQ manifesto.

And as a political blockbuster, it is more powerful than that famous report of the controversial commission on bilingualism and biculturalism.

This 488-page book [plus a summary of recommendations], in its discreet green, white and blue cover, demands radical change not just in Quebec, but in every community across Canada. It is concerned not merely with relations between French and English, but between man and woman.

The history of the problem it describes and seeks to solve is not 100 years of Confederation but the story of mankind.[11]

SOME OF THE QUEBEC WOMEN'S ASSOCIATIONS
WHICH PRESENTED BRIEFS TO THE BIRD COMMISSION

The Cercles de Fermières • The AFEAS • The Quebec Federation of Women • The University Women's Club • La Fédération des unions de famille • La Ligue des femmes du Québec • La Société d'étude et des conférences • L'Association des religieuses enseignantes du Québec • The Montreal Council of Women • Women's Federation, Allied Jewish Community Services of Montreal • The Voice of Women (Montreal)

The report highlighted the acute problems of a particularly neglected group of women: Indian women. During the nineteenth century, the law deprived an Indian woman of her status if she married a non-Indian. Subsequent laws put even greater limits on the rights of Indian women. In fact, it had become clear that the government intended in the long run to assimilate the Indian population; to achieve this, it was slowly taking away Indian status from women. The government had always seen emancipation – loss of special status – as an advantage for Indians. However, most Natives preferred to keep their culture and their Indian values alive. Ninety-five percent of all emancipations between 1965 and 1975 involved women who had not chosen to be emancipated, but who had lost their status because of the law.

Discussions concerning the rights of the individual made many different groups in the community aware of the flagrant injustice done to Indian women. But these discussions produced few concrete results because Native representatives were almost entirely male. Indian men were opposed to any change in Canadian laws because they were afraid that they would lose the privileges they had won with so much difficulty.

The Bird Commission provided an opportunity for many Indian women's groups to explain their lot. After the commission, a number of events kept Indian women in the public eye. A lawsuit launched by Jeannette Lavell in 1970 finally led a Supreme Court judge to declare "that inequality based on sex within a group or class is not necessarily an offence against the Declaration of Human Rights. As a result, the situation of Indian women today is disastrous: Indian women continue to be the victims of white laws. To be sure, there are not many of them in Quebec, but their situation is typical. The Quebec Native Women's Group is attempting to change the situation, but is finding it difficult."

The Bird Commission had considerable impact in Quebec, not because of

345

its recommendations – women in the movement thought they were conservative – and not because of its findings – they revealed nothing new – but because of the ferment it aroused in women's associations. Most of the associations had consulted with their members before presenting briefs to the commission. After the Bird report was published, the Quebec Federation of Women published its *Guide de discussion,* a booklet used by almost all women's groups in Quebec.

Debates in women's groups seemed to follow naturally upon the lengthy and impassioned discussions caused by *Humanae Vitae,* Paul VI's famous encyclical on contraception in 1968. The link between contraception and the female condition was fundamental: the availability of contraception enabled women to get an education, become active in the work place and society and change attitudes. Feminist analysis took a different approach when women began to regain control over procreation.

At the end of the Sixties, Quebec women were openly discussing contraception. The publication of *Humanae Vitae,* which specifically condemned the use of the pill, widened the gap between the Church's view of marriage and more liberal viewpoints. Many Catholics refused to obey papal instructions. On 20 November 1968, the daily newspaper *Photo-Journal* launched a survey on birth control; 2,394 people, 85 percent of them women and most of them Catholic Francophones, replied. An analysis of the results was presented in April 1979 on the Radio-Canada program *5D*; it revealed that the Church had lost control over the fertility of Catholic couples. Only 12 percent of the respondents "saw themselves as obliged in conscience to submit to the conclusion of the *Humanae Vitae* encyclical." Scarcely 1.5 percent of married couples had totally abandoned the use of any contraceptives and 3.6 percent had changed methods. The survey revealed that scarcely 15 percent of married couples and 6 percent of unmarried people consulted a priest on matters of contraception.

These changes were fundamental. Catholics quietly learned to free themselves from guilt associated with questions of family planning. The law supported the trend. In 1969, the advertising and sale of contraceptives and the diffusion of information relating to contraception were removed from the Criminal Code. Therapeutic abortion was also authorized. The state, declared Prime Minister Trudeau, "has no business in the bedrooms of the nation."

ORCHESTRA WIVES GO ON STRIKE

Nature and culture had joined forces for thousands of years to subject women to marriage and procreation, but societies had established avenues of escape for women wanting to avoid their double bind. However lacking in prestige, at least these avenues existed. Now however, there was no way out of the double bind. Convents emptied – they were no longer an alternative to marriage. The marriage rate rose, and marriage became the lot of most women. The "old maid" became a rarity, and childless couples an endangered species. At the end of the Sixties, unmarried mothers were keeping their children. The waiting lists of adopting parents became extremely long.

Women were having fewer children, but motherhood became increasingly difficult socially (read, "biologically") to escape. Life as a housewife became the fate common to all women: those who could hire servants experienced a "domestic crisis" even greater than that at the beginning of the century. Women became, in spite of themselves, servants within their own families.

During the Quiet Revolution, girls found themselves in the same educational programs as boys. Domestic-science schools shut their doors and men began to teach young girls. Textbooks for girls disappeared. In principle, the democratization of education opened avenues to females and males alike; but girls found themselves in courses where their class-mates were mainly girls. When they were hired for their first job, most girls found themselves working with women. When they prepared a budget for their future household with their fiancé, they inevitably discovered that their pay cheque was the smaller.

A real woman was, at once, a good lover, a good wife, a readily available mother, a competent worker, a good cook and a good trade-unionist; as in the past, a real woman was expected not to disturb the traditional order. At the same time, she had to take her job seriously. Any woman who kept up this pace for a few years found herself in a tighter fix than ever, paying dearly for the illusion of equality.

Women who wanted to devote themselves to bringing up their children did so in an ambiguous atmosphere. On the one hand, they were respected as long as they accepted the advice of all kinds of experts; on the other hand, they were suspected of leading an easy, comfortable life, that was much less difficult than those of their forebears and of their husbands, who were killing themselves at work so as to make their women happy.

The process of "scientific" and rational change that, during the first half of the century, had transformed mothers and working women into simple executors of male knowledge continued throughout the Quiet Revolution. The changes also affected new areas. With the advent of economic prosperity, the infrastructure of social, educational and hospital services no longer needed to depend on charity or cheap labour provided by nuns. As a result, the women who, for three hundred years, had run hospitals, schools, convents and homes became the target of the new managerial class. First there was a campaign of denunciation; then there was a purge. Some years after the Quiet

Revolution, there were few women left in administrative posts in the new "parapublic." They had been replaced by young, allegedly competent (male) administrators.

For most wage-earning women, work meant being exploited. There were few community services or day-care centres, and no maternity leave or domestic help. Women at home were dependent mothers and their work was undervalued. Women experienced great difficulty getting back into the work place and unionized women began to talk about barriers to female employment. The feminist movement began to reappear around 1965. The Bird Commission provided an opportunity for an examination of women's lives and for a diagnosis of the injustices they were suffering.

But already in 1969, a new type of feminism was making its appearance. Women questioned the view that it was important that woman combine an interesting life in society with a life at home. New ideas, new demands, new customs, new magazines and new associations began to appear in every sector of society. This time it was society itself and relations between the sexes that were being called into question.

NOTES

1 Account given by Laurette Lepage, quoted by Laetilia Bélanger in "Les femmes qui s'en sont sorties" in *Madame au foyer,* October 1975, p. 18.

2 Ghislaine Meunier-Tardif. *Vie de femmes* (Montreal, Editions Libre-Expression, 1981), p. 174.

3 Théo Chentrier. *Vivre avec soi-même et avec les autres,* unpublished texts selected and edited by Monique Chentrier-Hoffmann (Montreal, Editions de Mortagne, 1981), p. 103. Théo Chentrier was *animateur* of the Radio-Canada series *Psychologie de la vie quotidienne* (The Psychology of Everyday Life).

4 Conference Program "La femme du Québec. Hier et aujourd'hui."

5 Archives of the Quebec Federation of Women.

6 Ibid.

7 Yvonne Rialland Morisette. *Le Passé conjugué au présent,* Cercles de Fermières, Historique 1915-1980 (Laval: Editions Pénélope), *passim.*

8 Interview with Azilda Marchand.

9 Report of the Royal Commission of Enquiry on the Status of Women in Canada, Ottawa, 1970, p. 1, footnote 1.

10 Ibid., n.p.

11 Anthony Westell in the *Toronto Star,* 8 February 1970. Quoted by Florence Bird in *Anne Francis an Autobiography* (Toronto: Clarke Irwin & Co., 1974), p. 302.

FURTHER READING

Auger, G. and R. Lamothe, *De la poêle à frire à la ligne de feu,* La Vie quotidienne de Québécoises pendant la guerre de '39-'45. Montreal: Boréal-Express, 1981.

Barry, Francine, *le Travail de la femme au Québec: l'évolution de 1940-1970.* Montréal: Presses de l'Université du Québec, 1977.

Bouchard, Jacqueline, *Facteurs des sorties des communautés religieuses du Québec,* Ph.D Thesis, Institut de Psychologie, Université de Montréal, 1970.

Brault, Rita Henry, *Les Idées nouvelles viennent de la base, Historique de Serena.* Ottawa: Serena, 1974.

Caldwell, Garry, "La baisse de la fécondité au Québec à la lumière de la sociologie québécoise" in *Recherches sociographiques,* 1976, pp. 7-22.

Casgrain, Thérèse, *Une Femme chez les hommes.* Montreal: Editions du Jour, 1971.

Cuthbert-Brandt, Gail, "Weaving It Together: Life Cycle and the Industrial Experience of Female Cotton Workers in Quebec, 1910-1950" in *Labour/Le Travailleur,* no. 7, Spring 1981, pp. 113-125.

Dardigna, Anne-Marie, *La Presse féminine, fonction idéologique.* Paris: Maspéro, 1979.

Descarries-Bélanger, Francine, *L'Ecole rose ... et les Cols roses.* Montreal: Editions cooperatives Albert Saint-Martin/Centrale de l'enseignement du Québec (CEQ), 1980.

Dumont-Johnson, Micheline, "Les communautés religieuses et la condition féminine" in *Recherches sociographiques,* 1978, no. 1, pp. 79-102.

———, "Les infirmières, cols roses?" in *Nursing-Quebec,* September 1981.

———, "La parole des femmes. Les revues féminines au Québec 1938-1968" in *Idéologie au Canada français,* vol. IV, Book II, pp. 4-45.

Dunnigan, Lise, *Analyse des stéréotypes masculins et féminins dans les manuels scolaires au Québec.* Conseil du statut de la femme, 1976.

———, "L'orientation des filles en milieu scolaire," Conseil du statut de la femme, 1977.

Friedan, Betty, *The Feminine Mystique*. New York: Dell, 1977.

Gagnon, Mona-Josée, *Les femmes vues par le Québec des hommes: 30 ans d'histoire des idéologies 1940-1970*. Montreal: Editions du Jour, 1974.

Jean, Michèle, "L'anniversaire du droit de vote" in *Bulletin de la Fédération des femmes du Québec*, vol. 6, no. 4, pp. 2-5.

Lapointe, Huguette, "Historique de la Fédération des femmes du Québec," vol. 6, no. 4, pp. 5-12.

Monet-Chartrand, Simonne, "L'urgence de la communication" in *Bulletin de la Fédération des femmes du Québec*, vol. 7, no. 1, pp. 8-11.

Morris, Cérise, "Determination and Thoroughness: The Movement for a Royal Commission on the Status of Women in Canada" in *Atlantis*, vol. 5, no. 2, Spring 1980, pp. 1-21.

Patoine, Marcelle, *L'Eglise et l'éducation au Québec*, s.1, 1977.

Pierson, Ruth, "Ladies or Loose Women: The Canadian Women's Army Corps in World War Two" in *Atlantis*, vol. IV, no. 2.

———, "'Jill Canuck': CWAC of All Trades But No 'Pistol Packing Momma'" in *Communications historiques*, 1978, pp. 106-133.

———, "Women's Emancipation and the Recruitment of Women into the Labour Force in World War II" in Trofimenkoff, S. M. and A. Prentice *The Neglected Majority*. Toronto:, McClelland and Stewart, 1977, pp. 125-145.

Rialland-Morisette, Yolande, *Le Passé conjugué au présent*, Cercles de Fermières du Québec historique. Laval: Pénelope, 1981.

Sullerot, Evelyn, *La Presse féminine*. Paris: Armand Colin, 1966.

Tessier, Albert, *Souvenirs en vrac*. Montreal: Boréal-Express, 1975.

Thivierge, Nicole, "L'enseignement ménager: Une entreprise de récupération des modèles et des valeurs traditionnels" in *Maîtresses d'écoles, Maîtresses de maisons*, selected articles, with an introduction by Micheline Dumont and Nadia Eid. Montreal: Boréal-Express, 1983.

VI
THE EXPLOSION
1969-1979

IN 1970, THE LIBERAL PARTY regained power in Quebec with a promise to create ten thousand jobs. But the government was unable to keep its promise, and the decade slowly descended into economic crisis. In 1970, nationalism and the October Crisis took centre stage. The political repression that followed, and the inability of the provincial and federal governments to come to terms with Quebec's nationalist aspirations, led to the election of the Parti québécois in 1976.

In 1970, the province faced pressing social problems. In 1972, Quebec's three major unions formed a common front, and union leaders were imprisoned for defying the law. These events were followed by long and difficult labour conflicts in all sectors, which created a climate of dissatisfaction throughout Quebec. The political experience of women active in these confrontations played a significant part in the growth of Quebec feminism.

Quebec's economic situation deteriorated as it faced the oil crisis, endemic unemployment, galloping inflation, recession, rising interest rates, public-finance disasters and scandal, the most famous involving Montreal's Olympic Stadium. While violence erupted in Lebanon, Egypt, Uganda, Rhodesia, Cambodia, Pakistan, Chile, Greece and Poland; while injustice was spreading through the world's shanty towns, prisons, refugee camps and gulags; while the superpowers were stockpiling armaments capable of blowing up the entire world; while new religious cults, music, sports and sexual practices were flourishing; while international terrorism was challenging the democratic process – feminists were trying to see the world differently. They were accused of being militant, but they had never declared war, hijacked planes or taken hostages in the name of women's rights. Many people thought the "new" women's movement was just a passing phase, like the hippie movement, but feminist theory was becoming increasingly structured. Feminists were labelled hysterical; but more and more women, either publicly or privately, agreed with the feminists and were trying to change the world around them.

This latest chapter in the history of women in Quebec is unique. By the end of the Sixties political parties, governments, churches, unions and businesses were obliged to take women into account. During the Seventies, women began to break through the barriers between private and public life and the lives of women and men. Women were no longer willing to remain in limbo, caught between social expectations and the new roles they had chosen.

But men continued to downplay the significance of the women's movement. Political and economic analyses seldom mentioned it, and when they did, the movement was described as a transplant slow to take root in Quebec soil.

The following pages will focus on the growth of the women's movement and of feminist ideas. We will view the explosion of the Seventies as the culmination of tensions experienced by women in preceding generations.

CHAPTER FIFTEEN

THE TURBULENT YEARS: FEMINISM IGNITES

DEBUNKING THE FEMININE MYSTIQUE

THE 1970S WERE A TIME of protest and conflict in Quebec. In Montreal, the authorities attempted to stifle opposition; demonstrations on city streets were forbidden. In November 1969, close to two hundred women, activists from socialist and nationalist groups as well as women who advocated social change, staged a nighttime demonstration in which they paraded in chains. They thought police officers would not dare interfere with them; but the police packed the demonstrators into vans and took them to the police station, where they spent the night.

These demonstrators, whose previous experience had been in social movements defined and dominated by men, now felt the need to regroup as women. By their action that night, they heralded a new wave of feminism in Quebec. In five or six years, these women would radically change people's perceptions of women's position in society. For centuries, there had been solidarity amongst women during childbirth and when tending the sick and raising children. At the turn of the century, female political solidarity began to develop; its aim was to bring about changes for all women. The new solidarity of the Seventies went much farther and led to the discovery of a new world, redefined by the experience of women.

Women were accustomed to seeing themselves through men's eyes, evaluating themselves according to male norms, perceiving their lives in terms of the absence or presence of a man. But during the Seventies, women discovered the new reality of female experience that only other women could really share.

The first phase of the new feminism was one of defiant protest: a radical, violent, even destructive questioning of women's lives. Everything was thrown into question: marriage, sexuality, the family, education, the job market and stereotypes of beauty and behaviour. Beneath it all was a basic question: what was the relationship between women and men?

Taboos were shattered. Moral attitudes had broadened during the Sixties, and women were encouraged to speak publicly about their sexuality. They also began to ask questions. Why have a sexual relationship with a man if we get no pleasure from it? Why are children given only their father's name, when their mothers invest years of sacrifice and care? Why is this contribution not fully recognized? Isn't marriage economic servitude that uses the myth of romantic love to reduce women to working without pay? Their questions went beyond historical demands for political and legal equality; they would transform relationships between women and men, and, indeed, amongst women themselves.

Women were angry; they felt exploited by the male world. Their anger fueled female protest, but it also created change. Denunciations of the status quo were accompanied by new projects and new ways of living. Feminism attacked everything that had been thought, defined, controlled and used exclusively by men; but it also proposed a new equality defined by women. Women stopped thinking about what women should do for others and began thinking about what women wanted for themselves.

The feminist themes of the period were autonomy, self-definition and equality between the sexes. Many people thought sexual equality had been won with the right to vote in provincial elections in 1940 and the act respecting the legal capacity of married women in 1964. The new feminism exposed such "equality" for what it was: women had been granted rights, but there was no real equality. Economically, women were discriminated against; they were absent from public life; they were still wholly responsible for childrearing; they were underrepresented in the arts. Economically and socially, women were still dependent on men.

Feminist critiques revealed the extent of that dependence, and the degree to which women desired autonomy. This new concept of autonomy placed individual growth before self-sacrifice, a revolutionary idea in Quebec, where sacrifice was almost synonymous with femininity. Autonomy meant that a woman could plan her own life; it need not comprise only relationships with men, children and family.

For a long time, women denigrated and under-estimated themselves, often quite unconsciously, because they did not measure up to the norms determined by men. Men glorified their own physical strength and used it to explain their domination of women. Men also claimed a monopoly on rationality – women were naturally emotional and passive, while men were psychologically predisposed to impose their will on others.

Women, feminists said, should define themselves and stop accepting men's definitions. Feminists queried the underlying values of a society that often preferred the male child. They explored the real nature of women, hitherto hidden behind male myths. They contested men's essentially negative image of women. Was it true? Was it possible to reinterpret the reality of women in female language?

Women came to discover that there was no reason "normal" should be equated with masculine norms set by men, and no reason women should be evaluated by male standards. This discovery of the intrinsic value of femaleness was one of the most revolutionary aspects of the feminist movement. When it was proclaimed that the entire female body was beautiful, established values were overturned. The reinterpretation of the female body image shocked and fascinated the public. The popular stereotype of a woman as mother or sex symbol was attacked. When feminists spoke of menstruation as a natural phenomenon, when they refused to wear girdles, high heels and make-up, there were far-reaching implications. Women were, quite simply, what they were. They could be women without conforming to the traditional definition of femininity.

THE NEW FEMINISM:
AN INTERNATIONAL MOVEMENT

Radical feminism first emerged in the United States and was the initial driving force behind feminism in Quebec. Young American women, who had had their political initiation in the civil-rights movement and anti-Vietnam war protests began to wonder why they were fighting for the freedom of others while they themselves were oppressed. These women, many of them well-educated activists from left-wing groups, observed that they were expected to make coffee, to do the typing, and to be at the beck and call of male activists, but they were not called on to make strategic decisions or to hold responsible positions. Being subordinate, ancillary was intolerable. The contradiction between their college or university educations and their ambitions and the reality of their status as women became more obvious. Male domination seemed total, absolute; only radical change could overthrow it.

Feminist Kate Millett was one of the first women to expound a theoretical basis for radical feminism. She analyzed Western culture through its great literature and demonstrated that the basic power relation in society was that of men dominating women. All other oppression sprang from this oppression. The organization of institutions in our society perpetuated male domination; they constituted a patriarchy by which power was passed from male to male. When Millett's *Sexual Politics* was published in 1969 it was a bestseller everywhere. In 1971, it had equal success in French. Thousands of women who were neither activists nor intellectuals conceded that Kate Millett's analysis captured what they experienced and felt but could not articulate.

The radical-feminist movement was born at the end of the Sixties. It was radical because it aimed to abolish the domination of women by men in sexual relationships, the family, the work place and the media. Within a few years, radical feminism spread beyond the United States, for the situation described by American women was that of women everywhere in the West. Education and the growing number of working women in industrialized countries made the gulf between the old and new women's roles unbearable.

Feminist theories immediately caught the attention of the media. The most radical women declared war on men – they were enemy number one of women – and on the traditional family as a form of servitude for women. Although the media (controlled by men) took pleasure in depicting feminist demonstrations as the work of crazy, abnormal women driven by a pathetic hatred, they could not discredit feminists. Wherever there were feminist

---

THE THEORETICIANS OF THE NEW FEMINISM

KATE MILLETT – *Sexual Politics,* 1969 (translated into French, 1971). "The term 'politics' shall refer to power-structured relationships, arrangements whereby one group of persons is controlled by another."

SHULAMITH FIRESTONE – *The Dialectic of Sex,* 1970 (translated into French, 1972), develops the idea that men as a group have dominated women because of women's reproductive capacity. Women's liberation will be made possible by scientific progress. The reproductive function will be taken away from women and entrusted to the laboratories, where test-tube babies will be nurtured.

GERMAINE GREER – *The Female Eunuch,* 1970 (translated into French, 1971), depicts how women are rendered disfunctional as complete human beings and gives a devastating description of a society orientated to male sexuality. Women's role is reduced to producing children, and to working for and gratifying males.

In 1969 and 1970, the French publication *Partisans* put out a special edition – a collection of writings by new radical and Marxist feminists. Included was an article by a Canadian, Margaret Benston, which demonstated that the capitalist system was built on women's work in the family.

THE NEW VOCABULARY OF THE RADICAL FEMINISTS

Consciousness-raising groups – meetings where women learn about oppression and the possible options for change. Usually, men are excluded from these groups.

Male chauvinism – a cultural attitude of superiority found in men; the sexual equivalent of racism.

Sexism – the systematic characterisation of one group by another as inferior, based on sexual identity.

Male chauvinist pig – a man who displays an attitude of male chauvinism and sexism.

Sexist – a person who displays prejudice on the basis of sex.

---

protests, there were women who sympathized and wondered if they didn't have the same reasons to revolt.

In Quebec, young women became the voice of the new feminism. Many of these women were university educated or already belonged to left-wing groups. The first women's liberation groups in Canada were formed in Anglophone communities in Toronto and Vancouver. The movement spread to England and then to France after the student uprisings of May 1968. By the end of 1969, writings by American and French feminists were circulating in Montreal. Women activists in the nationalist movement began to question their own political role. The demonstration in chains on the first of November 1969 formed part of this new questioning.

FEMINISM GAINS A FOOTING IN QUEBEC

The Quebec women's liberation movement first emerged in 1969. A number of Anglophone women, in close contact with radical elements at Sir George Williams (later Concordia) and McGill universities were influenced by American feminists. (One of their spokespersons, Marlene Dixon, was teaching at McGill.) These women founded the Montreal Women's Liberation Movement in 1969. Also in 1969, two medical students published the *Birth-Control Handbook,* which sold more than two million copies. The Montreal Women's Liberation Movement opened a centre on Sainte-Famille Street with the financial help of Dr. Henry Morgentaler. (Morgentaler was one of the few doctors who performed abortions outside of a hospital – an illegal act, according to the Criminal Code, which, since 1968, had authorized "therapeutic" abortions performed in a hospital.)

Historian Martine Lanctôt describes how Anglophones tried to contact Francophone women, who were reluctant to respond because of their preoccupation with Quebec nationalism. The Francophone women admitted later that their reluctance to ally themselves with the Anglophones sprang from a fear of being ridiculed and of being accused of dividing the nationalist movement. But some became convinced that the nationalist and socialist movements should recognize the specific oppression of women. In January 1970, they founded the Front de libération des femmes du Québec (the Quebec Women's Liberation Front). The Front de libération des femmes (the FLF) was made up of Anglophone and Francophone activists. The Anglophones responded easily to American ideas and saw the oppression of women as a universal fact. The Francophones, whose political education had been the struggle for national liberation, were reluctant to collaborate with feminists from other provinces. They were looking for a way to reconcile three objectives: women's liberation, national liberation for Francophones and social liberation, which would lead to the overthrow of the existing class structure. Before long, the FLF expelled the Anglophones and moved into their own offices on Mentana Street in Montreal.

During the October Crisis, in 1970, nationalist and socialist groups were harassed by the police. This persecution sharpened feminists' awareness of oppression. In 1971, two militant feminists, copying the famous FLQ manifesto, published the *Manifeste des femmes québécoises* (The Quebec Women's Manifesto). They denounced the discrimination they experienced in left-wing groups and rejected national- and social-liberation projects that did not include women's liberation. They stated that women were victims of capitalist and patriarchal systems. They wanted to establish a militant movement specifically for women, but they also wanted to ally themselves with groups struggling for social change in general. Their feminism was closely linked to the fight for national liberation, as a popular slogan of the time indicated: *Pas de Québec libre sans libération des femmes! Pas de femmes libres sans libération du Québec!* (No Free Quebec without Freedom for Women! No Free Women without Freedom for Quebec!)

The FLF, which had only about sixty members, organized independent cells. The group protested the exclusion of women from the jury that was to try Paul Rose, a terrorist accused of killing a cabinet minister during the October Crisis. They denounced the Salon de la femme, an annual commercial fair held in Montreal, which they claimed strengthened the consumer society's paralyzing grip on women. One of the cells organized a public day-care centre. However, it was difficult to get a consensus among the various cells. One wanted to pursue women's liberation through revolutionary Marxist groups and published one issue of a newspaper called *Québécoises deboutte!* (Women of Quebec Arise!). Then, at the end of 1971, the FLF disbanded.

The formation of the FLF was an important event in the women's movement in Quebec: for the first time women had dared to dissociate themselves from left-wing movements dominated by men. The FLF introduced the idea of a revolutionary feminism – women could be liberated only if society fundamentally changed. But their ideological stance was not clearly formulated and members split into two groups: those with a Marxist background, who linked the oppression of women to the class struggle, and those who saw the source of their oppression in patriarchal female-male relations.

From 1972 to 1975, the Centre des femmes (the Women's Centre) on Sainte-Famille Street in downtown Montreal continued to operate, thanks to members of the FLF and women who had worked in left-wing movements. The centre was quickly perceived to be the base of the revolutionary feminist movement in the Francophone community. With the publication of *Québécoises deboutte!*, it became a place for exchanging ideas and making contacts. The centre attempted to produce a socialist feminism that integrated women's issues into the class struggle. However, the centre was outside the fashionable intellectual trends of nationalism and Marxism. It was also somewhat removed from broadly based feminist groups and women's groups, such as the Quebec Federation of Women and the AFEAS. Socialist groups remained hostile to the feminist ideology; but people began to talk about the centre, which was very active in the Comité de lutte pour l'avortement et la contraception libres et gratuits (Action Committee for Free Abortion and Contraception). The centre's objectives were: the analysis of the status of women, consciousness-raising, and the training of activists. Its aim was to set up small feminist community groups from which a women's liberation movement would eventually grow. Its activities included setting up an abortion service, which it hoped would politicize the issue, opening an information centre and the publication of eight issues of *Québécoises deboutte!*, which had more than two thousand subscribers.

Marxist feminists, socialist feminists and nationalist feminists found fertile ground in trade unions. At the CEQ, most of whose members were women, a committee was established in 1973 to study the status of women. The Gaudreault committee (named for the woman who introduced trade unionism to teachers) studied the link between the educational system and the status of women. The CEQ questioned the popular image of women as passive beings limited mainly to "women's" work, an image planted in the minds of very young children, through their school books.

Women constituted about a fifth of the members of the Fédération des travailleurs du Québec (FTQ)/Quebec Federation of Labour (QFL), but they had only a miniscule say in decision-making. In 1972, the QFL formed a study committee to look into the low participation rate by women in union decision-making. The committee's report, entitled *Travailleuses et syndiquées* (Women Workers and Unionists), drew attention to numerous aspects of a woman's life: family responsibilities, lack of day-care centres, and the burden of two jobs, which prevented women from participating in after-hours union activities.

In the Confédération des syndicats nationaux (CSN)/Confederation of National Trade Unions (CNTU), a third of the members were women. The CNTU, a federation of unions, had a women's committee, but it was dissolved in 1966, on the pretext that this would allow for more effective integration of women into the union. This neatly pushed the problems of women union members into the background. But the rise of the feminist movement in the Seventies forced the CNTU to see women's issues in a new light. In 1973, a new committee was formed which attempted to convince women union members that women's issues were important.

The three union centrals formed a committee to support Dr. Morgentaler. In the years that followed, the union's adoption of certain feminist demands – for maternity leave, child care centres and legislation guaranteeing equal pay for work of equal value – increased the credibility of these social goals. For example, women workers in the public and parapublic sectors obtained, in 1979, seventeen weeks' paid maternity leave at 93 percent of their salary.

The arrest, trial and imprisonment of Henry Morgentaler provided feminist and progressive forces with an opportunity to regroup. The feminist movement participated in the campaign to support Dr. Morgentaler, thus helping to publicize the feminists' position. The Comité de lutte pour l'avortement et la contraception libres et gratuits, comprising representatives from the Corporation des enseignants du Québec (Quebec Teachers' Association, known as "CEQ" in both French and English), the Association pour la défense des droits sociaux (Association for the Protection of Social Rights) and the Centre des femmes saw the protests against laws restricting the practice of abortion and contraception as a stage in a long-term struggle. In 1974, the committee published a play by a feminist troupe, Théâtre des cuisines (Kitchen Theatre). Appended to the play was a manifesto entitled *Nous aurons les enfants que nous voulons* (We Shall Have the Children We Desire). It also published, in 1975, the *Dossier sur l'avortement et la contraception libres et gratuits* (Information Booklet on Free and Readily Available Abortion and Contraception).

Most women's groups in Quebec – although not those affiliated with the Catholic Church – supported Dr. Morgentaler. Marches were held; shows were organized; badges were sold. Morgentaler's trial demonstrated the difficulty encountered by women wanting therapeutic abortions. For an abortion to be legal, it had to be approved by a committee of doctors. In Catholic hospitals, doctors refused to set up therapeutic-abortion committees or refused to approve abortion requests. The doctors' actions were supported by the "pro-life" movement.

A jury found Dr. Morgentaler not guilty, but the Court of Appeal overturned the verdict; the appeal court's decision was upheld by the Supreme Court of Canada. Public opinion condemned the arrogance of judges who convicted a man already acquitted by a jury of his peers. As a result of this outcry, an amendment to the Criminal Code was introduced that would eliminate such judgements in the future, but Dr. Morgentaler served a prison sentence before he was freed to continue practising in Montreal.

FEMINISM BECOMES A SOCIAL INSTITUTION

During the Seventies, women in Quebec became familiar with feminist language. Although many did not identify with the feminists, whose revolutionary image frightened them, women in Quebec responded to the feminist message and incorporated it into their daily lives. When radical feminists said the family was exploitative and should be abolished, not many women agreed immediately; but they did begin to question their role in the family. Did they have a life of their own, outside of their family responsibilities? Did they have financial security? Why wasn't housework recognized or paid? What would they do when their children grew up? Marxist feminists argued that the production of goods and services, the daily work of housewives, was integral to the economy; why had no one recognized the value of their "invisible work"? When feminists pointed out that women who worked outside the home had two jobs, women began to ask their husbands to prepare supper or do the dishes. When Australian feminist Germaine Greer came to Montreal in 1971, she brought radical feminism into Francophone homes. A beautiful woman who spoke fluent French, she received a lot of media attention. Kate Millett visited Montreal in 1973. (In her autobiography, she recalls how the enthusiasm of the women of Montreal almost overwhelmed her.) But the process of consciousness-raising was a long one; ten years passed before some radical-feminist ideas were adopted, reworked and promoted by women in Quebec.

The Report of the Royal Commission on the Status of Women, the Bird Commission, which appeared in 1970, helped awaken Quebec women to feminism. Studies prepared for the Bird Commission were published and served to direct the thinking of study groups in the province.

The radical-feminist message injected new energy into liberal feminism, which had existed in Quebec for more than seventy years. The Quebec Federation of Women, which drew its inspiration from liberal feminism, slowly became more radical. In 1975, they adopted a resolution seeking to remove abortion from the Criminal Code. This Federation was a regular recipient of grants; its leaders came from more affluent sections of the community and from the prestigious professions. It had a powerful voice. Also in 1975, several small groups were founded; one of the best-known was the RAIF – Réseau d'action et d'information pour les femmes (Women's Network for Action and Information).

Governments began to react to demands from women and to recommendations from commissions of enquiry in a concrete way. Since the publication of the Bird Report, there had been discussions about the possible creation of a "women's bureau." The Quebec Federation of Women made the bureau the theme of its 1971 convention. Pressure from the federation and other groups resulted in the setting up, in 1973, of the Quebec Council on the Status of Women. The council – called the CSF in French – had two mandates: to advise the government on questions relating to the status of women, and to keep women up to date on its analysis and policy positions. The creation of the Quebec Council was considered a victory by many women, although it was viewed sceptically by an important part of the movement. Some militant women thought the CSF's mandate was too restricted; others thought the council was an attempt by the State to co-opt women.

In 1973, the Canadian Advisory Council on the Status of Women was established in Ottawa. Again, some women were pleased, others upset. The federal and provincial councils launched numerous studies that bolstered university research. Feminism had invaded the institutions where knowledge was produced.

On the Anglophone college and university campuses of Montreal, discussions of American and English feminist writings began. Anglophone academics introduced courses on the position of women in society and encouraged their students to research this much "neglected" topic.

In Francophone universities, developing a quite separate field of knowledge, namely the female experience, took longer to get off the ground, because Francophone feminists were linguistically isolated from the Americans, the most innovative feminists of the time. In 1972, a university course on the status of women was taught at the Université du Québec à Montréal. There was also a "teach-in," attended by several hundred women. The publicity surrounding the teach-in, the fact that it was held at a university and its

---

GOVERNMENT ORGANIZATIONS CREATED IN 1973

IN QUEBEC

Quebec Council on the Status of Women (QCSW)
Chairpersons:
  1973: Laurette Robillard – administrator
  1976: Claire Bonenfant – bookseller

IN OTTAWA

Canadian Advisory Council on the Status of Women (CACSW)
Chairpersons:
  1973: Katie Cook – sociologist
  1976: Yvette Rousseau – trade-unionist
  1979: Doris Anderson – journalist
  1981: Lucie Pépin – nurse

---

success helped the feminist movement gain respectability amongst Francophones.

Also in 1973, at the Faculty of Continuing Education, at Université de Montréal, a course was taught on the history of women. At several universities, women academics undertook major research projects on the psychology of women, their daily behaviour, their economic profile, their sexuality and their history. Traditionally, knowledge dispensed by universities had been almost entirely based on the experience of men; women were hardly mentioned. When scholars did deign to consider women, it was always from the male point of view. Using their professional analytical tools, women intellectuals began to reconstruct knowledge from a woman's point of view.

Feminist economists stressed that traditional ways of measuring collective or individual wealth could not be used to evaluate housework. Women sociologists examined the universal oppression of women. Discrimination against women, their status under the law, their confinement in marriage, whose basic values had changed little since the Victorian era, their chronic poverty and the daily violence to which they were subjected were all part of traditional oppression. Yet women's oppression had been accepted: few people even discussed it until these new intellectuals came onto the scene.

Feminist psychologists declared war on Freud, who was largely responsible for the profound misogyny of Western psychoanalysis. They denounced the theory of vaginal orgasm since most research suggested that most women are physically incapable of achieving vaginal orgasm. By focusing on this issue, they undermined the foundations of the Freudian school, which did not understand many aspects of female sexuality. Freudians stated that women who did not reach orgasm through vaginal penetration were frigid, and that frigidity was innate to females (as were passiveness, childish behaviour, dependence, masochism and so on). When some women questioned the traditional definition of female sexuality and female-male relationships, other women realized that they need not stay in unsatisfying sexual relationships, and that they need not succumb to the male libido.

Feminist political scientists began to ask why there were no women in power centres such as legislatures and boards of directors. Formal political equality for women, they said, was an illusion that masked male domination in the outside world as well as in the home.

Feminist linguists and writers began to explore language. Language and literature seemed to reflect mostly male experience and male values. Women writers also began to invent a female language, to rewrite life in their own terms. Feminist historians rejected a male approach to history, which ignored half the population; they taught women to question the intellectual fraud of passing off writings about a few men as the history of humanity.

Film-makers from the National Film Board began to portray the experience of women. In 1973, several of them produced a documentary series entitled *En tant que femmes* (Speaking as Women), which examined the daily lives of married women, child care arrangements, nervous breakdowns, housework and marriage. The series was televised in Quebec and helped a number of isolated women realize that many others shared the same problems, that they were not alone.

In May 1979, several women professors organized an interdisciplinary colloquium at the Université du Québec à Montréal. Activists and researchers focused on research done by women about women and for women. One organizer concluded: "We have come to understand the need to identify ourselves both as women and as feminists and the need to channel our solidarity into organized groups."

THE NEW FEMINISM TAKES ROOT

The new feminism attracted a wide range of women. The year 1975 was declared International Women's Year by the United Nations, and this event gave thousands of Quebec women the incentive to question traditional male power structures.

Radical ideas had been circulating in Quebec for more than five years.

They were nurtured in left-wing women's groups and among intellectuals. Socialist and nationalist movements had influenced Francophone women, who had not yet attempted to articulate a radical-feminist program without allying themselves with these two groups. English-speaking feminist action groups were autonomous and less inclined to work within the framework of Marxism and nationalism. Amongst Anglophone feminists, lesbians asserted themselves publicly as a political group for the first time.

During International Women's Year, women came to grips with their disillusionment with male-dominated politics. Women in left-wing groups and activists in the nationalist movement realized that the Marxists and nationalists wanted to include feminist activism in their programs, but did not want to give feminism priority. A number of other women concluded that there was nothing to be gained through traditional channels, and began to rethink their position. Regional conferences organized by the federal government's International Women's Year Secretariat mobilized two thousand women, new recruits to militant feminism. The conferences led to a convention, Carrefour 1975 (Crossroads 1975), held at Université Laval. Using carefully prepared resource material, five hundred women discussed education, child care, sexuality and politics.

In 1975, feminism underwent a marked transformation. All kinds of feminists began to work together. Freed from the domination of Marxism and nationalism, Francophone women leaned increasingly toward a more autonomous type of feminism. Women's liberation in Quebec no longer took second place on the political agenda; women's demands were no longer drowned in a flood of requests from unions, political parties and left-wing groups. Increasingly, feminists defined their own political strategy.

This change of direction brought the women's movement closer to radical feminism. One collective began the newspaper Les Têtes de pioche in 1976; the paper became the voice of radical feminism. It expounded the view that all oppression was rooted in the exploitation of women by men, and that domination by men was the unifying experience of all women. The collective of six people attempted to join the Marxist feminists; however, incompatible political perspectives reduced the collective to three women and the newspaper ceased publication in June 1979. In spite of its limited circulation, Les Têtes de pioche exerted considerable influence on the women's movement.

Women who carried on the struggle within the Parti québécois made sure the party platform included measures to extend access to child care, abortion and maternity leave. Many women had high hopes when the party took office in 1976, especially as more than half of the party members were women. But it quickly became obvious that the Parti québécois, like other political parties, was male dominated. Disappointed, a few militant feminists left the party in

1978 and formed the Regroupement des femmes québécoises, believing that they could better pressure the government from an independent base.

WHAT DO FEMINISTS WANT?

After the political awakening of 1975, the women's movement developed cohesion and strength by working on concrete projects rather than an all-embracing, theoretical explanation of the origins of female oppression. Feminists of all persuasions joined forces with women who, although they did not see themselves as feminists, were also demanding change. Activities and debate within the movement were focused on four major themes: the body, work, speaking out and power.

THE BODY

One tenet of the new feminism was that the female body must be intrinsic to the definition of the position of women in society. Never before had women wanted to discuss at such length their relationship with their own bodies and the role their bodies played in relationships with men. For generations, men had justified their ongoing oppression of women through the myth that the female body was genetically inferior, best suited to procreation. Women became prisoners of their own bodies: just as men defined beauty and controlled health, so they controlled access to women's bodies.

For many women, questioning the status quo began with something quite immediate – their own bodies. In the Seventies, female sexuality was already being discussed. New contraceptive methods, the pill and the IUD, had permitted hitherto unheard-of sexual freedom, but they caused problems. Thousands of women experienced side effects from these contraceptives, some very serious, and they began to ask why it was that women always had to bear the burden of contraception. Why were pills and IUDs prescribed with so little concern for their side effects?

Some women realized they were at the mercy of a science that was controlled by males and often reflected male biases or indifference to women. Childbirth, at one time a natural act and the province of women, had become a medical procedure like any other – the "patient" had no say in the treatment. Women began to reject "medicalized" births. Some hospitals responded by trying to make childbirth more "human;" but the reforms were not fast enough or sweeping enough for women who wanted to retake control of childbirth and be attended by midwives at home. Midwifery was illegal: the powerful medical profession opposed all attempts to take control of childbirth from doctors.

A battle developed between doctors and feminists. Family doctors who prescribed tranquillizers and psychiatrists who diagnosed women who were "thinking too much about themselves" as "crazy" were challenged to defend their methods. The dependence of women on prescribed drugs was seen as a consequence of doctors seeing women as hysterical, childlike and easily manipulated. Psychiatry, which had given itself the power to define "normal" female behaviour, was challenged by women who saw this as an attempt to control them.

The issue of health united large numbers of women, for most women had had at least one negative experience with a doctor. There were conferences on the subject; health centres for women were set up throughout the province to free women from the grip of male medical practice. Government-established family-planning clinics, where abortions were performed, were set up at the end of the Seventies as part of the official responses to pressure from women demanding the right to control their own bodies.

Being a woman often means being the object of violence: direct and personal violence in the home and in sexual assault, indirect and impersonal violence in pornography and in television and movie images. Feminists attempted to sensitize other women to question this violence and urged them to refuse to live in a society in which rape was a metaphor for male power. At one time, rape was a taboo subject, kept as an ugly secret by its victims. In the 1970s, it became the symbol of all women's lack of personal freedom. Gone were the days when women who went out alone at night or ventured into certain areas were to be blamed for what happened to them. During the 1970s, nighttime demonstrations proclaimed that the night also belonged to women. Why is rape one of the least punished of all crimes? What is justice from a woman's perspective?

Women's groups started centres for victims of sexual aggression and for battered women. But all women were victims of sexual aggression at one time or another; all women knew women who had been beaten. All women were afraid of being attacked in everyday situations: taking an elevator, crossing a deserted parking lot, leaving the office late at night, being followed in the street. Sexual aggression and domestic violence attracted the attention of radical feminists and female lawyers. Self-defence and martial-arts courses became popular; women were no longer willing to accept that they were potential victims.

But the sexual liberation of the Sixties and Seventies had barely altered the balance of power between the sexes. On the contrary, sexist interpretations of sexuality took on alarming dimensions: the pornography industry boomed. Pornographic material was introduced into magazines, films and shows aimed at the male consumer. Some pornography depicted acts of sadism and violence, in which women were bound or whipped. Thus, the idea that women accepted or enjoyed male violence was perpetuated.

The contempt for and the degradation of women in certain types of pornography won over many women who had previously believed that feminists were exaggerating women's problems. Believers in freedom of speech began to wonder whether the very concept of free speech should be revised. In its present form, it permitted the trivialization of violence against women.

A few feminists glorified lesbianism as the single true expression of female sexuality. This point of view was often raised by anti-feminists to scare people and to discredit feminism. Few people realized that the word "feminism" included a wide variety of movements, just as "liberalism" and "socialism" did.

"ALL WOMEN ARE HOUSEWIVES"

This slogan, painted on a wall outside a Montreal subway station, bore witness to the growing conviction among women that their "invisible work" must be recognized. Every woman was primarily a housewife; although many women also held down another job. By the 1970s, women were wondering why they agreed to do two jobs when the first, housework, was not recognized as "work."

Convincing society that what women had always done out of "love," "duty" or "instinct" was work became one of the principal goals of the women's movement. Women demanded recognition of housework as a material contribution to the marriage; housewives, like other workers, should receive pensions and salaries. The AFEAS demanded recognition of the work done by women alongside their husbands. The tax system was changed somewhat to encourage the payment of a salary to wives working in a family business. The Régime des rentes du Québec (Quebec Pension Plan) allowed couples whose marriage had ended to share equally their accumulated pension rights. (These changes brought about virtually no improvement for women who were solely mothers or housewives.)

Women who stayed at home after marriage or the birth of a child became aware of the precariousness of their position and inflation and the rising cost of living lured many of them back to the job market. The growing number of divorces and separations made them realize the need for an adequately paid job. CEGEP and community-centre courses could not accommodate all the women who wanted to learn a skill.

The economic crisis worsened toward the end of the decade, and more women were forced to combine the roles of housewife, mother and wage earner. They learned that, for a worker, being a mother and having young children was a handicap. Many women had to give up a job when they had a child; others were fired. Child care centres were in short supply and expensive; a child's illness or a school professional-development day turned working into a nightmare. Recognition for the role of parent was one objective of the women's movement. During union negotiations, activists fought for recognition of maternity leave and parental leave for both mother and father. Attempts were made to organize child care centres at work, but few employers welcomed the initiative. New labour standards allowed a pregnant or nursing woman to change her job if working conditions proved harmful to her or her child. Many women could manage two jobs only part-time; but part-time work was often badly paid, rarely offered fringe benefits, and offered little recognition for job experience or little opportunity of moving out of job ghettos.

Immigrant women had the most poorly paid and insecure jobs. The clothing industry in Montreal depended on the labour of women immigrants, who had considerable difficulty reading or writing French or English and who were poorly educated. Sewing at home or cleaning offices or homes were their only options. Immigrant women groups helped new arrivals escape isolation and adjust to a society in which sex roles were changing rapidly. The Ligue des femmes du Québec also devoted most of its energies to this cause.

Women in Quebec dared to complain about things that preceding generations had endured in silence. For a long time, employers had increased their profits by paying female employees a fraction of what male workers would have received for the same or similar jobs. Male-dominated unions had long been accomplices in this exploitation. The new Quebec Charter of Rights and Freedoms set forth the right of equal pay for work of equal value, and hundreds of women launched grievances. Several companies, including Imperial Tobacco, were ordered to pay compensation to women employees who had been the object of such discrimination. In Montreal, a group called Action-Travail des femmes (Women Workers' Action Group) devoted itself to the problems of women in the work place: sexual harassment, wrongful dismissal, discriminatory hiring practices, lack of access to training programs and low wages. Action-Travail des femmes convinced many women that they should no longer tolerate overt discrimination and that they should seek redress for injustices.

At the Etats généraux des travailleuses (Congress of Women Workers) held in 1979, it was agreed that conditions for working women had changed little. Four of every ten working people were women but, like their mothers, their grandmothers and their great-grandmothers, they had to be content with two-thirds of the average male wage. There were female stars, female engineers, female lawyers, businesswomen and women in high-level positions in the public service, but most women worked in job ghettos where wages were low and chances of promotion almost nonexistent: office worker, secretary, saleswoman, waitress, cashier, sewing-machine operator. Life in the work place had changed very little. Profound changes for women could not be expected until the working world accommodated the domestic responsibilities not only of women but also of men.

SPEAKING OUT

Speaking out is the first step to self-assertion. Speaking out means refusing to hide one's anger, fear or hope, expressing how you feel as a woman, making women's issues a subject of discussion for everybody, and describing the world from a woman's perspective.

Talking about what it is like to be a woman is the only way to reassure every woman that her experience is not an isolated one; it is also the only way to change the rules of the game. We must speak out to convince women that they should refuse to remain marginal, concealing their problems and repressing their real desires. First, you have to talk to women to instil a sense of solidarity; then you have to talk to men to explain what women feel.

In an age when information is power, women began to speak out and to use this power to spread new ideas. On radio, on television and in newspapers, people began to discuss women's ideas and women's issues such as sexism, child care and health.

Women's opinions were gaining credibility. Women journalists once relegated to the women's pages and to programs about domestic problems, wrote about culture, politics, science and the economy. Because of the new female presence in the media of the Seventies, there was a little more interest in news concerning women. The public got used to women speaking out.

The female viewpoint became an accepted theme. Artists and actresses expressed ideas that would not previously have been considered worthy of artistic expression.

Scientific and literary conferences now included countless workshops on the status of women. Women's bookstores and publishing houses began to spread feminist ideas. Businesses, magazines, bookstores, research projects and conferences brought feminists together.

The feminist influence can be seen in the astounding literary output of the Seventies. From 1975 on, feminist authors left their mark on Québécois cultural expression. The production of *La Nef des sorcières* (The Ship of Witches), a play in which the characters voiced what women had never dared say about their social status, was a collective assertion of an authentic femininity. Denise Boucher's 1977 play *Les fées ont soif* (The Fairies Are Thirsty) illustrates female stereotypes by associating the Virgin Mary with a prostitute. When it was

---

FEMINIST MAGAZINES IN QUEBEC

Québécoises deboutte! 1971-1974
Les Têtes de pioches 1976-1979
L'Autre Parole 1976-
Pluri-elles 1977-1978
Des Luttes et des rires de femmes 1978-1981

---

staged, conventional morality was scandalized. But opponents of the play did not succeed in having it closed by the courts; in fact, it was one of the hits of the season.

Many feminists began to analyze sexist stereotypes. Their ideas were taken up by women no longer willing to see themselves portrayed as housewives and sex objects. In a consumer society, where advertising is all-pervasive, images of women influence public opinion: Changing school textbooks and advertising to present women as people became an issue, supported almost unanimously by Quebec women.

The best example of the new self-assertion amongst women was the celebration of International Women's Day, on 8 March. IWD was created to commemorate U.S. women workers' struggles in 1858; it became a day of celebration in Quebec. By the end of the Seventies, IWD was a day for collective demonstration: women from all milieux – workers' groups, unions, artists' groups, the government and universities – took stock of the struggles, achievements and failures of the women's movement.

EMPOWERMENT

Since the nineteenth century, the theme of power had been a constant among feminists struggling for the right to vote. But the realization that even the most intimate links between women and men involved a power relationship beyond each couple's unique relationship led feminists to take a close look at their own personal lives. The relative wealth of men compared to the poverty of women, women's responsibility for the children and the household, even if they worked outside the home, and male sexual expression that often did not consider women's needs – these phenomena led women to conclude that the personal is political. Women in all milieux identified with this theme, which had been popularized by radical American feminists. To change the situation, women had to gain power everywhere, and the process had to begin at home. The issue of male power in the home was a troubling one, creating tremendous anxiety for women who found it difficult to question traditional domestic relationships. It seemed to threaten some men's very identity, for they were temporarily incapable of creating an identity for themselves that did not stem from their domination of women. Not surprisingly, they reacted with overt hostility when women took control of their own lives.

Women's growing awareness of the importance of power involved them in complex political dilemmas. They were constantly confronted by one question: should women cooperate with political authorities or fight against them? The dilemma became greater when the Parti québécois came to power. The party seemed sympathetic to feminists, and there were many women party members. Indeed, the Parti québécois government proved more responsive to women's demands than any government in the history of Quebec. Elected in 1976, the Parti québécois asked the Conseil du statut de la femme to develop an overall policy on the status of women in Quebec. The council's report, *Pour les Québécoises: égalité et indépendance,* published in 1978, touches on all aspects of women's lives. Each analysis is followed by recommendations of ways in which the government could reduce inequality and create true independence for women.

Although the recommendations were officially endorsed by the government, they were taken up slowly by the various ministries. Women who placed all their hopes in the Parti québécois concluded that women's priorities were not those of men. Women who had been elected realized that as long as there were fewer women's voices than men's in the National Assembly, they would have little opportunity to shift the balance of power.

Women knew that power almost always eluded them in unions, boards and professional associations. Moreover, power could be a trap. Assuming it, or even sharing it, pressured women to think and act like men. Women gained power because they learned to come to terms with a power that was essentially male. How could they keep power and at the same time introduce new ways of using it? How could they "feminize" it without losing it? Women who exercised power admitted that their lives and their values came to resemble those of men. Is that what the women's movement had been fighting for?

SOME FEMINIST WRITERS

Louky Bersianik – *L'Euguélionne*   1976
Nicole Brossard – *L'Amer*   1977
Madeleine Gagnon – *Retailles*   1977
Denise Boucher – *Cyprine*   1978

"I'M NOT A FEMINIST, BUT ..."

At the beginning of the 1980s, this familiar refrain was nearly always followed by a statement that could have been directly lifted from a feminist agenda. Yet how often do we hear this today? Many women were in favour of feminist demands, but did not always want to be identified with them. They adopted feminist arguments and supported feminist struggles, but they rejected solidarity with the feminists.

This phenomenon exemplifies the real extent of change in women's attitudes and expectations. Women were still afraid to appear aggressive, to risk male disapproval by openly identifying themselves with women often caricatured as unbalanced or frustrated. Was this the reaction of women who still saw themselves through the eyes of men? Or was it an unconscious strategic move to soften the feminist message by qualifying it? Whatever it was, women's lives would no longer be what they had been in the past.

FURTHER READING

1. *Major Québécois Feminist Works*

Dolment, Marcelle and Marcel Barthe. *La Femme au Québec*. Les Presses libres, 1973.

Le Droit au travail social pour les femmes. CEQ, 1979.

Dossier spécial sur l'avortement et la contraception libres et gratuits. Agence de Presse libre du Québec, 1975.

La Lutte des femmes, combat de tous les travailleurs. CSN, 1976.

Manifeste des femmes québécoises. Montreal: L'Etincelle, 1971.

Nous aurons les enfants que nous voulons. 1974.

The Birth Control Handbook. 1971.

Québécoises deboutte! vol.1, Les Editions du Remue-Ménage, 1981 (New edition of major publications of the Centre des Femmes).

Les Têtes de pioche. 1976-1979, New edition, Les Editions du Remue-Ménage.

Travailleuses et Syndiquées. FTQ, 1974.

2. *Personal Accounts*

Lanctôt, Louise. *Une sorcière comme les autres*. Quebec/Amérique, 1981.

Payette, Lise. *Le pouvoir connais pas*. Quebec/Amérique, 1982.

3. *Government Publications*

Dulude, Louise. *Women and Ageing*. Ottawa: CACSW, 1978.

Macleod, Linda. *Wife Battering in Canada: the Vicious Circle*. Ottawa: CCCSF, 1980.

Messier, Suzanne. *Chiffres en main*. Quebec City: CSF, 1982.

――――. *La condition économique des femmes au Québec*. Quebec City: CSF, 1978, two volumes.

――――. *Ten Years Later*. Ottawa: CACSW, 1979.

――――. *Towards Equality for Women*. Ottawa: CACSW, 1979.

White, Julie. *Women and Unions*. Ottawa: CACSW, 1980.

――――. *Pour les Québécoises, égalité et indépendance.*, Quebec City: CSF, 1978.

――――. *Les travailleuses non syndiquées*. Quebec City: CSF, 1980.

4. *Other*

Bernier, Colette and Hélène David. *Le Travail à temps partiel*. Montréal: Institut de recherche appliquée sur le travail, no. 12, April 1978.

Guyon, Louise, Roxane Simard and Louise Nadeau. *Va te faire soigner, t'es malade!* Montreal: Stanké, 1981.

Lanctôt, Martine. *La Genèse et l'évolution du mouvement de libération des femmes à Montréal, 1969-1979*. Master's Thesis, UQAM, 1980.

Laurin-Frenette, Nicole. "La libération des femmes" in *Les Femmes dans la Société Québécoise*. Montreal: Boréal Express, 1977.

Lemieux, Denise and Lucie Mercier. *La Recherche sur les femmes au Québec. Bilan et Bibliographie*. Quebec City: Institut Québécois de recherches sur la culture, 1982.

O'Leary, Véronique and Louise Toupin. "Introduction" à *Québécoises Deboutte!*, vol. 1. Montreal: Editions du Remue-Ménage, 1982.

――――. *Le mouvement des femmes au Québec* Montreal: Centre de formation populaire, 1980.

5. *Collected Papers*

Art et féminisme. Quebec City, Musée d'Art contemporain, ministère des Affaires culturelles, 1982.

Brisson, Marcelle and Louise Poissant, eds. *Célibataire, pourquoi pas?* Montreal: Serge Fleury, 1981.

Cohen, Yolande, ed. *Femme et politique*. Montreal: Le Jour, 1981.

Devenirs de femmes. Montreal: Fides, 1981.

Des femmes et des luttes. Special edition of *Possibles,* vol. 4, no. 1, 1978.

Lacelle, Elizabeth J., ed. *La Femme et la Religion au Canada français*. Montreal: Bellarmin, 1979.

Mon héroïne. Montreal: Editions du Remue-Ménage, 1981.

EPILOGUE

Women are well and truly a part of the history of Quebec. They left homelands to settle here; they founded schools and hospitals; they loved, had children, colonized, looked after others, taught – in short, built the country alongside men.

Anne's great-great-great-grandmother *is* a part of this history, a history whose vital thread remains undiscovered. As we traced the history of Quebec women, we asked what factors brought about change and what strategies should be adopted for the future – a somewhat perilous undertaking, but we have tried to draw a few conclusions. The lot of a woman was tied to the survival of the family during the eighteenth century. Gradually, the traditional role – the essential, productive role – of women was taken away. They were exploited in the job market, which was being industrialized and wanted to make use of women's domestic skills – sewing, cleaning, cooking and spinning. At the end of the nineteenth century and in the twentieth century, women became involved in consciousness-raising; they realized they did not have certain rights and that they could only obtain those rights through struggle. Women were far from being passive victims of events, and changes they had hoped for finally became reality; for women demanded justice and the right to participate. Women's struggles over the years form the backdrop to feminism. Feminism is not the whole history of women, but it represents some of the important pieces in the quilt.

After the Contradictions and the Impasse, women spoke out. The family was no longer central to society. Women demanded independence and respect. According to the Civil Code, women now have equal rights and equal responsibility for marriage and children. This legal revolution, however, is still more an ideal than a reality. Yet, although women have not yet attained true equality in their daily lives, they are becoming independent – of men and children. Modern women's desire to escape from dependency clearly distinguishes our lives from those of our ancestors.

Women are unlikely to return to the traditional female role; our daughters have greater freedom to choose the life they want to live, but they will grow up in an uncertain future. In the end, if women and men are no longer defined and confined by the concept of the two spheres, if they talk to each other differently, is it not possible that a new approach will be taken to the history of women and to the history of humanity?

GLOSSARY

Ancien Régime – system of government in France before the revolution of 1789

Cent Associés (One Hundred Associates) – a group involved in commercial activities in New France

Coutume de Paris (Paris Custom) – the law governing New France during the Ancien Régime

Engagés – indentured labourers

Epistolière – well-to-do woman who engaged in letter writing as an art form.

La femme forte de l'évangile – traditional expression meaning highly competent woman

Minot – Canadian measure equivalent to eight gallons.

Pays d'en haut – refers to the area of Northern Quebec, but in some contexts can refer to Northern Ontario.

LIST OF ACRONYMS

AFEAS	Association féminine pour l'éducation et l'action sociale
CACSW	Canadian Advisory Committee on the Status of Women
CCCL	Canadian and Catholic Confederation of Labour
CCF	Co-operative Commonwealth Federation
CEGEP	Collège d'enseignement général et professionnel
CEQ	Corporation des enseignants du Québec
CNTU	Confederation of National Trade Unions (formerly Canadian Confederation of Labour)
CSF	Conseil du statut de la femme (Québec)
CSN	Confédération des syndicats nationaux
CWAC	Canadian Women's Army Corps
FLF	Front de libération des femmes

FLQ	Front de libération du Québec
FNSJB	Fédération nationale Saint-Jean-Baptiste
FTQ	Fédération des travailleurs du Québec
MLCW	Montreal Local Council of Women
NATO	North Atlantic Treaty Organization
NDP	New Democratic Party
NFB	National Film Board
QFL	Quebec Federation of Labour
QFW	Quebec Federation of Women
RAIF	Réseau d'action et d'information pour les femmes
UCC	Union des cultivateurs catholiques
UCF	Union catholique des Fermières
UCFR	Union catholique des femmes rurales
UNO	United Nations Organization
UQAM	Université du Québec à Montréal
VOW	Voice of Women
WD	Women's Division of the Royal Canadian Air Force
WREN	Women's Royal Canadian Navy Service
YWCA	Young Women's Christian Association

AN ANNOTATED INDEX
OF NAMES AND ORGANIZATIONS

Abby-Finestone, Sheila (QFW president) 338

Abenakis 19

Aberdeen, Lady (founded National Council of Women, 1893) 250

Académie Marie-Rose (school for girls 1876-1911) 144-145

Action catholique 237, 287, 305, 314

Action Committee for Free Abortion and Contraception (see Comité de lutte pour l'avortement et la contraception libres et gratuits) 361

Action de la jeunesse canadienne (nationalist group in 1950s) 314

Action-travail des femmes 371

Actualité (magazine) 306

AFEAS (see Association féminine pour l'éducation et l'action sociale)

Albani, Emma Lajeunesse (famous singer) 178-179, 225

Algonquins 17, 19, 20, 26, 34

Alliance canadienne pour le vote des femmes au Québec 256, 264

Alliance des professeurs de Montréal 295

Amoskeag Corporation (U.S. textile factory; employed Québécois) 129

Anciennes de Pédagogie familiale 336

Anderson, Doris (CACSW chairperson, 1979) 365

Angers, François Albert (economist) 287

Asile de la Providence 171-172

Asile de Montréal (nineteenth-century asylum for elderly women) 125

Asile du Bon-Pasteur 172

Assistance maternelle (founded in 1912) 200

Association catholique des institutrices rurales (founded by Laure Gaudreault) 230

Association de familles monoparentales bas-Saguenay "La Ruche" 340

Association de familles monoparentales de l'Estrie Inc. 340

Association d'économie familiale du Québec 340

Association des cadres et professionnels de l'Université de Montréal 340

Association des dames de la charité 171

Association des dames patriotes du comité des Deux-Montagnes 118

Association des demoiselles de magasin (see Shop Girls' Association) 217

Association des femmes collaboratrices 341

Association des femmes propriétaires 256

Association des puéricultrices de la province de Québec 340

Association des religieuses enseignantes du Québec 346

Association des veuves de Montréal 340

Association féminine pour l'éducation et l'action sociale (AFEAS) 316, 318, 339, 340, 346, 361, 370

Association for the Protection of Social Rights (see Association pour la défense des droits sociaux) 363

Association pour la défense des droits sociaux (see Association for the Protection of Social Rights) 363

Association syndicale féminine catholique 228

Assomption de la Sainte-Vierge, nuns of 168

Au bas de l'Echelle 340

Auger, Geneviève (historian) 280, 289, 290

Automatistes (artists who opposed traditional values) 274

Baby, Marie-Thérèse (eighteenth-century widow) 78-79
Baby Welfare Committee 198
Bank Act 253
Barbel, Marie-Anne (eighteenth-century businesswoman) 90
Barry, Francine (historian) 63, 109, 294, 310
Barry, Robertine (or Françoise, writer and editor of *Le Journal Françoise*) 179, 224
Beach, G. Mrs. (introduced Homemakers Clubs to Quebec, 1911) 236
Beauchamp, Colette (journalist) 337
Beaudet, Céline 192
Beaulieu, A. (historian) 178, 181
Beaver Hall Hill Group (1920s painters) 226
Beauvoir, Simone de (author of *The Second Sex*) 314
Béchard, Monique 314-315
Bégin, Monique (sociologist and politician) 337, 343
Bégon, Elizabeth (eighteenth-century letter writer) 59, 61-62, 66-67, 76, 88, 90-91, 93, 101, 109
Béique, Caroline (early twentieth-century feminist; co-founder of FNSTB) 200, 251, 253
Benston, Margaret 359
Bernhardt, Sarah 178
Bernier, Jacques 170
Bernier, Jovette (novelist) 224
Bersianik, Louky (feminist writer) 374
Bertrand, Janette (writer for *Le Petit Journal*) 317
Bibaud, Adèle (novelist) 179
Bilodeau-Parent, Janette (rejected mistress of Judge de Bonne) 106
Binmore, Miss (teacher who protested against low salaries) 166-167
Bishop's University, Faculty of Medicine 135, 164
Bill 16 321-323
Bird Commission 343-346, 348, 363-64
Bird, Florence 343

Blais, Marie-Claire (novelist) 318
B'nai B'rith Women's Council 340
Board of Catholic Examiners 165, 179, 298
Boileau-Kimber, Emilie (Patriote supporter) 119
Bonenfant, Claire (QCSW chairperson, 1976) 365
Borduas, Paul-Emile (painter, author of *Refus global*) 274, 314
Boston School of Domestic Science 149
Bouchard, Georges (founded first Cercle de fermières in 1915) 236
Bouchard, Jacqueline (psychologist) 326
Boucher, Denise (feminist writer) 374
Boucher, Pierre 25-26, 59
Bourassa, Henri (politician and journalist) 263
Bourassa, Père 134
Bourgeoys, Marguerite (founded Congrégation de Notre Dame) 31, 33, 36, 37, 38, 39
Bourget, Monseigneur (Bishop of Montreal, 1800s) 114, 137, 139, 171, 172, 175
Bradbury, Bettina (historian) 140
Brault, Gilles (birth control method) 304-305
British North America Act (1867) 115
British Women's Emigration Association (recruiter of servants 1880-1920) 158
Brooke, Frances (author of *The History of Emilie Montague*) 86, 109
Brossard, Nicole (feminist writer) 374
Bruchési, Monseigneur 247, 248
Bruneau-Papineau, Julie (wife of Louis-Joseph Papineau) 80, 91, 92, 118, 157, 171, 176, 177
Buller, Annie (political activist) 249

CACSW (see Canadian Advisory Council on the Status of Women)
Cadieux, Henriette (widow of notary Chevalier de Lorimier) 120-121

Cadieux, Rita (social worker, QFW president) 338

Cadron-Jetté, Rosalie (founded hospice Sainte-Pélagie for unwed mothers, 1848) 171, 172

Canadian Advisory Council on the Status of Women (CACSW) 364-365

Canadian Catholic Confederation of Labour, CCCL (see Confédération des travailleurs catholiques du Canada CTCC) 196, 226, 283, 287

Canadian Federation of University Women's Clubs (Laura Sabia, president) 341

Cantero, Fernande (homemaker, QFW) 337

Caron, Fredeline (president, Cercles de fermières) 339

Cartier, Jacques 15

Casaubon, family (women weavers and spinners) 146-147, 148, 150

Casaubon, Madame (head of family) 148

Casgrain, Abbé 179

Casgrain, Thérèse (1896-1981) 256, 258, 264, 284, 285-286, 292, 314, 321, 336, 337, 338, 343

Casti connubbi (papal encyclical forbidding contraception 1930) 187, 193-194

Catholic Church 28-29, 31, 68, 69-70, 71, 72, 73, 75, 77, 93, 114, 137, 139, 193-194, 197, 218-220, 235, 304-305

Catholic Committee of Public Instruction 246

Catholic Orphanage of Montreal 171, 172

Catholic Women's League 253, 291

Catholic Workers' League (see Ligue ouvrière catholique) 282

CEGEP 326, 327, 328, 330, 370

Cent Associés (the One Hundred Associates) 41

Centre bénévole de Mieux-être de Jonquière 340

Centre des femmes, Montréal (see the Women's Centre) 361, 362

Centre d'information et de réfèrence pour femmes 340

Cercle des femmes journalistes 340

Cercles d'économie domestique (founded in 1952 by bishops and Mme Savard) 288, 315, 316, 339

Cercles de fermières (see Farm Women's Circles) 236-237, 258, 288, 291, 292, 315, 316, 318, 339, 346

Cercle des rencontres du mercredi inc. 340

César, Marie-Madeleine (battered wife) 76

Champlain, Samuel de 15, 17, 18, 31

Charbonneau, Hubert (demographer) 41, 45, 47, 65, 68, 109

Charbonneau, Monseigneur (Archbishop of Montreal) 287, 288

Charbonneau, Bill (1909) 253

Charities Organization Society (founded in 1900) 199

Charpentier, Yvette (ILGWU organizer) 228, 282, 313

Châtelaine 303, 320, 321, 431

Cité libre (magazine) 314

Civil Code (1866) 114, 124-125, 253, 255, 256, 257, 258, 284, 287, 377

Cleverdon, Catherine L. (historian) 122

Closse, Lambert (husband of Elizabeth Moyen) 25

Club des femmes patriotes 117

Club Wilfrid-Laurier des femmes libérales 340

Colas, Réjane (lawyer, QFW) 337, 338

Colbert (French politician) 40

Colborne, Lady 120, 121

Colborne, Sir John 120

Collège des Jésuites de Québec 63

Collège Jean-de-Brébeuf 300

Collège Marie-Anne 300

College of Physicians and Surgeons 135

Collet, Marie Anne 1797 (eighteenth-century single mother) 67

Colonists 20, 46, 56

Comité consultatif féminin de Montréal 292

Comité consultatif féminin des finances de guerre (see the Women's War Finance Committee) 292

Comité de lutte pour l'avortement et la contraception libres et gratuits (see Action Committee for Free Abortion and Contraception) 361, 362

Comité de retour à la terre 235

Committee for the Equality of Women 342

Common Law 70, 126

Communauté sépharade du Québec 340

Communist Party of Canada 227, 249, 261, 295

Compagnie du gaz de Montréal (Montreal Gas Company) 149

Compulsory School Attendance Act (1943) 297, 299-300, 307

Conan, Laure (novelist, author of *Angéline de Montbrun*) 179

Concordia University 359

Confédération des syndicats nationaux, CSN (see Confederation of National Trade Unions, CNTU) 313, 362

Confédération des travailleurs catholiques du Canada, CTCC (see Canadian Catholic Confederation of Labour) 287, 313

Confederation of National Trade Unions, CNTU (see Confédération des syndicats nationaux, CSN) 362

Conférence de Saint-Vincent-de Paul de Québec (shelter for female ex-prisoners) 171

Confrérie de la Sainte-Famille 93

Congrégation des Filles séculières de Ville-Marie (founded by Marguerite Bourgeoys, 1669) 33, 34, 35

Congrégation Notre-Dame 36, 168, 173, 242, 246

Congress of Industrial Organizations (CIO) 226

Conseil d'hygiène de la province de Québec (founded 1887) 198

Conseil du statut de la femme (see Quebec Council on the Status of Women) 374

Conseil local des femmes de Montréal (see Montreal Local Council of Women) 217

Constitutional Act (1793) 113

Convent of Sacré-Coeur 296

Cook, Katie (CACSW chairperson, 1973) 365

Cooperative Commonwealth Federation (CCF) 199, 285, 321

Copp, Terry (historian) 202, 208

Corporation des enseignants du Québec (CEQ) 362-363

Corporation des instituteurs et institutrices catholiques de la province du Québec, CIC (teachers' union, 1946) 295

Corriveau, Marie-Josephe ("La Corriveau") 94, 98-99

Couc, Elizabeth (see Isabelle Montour)

Council of Canadian Unions 295

Cours de Préparation au mariage (Church marriage manual) 304

Coutume de Paris 66, 68, 69, 70, 80, 83, 90, 106, 107, 122-123, 124, 125

Criminal Code 138, 193, 360, 364

Cross, D.S. (historian) 160

Cross, Suzanne (historian, garment industry) 151

CTCC (see Confédération des travailleurs catholiques du Canada)

Cushing-Foster, Eliza (writer) 177

Cuthbert-Brandt, Gail (historian) 213, 294

D'Allaire, Micheline (historian) 34, 109

Dandois, Marie-Paul (QFW president) 338

Dandurand, Josephine (writer, member of MLCW) 179, 180, 200-201, 224, 251

Danylewycz, Marta (historian) 144, 173

Daveluy, Marie-Claire (writer) 224

Davis, Susannah (servant and rape victim) 100

Day Nursery 198

Dechêne, Louise (historian, Ancien Régime) 22
Delta Sigma Society (founded in 1885, McGill) 247-248
Department of National War Services (created in 1940) 291
Department of Public Instruction 242, 243
Derrick, Carrie (McGill professor) 244, 251, 263, 285
Descarries-Bélanger, Francine 309, 332
Deschamps, Yvon (comedian) 335
Désilets, Alphonse (founded first Cercle de fermières in 1915) 236
Desilets, Rolande S. 258
Desjardins, Alice (lawyer, QFW) 337
Des Luttes et des rires de femmes (feminist magazine) 373
Dessaulles, Henriette (diarist, "Quebec woman of mid-1800s") 132-135, 137, 159
Dessaulles, Rosalie (*seigneuresse* of Saint-Hyacinthe) 120
Desranleau, Monseigneur (church union specialist) 288
Dixon, Marlene (Montreal Women's Liberation Movement) 359
Dominion Textile strike 226-27, 294-296
Donalda, Pauline (opera singer) 225
Dorchester, Lady (governor's wife) 91
Dorion Commission 255-261
Dossier sur l'avortement et la contraception libres et gratuits (Information Booklet on Free and Readily Available Abortion and Contraception) 362
Drapeau, Jean (mayor of Montreal) 283
Drummond, Lady Julia (MLCW president) 251
Dubé, Angéline (Solidarité féminine) 261
Duberger, Françoise ("la Galbrun" found guilty of killing her husband, 1671) 93-94
Dumais, Rose-Marie (housekeeper) 215

Dumas, Sylvio (historian; King's Daughters) 43, 51
Dunnigan, Lise (1975 study of school texts) 329
Duplessis, Maurice (Quebec premier 1936-39, 1944-59) 186, 187, 203, 273, 274, 283, 286, 294, 295, 296, 297, 318, 321
Dupuis Frères (Montreal department store) 233, 295
Duval, Jeanne (vice-president, CTCC) 313, 337
Duval-Thibeault, Anne-Marie (poet) 179

Eaton's catalogue 138, 148, 149, 233, 234
Eccles, William (historian) 99
Ecole d'enseignement supérieure (founded in 1908) 247, 248
Ecole des arts domestiques (founded in 1930) 248
Ecole ménagère de Roberval (founded in 1882) 242-243
Ecole ménagère provinciale (founded in 1904) 243
Ecole normale Jacques-Cartier (teachers' college) 246
Ecole sociale populaire 236
Ecole supérieure de pédagogie familiale 297
Editions du jour (Montreal publisher) 306
Educational Record 166
Elle (magazine) 320
Ellice, Jane (wife of the Seigneur de Beauharnois) 106, 119, 120
Enard, Jeanne (seventeenth-century brandy trader) 23
Etats généraux des travailleuses (Congress of Women Workers) 371-372

Fareau, Madeleine (homemaker, QFW) 337
Farm Women's Circles (see Cercles de fermières) 236

Fédération des oeuvres de charité canadienne-française (founded by T. Casgrain) 286

Fédération des travailleurs du Québec, FTQ (see Quebec Federation of Labour, QFL) 287, 313, 362

Fédération des unions de famille 346

Fédération nationale Saint-Jean-Baptiste FNSJB, (founded in 1907 by Marie Gérin-Lajoie) 198, 211, 217, 226, 236, 246, 248, 251-252, 253, 256, 262, 284, 285, 291, 292, 336, 337

Federation of Textile Workers 227

Fédération provinciale du travail du Québec 226

Fédération québébécoise des infirmiéres et infirmiers 340

Female Benevolent Society (founded in 1817) 102, 103

Female Compassionate Society (founded in 1822) 102, 103

Fémina (radio program) 285, 341

Femmes d'aujourd'hui (TV show) 341

Femmes rurales (rural magazine) 320

Filion, Gérard (member of Action catholique and *Le Devoir* director) 287

Filles de la Congrégation 38-39

Filles du roy (see King's Daughters) 18, 43

Firestone, Shulamith (author of *The Dialetic of Sex*, 1970) 359

Fitzbach-Roy, Marie 171, 172

Fleury-Deschambault, Marie-Catherine (Baron de Longueuil's widow) 66-67

FLQ (see Front du Libération du Québec)

FNSJB (see Fédération Nationale Saint-Jean Baptiste)

Forestier, Marie (supervisor, Hôtel-Dieu de Montréal) 32

Foucher, Antoine (registered children's births 1744-1767) 79

Fournier, Marcel (historian) 249

Foyers Notre-Dame 304

Francoeur Bill (1935) 196-197

François, Bishop of Quebec 74

Françoise (see Robertine Barry) 179

Fraternité canadienne des cheminots 205-206

Fréchette, Louis (poet) 178

Frémont, Gabrielle 224

Freud, Sigmund 320, 365, 366

Friedan, Betty (American feminist) 301, 318

Front de libération des femmes du Québec (see Quebec Women's Liberation Front) 360

Front de Libération des Femmes (FLF) 360-361

Front du Libération du Quebec (FLQ) 275, 348, 360

Gaffield, Chad (historian) 129

Gage, Governor 67

Gagné, Christine (AFEAS president) 339

Gagnon, Madeleine (feminist writer) 374

Garderie de Nourrisons (see Infant Nursery) 198

Gardeur de Repentigny, Pierre (raped servants) 77

Gaspé, Philippe Aubert de (early novelist) 94

Gaudet-Smet, Françoise (founded *Paysana* magazine, 1937) 236, 264

Gaudreau, Germaine (QFW) 339

Gaudreault, Laure (1930s teachers' union organizer) 229-230, 313

Gauthier, Abbé Georges (teacher at Mont-Saint-Marie Convent) 246, 247

Gauvreau, Dr. Joseph 192-193, 201, 202

Gazette du Travail 227-228

Gélinas, Blanche (Solidarité féminine) 261

Gendron, Abbé (Saint-Hyacinthe Seminary) 174

Généreux, Georgiane and Léontine 200

Gérin-Lajoie, Antoine (novelist) 128

Gérin-Lajoie, Dr. Léon (son of early feminist Marie Gérin-Lajoie) 193, 194

Gérin-Lajoie, Marie (mother) 137, 180, 193

Gérin-Lajoie, Marie (daughter, founder of FNSJB) 199-200, 201, 220, 243, 246, 247, 251, 252, 253, 256, 257, 258, 262, 263, 285, 314
Gérin, Léon (sociologist) 134, 137, 148, 150, 153
Gérin, Louis 132
Gervais, Solange (AFEAS president) 339
Gillecey, Mary (widowed after Rebellion of 1837) 120
Girls Friendly Society 250
Girouard, Madame (founder of the Association des dames patriotes du comté des Deux-Montagnes) 118
Globensky, Hortense (opposed the Patriotes) 118
Godbout, Adélard (Quebec premier 1939-1944) 187, 264, 265, 287, 294, 297
Gosselin, Madame (founded the *Museum of Montreal,* 1832) 132, 177, 178
Gosselin, Madame Charles (president, Cercles de fermières) 339
Gouin, Sir Lomer 253
Gouttes de lait (Drops of Milk, founded in 1910 by Monseigneur Le Pailleur) 198, 201, 251, 266
Grand Council of Indian bands 127
Grandmaison, Eléonore de (seventeenth-century businesswoman and widow) 48
Gray, Hugh (British traveler) 123
Greer, Allan (historian on illiteracy) 142
Greer, Germaine (author of *The Female Eunuch,* 1970) 359, 363
Grey Nuns of Montreal (see Soeurs grises de Montréal) 37, 81, 91, 95, 140, 141, 172
Guay-Ryan, Madeleine (wife of Claude Ryan) 314
Guenet, Marie (supervisor of Hôtel-Dieu de Québec) 32
Guertin, Catherine (midwife) 79
Guide de discussion (published by Quebec Federation of Women) 346
Guindon, Léo (leader of Alliance des professeurs de Montréal) 295-296
Guy, Pierre (merchant) 79, 97
Guyart, Marie (see Marie de l'Incarnation) 33

Hall-Gould, Bella (social worker) 199, 249
Hamelin, Jean (historian) 115, 178, 181
Hamel, Thérèse (sociologist) 242
Harvey, Fernand (historian) 161, 162
Hébert, Anne (writer) 318
Hébert-Couillard family (extended seventeenth-century family) 18, 20
Hébert, Louis (husband of Marie Rollet) 17-18
Heller, Geneviève (historian on housework) 150-151
Henripin, Jacques (demographer) 56, 65, 136, 304, 343
Henry, Rita (birth-control method) 304-305
Home and School of Industry (trained domestic workers) 160
Homemakers Clubs (founded in 1897) 236
Homestead Act, 253
Hoodless, Adelaide 243
Hôpital-Général (in Paris) 43, 49
Hôpital-Général de Montréal 76, 95, 102, 220
Hôpital-Général de Québec (founded in 1701) 76, 94, 95, 101
Hôpital Notre-Dame 221
Hôpital Sainte-Justine (see also Sainte-Justine Hospital for Children) 200, 251
Hospice Saint-Pélagie (founded in 1848 by Cadron-Jetté) 172
Hospitalières de Dieppe 32
Hospitalières de la Flèche 33, 35
Hospitalières de Montréal 36
Hôtel-Dieu de Montréal (founded by Jeanne Mance, 1643) 32, 35, 170
Hôtel-Dieu de Québec (founded in 1639) 21, 32, 35, 39, 95
Hotte, Gabrielle (QFW president) 338
Hudson's Bay Company 75

Huguenin, Madeline (founded *La Revue Moderne*) 224

Humanae Vitae (Paul VI's encyclical on contraception, 1968) 346

Humphrey, John (lawyer; Bird Commission) 343

Hurlbatt, Ethel (principal of Royal Victoria College until 1929) 244

Hurons 15, 19, 24, 34, 35

Hurteau, Laure (journalist) 284

Hygiène et physiologie du mariage (1871 handbook on sexuality condemned by Monseigneur Bourget) 139

Idéal féminin (religious magazine) 320

Igartua, J. 65, 109

Imperial Order of the Daughters of the Empire 291

Imperial Tobacco strike (1951) 295

Infant Nursery 198

Institut des soeurs Notre-Dame-du-Bon-Conseil de Montréal (founded in 1923) 200

Institut familial de Saint-Jacques 315

International Ladies Garment Workers Union (ILGWU) 227, 228

International Women's Day 373

International Women's Year 366-367

Iroquois 15, 16, 19, 23-24, 25, 26, 27, 34, 49, 126

Jasmin, Judith (journalist) 317

Jean, Sister Marguerite (historian) 174, 175

Jesuit Relations, The (see Rélations des Jésuites) 32, 41

Jesuits 18, 19, 23, 24, 41, 57, 114

Jeunesse ouvrière catholique (see Young Catholic Workers) 282, 293

Jodoin, Mariana (Quebec senator; headed Comité consultatif féminin de Montréal) 292, 336

Johnson, Daniel (Quebec premier 1966-1968) 287

Jolin, Madame Adélard (president,

Cercles de fermières 339

Jones, Richard (historian) 187

Joybert de Soulanges, Elizabeth (wife of Marquis de Vaudreuil) 90-91

Junior League of Montreal Inc. 340

Kalm, Pehr (Swedish traveler, 1749) 68, 87, 89

King, Louisa (1898 factory inspector) 152

King, William Lyon Mackenzie (Canadian prime minister 1921-1930, 1935-1948) 152, 285, 286, 287

King's Daughters (see Filles du roy) 18, 41-45, 189

Kirkes (seventeeth-century pirates and adventurers) 18

Kirkland-Casgrain, Claire (first woman MNA, 1961) 321-322, 336

Kitchen Theatre (see Théâtre des cuisines) 362

Knights of Labour, The 163

Labelle, Cécile (businesswoman,QFW) 337

Laberge, Albert (novelist) 223

La Bonne Fermière (agricultural magazine) 236

Lacelle, Claudette (historian) 64, 67, 109, 156

Lachance, André (historian) 97, 100, 109

Lacoste-Beaubien, Justine (founder of Saint-Justine Hospital for Children) 125, 200

Lacoste-Frémont, Thaïs (sister of Marie Gérin-Lajoie) 256

Ladies Benevolent Society 171

Lamarsh, Judy 342

Lamontagne-Perrault, Euphrosine (mother of two Patriotes) 121

Lamothe, Raymonde (historian) 280, 289, 290

Lanctôt, Martine (historian) 360

Landry, Yves (demographer) 41, 47, 65, 109

La Nef des sorcières 372

Lange, Lola M. (farmer, Bird Commission) 343

Langstaff, Annie Macdonald (first woman McGill law graduate) 245

La Patrie 164, 201, 246, 306

La Petite Feuille (teachers' union newsletter) 230

Lapointe, Jeanne (professor, Bird Commission) 343

Lapointe, Michelle 228-229

Lapointe, Renaude (journalist) 317, 337

Lapointe-Roy, Huguette (QFW president) 338

La Presse 164, 317, 337

Lasnier, Rina (writer) 318

La Revue moderne (magazine, founded in 1919) 224, 319, 320

La Revue populaire (magazine) 306, 319

Le Samedi (1950s magazine) 319

La Semaine (nineteenth-century teachers' newspaper) 166

La Semaine religieuse 247

La Terre et le Foyer (magazine of Cercle de fermières) 316, 319, 320

Laurendeau, André (editor of *Le Devoir*) 283

Laurendeau, Francine 318

L'Autre parole (feminist magazine) 373

Laval, Monseigneur de 63

Lavell, Jeannette 345

Lavigne, Marie 208

League for Human Rights (founded by T. Casgrain) 286

League for Women's Rights (see Ligue des droits de la femme, founded by Casgrain) 256, 264, 265, 284, 286, 336

Lebrun, Bernadette (Solidarité féminine) 249, 261-262

Le Canadien 106, 117

Leclerc Hamilton, Caroline 200

Le Devoir 263, 264, 283, 287

Leduc, Alec 314

Le Film (1950s magazine) 319

Legardeur de Repentigny, Marguerite (early French colonist) 46

Le Journal 164

Le Journal de Françoise (published 1901-1908, edited by Robertine Barry) 157, 224

Leman, Madame (wife of Beaudry Leman) 201

Le Pailleur, Monseigneur (founder of Gouttes de lait, 1910) 201

Le Petit Journal (women's advice column in 1950s) 317

Lesage, Jean (premier of Quebec, 1960-1966) 274, 275

Les auxiliaires bénévoles de l'hôpital de Jonquière 340

Les fées ont soif (play by Denise Boucher) 372-373

Les Grands Ballets Canadiens (founded by Ludmilla Cheriaeff) 318

Leslie, Geneviève (historian) 213, 234

Les Têtes de pioche (radical feminist magazine) 367, 373

Le Temps 164

Levasseur, Irma (first woman doctor) 200

Lévesque-Martin, Jeanne d'Arc 237

Lévesque, René (founder of Parti québécois) 275

Liberal Party of Quebec 353

Ligue de la jeunesse féminine (see Young Women's League) 285

Ligue des citoyennes de Jonquière 340

Ligue des droits de la femme (see League for Women's Rights) 264, 284

Ligue des femmes du Québec (founded by Laurette Sloane, 1958) 315, 346, 371

Ligue des petites mères (Young Mothers' League) 198

Ligue nationale de la colonisation 235

Ligue ouvrière catholique (see Catholic Workers' League) 282, 304

Loi des sièges (Chair Law) 217

Loiselle, Georgina (factory apprentice) 161

Longueuil, Baron de 67-68

Loranger, Françoise (writer) 318

Lorrain, Dorothée (biologist, QFW) 337
Lorrain, Louise (Action de la jeunesse
    Canadienne) 314
Louis XIV 16, 55
Louis XV 55
Loyalists 56
Lyman, Mrs. Walter (founded Provincial
    Franchise Committee) 263

Macdonald College (McGill) 236, 243,
    300
McGill, Elsie Gregory (engineer, Bird
    Commission) 343
McGill University 143, 164, 199, 220,
    221, 244-245, 246, 247, 248, 296, 300,
    359
McGill University, Faculty of Arts
    (admitted women in 1884) 244, 245
McGill University, Faculty of Law
    (admitted women 1911) 220, 246
McKenzie, Nancy (wife of J.G.
    McTavish) 75
McLaren, Angus (historian) 138, 139-
    140
McTavish, J.G. (Hudson's Bay
    administrator and bigamist) 75
Mademoiselle de Muy 68
Mailloux, Sophie (left destitute after
    Rebellions of 1837-38) 120
Maintenant (magazine) 320-321
Maisonneuve, Paul Chomedy de 36
Maison Notre-Dame-de-la-Merci,
    Quebec City (maternity hospital
    founded in 1840 by Mademoiselle
    Métivier) 136
Malouin, Marie-Paule (studied the
    Académie Marie-Rose) 144, 154
Mance, Jeanne (French-Canadian
    heroine, founder of Hôtel-Dieu de
    Montréal) 31, 33, 34, 35, 39
Manifeste des femmes québécoises (see
    Quebec Women's Manifesto) 360
Marchand, Azilda (AREAS
    president) 339, 341
Maréchal, Abbé 175, 176
Marguerite (servant of Julie Bruneau-
    Papineau) 157

Maria Chapdelaine (novel by Louis
    Hémon) 129
Marie-Anne, Mother Superior (founder
    of the sisters of Sainte-Anne) 175-
    176
Married Women's Property Acts 126
Marie Claire (magazine) 306, 320
Marie de l'Incarnation, Sister (Ursuline,
    1599-1672) 22, 31, 32, 33-35, 39, 44, 47,
    83
Marie-Joseph, Black slave in 1700s 97
Martel, Florence 284
Martin-Ondoyer, Charlotte (battered
    wife, 1734) 76
Menorah Society for Jewish Women
    (founded in 1915) 248
Mercier, Catherine, (captured by
    Iroquois, 1651) 25
Merleau, Josephte 121
Messier, Martine (fought off Iroquois,
    1652) 25
Métis 25
Métivier, Madame (see Maison Notre-
    Dame-de-la-Merci) 136
Micmacs 19
Millet, Geneviève (adulteress
    sentenced in 1733) 76
Millet, Kate (author of *Sexual Politics*,
    1969) 357, 359, 363
Milkman, Ruth (women's labour) 196
Miner, Horace (sociologist) 192
Ministry of Agriculture 236, 243
Ministry of Education (created in
    1964) 325, 327
Ministry of Social Affairs 325
Missionaries 20, 24, 73
MLCW (see Montreal Local Council of
    Women)
Mondin, Anthoine (seventeenth-
    century colonist) 21
Mongeau, Serge (opened first family-
    planning clinic) 306
Monk, Elizabeth (MLCW feminist) 251
Monk, Maria (author of *An Exposé of
    The Horrible Crimes Committed at
    Hôtel Dieu de Montréal*, 1835) 170
Monseigneur de Laval 34, 63

Montagnais, women and French settlers 17, 18, 19
Montcalm, Marquis de 87
Montour, Isabelle (1667-1749, interpreter, wife of Iroquois chief) 25, 26, 27
Montreal Catholic School Board 295
Montreal Council of Social Agencies (founded in 1919) 199, 261
Montreal Council of Women 346
Montreal Gas Company (founded in 1847) 149
Montreal General Hospital (founded in 1821) 76, 95, 102, 220
Montreal Home for Fallen Women 170
Montreal Lakeshore University Women's Club 340
Montreal Local Council of Women, MLCW (feminist organization founded in 1893; see Conseil local des femmes de Montréal) 180, 217, 250, 251, 253, 256, 262
Montreal Orphan Asylum 125
Montreal Prostestant Orphan Asylum 102
Montreal Star 164, 200
Montreal Suffrage Association (founded by Carrie Derrick in 1912) 263
Montreal teachers' strike, 1949 295
Montreal University Settlement 199, 249
Montreal Women's Liberation Movement 359
Montreuil, Gaétane de (editor) 224
Moodie, Susanna (early Canadian writer) 102
Moreau de Bresoles, Judith (nurse in New France) 39
Morel, André 45
Morgentaler, Dr. Henry 359, 360, 363
Morin, Sister Marie, (first woman writer in New France) 36
Mouvement des femmes chrétiennes 340
Mouvement laïc de la langue française 314
Mouvement: services à la communauté;

Cap. Rouge 340
Moyen, Elizabeth (captured by Iroquois, 1665) 25
Mullins-Leprohon, Rosanna (novelist) 177
Murdoch, Mrs. (Murdoch case) 335
Murray, Commander 99
Museum of Montreal (magazine founded by Madame Gosselin in 1832) 132, 177, 179-180

Napoleonic Code 124, 125
Nascapis 19, 29
National Council of Jewish Women 291
National Council of Women (founded in 1893 by Lady Aberdeen) 250, 281, 291, 337
National Film Board 320, 366
National Salvage Office 290
Native peoples 15, 19-20, 21, 23, 33, 38, 73-74, 126
NDP (see New Democratic Party)
Needleworkers' Industrial Union 227
Nelson, Wilfred Nelson (authored report on prisons in Lower Canada) 172
New Democratic Party (NDP) 285, 314, 342
Newman Society for Catholics 248
North-west Company 75
Nous aurons les enfants que nous voulons (We Shall Have The Children We Desire) manifesto 362
Nouveau Journal (begun in 1961) 317

October crisis, 1970 353, 360
Ogilvie, Doris (lawyer, Bird Commission) 343
O'Sullivan Business College 216
Ottawa (Indians) 19

Padlock Law 294
Palmer, Dorthea (nurse arrested for distributing contraceptives in 1936) 193-194
Papineau, Louis-Joseph (Patriote leader) 91, 92, 104, 118, 122, 157, 171, 177

Paradis, Suzanne (writer) 318
Parent Commission 309
Parent Madeleine (trade unionist) 282, 295-296
Parent Report (1964) 307-309
Parents' Information Bureau of Kitchener 193-194
Parizeau, Germaine 292
Parti canadien (became Parti patriote after 1826) 104, 106
Parti patriote (or Patriotes) 118, 119, 121-122
Parti québécois 353, 367, 374
Partisans (French magazine) 359
Parti socialiste ouvrier (1894 manifesto) 163
Patry-Buisson, Ghislaine (QFW president) 338
Paul VI 364
Payeur, Denis (homemaker QFW) 337
Paysana (magazine founded by Françoise Gaudet-Smet, 1937) 236
Péan, Madame (popular upper-class hostess in 1700s) 91
Peltrie, Madame de la 83
Pendant que les hommes travaillent, les femmes elles... ("While the men work, the women...") 341
Pépin, Lucie (CACSW chairperson, 1981) 365
Pérodeau Act (1915) 253
Perreault, Madeleine (Women's War Finance Committee) 292
Perot The Younger, Pierre Thomas (father of Marie Anne Collet's child) 67
Picoté de Belestre, Marie-Anne (married English captain) 67
Pierre-Deschênes, Claudine (historian) 198
Pierson, Ruth (historian) 281
Pinard, Yolande 250
Pinzer, Maimie (letters on prostitutes) 218
Plamondon, Huguette (union official, QFW) 313, 337
Plante, Lucienne 246

Pluri-elles (feminist magazine) 373
Poulliot, Marie (early French colonist) 21
Pour les québécois: égalité et indépendance (QCSW report, 1978) 374
Prentice, Alison (historian; teachers) 165
Price, Enid (effects of World War One on women's work) 195-196
Primeau, Marielle (president, Cercles de fermières) 339
Professional Corporation of Physicians 195
Protestant Board of School Commissioners 262
Proulx, Marcienne (historian) 199
Provincial Franchise Committee (founded in 1921 by Marie Gérin-Lajoie; see also Provincial Suffrage Committee) 263, 285
Puritans 29, 31, 32, 93

QCSW (see Quebec Council on the Status of Women)
QFW (see Quebec Federation of Women)
Quadragesimo anno (papal encyclical, 1931) 187
Quakers 29, 31, 77
Quebec Charter of Rights and Freedoms 372
Quebec Council on the Status of Women, QCSW (see Conseil du statut de la femme) 364, 365, 374
Quebec Factories Act (1885) 152
Quebec Federation of Labour QFL (see Fédération des travailleurs du Québec) 287, 362
Quebec Federation of Women (founded by Casgrain in 1966) 285, 286, 336, 337, 339, 340, 341, 346, 361, 364
Quebec Industrial Establishments' Act (1894) 152
Quebec Labour Code 294

Quebec Native Women's Group 345-346

Quebec Old Age Pensions Act, 1936 203

Québécoises deboutte! (feminist magazine in 1970s; see *Women of Quebec Arise!*) 361, 373

Quebec Public Charities Act, 1921 202, 218

Quebec Social Insurance Commission (Montpetit Commission) 202-203

Quebec Women's Liberation Front (see Front de libération des femmes du Québec) 360

Quebec Women's Manifesto (see Manifeste des femmes québécoises) 360

Quiet Revolution 274-275, 318, 325, 327, 331, 347, 348

Racette, Rita 314

Radio-Monde (newspaper) 192

Ramezay, Louise de (sawmill owner) 94

Ramkhalawasingh, Ceta (historian)195, 196

Rebellion of 1837-38 87, 113, 114, 118-121

Red Cross 291

Régime des rentes du Québec (Quebec Pension Plan) 370

Regroupement des femmes québécoises 368

Regroupement des garderies, région "six C" 340

Relations (magazine) 312

Relations des Jésuites (see *Jesuit Relations*) 32

Rerum novarum (papal encyclical 1891) 187

Réseau d'action et d'information pour les femmes, RAIF (see Women's Network for Action and Information) 340, 364

Réseau d'action et d'information pour les femmes (Saguenay) 340

Richard, Juliette (rural telephone operator) 238

Ringuet (author of novel *Trente Arpents*) 193

Ritchie-England, Dr. Grace 251, 253, 285

Roback, Léa (political activist and union leader) 194, 206, 214, 217-218, 229, 248, 282, 313

Robillard, Laurette (QCSW chairperson, 1973) 365

Rollet, Marie (seventeenth-century colonist) 17-18

Ronde, Mademoiselle de la (eighteenth-century bride) 72-73

Rose, Fred (union organizer and communist MP 1943-46) 230

Rose, Paul (FLQ member) 360

Rotenberg, Lori (historian) 214

Rousseau, Louise (secretary, QFW) 337

Rousseau, Yvette (trade unionist) 338, 365

Rowley, Kent (United Textile Workers of America) 294-296

Roy, Adeline (teacher) 168

Royal Commission on the Relations of Labour and Capital (1886) 151, 161, 163

Royal Commission of Enquiry on the Status of Women (see also the Bird Commission) 343

Royal Victoria College, McGill 244

Roy, Catherine 121

Roy, Gabrielle (novelist) 318

Roy, Josepht 121

Roy, Raymonde (real estate agent, QFW) 337

Roy, Raymonde (demographer) 47

Rumilly, Robert (historian) 288

Sabia, Laura 314, 341, 342

Sacré-Coeur hospital (founded in 1897) 200

Saint-Augustin, Mother Catherine de 93

Saint-Germain, Eugénie (widow of J.-N. Cardinal, politician) 120

Saint-Jean, Idola (McGill professor and founder of Alliance canadienne pour le vote des femmes du Québec) 244, 256, 264, 314

St. John's Ambulance Brigade 291

Sainte-Anne, sisters of 175

Sainte-Anne-Marie, Mother (teacher) 246, 247

Sainte-Justine Hospital for Children (see also Hôpital Sainte-Justine) 125, 313

Sainte-Marte de Saint-Hyacinthe, sisters of 174, 175

Saint-Laurent, Madeleine (major in Women's Army Corps) 279

Saint-Martin, Albert (workers' university) 249

Saint-Martin, Fernande (*Châtelaine* editor; QFW) 337, 341

Saint-Vallier, Bishop 97

Saint-Vincent-de-Paul 199, 200, 261

Saints-Noms-de-Jésus-et-de Marie, soeurs de 144

Sauvé, Jeanne (first woman Speaker of the House of Commons) 286, 342

Sauvé, Paul (Quebec premier, 1959-1960) 274, 275

Savard, Madame (founded Cercles d'économie domestique) 288

Savary, Charlotte (writer) 318

School for Household Science (founded by Mcdonald College, 1907) 243

School for Teachers, Macdonald College 300

Séguin, Normand (historian) 128, 166

Séguin, Robert-Lionel (historian; New France) 88, 110

Séminaire de Québec 63

Serena (first family-planning association, 1955) 305

Service d'orientation des foyers 304

Sherbrooke and District University Women's Club 340

Shop Girls' Association 217

Simcoe, Lady 96, 106

Smith, Donald (Lord Strathcona) 244

Société d'étude et des conférences 346

Société Notre-Dame-de-Montréal 35

Société Saint-Jean Baptiste 243

Soeurs de la Congrégation 62

Soeurs de la Miséricode 172, 173, 218

Soeurs de la Providence (founded by Emile Gamelin) 172

Soeurs du Bon-Pasteur 172

Soeurs Grises de Montréal (see Grey Nuns of Montreal) 37

Solidarité féminine (founded in 1932) 261-262

Stoddart, Jennifer (historian) 208, 216

Strasser, S.M. (historian on technology) 149, 151

Strong-Boag, Veronica (historian) 203, 216

Syndicat des allumettières (Matchgirls Union) 228

Syndicats d'économie domestique (set up by bishops, 1946) 288

Taschereau, Louis-Alexandre (Quebec premier) 186, 235, 263

Talon, Jean (Intendant) 16, 41, 46

Tardivel, Jules (the Ultramontane) 179

Tavernier-Gamelin, Emilie (organized shelters for poor and sick) 171, 172

Tekakwitha, Kateri, "Lily of the Mohawk" 24-25

Tessier, Abbé (reorganized domestic-science school system) 297-298, 315

Théâtre des cuisines (Kitchen Theatre) 362

Thérèse de Jésus, Soeur 96

Thibaudeau, Marie (MLCW activist) 201, 251

Thivierge, Maryse (historian) 222, 223, 248

Thivierge, Nicole 242

Tisserand, Cardinal 314-315

Trades and Labour Congress of Canada (TLCC) 226

Travailleuses et syndiquées (*Women Workers and Unionists*; FTQ report, 1972) 362

Treaty of Paris (1763) 55

Tremblay, Marie (president, Cercles de fermières) 339
Trente Arpents (Thirty Acres) by Ringuet 193
Trofimenkoff, Susan (historian, women's work) 161, 163, 263
Trudeau, Lise (homemaker, QFW) 337
Turgeon Commission, 1938 211

Union Bill (or Act of Union, 1840) 113
Union catholique des cultivateurs (UCC; see Union of Catholic Farmers, founded in 1924) 235, 287, 288
Union catholique des femmes rurales (UCFR) 315, 316, 317, 336, 339
Union des fermières catholiques (see Union of Catholic Farm Women) 287, 288
Union of Catholic Farmers (see Union catholique des cultivateurs) 287
Union Nationale 273, 274, 275
Union of Catholic Farm Women (see Union des fermières catholiques) 287, 288
Unions de famille 336
United Textile Workers of America 294, 295, 296
Université de Montréal 220, 246, 247, 297, 365
Université du Québec 327, 328, 364, 366
Université Laval 246, 297, 367
University Women's Club 314, 336, 346
Ursulines de Québec (founded in 1639 by Marie de l'Incarnation) 32, 33, 37, 38, 48, 62, 63, 91, 95, 96
Ursulines de Trois-Rivières (founded in 1702) 94, 96

Van Kirk, Sylvia (historian) 75, 110
Vaudreuil, Governor 87, 90, 97
Veillées des berceaux (Watching over the Cradles) 198
Verchères, Madeleine de (seventeenth-century heroine) 26-27, 30, 97
Viger, Jacques (1825 census) 90, 95
Villebois de la Rouvillière, Maria-
Catherine de (Elizabeth Bégon's granddaughter) 59, 61
Villeneuve, Cardinal 265, 297
Voice of Women, Quebec chapter (founded 1961 by Casgrain) 286, 314, 318, 336, 341, 346

Wallot, Jean-Pierre (historian) 76, 101, 110
War of 1812-18 56
Wartime Prices and Trade Board 290, 292
Washington International Council of Women (founded in U.S. in 1888) 250
Werner, Pascale (historian) 206
West Island Woman's Centre 340
West Island Woman's Shelter 340
Whitton, Charlotte 292
Wollstonecraft, Mary 105
Women of Canada 136, 160
Women of Quebec Arise! (see *Québécoises deboutte!*) 361
Women's Centre, Montreal 361
Women's Christian Temperance Union 250
Women's Corp of the Canadian Army (CWACs) 279-281
Women's Corp of the Royal Canandian Navy (WRENSS) 270-281
Women's Division of the Royal Canadian Air Force (WDs) 279-282
Women's Federation, Allied Jewish Community Services of Montreal 346
Women's Institute 236
Women's Liberal Federation of Canada 264
Women's Minimum Wage Act 210-211, 215
Women's National Immigration Society 158
Women's Network for Action and Information (see Réseau d'action et d'information pour les femmes) 364
Women's Voluntary Services (WVS) 291

Women's War Finance Committee (see Comité consultatif féminin des finances de guerre) 292

Woodsworth, J.S. (founder of CCF) 199

Workers' Unity Leaque (founded in 1929) 227

Young Catholic Workers (see Jeunesse ouvrière catholique) 283

Young Women's Christian Association, YWCA (founded in Montreal in 1874) 160, 173, 250, 291, 340

Young Women's League (Ligue de la jeunesse féminine founded by T. Casgrain) 285

Youville, Marguerite d' (founder of Grey Nuns) 31, 37, 82, 83, 91, 93, 95, 97, 101